Augsburg Commentary on the New Testament
REVELATION

•

Gerhard A. Krodel

Augsburg Publishing House

Minneapolis, Minnesota

AUGSBURG COMMENTARY ON THE NEW TESTAMENT
Revelation

Library of Congress Cataloging-in-Publication Data

Krodel, Gerhard, 1926–
Revelation / Gerhard A. Krodel.
p. cm.—(Augsburg commentary on the New Testament)
Bibliography: p.
ISBN 0-8066-8880-7
1. Bible. N.T. Revelation—Commentaries. I. Title.
II. Series.
BS2853.3.K76 1989
228'.07—dc19 89-30828
CIP

The paper used in this publication meets the minimum requirements of American National Standard for Information Sciences—Permanence of Paper for Printed Materials, ANSI Z329.48-1984 ∞™

Manufactured in the U.S.A. AF 10-9038

93 92 91 2 3 4 5 6 7 8 9 10

To Elizabeth, Katie, Karla,
and Joan

We have a vast amount to learn from the Revelation of John that, for those of orthodox and liberal views, has never properly fitted into the traditional system.

Ernst Käsemann

CONTENTS

FOREWORD

The AUGSBURG COMMENTARY ON THE NEW TESTAMENT is written for laypeople, students, and pastors. Laypeople will use it as a resource for Bible study at home and at church. Students and instructors will read it to probe the basic message of the books of the New Testament. And pastors will find it to be a valuable aid for sermon and lesson preparation.

The plan for each commentary is designed to enhance its usefulness. The Introduction presents a topical overview of the biblical book to be discussed and provides information on the historical circumstances in which that book was written. It also contains a summary of the biblical writer's thought. In the body of the commentary, the interpreter sets forth in brief compass the meaning of the biblical text. The procedure is to explain the text section by section. Attempts have been made to avoid scholarly jargon and the heavy use of technical terms. Because the readers of the commentary will have their Bibles at hand, the biblical text itself has not been printed out. In general, the editors recommend the use of the Revised Standard Version of the Bible.

The authors of this commentary series are professors at seminaries and universities and are themselves ordained. They have been selected both because of their expertise and because they worship in the same congregations as the people for whom they are writing. In elucidating the text of Scripture, therefore, they attest to their belief that central to the faith and life of the church of God is the Word of God.

The Editorial Committee
Roy A. Harrisville
Luther Northwestern Theological Seminary
St. Paul, Minnesota

Jack Dean Kingsbury
Union Theological Seminary
Richmond, Virginia

Gerhard A. Krodel
Lutheran Theological Seminary
Gettysburg, Pennsylvania

ABBREVIATIONS

ACNT	Augsburg Commentary on the New Testament
BR	*Biblical Research*
CBQ	*Catholic Biblical Quarterly*
Exp. Times	*Expository Times*
HTR	*Harvard Theological Review*
Interp.	*Interpretation*
JBL	*Journal of Biblical Literature*
KJV	King James Version of the Bible
LW	*Luther's Works,* American edition
LXX	Septuagint (the Greek Old Testament)
MT	Masoretic text (Hebrew) of the Old Testament
NEB	New English Bible
Nov. Test.	*Novum Testamentum*
NTS	*New Testament Studies*
Pss. Sol.	*Psalms of Solomon* (see Charlesworth, ed., Pseudepigrapha)
1QH	The Thanksgiving Scroll (Qumran, cave 1)
1QM	The Scroll of the War of the Sons of Light Against the Sons of Darkness (Qumran, cave 1)
1QS	The Manual of Discipline (Qumran, cave 1)
4QpIs	Commentary on Isaiah (Qumran, cave 4)
4QPatrBl	Patriarchal Blessings (Qumran, cave 4)
4QTest	Testimonia (Qumran, cave 4)
4QFlor	Florilegium (Qumran, cave 4)

11QT	The Temple Scroll (Qumran, cave 11)
RSV	Revised Standard Version of the Bible
WA	Weimar edition of Luther's works
ZNW	*Zeitschrift für die neutestamentliche Wissenschaft*

INTRODUCTION

1. Voices from the Past and Present

The last book of the Bible, the Apocalypse—what are we to make of it? For some Christians it is the most important book, for others it is the most ignored. Certainly it is the most misunderstood book of the New Testament. To some it is the key that unlocks all of Scripture, the capstone that gives unity and meaning to the diversity of biblical writings. Others ignore it or view it as a book locked with the seven seals.

Yet the vivid, evocative language of the Apocalypse and its symbols and images have influenced the church's liturgy and hymnody, its art and architecture, as has no other book of the Bible. Seventy-eight hymns in the *Lutheran Book of Worship* draw their poetry from the richness of this last book of the Bible. The arches of Roman basilicas like St. Mary Major (A.D. 440), the mosaics of St. Paul Outside the Walls (Rome) which display the adoration of the Lamb in majestic beauty, the rose windows of Chartres, the horsemen on the portals of cathedrals in Paris and Amiens, the frescoes in the cathedral of Padua, Michelangelo's *Last Judgment* in the Sistine Chapel, Dürer's woodcuts, the tapestry of Angers, the illustrations in Latin Bible manuscripts, and Handel's "Hallelujah Chorus"—these and countless more testify to the power of the Apocalypse in Christian art, piety, and imagination. The dome of every Greek church is graced by the image of Christ, the Pantocrator, who, like the Father, is "the beginning and the end." Indeed, the church would be poorer without this book. In times of distress and persecution it gave strength to the victims of terror beginning with the martyrs of Lyons and Vienne in Gaul (A.D. 177) and of Scilli in North Africa (July 17, A.D. 180), and it continues to do so even in our century. The vision that they, the brutalized and despised followers of the Lamb, are conquerors of beasts by the blood of Christ and by their own suffering (Rev. 12:11; 14:1) gave meaning to their life, their suffering and death. They manifested an alternative to the quest for self-fulfillment in its countless varieties and drew their strength from the Revelation of Jesus Christ to John.

A Sorry Story of Misinterpretation

It is also true, however, that those who ventured to interpret the Apocalypse more often than not contributed generously to a history of misinterpretation that stretches from the first Latin commentary by Victorinus of Pettau (who died a martyr's death about A.D. 303) to Hal Lindsey's best-seller, *The Late Great Planet Earth*.

According to the Jehovah's Witnesses, Jesus Christ "arrived to sit down on his own Messianic throne as King and Judge in 1914" and "the judgment began in 1918." Never mind that they had to modify the view of their founder Charles T. Russell, who, prior to World War I, had brazenly proclaimed, "Millions now living shall never die." He died in 1916. When his original forecast of the end of the second world, or dispensation, in 1914 was not fulfilled (the "first dispensation" ended with the flood) he simply announced that he had overlooked another necessary step in his apocalyptic computation and what really happened in 1914 was the casting out of Satan from heaven (Rev. 12:7-9) and the establishment in heaven of God's invisible organization, whose earthly representatives are the Jehovah's Witnesses.

How did Russell arrive at the date of 1914? He began with the obscure date of A.D. 539, which he discovered as the year in which tremendous events took place. First, there was the conquest of the Ostrogoths and their king, Vitiges, in Ravenna, Italy, by the great Byzantine marshal Belisarius. Ignore the fact that the Ostrogoths actually surrendered a year later and rallied again under their new king, Totila, conquering

Rome twice, in A.D. 546 and 550. Second, the establishment of the papacy took place in A.D. 539, according to Russell. This would be a rather surprising discovery, for Pope Vigilius (A.D. 537–555), whose life story makes any soap opera sound stale, was anything but a strong pope. Leo I (A.D. 440–461) would have been a better candidate for the establishment of the primacy of the bishop of Rome than poor, wily, but weak-kneed Vigilius, who was manipulated and humiliated by Emperor Justinian and his wife Theodora, the bear keeper's daughter. Pope Leo I had stood up to Attila the Hun in A.D. 452, saving Italy from devastation. He had forcefully and successfully claimed that as successor to Peter he was the vicar of Christ and that the church of Rome "always has primacy." In comparison to Leo I or Gregory I (A.D. 590–604), Pope Vigilius was a pathetic figure rather than the establisher of the papacy. But Russell needed the date A.D. 539 in order eventually to get to A.D. 1914. How did he do that?

Daniel 12:12 contains a beatitude for him who waits and comes "to the thousand three hundred and thirty-five days." These prophetic days are identical with calendar years, Russell argued. In 1874 Russell had published his first book. By subtracting 1,335 years from that date, he arrived at A.D. 539. He then labeled 1874 the date of Christ's invisible return. Now only one more step was needed. Since God had granted for the gathering of Israel's remnant (the Jewish harvest), a 40-year period, which lasted from the first Pentecost of Acts 2 in A.D. 30 to the destruction of Jerusalem in A.D. 70, he will grant a second 40-year period for the gathering of the Gentile church (the Christian harvest). Add 40 to 1874 and you get A.D. 1914, the end of the world. When the end did not occur, he decided that in 1914 Jesus sat down upon his throne as king and judge, casting out Satan from heaven. With that kind of approach one can do just about anything with the Apocalypse.

We would do well to recall, however, that it was not just dispensationalist sectarians in America and England who constructed apocalyptic timetables. The outstanding Lutheran interpreter of the New Testament in the 18th century also engaged in this enterprise and did so with a vengeance. Johann Albrecht Bengel (1687–1752) was one of the foremost scholars of his day of the Greek text of the New Testament. His work on the text of Revelation was a milestone in the history of biblical scholarship. He recognized, for instance, that Erasmus's Greek text of Revelation was based on only one late and mutilated minuscule, a fact that obliged Erasmus to supply the missing portions by translating the Latin text into Greek. Bengel's conclusion was confirmed a century later, when Franz Delitzsch discovered the manuscript with Erasmus's notes on it.

But Bengel's passion was the interpretation of the New Testament. His *Gnomon* (= the raised part of a sundial) of 1742 contained his interpretation from Matthew to Revelation and was read by many Lutheran pastors of the 18th and early 19th centuries and was translated into English (1858). Since God acts in history, it is not Luther's dialectic of law and gospel, of judgment and grace, which opens the Scripture as Word of God. Rather, the unity of the acts of God as witnessed by both testaments constitutes the key to the Scripture. Moreover, God's acts find their climactic conclusion in the eschatological future as written in the Apocalypse. What Paul's letter to the Romans was for Martin Luther, the book of Revelation was for Johann Bengal—the key to the Bible. Since one cannot speak of God acting in history without taking biblical chronology seriously, Bengel constructed a chronology as "the most important aid" for the interpretation of the acts of God in history culminating in Christ's parousia, the millennium, and the new creation.

One might ask, Did Bengel not consider texts such as Mark 13:32, "Of that day or that hour no one knows, not even the angels in heaven, nor the Son, but only the Father," or Acts 1:7, where Jesus tells his apostles immediately prior to his ascension that "it is not for you to know the times or seasons" of the end? Of course he knew. His answer was that before his ascension Jesus did not know the time of the end, but in the Apocalypse the exalted Jesus himself communicated to John the revelation which God gave to him after his exaltation (1:1-3). This new revelation concerning the end time can be mapped out in terms of chronology. Bengel's chronology was meant to inspire trust because it was based on the only New Testament book that the exalted Christ himself had "dictated" and legitimated (22:6, 16, 18-19). John of Patmos functioned merely as scribe of the Revelation of Jesus Christ. Its author is the Lord of the church himself who is "coming soon" (22:7, 12, 20; cf. 1:1, 3). This promise, Bengel believed, refers to his own time. The numbers found in the Apocalypse disclose the chronology of the salvation history of the end time. The most important number is 666 (13:18), which Bengel understood as a reference to a span of time.

Bengel took the number 666 to refer to a span of years identical with the 42 months of Rev. 13:5. A "prophetic" month therefore lasts exactly $15\frac{6}{7}$ chronological years. With this insight he had the basic data for constructing an apocalyptic timetable. Elated by his discovery, he next determined the meaning of "a half time," which is $111\frac{1}{9}$ years. The apocalyptic "time" of Daniel and Revelation consists of $222\frac{2}{9}$ years, "two times" consequently are $444\frac{4}{9}$ years; a "half a chronos" is $555\frac{5}{9}$ years; the number of the beast (Rev. 13:18) refers to exactly $666\frac{6}{9}$ years. The "time and times and half time" (12:14) lasts $777\frac{7}{9}$ years; a "little time" (5:11) lasts $888\frac{8}{9}$ years; a full "chronos" lasts $1{,}111\frac{1}{9}$ years (hence the "non chronos" of 10:6—which the RSV translates with "no more delay"—must be shorter than 1,111 years); an "age" (Greek, *aiōn*) lasts $2{,}222\frac{2}{9}$

years, while the world will last 7,777⁷⁄₉ years, and so forth. Bengel's calculations, in abbreviated form, can be shown as follows:

A.D. 96 the Revelation is written and the future is disclosed.

A.D. 97–98 the seals are opened as promised in Revelation 6 and the "chronos" is indicated in the fifth seal (6:11).

The second, third, fourth, and fifth centuries are filled with the blasts of the first *four trumpets* (8:6-13); the second century is marked by the scattering of the Jews by Hadrian (8:7); the third century sees the invasion of the barbarians (8:8); and the fourth century witnesses the Arian heresy (8:10).

Through the *fifth* trumpet the Roman empire in the West comes to an end (8:12). The "first woe" (cf. 8:13; 9:12) is dated between A.D. 510 and 589 and comprises the tribulation of the Jews in Persia (9:1).

From 589 to 634 is the interval between the first and the second woe. The second woe lasts from A.D. 634 to 847 (9:13-19) and is filled with murder perpetrated by the Islamic "Saracenes" (9:13) as well as with the unsuccessful struggle against idolatrous images (9:20) in the East.

In A.D. 800 begins the "non chronos" of 10:6 with the coronation of Charlemagne, followed by a line of many "kings" (10:11).

A.D. 847–947 is the interval between the second and the third woe.

The third woe lasts from 947 to 1836 (cf. 12:12).

A.D. 940–1617 comprises the 1,260 days of the woman (12:6).

A.D. 1058–1836 is the "time and times and a half time" of 12:14.

In 1614 the angel with the eternal gospel appears—Johann Arndt—the father of Lutheran Pietism (14:6).

June 18, A.D. 1836, will see the beginning of the thousand-year imprisonment of Satan and the destruction of Antichrist (Rev. 19:11—20:3).

During the millennial imprisonment of Satan in the abyss, the church will expand and the Jews will be converted in accordance with Rom. 11:25-36; a millennium of peace, prosperity, and happiness will come about. However, sin, death, and temptations are still present during this millennium. Also, the law of God remains in force (Matt. 5:18), including governmental authority, marriage, and occupations.

After this first millennium, Bengel tells us, we shall find a second millennium in which the saints reign with Christ in heaven (20:4-6). At the end of the first millennium and overlapping with the beginning of the second there comes the release of Satan and the war of Gog and Magog against the people of God on earth, especially the believing Jews. Gog and Magog were identified by him (and also by Vitringa) as Russia on the basis of the Hebrew word *rosh* of Ezek. 38:2, a text to which

Rev. 20:7-9 alludes. *Mesech,* which is mentioned with Magog in Gen. 10:2, thus refers to Moscow. When the destruction of Satan, Gog, and Magog occurs, believers will discover themselves in the second millennium, in which they are raised from the dead in order to reign with Christ in heaven (20:4-6), followed by the final judgment (20:11-15), the new creation, and the eternal bliss and resurrection of the blessed (21:1—22:5).

Bengel's twofold millennium distinguished him from other Lutheran chiliasts (from Greek, *chilioi,* 1,000) such as Spener or Loehe. He reached this strange conclusion because he read the literary sequence of the text in terms of chronological sequences. Since 20:1-3 with its thousand years precedes the thousand years mentioned in 20:4-6, there must be two millennia in tandem with each other. In short, Bengel rejected the notion that the sequence of visions in the Apocalypse is like the sequence of images seen in a kaleidoscope, which recapitulate, that is, repeat in new forms the same material. This theory of recapitulation was first advanced by Victorinus of Pettau (the present Ptui in Slovenia, Yugoslavia). He died as martyr about A.D. 303. His commentary, which is the oldest in Latin, is one of the most interesting interpretations of the Apocalypse that has ever been written. He saw more clearly than those who came after him that the sequence of visions in Revelation must be understood thematically, not chronologically. The thematic repetitions of judgment visions and of salvation visions refer to the same eschatological events. In contrast to Bengel, Victorinus held that the sequence of visions in Revelation does not constitute a sequence of predicted historical events. While we might disagree with some of Victorinus's interpretations of particular texts and images, his recapitulation theory represents an alternative method of interpreting Revelation. Instead of focusing attention on trying to discover a chronological table of historical events that are predicted in encoded form in the Apocalypse and await our discovery, the recapitulation theory approaches Revelation by focusing attention on themes and cycles of visions. Bengel's fundamental error lay in his basic assumption that the prophecy of the Apocalypse consists of coded predictions of the course of history from John's time to Bengel's and to the parousia beyond. This approach, which has engaged countless interpreters before and after him, has always produced bizarre results.

Even Martin Luther must be located among those who grossly misunderstood the last book of the Bible in terms of coded predictions of the course of history. (For the following, see *LW* 35:398–411.) "My spirit cannot accommodate itself to this book," he wrote in his first preface to the Apocalypse in 1522. Luther's admission that he could not understand the Apocalypse was the best thing he ever wrote concerning it. To acknowledge one's inability to understand something is an expression of honesty and surely preferable to faking insight where there is none. In his preface to the Apocalypse of 1522, he made it clear that he considered this book to be "neither apostolic, nor prophetic" and that "many fathers" of the ancient church had "also rejected this book a long time ago." For Luther, the Apocalypse was not an apostolic writing, because "apostles do not deal with visions," but speak and write "in clear plain words" which can be understood by anyone. "Moreover there is no prophet in the Old Testament, to say nothing of the New, who deals so exclusively with visions and images" as did the author of the Apocalypse.

Recognizing its link with Jewish apocalyptic literature, Luther commented, "For myself, I think it approximates the Fourth Book of Esdras." This insight is quite correct. Revelation belongs to the apocalyptic genre which is a type of literature that Luther did not appreciate. When he was engaged later in the translation of the Old Testament Apocrypha he did not even bother to translate 4 Ezra. Incidentally, the Lutheran publisher, Christopher Sauer, of Germantown, Pennsylvania, added 4 Ezra to the first Bible published on the American continent in a European language (German) in A.D. 1743. Sauer's Bible also included the section of 4 Ezra 7:36-105 which for doctrinal reasons is missing in most Latin manuscripts and which appeared in an English Bible for the first time in 1895.

Since Revelation is an apocalyptic book that narrates visions and uses images and symbols, Luther could not "detect that the Holy Spirit produced it"; nor is Jesus Christ "taught" or "known" in it. It showed considerable self-confidence on Luther's part to admit his own inability to understand it and simultaneously to use his lack of comprehension to make sweeping negative value judgments. Having stated his own preference for those New Testament writings which "present Christ to me clearly and purely," he also told his readers that they were welcome to their "own opinions" with respect to the authorship and value of the Apocalypse. One would have thought that Luther's own condemnations by Pope Leo X and by the imperial Diet of Worms (1520–1521), the prospect of persecution and possible martyrdom, together with his fervent expectation of the imminent end of the world, might have enabled him to gain a new understanding of Revelation. But this was not to be. The Apocalypse interested him only as a quarry from which he could gather stones for his antipapal polemics. Already one year earlier, in 1521, he had used the Apocalypse to show the anti-Christian nature of the papacy. He identified Thomas Aquinas as the star of Rev. 9:1 and Aristotle as the Apollyon of 9:11; the locust plague refers to false teachers of the church. The identification of the papacy with the beast and the harlot of Revelation 13 and 17 remained with Luther to the end and was then taken over by his followers. Yet even this particular allegorical interpretation was not an innovation. Followers of Wycliffe in the 14th century and radical Franciscans of the 13th century had already denounced the papacy in terms of the Antichrist of Revelation 13 and 17.

The radical Franciscans were dependent on Joachim of Floris (about A.D. 1200), who produced one of the most influential interpretations of the Apocalypse. He divided world history into three periods. The time of the Father, which is the period of the Old Testament (a time of marriage), is followed by the time of the Son, which is the church and its unmarried clergy. The second appearance of Christ will usher in the period of the Holy Spirit in conjunction with the establishment of a new monastic order. Joachim himself was a monk. Moreover, the period of the Holy Spirit, Joachim believed, would begin in A.D. 1260. Then 42 generations will have passed during the period of the church (cf. Rev. 11:3), just as there had been 42 generations during Old Testament times (cf. Matt. 1:1-17). While Joachim did not identify the papacy with Antichrist, his followers from among the recently established Franciscan order had no such compunctions. Pope and emperor were now seen as the beasts predicted in Revelation 13, and the task of the radical Franciscans was to reform the church from ecclesiastical scum.

Luther made use of this tradition in his new preface to the Apocalypse of 1530. The imperial papacy, which used the temporal sword, and the empire, which was subservient to the papacy, are the two beasts of Revelation 13 (*LW* 35:405). Otherwise Luther was primarily dependent on Nicholas of Lyra's commentary of 1329.

Nicholas used Revelation to interpret world history in the following manner: The seals (chap. 6) lead to the time of Domitian; the trumpets are the period of the heretics (Arius and others). In Revelation 12 he saw the struggles between the Parthian king Chosroes (the dragon) and the Byzantine emperor Heraclius. The first beast of Revelation 13 is Chosroes's son, the second in Mohammed. Revelation 14 refers to Pipin and Charlemagne. The seven bowls of wrath are the crusades. The rider on the white horse (Rev. 19:11) is not Christ but Baldwin, king of Jerusalem during the Crusades. Note that Nicholas was a Frenchman, like Baldwin. Revelation 20 refers to the struggle between Pope Calixtus II (1119–1124) and Emperor Henry V. The binding of Satan took place (Rev. 20:1-3) in the establishment of the new monastic orders which open up the millennium. While Luther could hardly follow Nicholas of Lyra in every detail, he was clearly dependent on him in his general approach to the Apocalypse and in several particular items. For Luther, "the surest step toward finding its [the Apocalypse's] interpretation is to take from history the events and disasters that have come upon Christendom till now and hold them up alongside of these images" (of Revelation). This approach is not basically different from the one used by

Hal Lindsey and others. The difference lies in the times in which Nicholas, Luther, and Lindsey lived.

Like Nicholas before him, so Luther in 1530 identified the trumpet plagues with sundry heresies, beginning with Tatian and "the Encratites who forbade marriage and wanted to become righteous by their works" (first trumpet), followed by Marcion, the Manichaeans, and the Montanists "who extol their own spirituality above all Scriptures, and move—like this burning mountain (Rev. 8:8)—between heaven and earth" (second trumpet). Origen, Novatus, and the Donatists were the third and fourth trumpet plague; the fifth (= the first woe) is Arius, and the sixth (= second woe) is "the shameful Mohammed with his companions," who have inflicted "great plagues on Christendom." Along with this sixth (evil) angel comes "the mighty angel with the rainbow (Rev. 10:1 who is also evil!) and holds the bitter scroll, that is, the holy papacy, with its appearance of great spirituality." In short, the second woe consists of two plagues, Islam and the papacy. Referring to Rev. 11:1-3 and misconstruing the Greek text, Luther commented, "They [the papists] measure and enclose the temple with their laws, leave out the inner sanctuary and start a counterfeit church of external holiness." In Rev. 11:4—12:17 Luther found "comforting images" which indicate "that some pious teachers and Christians are nevertheless to remain" under all three woes. The two beasts of Revelation 13 are the empire and the papacy. So one can see that "the devil's final wrath gets to work" in the East with "Mohammed and the Saracenes" and in the West with "the papacy and the empire." "To these are added for good measure the Turk, Gog and Magog," as Revelation 20 will show. With chap. 14 begins the slaying of Antichrist through the proclamation of the eternal gospel. Luther's friend Bugenhagen identified Luther with the angel who proclaims the eternal gospel of Rev. 14:6. Chapters 15 and 16 increase the gospel's attacks upon the papacy. The frogs of 16:13 are "the sophists, such as Faber, Eck and Emser," contemporary opponents of Luther who "croak much against the gospel, but accomplish nothing and remain frogs." Chapters 17 and 18 depict the destruction of the "imperial papacy and the papal empire." A beginning has already been made with the sack of Rome in 1527 by the army of Charles V, which Luther saw reflected in Rev. 17:16. Revelation 19:11—20:10 is treated by him in a rather perfunctory manner. It is not clear whether for him Christ's victory over the anti-Christian kings in 19:11-21 refers to his parousia or not. But one thing is clear. The millennium during which Satan is bound (20:1-3) and during which the saints reign with Christ (20:4-6) "begins about the time this book was written." This means that the millennium is not a future period but comprises the period of the church beginning with John of Patmos. Luther received this idea from Augustine, who in turn took it over from the anti-chiliast Tyconius (about A.D. 380), a Donatist theologian from North Africa whom his own church excommunicated.

For Tyconius, the millennium stretched from the first to the second coming of Jesus, which is the time of the church. He expected the second coming to occur shortly after A.D. 380. According to him, all prophetic time references must be understood "spiritually" and the thousand years of Rev. 20:2 are identical with the 3½ times of Daniel (cf. Rev. 11:2; 12:14) and refer to 350 calendar years. By adding the thirty years of Jesus' life, one arrives, according to Tyconius, at the date of his second coming. Of course, Augustine, writing after A.D. 380, did not accept Tyconius's parousia date (*City of God,* chaps. 20–22). But his interpretation of the millennium as the time of the church became the official opinion during the Middle Ages, as well as of Luther and his followers, including the Missouri Synod theologians Franz Pieper and J. T. Mueller.

Between Luther's two prefaces of 1522 and 1530 lay the rise of radical groups who, with peaceful or with revolutionary means, hoped for the establishment of the millennium that lay ahead. They drew their inspiration from the last book of the Bible, and for them it was absurd to hold that the millennium covered the past period of the Roman church, including the Lutheran reform which was a halfway affair at best to them. In 1530 it was no longer feasible for Luther to state simply: "My spirit cannot accommodate itself to this book." He had to say something positive concerning this book which was eagerly studied by the leaders and the people of the diverse groups of "Enthusiasts," as Luther labeled his Protestant opponents. Yet instead of entering into a dialog with them on the basis of the text of Revelation, he merely presented the stale bread of Tyconius-Augustine, of the radical Franciscans, and of Nicholas of Lyra. What Luther wrote in his new preface of 1530 shows that he really was not in tune with this book; it always remained a strange book for him. It never occurred to him that John of Patmos could no more preach against the papacy than he himself could preach against star wars, both of which were beyond their horizons and irrelevant to their situations. He concluded his thumbnail sketch of interpretation by stating that "through and beyond all plagues, beasts, and evil angels Christ is nonetheless with his saints, and wins the final victory" (*LW* 35:411). True enough, but hardly sufficient! One can, however, be grateful that Luther did not try to set a date for the parousia.

One of his devoted followers, Michael Stifel, did just that and calculated October 19, 1533, 8 A.M. sharp, as the hour of Christ's second coming. Stifel arrived at this date on the basis of reading Daniel in combination with Revelation. In February 1533, Luther still called him a pious and learned man (WA *Tischreden,* 3:2955b), but Luther himself consistently abstained from such foolishness. Incidentally Stifel, like

Bengel two centuries later, argued that texts such as Mark 13:32 were true only with respect to Christ's state of humiliation and have been superseded by the exalted Christ in his Apocalypse.

In 1530 the Lutherans presented their Augsburg Confession to Emperor Charles. Its seventeenth article issued another condemnation of "the Anabaptists," without any attempt to distinguish between different Baptist groups. One can only be glad that the actual formulation of Article 17 did not involve an implicit condemnation of Revelation 20–21, but limited itself to the rejection of revolutionary chiliasts and their teaching. The pertinent text reads: "Our churches . . . also condemn others who are now spreading Jewish opinions to the effect that *before the resurrection* of the dead the godly will take possession of the kingdom of the world, the ungodly being suppressed everywhere." The German text reads in its final clause: (the saints will) "annihilate all the godless." What is condemned here is not John's expectation of a millennium (Rev. 20:4-6), nor does Augustine's and Luther's false interpretation of the millennium receive confessional status. Augustana 17 rejected the revolutionary chiliasm of persons such as Thomas Müntzer and Hans Hut. The latter preached rebellion even after the catastrophe of the peasant revolt in 1525 and expected that God would give the signal in 1531 for the annihilation of the godless (especially the princes and preachers). Statements similar to Article 17 of the Augsburg Confession are found in other Protestant confessional writings, such as the Second Helvetic Confession of 1566, chap. 11. For John of Patmos, a millennium *prior* to the resurrection would be as ludicrous as its establishment through human revolutionary action.

Rejection and Neglect

If a book can be so grossly misused and so frequently misunderstood as the Apocalypse has been, it might seem to some best to ignore it or to reject it outright.

Rejection of the Apocalypse along with all other Johannine writings came early toward the end of the second century. The anti-Montanists of Asia Minor, to whom the church father Epiphanius assigned the label "Alogoi," blamed the Fourth Gospel with its "Logos" Christology (John 1:1, 14) for the rise of Montanism. They and the Roman presbyter Gaius at the beginning of the third century went one step farther and declared the Gospel of John and Revelation to be the work of the arch-heretic Cerinthus. In so doing, Gaius thought he could undermine the scriptural basis of the Montanists, who taught that the Paraclete (RSV, "Counselor") of John 14:16, 26; 15:26; 16:7-15 was speaking through Montanus and his two prophetesses Priscilla and Maximilla. Like the author of Revelation, Montanus advocated rigorous ethical demands within a church that had become morally lax, and he proclaimed the imminent end of the world just as the apocalypticist had done. But he went farther. Claiming the power of the Paraclete speaking through him and his two companions, he promised that the heavenly Jerusalem (21:2-4), which would last millennium (20:4-6), would descend from heaven in Asia Minor, near the little town of Pepuza in Phrygia. He and his followers requested all believers to gather there and await the end, or rather the new beginning. The Montanist prophecies, which had claimed to guide believers "into all truth" as promised in John 16:13, went unfulfilled, because obviously the end did not come. The Montanist movement, however, continued and became a counterchurch with stern moral demands that attracted the great North African theologian Tertullian into its fold. In opposition to Montanism the group of the Alogoi in Asia Minor and the presbyter Gaius of Rome sought to exclude the Fourth Gospel and the Apocalypse from the writings of the church. The rest of the church would have none of it.

The next attempt to exclude or at least to downgrade the Apocalypse came from the school of Origen. Around A.D. 250, Dionysius, bishop of Alexandria, wrote a learned tract which is partially preserved in Eusebius's *History of the Church* (7.24–25). Dionysius sought to demonstrate that the linguistic and stylistic differences that exist between the Fourth Gospel on one hand and the Apocalypse on the other make the apostolic authorship of Revelation improbable. Thus its position among what came to be known as the canonical writings of the New Testament was in doubt among Origen's theological heirs. The chief reason for Dionysius's antipathy against Revelation lay in the realistic eschatology of this book. Most objectionable to him was the notion of Christ's millennial reign on earth (20:4-6; 21:1—22:5). The spiritualizing Origenists preferred an individualistic eschatology of souls with Christ in heaven, and they rejected the expectation of Christ's reign on a new earth free from sin, death, and the devil. Origen's followers slandered the hope for the kingdom of Christ on earth as an expression of the desires of the flesh. Hence Dionysius repeated the defamation, perpetrated by the Alogoi, concerning Cerinthus's authorship of this book. In order to undercut the chiliasm of the Apocalypse, he added that it had been Cerinthus's doctrine "that the kingdom of Christ would be on earth; and he dreamed that it would consist in . . . the satisfaction of the belly and the sex drive." As if Christian chiliasts, such as Justin Martyr or Irenaeus, or the author of Revelation, had taught that! Piously Dionysius added that for his part he would "not dare to reject the book, since many brethren esteem it highly." Excerpts from Dionysius became widely known, also to Luther (cf. his prefaces), through Eusebius's *History of the Church*. The Origenist Eusebius counted the Apocalypse among the "homologoumena," writings acknowledged by the churches, but he added the comment, "if one wishes." Simultaneously he counted it also among the spurious, rejected writings, adding the same comment, "if one wishes." His own preference was clearly for exclusion of this book from the canonical writings of the New Testament.

Revelation found its place in the canon because of its wide use in the church of the West, the tenacity of Greek-speaking pockets in the East, and the prestige of Athanasius, who included it among the canonical writings of the New Testament in his famous 39th Easter festival letter of A.D. 367. Yet the Apocalypse is absent in the list of canonical books of Cyril of Jerusalem (about A.D. 350) and of Gregory of Nazianzus (died A.D. 390). Amphilochius of Iconium (died A.D. 394) mentioned its widespread rejection. The 59th canon of the Synod of Laodicea (cf. Rev. 3:14), about A.D. 360, omitted Revelation from its list of canonical books—and "all the canons" of this synod were accepted by the Quinisextine Council of A.D. 692. Oddly enough, the same council also accepted another list which did contain Revelation. The Syriac-speaking church did not have Revelation in its Bible until the sixth century, and the East Syrian Nestorian church excludes it to this day. In the Greek-speaking church it was in the canon but widely ignored in preaching and teaching. Greek manuscripts containing the text of Revelation are few in number in comparison with Gospel or Epistle manuscripts, which reflects the broad neglect of the Apocalypse in Greek-speaking churches. Not infrequently these manuscripts were bound together with apocryphal material. Thus, for instance, minuscule 2084, a 14th- or 15th-century paper manuscript of Revelation, is found in a volume that contains medieval legends, like Pilate's letter to Emperor Tiberius and Augustus's letter to Pilate.

It was not just the Greek-speaking church which largely ignored this book. John Calvin wrote a commentary on every New Testament book except Revelation. In modern times the theological problems posed by the Apocalypse resulted in neglect and open rejection. Adolf Jülicher's famous judgment that "Apocalyptic is prophecy turned senile"; E. F. Scott's verdict that this "book cannot be placed on the same religious level as the other New Testament writings"; Rudolf Bultmann's opinion that Revelation presents a "weakly Christianized Judaism"; and C. H. Dodd's conclusion that "the God of the Apocalypse can hardly be recognized as the Father of our Lord Jesus Christ, nor has the fierce Messiah whose warriors ride in blood up to their horses' bridles" much in common with "the primitive kerygma"—these conclusions by widely respected scholars hardly enhance the prestige of our book. Laypeople such as

D. H. Lawrence joined the chorus, denouncing the Apocalypse as "the Judas of the New Testament." Johann Wolfgang von Goethe in a letter expressed his distinct preference for Jesus' parables over against "the seven messages, lampstands, seals, stars and woes," and he opined that should there be "something divine" in the New Testament it might be found in the parables.

The Apocalypse has always been misunderstood when it is approached as code containing predictions for the interpreter's own past and future; it has frequently been neglected and occasionally been maligned. Those who regarded it as key to the Scripture generally misused it most.

Modern Premillennialists

The misuse of the Apocalypse reached its pinnacle in the diverse groups of premillennialists (those who expected Christ's parousia *prior* to the millennium, in contrast to the postmillennialists, who expected the parousia *after* the millennium).

Their spiritual ancestors were the Plymouth Brethren in England, the Millerites, and similar groups in 19th-century America. The most influential premillennialist of our time is Hal Lindsey, and his best-seller of 1970 infused new strength into fundamentalistic premillennialism which through a network of publication enterprises and missionary societies has spanned the globe. Common to all premillennialists is the belief that after a brief reign of Antichrist, which generally is thought to last seven years, Christ will return and with his armies of raptured saints defeat the Antichrist in the battle of Armageddon. Then the millennium, the thousand-year reign of Christ on earth, begins. After this interim of a thousand years comes the final judgment and the new creation.

All "futurist" premillennialists combine texts from Daniel with texts from Revelation, Ezekiel, and Zechariah which they interpret literally and believe to be applicable not to the prophets' time but to our time. In contrast to the "historicist" premillennialists, who, like Luther, tried to discover the course of the church's history in these writings, and in contrast to postmillennialists, who expect Christ's second coming after a millennium of phenomenal expansion of Christianity, the "futurist" premillennialists expect the imminent appearance of Antichrist followed by Christ's second coming prior to the millennium. In short, they are oriented toward an imminent eschatological future. Some are buffs of apocalyptic time calculations; some locate the rapture of the saints (cf. 1 Thess. 4:15-17) prior to the appearance of Antichrist, others hold that it may take place during his early rise to power or his middle years, and still others insist that the rapture occurs at the end of the period of tribulation caused by Antichrist, but in every case the rapture will happen prior to Christ's coming for the slaughter at Armageddon. With Hal Lindsey, premillennialists shifted their emphasis from saving individual souls from the lake of fire and brimstone to apocalyptic interpretations of contemporary politics and to expectations concerning future political developments. The "prophetic countdown" began in 1948 with the establishment of the State of Israel, thus says Lindsey.

In *A Radio Bible Class Publication* on the subject "What Can We Know About the Antichrist?" (Grand Rapids, Mich., 1987), we read that the Antichrist, on the basis of Rev. 6:2, will appear at first as "a man of peace." "He will be so clever that the nation of Israel will be deceived by him" and he will make a covenant with the modern State of Israel. But at "midpoint of his seven-year treaty the Antichrist will suddenly turn against the Israelites" and greatly vex them. He will "halt their sacrifices" in the restored temple (!) and begin to desolate Jerusalem (with reference to Dan. 9:27; Matt. 24:15-22). He will also openly advocate homosexuality (Dan. 11:37). Besides Satan and the false prophet (Rev. 13:2, 11) he will have the harlot of Revelation 17 as his "third cohort." She will be working closely with him during his rise to power and establish an "ecumenical religion" tolerating "everything except biblical Christianity." But after the Antichrist shall have achieved world dominion, he will turn against the harlot and destroy her in accordance with Rev. 17:16.

The "seven heads" of the beast of Rev. 13:1 "represent a succession of great empires." The "sixth is the Roman empire of New Testament days" (Rev. 17:10). "The seventh will be the future restored empire under Antichrist. The eighth (cf. Rev 17:10-11) may be his kingdom after he is killed and resurrected by the devil" (cf. Rev. 13:3). Note that this particular view omits all of history from the end of the Roman empire in the West (A.D. 476) to the present in contrast to timetables of "historicist" millennialists. The "ten horns" (17:12), according to the Radio Bible Class publication, "will be a federation of Western nations organized by Antichrist during the time of his rise to power."

Other premillennialists identify the ten horns of the beast as the nations of the European Common Market (there are now already 12) who for a time will befriend the State of Israel and even defend it against the evil empire of the North, Russia, (cf. Ezekiel 38–39). But when Antichrist turns against Israel, then the ten nations of the European

Common Market will follow suit. Their leaders and Antichrist will enter the restored temple of Jerusalem and demand veneration by the people of Israel. This Israel will refuse. And then Christ and his raptured saints will appear for the slaughter of Antichrist and his army at Armageddon. Then many, or all, Jews will accept Jesus, and the millennium of peace, prosperity, and happiness will follow. Other schemes are still wilder, with Chinese and Indian armies appearing on the scene, making mincemeat of the Russians.

Not all premillennialists are so specific, but all use the Bible as God's gigantic jigsaw puzzle which he gave to us in order to figure out his end-time plan stretching from our present to the millennium. Some naturally claim to know more than others. Thus, for instance, Robert W. Faid, a former engineering supervisor and latter-day Master of Theology from Coatesville Bible College, is certain that the Antichrist is none other than General Secretary/President Mikhail Gorbachev whom "Satan branded in his mother's womb" with a birthmark. All biblical prophecies concerning Antichrist, save two, apply to Gorbachev. The two missing ones, which are the mortal wound and his miraculous recovery (Rev. 13:3), will surely happen in the immediate future. Faid has calculated that the odds that Gorbachev is the Antichrist are better than "seven hundred and ten quadrillion" to one! What odds, what calculation! So then, Gorbachev joins the list of candidates for the mysterious number 666, which includes among others Nero, Domitian, Mohammed, Frederick II, individual popes, the papacy as a whole, Martin Luther, Napoleon, Kaiser Wilhelm, Stalin, Hitler, Roosevelt, Kissinger, and yes, Ronald Wilson Reagan (the latter is the only U.S. president to have six letters in each of his three names—the significance of 666 is clear [Rev. 13:18]). The misuse of the Bible by premillennialists knows no bounds, but the flow of time makes nonsense of them all.

The notion of the divine rapture from the inevitable holocaust buttresses self-righteous, narcissistic smugness; the rejection of negotiations and compromise with our international opponents divides nations along lines of absolute good and absolute evil. The premillennialist ideologies concerning the State of Israel have made its devotees deaf to the cries of Palestinians and to the need of a shared humanity.

The Millennialists of the Ancient Church

The controversy surrounding the interpretation of the Apocalypse today has two aspects. One is the use of the Bible in general and of the Apocalypse in particular in an age of historical criticism. The other centers around the question, What did John, the apocalypticist, mean by the thousand-year reign of the martyred saints *with* Christ (Rev. 20:4-6)? Both issues already caused controversy in the ancient church.

Millennialism (= chiliasm) was rather widespread in the ancient church. Leaders such as Papias, bishop of Hierapolis (about A.D. 80–140), Justin Martyr (converted in Ephesus about A.D. 130), Melito of Sardis (about A.D. 170), Irenaeus, bishop of Lyon, Gaul (born in Asia Minor about A.D. 142), Victorinus of Pettau (martyred about 303), and many others were chiliasts. They roundly rejected an allegorical interpretation of Old Testament prophecies, as practiced by Gnostics in the second century, even as later chiliasts would oppose the Origenists. Chiliasts believed that the prophecies concerning the people of Israel and Jerusalem must be fulfilled literally. Moreover, these prophecies shall be fulfilled during Christ's millennial reign on earth. Finally, they held that the millennial reign will be an *interim* rule, bounded by the parousia and the final judgment. It will therefore be distinct from the eternal reign of God in a new creation. By making the millennium into an interim, and by locating the fulfillment of Old Testament prophecies within this interim reign, the chiliasts radically altered John's apocalyptic vision of 20:4-6. Except for the concept of a thousand-year reign, the chiliast vision has little in common with John's text. In fact, the chiliasts created an alternative vision, and having done so, they connected their millennial vision with Rev. 20:4-6.

This commentary will endeavor to show that John's millennium is not an interim but the beginning of the life of the world to come, that John's new Jerusalem descends from heaven at the beginning and not at the conclusion of the millennium, and that the millennial reign with Christ constitutes the prerogative of the saints over against the rest of humanity, who after the final judgment shall enter the new Jerusalem, provided their names are found in the book of life.

In contrast to John, however, the millennialists of the ancient church adopted Jewish apocalyptic notions of a Messianic interim reign on this earth, and they also attached Old Testament traditions to Rev. 20:4-6. Thus they, not John, created an interim kingdom between this world and the new creation. Undoubtedly John had been aware of such apocalyptic interim kingdom traditions within churches of Asia Minor and he had tried to accommodate their views in chaps. 20:1—22:5. But in spite of his threats in 22:18 he did not succeed. The interim kingdom millennialists won. In reaction to them, Tyconius and Augustine falsely identified Rev. 20:4-6 with the time of the church, while the modern "futurist" premillennialists have taken up the cause of the second-century chiliasts.

Papias, bishop of Hierapolis, which is a few miles north of Laodicea (cf. Rev. 3:14), lived at the beginning of the second century, and, like most theologians of Asia Minor, he was a chiliast. Eusebius therefore labeled him "a person with very little intelligence" and held him responsible for the chiliasm of a "great many churchmen after him," including Irenaeus. It is not impossible for Papias to have known the author of the Apocalypse. Andrew of Caesarea writing his commentary on Revelation in the sixth century thought that Papias knew John personally, and Irenaeus implied the same. Papias certainly must have known John's book in view of the short distance between his city and Laodicea. Unfortunately only a few fragments from his five books have survived in citations of other church fathers, especially Irenaeus (*Adv. Haer.* 5.33) and Eusebius (*C.H.* 3.39). However, these fragments clearly demonstrate that diverse views concerning the millennium circulated in churches of Asia Minor from the very beginning. Papias did not heed the demand of John, stated most emphatically in 22:18-19, that no one should add "to the words of prophecy of this book" on pain of plagues. On the contrary, Papias's millennial expectations were filled with traditions that are extraneous to Revelation and present a new version of the millennium in comparison to Rev. 20:4-6. Furthermore, he based his millennial vision on words of Jesus himself, thereby claiming absolute authority for it. Actually his vision is dependent on apocalyptic traditions, such as *2 Bar.* 29:5-6 and *1 Enoch* 10:19. According to Papias, the millennium will see "vineyards grow each with ten thousand vines, and on one vine ten thousand branches and on one branch ten thousand shoots and on every shoot ten thousand clusters and in every cluster ten thousand grapes and every grape when pressed will give twenty-five measures of wine; and when one of the saints grasp a cluster, another will cry out: I am better, take me, bless the Lord on my account. . . . And all animals will be using foods, produced by the earth and will live peacefully and in harmony together."

Moreover, we know that Papias, in contrast to John, indulged in speculations concerning the relationship between the six days of creation and the periods of world history. Unfortunately we no longer have his text. However, *Barnabas* 15 tells that just as God "finished" his work of creation so "everything will be finished in 6,000 years," because one "day of the Lord shall be as a thousand years." The *seventh* day corresponds to the millennium, and the *eighth* day is "the beginning of another world." According to *Barnabas* 15, the millennium is clearly an interim, and it is probable that Papias held the same view.

Already at the beginning of the second century, churches in Asia Minor held diverse millennarian hopes. In Justin new traditions come to the fore. According to him, Isa. 65:17-25 refers to the millennium. Jerusalem, which had been destroyed by Titus and Hadrian, will be rebuilt and shall become a place of rejoicing. Yet people shall still die during this interim period (*Dialog* 81). While Justin refers to the Apocalypse, he is no longer aware that his views are contrary to Rev. 20:4-6. The same holds true for Irenaeus, who added that the rebuilding of the earthly Jerusalem shall take place in accordance with the image of the heavenly Jerusalem (*Adv. Haer.* 5.35.2). In contrast to Rev. 20:4-6, he believed that the prophets and the patriarchs of the Old Testament shall participate in the millennium (*Adv. Haer.* 5.34.2-3). The Antichrist shall be a member of the tribe of Dan (*Adv. Haer.* 5.30.1-2), because he shall recapitulate every error and idolatry since the flood. Hence, contrary to Revelation 13 and 17 he is not related to imperial Roman power. Finally, Irenaeus not only divided history into periods in accordance with the seven days of creation (*Adv. Haer.* 5.28.3, etc.) but he also thought that the righteous after the final judgment will be assigned different locations. According to their merit, some will enter heaven, others paradise (distinct from heaven), and still others shall dwell in "the city." Believers shall progress through the Spirit to the Son and through the Son to the Father. This order of the saved is, according to Irenaeus, a tradition of "the presbyters" (*Adv. Haer.* 5.36.2). But it is a tradition that contradicts Revelation 20–22. Still another tradition is combined with the millennium. According to Victorinus of Pettau, it will be the returning Elijah, not Christian preachers, who shall convert the 144,000 of Rev. 7:4; 14:1. They are believing Jews who will be gathered around the Lamb on Mount Zion in the Holy Land. In short, traditions independent of and in conflict with Rev. 20:4-6 produced new forms of millennial expectations.

Opposing chiliasm, the Origenists with their allegorical method of interpretation hardly did justice to the text of Revelation either. The Antichrist of the Apocalypse is now transformed into the sum total of evil, and the seven heads of the dragon become seven sins. The millennium is changed by Tyconius and Augustine into the time of the church, understood either literally as a thousand-year period or, later on, symbolically, but in either case it has been robbed of its eschatological thrust. Augustine's interpretation of the millennium triumphed in all mainline denominations, Catholic and Protestant. Yet diverse apocalyptic traditions also continued, like a stream that went underground, in the churches of the East (see Kretschmar, 82–90) and of the West (see McGinn). Their resurgence at different times in the church's history and their presence in American premillennialism testify to the vitality of apocalyptic traditions. But they also became the reason why the last book of the Bible was generally misunderstood and why it was justly neglected.

2. Historical Interpretation

General Comments

Historical interpretation means that every text has a historical context from which it may no more be divorced than you and I may be presented as if we were Turks and lived in 16th-century Turkey or on Mars in the 23rd century. This insight makes it impossible to mix texts from Ezekiel with Daniel and with texts from Revelation and interpret one by means of the other(s). They were not written for the same historical situation, nor were they written with the same objectives in mind. Each had its own context and audience, and the audience is not "us" but "them." So long as fundamentalism refuses to take seriously that each text has a historical context, so long will there be vulgar misuses of the Scriptures in general and of the Apocalypse in particular. God's word indeed does speak to every age, but it does so through the medium of its first historical utterance in a given historical context. Shortcuts to "relevancy" have produced an abundance of oddities that blunt and pervert the Word of God.

A historical interpretation of the Apocalypse exacts a price, however—namely, that the present-day reader will realize that the millennium did not occur in John's immediate future, as envisioned in his book; the parousia of Christ did not happen "soon," as promised repeatedly (1:1-3; 22:7; 12, 20); Rome did not fall, as expected. When it fell in A.D. 410, it was not Antichrist and his minions who sacked it but the Visigoths under Alaric, an Arian Christian. Then followed the sack of Rome by the Vandals (A.D. 455), the Ostrogoths (A.D. 546 and 550), and others (e.g., A.D. 1527), and it still flourishes. No Antichrist has burned "her up with fire" and devoured "her flesh" (Rev. 17:16). The Apocalypse shares the problem of the nonoccurrence of the imminent-end expectation with Paul's letters, the Gospels of Mark and Matthew, and other New Testament writings.

What is most important when dealing with the imminent-end expectation of early Christianity is that we realize that there was no bitter disappointment over the postponement of the parousia in those churches. There are no texts that indicate that the early Christian communities were devastated by the delay of the second coming. Why was their *faith* not shattered when their *hope* proved to be wrong? Because their faith was not based on their hope but on the death and resurrection of Jesus Christ, as expressed in creedal and hymnic traditions (e.g., 1 Cor. 15:3-5; 1 Peter 3:18, 22b; Rev. 1:5-6; 5:9b-10). Their *faith* was determined by Christ's first coming, which included his resurrection. Their *hope* expressed the "not yet" of his second coming. For *faith*, Christ's resurrection was not just an isolated miracle, but it was God's eschatological deed which had cosmic significance. This faith generated the *hope* that the cosmic significance of Christ's resurrection would be made manifest in grace and in judgment in the near future, "soon." In between his first and second coming the believers are celebrating the Eucharist, the coming of Christ in bread and wine. With its closing words the Apocalypse, which was meant to be read during the liturgical assembly, forms a bridge to the celebration of the Eucharist in which Christ is present "in the midst of the lampstands" (1:12-13) as giver and as gift (22:14-21). And the Eucharist connects his past and present coming with the earnestly hoped for future coming in the millennium, when they shall eat with him and he with them (3:20). "Maranatha!" (1 Cor. 16:22); "Amen. Come, Lord Jesus!" (Rev. 22:20); "Let grace come and let the world pass away" (*Didache* 10.6). Not as a substitute for the postponement of the parousia, nor as compensation for the hoped for millennium, was the Eucharist celebrated (contrary to Gager) but as a way of enacting the presence of him who had already ransomed them "by his blood" and made them—little, despised, no-accounts— "a kingdom and priests to our God" (Rev. 5:10) and who has promised to return. Their *faith* did not quiver when their hope had to be adjusted because their faith was not based on the future hope, on the envisioned parousia, but on the past eschatological deed of God through Christ.

A historical interpretation of the Apocalypse will seek not only to find parallels to ideas, images, and visions of this book but also to delineate Jewish apocalyptic hopes from John's expectations. For instance, the notion of two successive aeons, the present aeon (*ha olam hazzeh*) and the future aeon (*ha olam habba*), is absent in Revelation for the simple reason that the future aeon is present already through Christ's exaltation. Moreover, we must also distinguish John's faith in God and Christ, who are "in charge" over present, past, and future from contemporary Hellenistic notions concerning Providence, Fate including astrology, and Chance. Moreover, Greco-Roman literature also contained "revelations" and prophetic predictions.

For instance, in his Fourth Eclogue, Virgil (70–19 B.C.) predicted the return of Rome's past golden age: "Come are those last days that the Sibyl sang; the ages' mighty march begins anew." The inaugurator of a new golden age will be a "new born babe" (son of Pollio, perhaps of Augustus) who "shall free the nations from perpetual fear." Small wonder that church fathers later on found a pagan prophecy concerning Christ in Virgil's Fourth Eclogue. It expressed his fervent hope for a divinely inaugurated age of peace under Roman rule. The sixth book of Virgil's *Aeneid* reveals, by means of a journey of Aeneas into the netherworld, that the blessed departed souls dwell on the Elysian Fields in beautiful surroundings awaiting their return after being purged of their sins over a period of a thousand years. Neither Virgil's millennium nor Jewish apocalyptic speculations concerning a messianic interim (4 Ezra 7:28-29) are the source of John's millennium of Rev. 20:4-6. Parallels are not sources! Hellenistic religion which formed part of the context of the seven churches in Asia Minor is a complicated and many-sided affair. John adopted and adapted pagan imagery also, like the combat myth in Revelation 12, or the Christological epithets "Alpha and Omega," "Beginning and End," and so forth, in order to communicate his revelation in relevant language. In the throne room vision (Revelation 4) he used features of Roman imperial ceremony in such a way that Roman pomp and emperor worship appear as the diabolical perversion of worship as it ought to be (see Aune, 1983). A few comments on emperor worship may be in order.

The Imperial Cult and Domitian

If you can image a staircase with five steps, then imagine the first step to be occupied by the animal kingdom. The second is occupied by slaves; the third, by free people who are no-accounts, like most of us; the fourth, by important persons, such as emperors and philosophers; and the fifth step by the gods. Just so, it takes only one step to become a god. Gods were not conceived by the Romans to be "the wholly other." They were superior to humans, but they also had their own shortcomings, like the love affairs of the great Jupiter. One expected the gods to reciprocate for favors done by humans. When they did not, then a Roman mob could be hystericized to destroy temples, as was done when Germanicus died in A.D. 23. He had been the adopted son of Emperor Tiberius and was very popular. Today one would burn down banks or stone embassies. Fear of the gods was not the Roman attitude but the characteristics of oriental "superstitions," as Romans labeled Judaism or Christianity.

Emperor worship came to Rome from the East. Alexander the Great may have thought of himself as son of the god Ammon after his visit to Ammon's shrine in Egypt. Rome, which had entered the East in the second century B.C., made Julius Caesar into a god by decree of the Senate after his assassination on the Ides of March in 44 B.C. Next, after Augustus had died, an eagle flew out of the funeral pyre—that was arranged rather cleverly—carrying the emperor's soul into heaven. Moreover, a senator swore—and senators knew the difference between oaths and perjury—that he had seen Augustus's spirit ascend, soaring into heaven through the flames of the funeral pyre (Suetonius, *Augustus* 100-101). Thus by decree of the Senate he became a god. Romans considered it tacky for a living emperor to promote himself to the rank of deity, as Caligula had done. On his deathbed, Emperor Vespasian, Domitian's father, sarcastically observed that his time of transformation into a god was at hand.

This reticence toward granting godlike honors to a living emperor, however, was not shared by sycophants and opportunists who hoped to ingratiate themselves with emperors. It was also absent in the Roman East. The Roman province of Asia developed into a hotbed of the imperial cult which, at least by the time of John, included the worship also of living emperors. Pergamum had become the official center of the imperial cult in this province (cf. "Satan's throne" in Rev. 2:13), having received official permission in 29 B.C. to build a temple in honor of the divine Augustus and the goddess Roma. But the cult also thrived in Ephesus, Smyrna, and Thyatira. It was never meant to be a substitute for the worship of other gods. In matters of religion Rome was tolerant. Participation in the imperial cult was an expression of political loyalty and gratitude toward Rome and its emperor.

It has frequently been said that Domitian (A.D. 81–96), the emperor during whose time John wrote the Apocalypse, claimed divinity for himself and demanded to be addressed as "our Lord and God" (*dominus et deus noster*). Revelation 13 and 17–18 are then seen as John's response to a self-deifying megalomaniac of an emperor. However, this matter is not so simple. In the first place, while Tacitus, Pliny, Suetonius, and Dio Cassius, a century after them, do paint pictures of a self-deifying tyrant, they had an ax to grind and they ground it with vengeance after Domitian's death. As persons of senatorial or equestrian rank whose influence Domitian had diminished in the interest of the empire, they lost no time maligning him in every conceivable way once he was dead. Their evidence is tainted, to say the least. In the second place, there is no evidence of a persecution of Christians by the state during Domitian's reign. The seven churches of the Apocalypse have one martyr! In the third place, if Domitian had demanded to be addressed as "our Lord and God," then those writers, like Statius, whom he employed and who wrote upon his specific request would have had to use such an address, but they do not address him with divine titles. In the fourth place, far from demanding divine honors, Domitian actually forbade them. When he was hailed by a mob as "Lord" he would have none of it. (Statius, *Silvae* 1.6.81-84). Like his father Vespasian, he probably held some cynical views about this deification nonsense. Nor is there any evidence from the coins issued during Domitian's reign that would indicate his claim to divine honors, as his detractors from Tacitus to Dio Cassius have maintained. In the fifth place, Domitian was actually a competent and social-minded administrator, which even Suetonius had to admit (*Domitian* 8.2). Domitian's legate in Asia Minor, for instance, prevented the rich landowners from ripping off the poor during a famine by setting a reasonable price for grain and by enforcing the surrender of grain. He also told them that "it is most unjust that hunger of one's fellow human beings should be the basis for profit." Roman rule brought economic improvement to Asia Minor. Simultaneously wealth remained in the hands of the few rich, while the vast majority there, as everywhere, worried at least sometimes about how they would get their next meal (see McMullen). Hence we hear of occasional bread riots and of special efforts by the government to alleviate food shortages.

Of course Domitian was cruel, like his predecessors and successors (e.g., Trajan, see below in this section). He had a vestal virgin buried alive because she had broken her vow of chastity. He ordered the execution of a senator, Flavius Clemens, who, according to Suetonius (*Domitian* 15), was Domitian's "own extremely stupid cousin" and the banishment of his niece Domitilla, probably on suspicion of plotting against him. Dio Cassius wrote that the reason for Clemens's execution lay in the charge of "atheism" leveled against him (*Hist.* 67.14). But this charge is as unlikely as is the notion that he was executed because he converted to Judaism or to Christianity which Romans denounced as "atheism." It was Domitilla's steward, Stephanus, who murdered Domitian as part of a large conspiracy which the emperor had been unable to uproot. Incidentally, if Domitilla was a Christian, then so was her steward, Stephanus, the first Christian assassin we know of. But there is no evidence of persecution of Christians by Domitian. Even Eusebius could point out only two banishments of Christians during his reign (Domitilla and the author of the Apocalypse). Simultaneously he narrated that Domitian released the Christian grandsons of Judas, the brother of Jesus, after an interrogation "concerning Christ and the kingdom" (*C. H.* 3.18-19). In short, there is no evidence that Christians in Asia Minor had it worse under Domitian than they had it before or after him.

Yet there was something nefarious about the imperial cult, because it gave opportunity for troublemakers to get Christians into serious difficulties. Not that there was a law that everyone in Asia Minor had to worship the emperor's genius, which is his divine double. But the expectation existed that one did so, when necessary, be it with genuine or hypocritical motives. Who would make a fuss about offering a mere pinch of incense (also called "manna," cf. Rev. 2:17b) to the emperor's genius as a sign of loyalty unless one was a Jew? The Jews, however, had received special privileges that apparently exempted them from the imperial cult. At any rate, emperor worship apparently posed no problems for the prosperous Jews of Sardis, as far as we know (cf. Kraabel). The Christians who were no longer part of the synagogue faced several kinds of difficulties. They were perceived by their pagan neighbors as stand-offish and clannish. Their rejection of pagan religion as "fornication" seemed absurd, and their expectation of the end of the world would strike their fellow citizens as downright dangerous. One could get at them most easily because of their refusal to worship the emperor. On another level, such refusal radically curbed their social life in private associations (collegia) and trade guilds where men met to enjoy each other's company—away from women and where joyous banquets were held with Caesar and some god as silent guests. But legal transactions, the theater, sporting events, and the gladiatorial spectacles were also held under the benevolent protection of Caesar, who in Asia Minor was thought to be the son of some god.

Christians of Asia Minor could and did enjoy the peace and prosperity that Domitian's reign gave to them. Beyond doubt they held different views concerning the emperor cult. Some may have followed the example of 1 Peter, which was probably written at that time, or a decade later, and was addressed also to "the exiles . . . in Asia." Categorically it stated: "Honor the emperor!" (1 Peter 2:17). Though this exhortation could be interpreted in more than one way, it allowed for honoring him by sprinkling a little incense before his statue, if need be. Jezebel of Thyatira may have thought along these lines (Rev. 2:20). The prophet John did not. While we have no evidence of persecution of Christians in Asia Minor by the state during Domitian's time, we do have evidence of various Christian responses to the emperor cult. According to Luke, some "Asiarchs," who were the representatives of the imperial cult in the region of the seven churches of the Apocalypse, had been "friends" of Paul (Acts 19:31). And what Paul wrote in Romans 13, we know and those who came after him in Ephesus probably knew likewise. But irrespective of which views concerning the state circulated in different churches, we can be certain that local magistrates (e.g., Acts 19:35) and eventually Caesar's representative would take notice of Christians if segments of the populace turned against them. This is what happened in Bithynia around A.D. 111 when Pliny was *legatus pro praetore*.

Persecution under Pliny

Since Pliny's proceedings against Christians illustrate one aspect of the general context in which Christians of Asia Minor had to live, we shall deal with this persecution, even though it took place some fifteen years after the composition of the Apocalypse. A drama in four parts unfolded before Pliny, which he reported in a letter to Emperor Trajan (*Epistles* 10.96).

Part I: Christians were brought before Pliny, and after asking them repeatedly whether they were Christians and warning them "of the punishment awaiting them" if they persisted in their admission, he ordered their execution. Pliny found it unnecessary to investigate whether or not they had committed actual crimes or whether crimes or disgusting behavior (*flagitia*) was inherent in the practice of Christianity. At this stage, the fact that a person confessed to being a Christian was sufficient ground for his or her execution. In retrospect he covered his tracks in his letter to Trajan by telling the emperor that their "obstinacy" ought "not to go unpunished," as if obstinacy in itself were a capital crime under Roman law. Roman citizens who admitted to being Christians were sent by Pliny to Rome for trial (cf. Acts 25:12).

Part II: When the populace found out that Pliny executed Christians, he faced a torrent of new charges against church members. Moreover, an anonymous pamphlet containing the names of Christians was also brought to his attention. He arrested the persons, and we may assume he executed those who confessed to being Christians. However, there were others who denied they had ever been Christians. Those he asked to repeat a formula of invocation to the gods and to make an offering of wine and incense before the emperor's statue and to curse the name of Christ. If they did that, he dismissed all charges against them (cf. Revelation 13).

Part III: "An informer" gave him the names of some who upon appearance before his tribunal stated "that they had ceased to be Christians," some as long as twenty years ago (that would be during Domitian's reign). They all did reverence to Trajan's statue, invoked the gods, and cursed Christ. But, significantly, Pliny did not dismiss their case. He may have thought that one does not release a criminal just because his crime happened to lie in the past and he has changed his mind in the meantime. Pliny's treatment of this group indicates that being a Christian constituted a capital crime in his own thinking at that time.

However, from this group of Christian apostates Pliny learned that Christianity was actually a harmless affair without inherent criminal activity. The apostates told him that formerly when they had been Christians "they had met regularly before dawn on a fixed day to chant verses alternately amongst themselves in honor of Christ as if to a god, and also to bind themselves by oath, not for any criminal purposes, but to abstain from theft, robbery and adultery, to commit no breach of trust and not to deny a deposit when called upon to restore it." Now Pliny faced a problem. Up to this point he may have thought that criminal activity was a regular part of Christianity. He had to be certain about this aspect of the problem.

Part IV: Pliny decided to get to the truth of this matter by subjecting two slave women who were deaconesses to torture. Such a procedure was admissible under Roman law if the persons subjected to torture were not Roman citizens (cf. Acts 22:24-25). These brave women corroborated the testimony of the apostates, and Pliny informed Trajan that he "found nothing but a degenerate sort of cult carried to extravagant length," but no inherent crimes. The absence of criminal activity placed Pliny's former executions of Christians in a new light, and therefore he decided to ask Trajan for advice, to suggest a way of dealing with the apostates and to cover his own tracks.

He began by telling Trajan: "I do not know the nature of the extent of punishments usually meted out to them," even though he had them summarily executed. Nor, he wrote, does he know how far investigations should be pressed. "Nor am I at all sure whether any distinction should be made on the grounds of age, or if young people and adults should be treated alike." But what interested him most was whether a pardon could be granted to apostates. Therefore he suggested to the emperor in his concluding sentence that "a great many people could be reformed if they were given an opportunity to repent" of being, or of having been,

Christians. Pliny postponed further executions until he heard from his emperor.

Trajan replied that Pliny had "followed the right course of procedure" when he had ordered the execution of "obstinate" Christians. He also informed his legate that it is "impossible to lay down a general rule" with respect to legal procedures against them. However, "these people must not be hunted out; if they are brought before you and the charge is proved, they must be punished," by execution presumably. But anyone who denied being a Christian and demonstrated it by "offering prayers to our gods" (Trajan omitted a reference to worship of his own image), such a person "is to be pardoned as result of his repentance." Anonymous accusations, the emperor insisted, should be ignored, because they "are quite out of keeping with the spirit of our age." These words of Trajan criticize Pliny's procedure only insofar as he had acted upon anonymous denunciations. In short, the goal of the government's dealings with properly accused Christians was to achieve their "repentance" through apostasy from the Christian faith. The government could forgo aggressive actions against them, because it knew of the absence of criminal activity within this "cult," or "superstition," as Pliny labeled the church. Simultaneously Trajan was unable to state that in the absence of crimes Christianity was to be tolerated, like all other religious associations.

Thus the situation of Christians in Asia Minor at Trajan's time and, we may suppose, also at Domitian's time was marked not only by general religious toleration within the empire but also by insecurity, harassment, and occasional outbreaks of violence against the church. The fact that Jews who rose three times in armed rebellion against Rome (A.D. 66–73 in Judea and Galilee; A.D. 115 in Egypt, Cyrene, and Cyprus; A.D. 132–135 in Judea under the messiah Bar Kochba) could practice their religion demonstrates the strength of the tradition of religious toleration within the Roman empire. Whether or not Christians were persecuted depended on the mood of the pagan and Jewish populace in a particular location, and it also depended on the zeal of individual provincial governors. In this situation, characterized by insecurity on one hand and by a tradition of religious toleration on the other, John wrote his book for seven churches in Asia Minor. For him, present and envisioned future persecution is a minor theme within the major theme of worship. Worship of the beast or worship of the Lamb—that will be the question. Is the emperor to be hailed as link between deities and people, guaranteeing peace, law, and order, or is the Lamb that was slain destined to be worshiped not only in heaven but also on earth (5:9-14)?

3. Jewish Apocalypses and John's Apocalypse

The word "apocalypse" comes from the first Greek word of John's book and means "revelation." Scholars assigned this word to a type of Jewish literature that is represented in the Old Testament by Daniel and sections of prophetic books such as Isaiah 24–27; 56–66; Ezekiel 34–48; Zechariah 9–14; and others. However, the bulk of the apocalyptic genre lies outside the Old Testament and consists of writings such as *1* and *2 Enoch,* 4 Ezra, *2 Baruch, Jubilees,* and other apocalypses. *1 Enoch* is itself a small library of originally separate apocalyptic writings, like The Book of the Watchers from the late third or early second century B.C. Fragments of it have been found in Qumran, and it now comprises chaps. 1–36 of *1 Enoch.* All apocalyptic books narrate, in autobiographical form, divine revelations that were mediated to the seers by a transcendent being, generally by an angel. The revelation pertains either to heaven above or to the future that lies ahead or to both. The mystery of heaven above and of the future with its final judgment are the boundaries of life on earth in terms of space and time, and these boundaries are opened up in apocalyptic literature. We find therefore two types of Jewish apocalypses. In one the seer is taken by an angel on a guided tour of heaven, where he sees and receives explanations of all kinds of heavenly mysteries. For instance, the first part of Enoch's heavenly journey in The Book of the Watchers concludes with Enoch seeing "seven stars which were like great burning mountains," and the angelic tour guide explains to him that "it is the prison house for the stars and the powers of heaven," that transgressed God's law and were bound by him till judgment day (*1 Enoch* 18:14-16).

The other type of apocalypse has its focus on time (e.g., Daniel and 4 Ezra), especially the time of the end. Frequently the past history is divided into periods and the course of past history is then "predicted" by the supposed author such as Daniel or Ezra from his imagined vantage point in the past. For instance, in Dan. 7:2-14 the supposed author in a first person singular report narrated his vision of four beasts that rise successively out of the sea. The focus of the vision changes to the "Ancient of Days" who executes judgment upon the beasts and who gives dominion, glory, and kingdom to "one like a son of man." The vision is then interpreted for the seer by an angel (Dan. 7:15-27). The four beasts represent four kingdoms (Babylonians, Medes, Persians, and Greeks). The fourth beast is a monstrosity with ten horns representing ten successive kings. After them there shall arise another one who shall "wear out the saints" for three and a half years, that is, "for a time, two times and half a time," until God's judgment destroys him. Then God shall give "the kingdoms under the whole heaven" to the saints of the Most High (Dan. 7:24-27). By paying attention to the focus of the angelic interpretation, modern scholars have rightly determined that this book was not composed during the exile (about 550 B.C.) but during the struggle of Judaism with Antiochus IV Epiphanes (about 165 B.C.). Antiochus wanted to force Hellenistic pagan religion upon the Jews, and the Maccabees rose up in revolt against him. But the author of Daniel expected the vindication of God's faithful people not from armed rebellion but from God's own intervention in judgment and salvation. For Daniel, the course of history is determined. The end, the judgment upon pagan oppressors and the vindication of the saints, is believed to be near.

Not all Jewish apocalypses were written in reaction to acute crises like Daniel during the Maccabeean revolt or 4 Ezra after the destruction of the temple in A.D. 70. But all Jewish apocalypticists expressed directly or indirectly dissatisfaction with the status quo. In this respect they are the heirs of the Old Testament prophets, and like the prophets they seek to mediate the truth of God to people living in a particular time and space. Israel's prophets had announced judgment over a sinful nation, and that judgment fell in the Assyrian conquest and the Babylonian captivity. But the prophets had also promised a new deliverance, a new exodus, a new covenant, a new law, a new David, a new nation, and a new Jerusalem. History apparently did not work out this way, at least not as they had envisioned it. Now it was the righteous, Torah-abiding pious people who in history were subjected to tribulations of one sort or another, while idolaters and the ungodly prospered. It would have been counterproductive simply to repeat ad infinitum that they, the obedient daughters and sons of Israel, remained under God's judgment in order to be purified since they, admittedly, were not yet perfect. Such an approach would not work for long, because it lacks a vision that reaches beyond the absurdities of history and death. Israel's prophetic hope therefore turned upward to heaven and forward to the ultimate future and produced the bewildering variety of apocalyptic texts.

Apocalypticism is the heir of Israel's prophetic tradition in that it interpreted history and the world below. It did not transform history into a never-ending series of cycles, patterned after the cycles of the day or the year, but it retained the prophetic perspective in which history has a goal that is determined by God. Apocalypticists could incorporate mythical material which originally expressed a cyclical view of history, like the story of the divine warrior who subdued the forces of chaos in primeval times. Such a story was reenacted annually in the cult, thereby guaranteeing order for another year. The apocalypticists, however, project that story from primal times to the end time (Isa. 27:1; Rev. 12:7-12) in the conviction that the goal of history will witness the destruction of all lunatic demonic forces that run rampant in history now.

While Jewish apocalypses differ greatly in terms of content, they all have the form of autobiographical reports about visions and auditions in which heavenly and/or end-time mysteries are disclosed. In terms of function, an apocalypse gives divine legitimation to its message. It interprets the present prophetically and seeks to facilitate behavior modifications or perseverance in faith under adverse conditions. By narrating visions and auditions, an apocalypse also invites its hearers/readers to participate in the author's original visionary experience. By presenting his message in symbols and images that at times border on the bizarre, the author teases his audience to use their imagination as he draws them into his "experienced" revelation.

Obviously, John's Apocalypse shares these formal peculiarities with Jewish apocalypses. He used a great variety of images, some of which have their origin in the Old Testament, especially in Daniel, Ezekiel, Isaiah, and Zechariah; others came from Jewish apocalypses, and still others had their origin in oriental mythology and Hellenistic syncretism. John's menagerie of animals is astounding. There are heavenly animals, like the four living creatures (representing creation, 4:6-8), and animals released by commands from heaven (6:1-8; 8:13; 9:3-11; etc.), and antagonistic animals (e.g., 12:3; 13:1). Heaven opens (4:1; 19:11), angels hold back apocalyptic winds (7:1), and plagues, earthquakes, and lightning rattle the audience out of its church-sleep. Other features that the seer shares with Jewish apocalypses are the use of colors (e.g., white, symbolizing holiness, or its counterfeit, e.g., 6:2) and the use of numbers and time references. Forty-two months is a short time (11:2-3; 12:14; 13:5) in comparison to a thousand years (20:4-6). In short, most of what strikes modern readers as odd about this book is quite traditional material that would have been understood by John's original audience.

Moreover, John, like other apocalypticists, gives explicit and implicit interpretations to some of his materials, lest he lose his audience. Explicit interpretations are given in 1:20; 7:13-17; and 17:6b-18. Implicit interpretations are given in 1:8, the mysterious Alpha and Omega is God who was and is and is to come; the angel of 8:3 with the golden censer filled with incense represents the church's prayers before God; the eating of the little scroll in 10:10 means the continuation of Christian prophecy; "the great city" of 11:8 is "where their Lord was crucified"; in 14:18-20, the grapes and the winepress are the execution of judgment upon those rejecting the "eternal gospel" of 14:6; the virgins of 14:4 (RSV, "they are chaste") are those who "had been redeemed from the earth" (14:3); the rider on the white horse of 19:11 is "The Word of God," and his "sword" is his own testimony; and so on. Quite a few other symbols, such as "the Lion" and "the Lamb" (5:5-6), would be readily understood by John's hearers. At any rate, John did not expect his first-century audience to experience "hermeneutical difficulties," as we would say, when they heard his Apocalypse during the worship in their churches. However, we also have to realize that John's symbols and images do not have a simple one-to-one meaning. For instance, Babylon is not just Rome; it is whatever political power is against the reign of God within the gigantic drama that leads from creation to a climax determined by God. Rome had its precursors, and so, for John, Babylon becomes again visible in Rome without the two being simply identical. Thus precision of meaning is not to be expected from an apocalypse using images and symbols.

Our Apocalypse can be read as one specimen within a genre that at least theoretically could also include apocalypses from outside Judaism and Christianity. The Apocalypse Group of the Society of Biblical Literature proposed the following definition of this genre: " 'Apocalypse' is a genre of revelatory literature with a narrative frame-work, in which a revelation is mediated by an otherworldly being to a human recipient, disclosing a transcendent reality which is both temporal, insofar as it envisages eschatological salvation, and spatial insofar as it involves another, supernatural world." This definition of the genre, which was articulated originally by J. J. Collins in 1979 (cf. *Semeia* 14, p. 9; 36, p. 2), suffices, as far as it goes. Suggestions about expanding the definition to include greater specificity in terms of form (autobiographical report) and functions (legitimation, exhortation, and audience participation) are being discussed. However, we must also recognize the differences between John's Apocalypse and other apocalypses, and it is to these that we now turn.

First, the last book of the Bible is unsurpassed among apocalypses in terms of literary beauty and artistry. Its structure is so clear and yet so puzzling that no outline, including the one attached to this introduction, can do it justice. Even its strange Greek grammatical constructions serve to evoke the sacred language of the Old Testament. Its 404 verses allude 518 times to the earlier sacred Scriptures. John was immersed in the text and language of the Bible of his people. Yet there is not one single citation of the Old Testament in his book and for good reasons. As prophet he does not quote Scripture but communicates the revelation of Jesus Christ (1:1). His communication is cast in Old Testament language because it is the climax of Old Testament prophecy. Hence the author inserted new prophetic oracles (e.g., 1:7-8; 13:10; 21:5-8; 22:18-19) and seven beatitudes (e.g., 1:3; 14:13; 16:15). He also focused attention on worship with the introduction of 16 hymns, because worship of God and the Lamb, or worship of beasts, emperors, and idols, is the central issue of this prophetic book.

Second, his revelation of Jesus Christ is cast in the form of a circular (a round-robin) letter for seven churches in the Roman province Asia, of Asia Minor. No Jewish apocalypse has the form of a letter. His epistolary prescript ending in a doxology bears similarity to Pauline letters (e.g., Gal. 1:1-5), not to Johannine letters. We will try to show that this longest letter of the New Testament is really a letter and not just an apocalypse with a letter framework. Moreover, this letter-apocalypse is not a pseudonymous writing. It bears the name of its author, John, unlike every other apocalypse before him where the author hides himself in a figure of the remote past, such as Enoch, Ezra, or Baruch. The author of our letter is known to the churches that are named in the address. Hence he does not indulge in fictional predictions of the past course of history, like Daniel, 4 Ezra, and *2 Baruch*.

Third, the ultimate reason for the absence of fictional predictions lies in its new point of view. For John, the future triumph of God over Satan, beasts, destroyers, and idolaters has already been inaugurated in the exaltation of the Lamb that was slain and has begun to reign. This point of view is new in comparison to all prior apocalypses. For him, like for the rest of the New Testament, the end time has already begun in the death and resurrection of Jesus Christ. The victory has already been won and is being celebrated in hymns by God's entourage in heaven. This point of view constitutes the basic conviction of John's prophecy.

Fourth, the future consummation of his prophecy differs from prior apocalypses. Nowhere in Judaism do we find the idea of a "first resurrection." John did not construct the consummation by projecting a reversal of present human needs onto an eschatological screen, but he gave new expression to the conviction that those who belong to the resurrected Christ shall be raised "first" (cf. 1 Cor. 15:23; 1 Thess. 4:16-17). "The first resurrection" and John's millennium prior to the final judgment constitute the prerogative of the followers of the Lamb. Nothing like that appears in Jewish apocalypses. In 4 Ezra 7 a messianic interim is followed by the Messiah's death, but the millennium in John's letter is no interim, as we shall see. Because the parousia of Christ shall bring the public manifestation of his reign which has already been inaugurated through his exaltation, the vocabulary and the apocalyptic structure of "two ages" are absent here.

Fifth, the material between the throne room vision of Revelation 4–5 and the vision of the new Jerusalem at the end also differs. There is no apocalyptic timetable to be found, nor do cosmic speculations clutter the pages of this letter. The material is determined by the exaltation of the slain Lamb. His exaltation sheds light upon Christian heretics and washed-out believers, upon beasts and harlots, in John's present and future. The exalted Christ reveals the true nature of the world and of the short time between John's own present and the envisioned end. This perspective turns traditional apocalyptic images upside down. "The Lion of the tribe of Judah" (5:5) is a traditional image for the warrior Messiah, and John heard about him from one of the heavenly elders. But what he actually "saw" (5:6) is not a killer lion but a Lamb that had been killed. The traditional expectation is radically reversed. The Lamb is not miraculously changed into a lion, like a frog who is turned into a prince. The lion *is* the

Lamb, and there will not be a Messiah other than the slain Lamb. Thus the Messiah's conquest takes place paradoxically through his death, through what to all appearances amounts to his total defeat. Hence the messianic community on earth conquers "by the blood of the Lamb" *and* by their own suffering (12:12). This is another inversion of a traditional image, namely, of Michael's defeat of Satan (12:7-9). Moreover, the parousia-Christ in the traditional image kills his opponents (19:11-21). Yet John narrates no battle, and the only "sword" that is used is the word of Jesus, who is "The Word of God" (19:13) and whose testimony is his death.

The inversion of traditional images is enclosed by a modification of the apocalyptic genre. What is revealed in John's letter are not secrets about heaven and the future that must be "sealed," as in Dan. 12:4, 9. On the contrary, such sealing is expressly prohibited (22:10), because the letter is sent to actual, specific communities, not to fictitious ones. Moreover, our letter in the three cycles of sevens does not disclose an apocalyptic timetable. What is disclosed is the sovereignty of God and Christ in the past (4:11; 12:5), present (chaps. 2–3), and future. After the Lamb received the scroll with its seven seals, the traditional apocalyptic pattern would require that the content of the scroll would be disclosed. Instead, what is revealed is the sovereignty of the slain Lamb. He does not reveal apocalyptic end-time information, but paradoxically he, the slain Lamb, discloses his power by enacting the end-time events. Likewise with respect to heaven this letter does not communicate information about heaven's "geography" or other heavenly secrets. What is important is the heavenly worship, the acclamation of the sovereignty of God and the Lamb. The church on earth is already participating (5:8) in this worship with angels and archangels and all the company of heaven. The hymns that John created unite the church's worship on earth with the angelic worship in heaven.

These differences demonstrate that John's literary achievement is unique within apocalypticism. In spite of obvious similarities to the apocalyptic genre we must also see the modifications of the genre itself. These differences also suggest his implicit criticism of certain apocalyptic traditions that were circulating in his churches. Just as the author of 2 Thess. 2:1-12 criticized a tradition concerning the end time within a church, so did John. He not only reversed traditional images, as we have seen, but he also modified an apocalyptic interim speculation, as we shall see (cf. comments to 20:4-6). Apocalypticism did not determine his Christology. On the contrary, he reworked apocalyptic traditions in the light of Jesus' death and resurrection.

John's all-embracing Christological perspective does not permit us to view his letter primarily as a reaction to actual or envisioned social deprivation, nor is it a response to political persecution. "Tribulations" for him belong to the structure of the Christian life, because the Lamb is victorious only as the slain one. In contrast to 4 Ezra 14:10-17 and 2 *Bar.* 85:10, the presence of evil and the resultant tribulations of the saints are not the consequence of the world having grown old, of "the power of creation" being "already exhausted." John worried not about the presence of tribulations in his churches but about their absence. That would reveal a lukewarm church which has accommodated itself to the pressures of the world (3:14-22). Tribulations reveal the shape of the Christian life and the Christians of Asia Minor needed to hear that, just as we do. John's letter-apocalypse is misunderstood if it is interpreted as compensation for real or imagined tribulations or as (unsuccessful) "catharsis" of feelings of powerlessness, fear, envy, resentment, and vengeance (Yarbro Collins, *Crisis*, 143–160). John's visions do not "overcome" the tension between faith and the brutal realities of everyday life of Christians in Asia Minor. His message does not grant "a fleeting experience of the millennium" (Gager, 153). On the contrary, his gospel creates and heightens the tension, because it is the word of Jesus' faithful endurance (3:10). There is no salvation without endurance of tribulations (cf. 7:14). Christology determines his response to tribulations and distinguishes it from apocalyptic ideas about suffering determined by this old evil aeon. The vision John is communicating to his people that Christ, the victim, *is* the victor embraces all of life, including the future, even as his alternative vision of the beast and its worship embraces every aspect of society, including buying and selling (13:11-17), present and future (18:9-21).

4. A Prophetic-Apocalyptic Circular Letter

General Comments

The visions, auditions, symbols, and images that comprise the content of this book are clearly apocalyptic. *Yet* traditional apocalyptic images and symbols are transformed by the Christian conviction concerning Christ's death and exaltation. "The words of the book" by John claim to be "words of prophecy" that dare not be altered on pain of plagues and condemnation (22:18-19), and *yet* John never explicitly claimed the title "prophet" for himself. He identified himself only as scribe of Jesus, as witness "to the word of God and the testimony of Jesus," and as "brother" who shares tribulation "in Jesus" with his sisters and brothers whom he addresses (1:2, 9, 11). Finally, the epistolary prescript and conclusion (1:4-6; 22:21) indicate that the book is sent as a circular letter to the seven churches. *Yet* John never used the Greek word *epistolē* (cf. 2 Cor. 7:8; 10:9) or *gramma* (Acts 28:21) when he referred to his letter, but always *biblion* (1:11; 22:7, 9, 10, 18, 19), a word that is not commonly used of letters (exceptions: cf. Josephus, *Against Apion* 1.101; Polyaenus, *Strategemata* 7.19).

John was probably aware of the oddity of his literary undertaking. As a prophetic letter (e.g., Jer. 29:1-23; *2 Bar.* 77:17-19), Revelation was somewhat long in comparison to Paul's letters, and an apocalypse had never been written as a letter before. So he called it a *biblion* but sent it as a letter. Why? As *biblion* it is meant to be part of the sacred, normative writings of his churches. It is not to be one apocalypse among others, but the only one, commissioned by Christ himself (1:11, 19; cf. 22:18-19). Because it was a letter, John could expect it to be read during the worship of the communities addressed, even as Paul's letters had been read during these gatherings.

But more, Revelation was meant to be a letter. The letter genre exhibits great flexibility in terms of content and composition, as Stanley Stowers has shown. With his letter, John communicates the revelation of Jesus Christ to his hearers, from whom he is separated, leading them into (1:9-11) and out of (22:6-21) the world of his visions, presenting their present situation from Christ's perspective and opening the future for them. In the process he conveys to them admonition, censure, exhortation, praise, and promises, together with threats of judgments. Revelation was meant to be a written communication for a specific purpose, or purposes, from John to his churches from which he is apart. This is what a letter is all about.

Reading a letter is like listening to one end of a telephone conversation in which one party does all the talking. The listener wonders why the speaker brings up a particular matter and is talking the way he or she does. To what questions is he or she responding? Or is the speaker pressing his or her own agenda? Every letter writer pursues one or more objectives. The seven messages of Revelation 2–3 reflect rather clearly John's specific aims for each of his churches. But also the second part of his letter expresses his intention. By narrating his visions, he draws them into his apocalyptic eschatology and communicates an alternative all-embracing point of view. God and the Lamb that was slain encompass past, present, and future in sovereignty. Because the Lamb is victorious as the slain one, tribulations in the present are the sign that Christians are followers of the Lamb. Far from aiming to dispense religious aspirin via his letter, which would alleviate the tension between the experienced pressures of everyday life on one hand and the faith commitments on the other, John heightened the tension by showing that faith commitment is irreconcilable with accommodation to the beasts. By constantly bringing up the theme of worship, he not only connected the reading of his letter with its worship setting in the seven churches but he encouraged his people to keep their focus on the sovereignty of him who shed his blood for them and who determines their present and their future. Worship enables his people to keep God in focus and gain the vision of ultimate reality beyond the pressures and nuisances of everyday life in Asia Minor. His letter also aims to draw a clear boundary between heretics and beast worshipers on one side and the community of the faithful on the other. Outside are "the dogs . . . fornicators . . . idolaters and every one who loves and practices falsehood" (22:15), and this is as it should be. If it is otherwise, a community gets contaminated and becomes society on Sunday, that is, a church to be spat out (3:16). John also endeavored to incorporate and to reinterpret different traditions, undercutting apocalyptic timetable speculations and notions about a messianic interim. With his letter he communicated an authoritative message to his churches, thereby bringing order into the chaos of apocalyptic traditions that were floating around in churches of Asia Minor. In short, John communicated to his churches his vision of the ultimate reality, God and the slain Lamb, placing his vision in opposition to other views of what is real and true. In so doing, he also revealed for his churches the nature of God's opponents and their futility. As a whole, his letter was meant to function as an exhortation to be conquerors, to worship God, to persevere, and to cut out accommodation and compromise.

According to Stowers's categories, Revelation would be a "protreptic" letter, written to urge his readers to accept the revelation of Jesus Christ "as normative" for their life. The seven messages of the first part (chaps. 2–3) were written for specific situations, even though simultaneously they should be heard by the whole church. In addition to the prescript, these seven messages underline the epistolary character of this writing. They are also thematically connected with the second part (4:1—22:5). This means that the audience is not left behind as we move into Part II. John's hearers are enveloped in visions that deal with their future and are challenged to listen to the message concerning their future. Hence they are also addressed directly (e.g., 13:9; 14:12-13; 16:15; 18:4; 19:5-8; 20:6). In short, there is every reason to accept our book as a prophetic, apocalyptic, circular letter.

The relationship between New Testament letters and Greco-Roman rhetoric has been discussed by scholars only in recent years. Rhetorical handbooks gave instructions on how to persuade people and deal with such items as external proofs (in Revelation, visions and allusions to the Old Testament) and internal proofs, namely, the credibility of the speaker/author (cf. 1:2, 9); his ability to arouse the emotions of his hearers, their "pathos" (Revelation certainly does that through its kaleidoscopic sequence of contrasting visions), and finally the need for logical presentation. Greco-Roman rhetoricians discussed three types of rhetoric. "Judicial" rhetoric, practiced in law courts, endeavors to persuade an audience concerning just or unjust deeds committed in the past; "deliberative" rhetoric seeks to persuade people about the appropriateness of certain actions in the future; "epideictic" rhetoric assigns praise or blame in the present on occasions such as honoring a benefactor, victory celebrations, political rallies, funerals, and so forth. A useful introduction is found in G. Kennedy, *New Testament Interpretation Through Rhetorical Criticism.* Helpful as such insights are, there are limitations because, as Stowers has shown, "the letter writing tradition was essentially independent of rhetoric" (p. 52).

Granting such independence, letters nevertheless have similarities to rhetoric, especially if a letter was to be used in an oral performance and read to an assembly. It was not for nothing that at the very beginning John announced the first beatitude for the person who reads his letter aloud and for all, gathered in the assembly, "who hear, and who keep" what they heard. Thus John began his letter as one would begin a deliberative speech, with a proem (1:1-8) in which he sought to gain the attention of the hearers (1:1-3). Next, he addressed them directly (1:4a) and established the common basis that exists between him and them (1:4b-6). This common basis is a christologically determined realized eschatology. Verses 7-8 state the theme, or proposition, which the letter will unfold in Part II: Christ shall come and God, who was and is, shall come. Next he deals with his own "ethos," showing his credibility from below, as an exile who shares with his audience "tribulation and the kingdom and the patient endurance" in Jesus. His credibility is also established from above by the vision of Christ (1:10-20). John indicated the structure of his letter as an aid for his audience. "Write what you see, *what is* [chaps. 2–3] and *what is to take place hereafter*" (1:19; cf. chaps. 4–22). Moreover, the Christ who is to come (1:7) is present in his churches (1:12) and therefore he can and does evaluate their present state of affairs authoritatively (chaps. 2–3). In short, the first three chapters exhibit not only "ethos" (John's credibility) and "pathos" (an appeal to the emotions of the audience) but also "logos" (logical arrangement and argumentation), as any decent speech would.

The opening of the second part of the "body" of the letter (4:1—22:5) contains other structural aids for the audience. The first two words, "after this" (Greek, *meta tauta*), signal the closure of one vision and the opening of another. The angel's word to John, "I will show you what must take place *after this*" (4:1c; again, *meta tauta*) refers back to 1:19. The seven messages to the churches have been completed. A new series commences with the vision of the open heaven, and it will deal primarily with the future which is present already in heaven. In the first part of his letter John had unfolded for his hearers the meaning of realized eschatology which he and they embraced (1:5-6). It involves the presence of Christ who calls to repentance, admonishes and censures, encourages and praises, and, if need be, threatens. Realized eschatology also involves the future and is inseparable from future salvation which the conqueror saying promised to those who persevere. This future will now be unfolded in Part II of his letter without ignoring the past and the present (e.g., chap. 12).

This second part contains three sections in an *A-B-A'* pattern. The center second (12:1—16:21) deals with the basic objection to the theme, or "proposition," of 1:7-8. John shows that antagonists to God and the Lamb shall appear on earth (13:1-18) challenging God's sovereignty, attacking his faithful people, and conquering them (13:7). John's audience already has a foretaste of what is to come. Their situation shall get worse. Yet the very appearance as well as the elimination of the satanic trinity is determined by God and the Lamb. This center section in which the antagonists appear gives credibility to the all-embracing vision of the sovereignty of God which John sought to communicate to his hearers.

Like a good speech, our letter also leads to a climactic conclusion, 19:11—22:5. Last, a letter should have a closure, or epilog (22:10-20). Such a closure, also called "peroration," should summarize the main point of the letter ("Behold, I am coming soon," 22:12, 20; cf. 1:1-3), reiterate the legitimation of the message (22:6, 10, 16a, 18-19), arouse the audience to heed the message (22:7, 9d, 14, 16), and, in our case, form a bridge from the experience of participating in John's visions to the celebration of the Eucharist in which Christ comes already before the end.

No one would suggest that John had studied Aristotle's *Rhetoric* or his *Topics*. However, our prophet could read and write in Greek and think in Hebrew, and such an ability was not commonplace in antiquity. In fact, reading and writing were rare among lower-class people. Education was the privilege of the rich and semi-well-to-do, because it was quite expensive. If John could produce a work of such exquisite literary artistry, like our book, then he was an educated person who knew about rhetoric, just as our high school graduates know about social studies even though they have never read Marx.

Techniques of Composition

Here we ask the question, How did John achieve literary unity in his writing? What literary techniques and devices did he employ and how did he structure his letter?

First: among the bewildering variety of symbols and images John has a central image, "the throne," which, beginning with 1:4 and ending with 22:3, gives unity to the message of his letter. His message is about the throne, the sovereignty, of God and therefore about worship.

Second: he placed two introductory visions (1:9-20 and chaps. 4–5) at the beginning of his two main parts and he carefully connected both parts. The command to listen (3:22) at the end of the letter septet connects with the exclamatory "behold" of 4:1

(RSV, "lo"). The throne of the Father of 3:21 is taken up in 4:2. The "first voice," like a trumpet, which John heard in 4:1, links up with 1:10 and connects both introductory visions. Finally, the promise, I will show "what must take place after this" (4:1) almost verbatim repeats the second part of the commission of 1:19.

Third: innumerable cross-references give unity to this letter. For instance, the descriptions of Christ in the inaugural vision (1:9-20) are taken up in the introductory formulae of the seven messages and reappear in the parousia vision (e.g., 19:12, 15). The promises to the conquerors (chaps. 2–3) are taken up in 21:1—22:5 (e.g., compare 2:7 with 22:1-5). The "one like a son of man" (1:13) appears as judge in 14:14.

Fourth: contrast images heighten the drama of the letter, give focus to the issue, and demand that the hearer decide between the throne of God and the dragon's throne (13:2; 16:10). Other contrast images are the beast from the sea and the Lamb in heaven; the false prophet who performs signs (13:11-14; 19:20) and the true witnesses who have power over "every plague" (11:46); the harlot and the Bride; Babylon and the new Jerusalem; the rejoicing of the idolatrous earth dwellers (11:9-10) and the rejoicing of the people of God who learn to sing a new song (14:3; 15:3-5; 19:6-8).

Fifth: with great deftness John used the literary device of intercalation. Sandwiched between two related, or contrasting, visions (= A and A′), like the sixth and the seventh seal (6:12-17 and 8:1), is another vision or group of visions (= B, 7:1-17). In short, he employed an *A-B-A′* pattern in which the focus lies in B. He used this technique for structuring the whole second part as well as some subsections (see outline). Thus, for instance, the vision of the fall of Babylon (17:1—19:10) not only evolves out of the seventh bowl vision (16:19) but is unit A. The descent of the new Jerusalem is its counterpart A′. (Compare the two introductions, 17:1-3 with 21:9-10, and compare the two conclusions, 19:9-10 with 22:8-9.) Intercalated between the fall of Babylon vision (A) and the new Jerusalem vision (A′) is a group of judgment and salvation visions (B), 19:11—21:8, the climax of which is the only direct word of God (21:5-8) within the body of the letter (cf. 1:8).

Sixth: John is also a master of suspense and delay. One would have expected a word spoken by God in the throne room vision of chaps. 4 and 5, but his word is delayed until 21:5-8. What we hear in the throne room vision is the worship, the hymns of his heavenly entourage. Moreover, one would have expected a vision of the end in the seventh seal, since the sixth seal brings us to "the great day" of wrath, but the vision of that day is also delayed. Finally, in 10:6 we hear, there shall be "no more delay," but "in the days" of the seventh trumpet blast (cf. 11:15-19) the end shall have come. Yet John's vision narrative continues after chap. 11 for eleven more chapters. John keeps his audience in suspense.

Seventh: additional structuring devices are (1) the use of four septets, namely, the seven messages, seven seals, seven trumpets, and seven bowls; (2) the use of interludes, or digressions in connection with the septets of Part II. The major interludes are chap. 7; chaps. 11:1—11:13; and chaps. 12:1—14:20, which are in fact an interlude, dealing with the antagonists and their destruction, between the trumpet septet and the bowl septet. A minor interlude is 16:13-15, which anticipates 19:11-21. And then there is the most troublesome interlude of Revelation, the millennium of 20:4-6, which is unfolded in 21:1—22:5.

Concerning the septets of Part II—seals, trumpets, and bowls—we note that the people of God appear in them only once, namely, in the fifth seal vision (6:9-11). There the martyrs under the altar cry in the language of psalms of lament: "Lord, . . . how long before thou wilt judge and avenge our blood . . . ?" The three septets of Part II and the parousia vision of 19:11-21 answer the martyrs' complaint. By means of interludes John provided previews of the church's future glory. These previews depict aspects of the millennium which is the beginning of the life of the world to come (see 7:9-17; 11:11-13; 14:1-5; 15:1-4; 20:4-6).

Eighth: some visions serve a dual purpose. They close one cycle of visions and simultaneously they introduce another. This technique of interlocking visions is found, for instance, in 15:1-4 which on one hand relates to 14:1-5 in an *A-B-A′* pattern and on the other hand introduces the subsequent bowl septet (cf. 15:1). Another example would be the transitional section of 22:6-9. The parallel to 19:9-10 requires that we consider it to be part of the new Jerusalem vision, but the change in subjects of the action in 22:6-8 indicates that it also belongs to the epilog (see commentary).

Ninth: John made use of "the encompassing technique," as J. Lambrecht has called it. This means that out of the seventh *seal* (8:1) evolves all further action narrated by John. The seventh *trumpet* (11:15-19) encompasses everything that follows. The seventh trumpet blast brought the announcement: "The kingdom of the world has become the kingdom of our Lord and of his Christ" (11:15). This announcement encompasses all subsequent visions up to 22:5. The destruction of the "destroyers of the earth" (11:18), accomplished through the seventh trumpet, will also evolve from it. And the same applies to the seventh *bowl* (16:17-21). The judgment on Babylon is not just announced (cf. 14:8) but executed through the seventh bowl of wrath. "It is done!" (16:17). The "last" of the plagues, with which "the wrath of God is ended" (15:1), has occurred. Yet it is not done, for the judgment narratives continue, evolving out of the seventh bowl. The destruction of Babylon is narrated in the following visions (17:1—19:10), and the parousia of Christ brings a new series of judgments (19:11—20:15).

John utilized the encompassing technique in other ways also, namely, as literary "brackets." The prolog (1:1-8) forms brackets with the epilog around the whole letter, as the verbal parallels indicate. The theme of the oracle of 1:7 is taken up, for instance, in the sixth seal, in the fear before "him who is seated on the throne" and the fear "from the wrath of the Lamb" (6:16). Its conclusion is found in the parousia vision of 19:11-21. The word of God in the prolog (1:8) is fulfilled in 21:3-8. The One "who is to come" (1:8) has come. Both texts serve as brackets, encompassing what lies in between. The throne room vision of chap.

4, which shows him dwelling in unapproachable, awe-inspiring splendor in heaven, has its counterpart in the vision of God dwelling among his people on earth (21:1—22:5).

Because John interconnected his materials through intercalations, interludes, cross-references, brackets, and encompassing, no "flat" outline will do justice to his artistic structure. One would have to apply different colors and also draw colored lines to show the connections, or better, make use of a hologram. At any rate, a "flat" outline, like the one that follows this introduction, suggests divisions, parts, and separate sections, whereas John interwove his material more deftly than this outline can show. The sequence of visions is indicated by him through simple markers, such as "then I saw," or "I heard," or "he said to me."

Tenth: we should not construct cycles of sevens where John did not number his visions. Had he desired additional numbered cycles, he would have done it himself. To construct a cycle of "seven unnumbered visions" out of 19:11—21:8 is to ignore John's eleven (!) markers of "I saw," "I heard," "he [God] said." John's three cycles of numbered visions are related to each other in that the trumpets and the bowls are modeled on the Egyptian plagues and flow from the seals. Yet each cycle also has a character of its own, as the commentary will show; for example, the bowls are directed specifically against the beast worshipers and they are also "the last" plagues (15:1).

If the bowl plagues are "the last" ones and if the trumpet plagues proceed from the seventh seal, must we not conclude that John presented these cycles in chronological sequence? In antiquity as well as in our time this view has found advocates, not only among fundamentalists but also among scholars, such as Charles, Rowland, Aune, and others. On the other side of the argument we find the advocates of "recapitulation" from Victorinus of Pettau to Elisabeth Schüssler Fiorenza. They rightly point to the thematic parallels between the three septets which recapitulate each other. Moreover, the interludes of chaps. 7 and 10–11 make it impossible to translate the sequence of visions into a chronological sequence. Thus, for instance, the redeemed of 7:9-17 are in the millennium already, while the trumpet plagues of 8:7—9:21 are blasts against a humanity that refuses to repent (9:20). At any rate, the seven trumpets are sounded prior to the millennium, not after it, and there is no use denying that. The conclusion is inevitable: the sequence of John's visions does not constitute a chronological sequence of historical/eschatological events.

Finally, the advocates of recapitulation point out that the visions of the sixth and seventh seals and the seventh trumpet already describe the eschaton. The day of judgment (6:16-17) as well as the final salvation (11:15-18) is present before the first bowl of wrath is poured out in 16:2. Therefore the sequence of the three septets cannot possibly constitute a chronological sequence. The three septets depict aspects of the approaching end. They refer to the short time between John's own time and the parousia/millennium. Recapitulation may not be understood as mere repetition. Later cycles intensify aspects of earlier ones, or refocus them. Temporal progression from John's present, or from his immediate future to the eschaton, is expressed *within* each of the three numbered cycles, rather, by the sequence of these three cycles.

The Author and Date of Composition

Who was the person who wrote this magnificent and quite unique prophetic-apocalyptic letter? He calls himself John (1:4, 9; 22:8), and the ancient church, beginning with Justin Martyr, identified him with the apostle John, son of Zebedee (*Dialog* 81.4). The dissenting voice of Dionysius of Alexandria (in Eusebius, *C.H.* 7.25.7-8) is interesting even though his argumentation is faulty and as antimillennialist he had an ax to grind. He argued that since we know that the apostle John wrote the Fourth Gospel and since the language of the Apocalypse differs greatly from that Gospel, the apostle John could not have written the last book of the Bible. Its author was another John. Dionysius never considered that the son of Zebedee might have written the Apocalypse rather than the Gospel that bears his name.

Modern scholarship in general agrees with Dionysius but assigns the authorship of all Johannine writings to persons (plural) other than the apostle John. Our author did not claim to be an apostle, nor did he give the slightest indication that he was an eyewitness to Jesus' ministry. When he refers to the twelve apostles they appear as past founders of the messianic people of God (21:14). He placed himself among the prophets (22:9) without explicitly claiming this title either. There is no internal evidence that would suggest that he was one of the twelve apostles. Moreover, if the testimony of Irenaeus (*Adv. Haer.* 5.30.3) is correct, as most scholars believe it is, that our letter/book was written at the end of the reign of Domitian, which would be about A.D. 95, then the son of Zebedee would have been 90 plus years old, an unlikely age for composing such an artistically constructed letter.

Some modern interpreters (e.g., Rowland and J. A. T. Robinson) suggested that the Apocalypse was written between A.D. 68 and 70. According to Robinson, the author had been a partaker of the suffering (1:9) "in Rome during and after the Neronian persecution" and composed our book around A.D. 69. One reason for Robinson's preference for this earlier date is the absence of persecution of Christians under Domitian. Robinson, however, goes one step farther when he states that the Apocalypse would be "the product of a perfervid and psychotic imagination," unless it grew out of the intense experience of "suffering at the hands of the imperial authorities" (p. 231). Hence the date of its composition is, according to him, the time subsequent to the Neronian persecution.

However, already the conservative scholar Zahn had pointed out in 1924 why this hypothesis is improbable. The fact is that *The Shepherd of Hermas*, an apocalypse written in Rome during the first half of the second century, as well as *1 Clement*, written from Rome around A.D. 100, does not know John's Apocalypse, even though it is addressed to the whole church through its seven churches. Both Roman writings highlight apostolic authority (cf. *Hermas, Vis.* 13; *1 Clement* 5; 42; 44; 47) and reflect familiarity with the Pauline corpus but not with the Apocalypse. Their unawareness of Revelation becomes understandable if we accept Irenaeus's date of origin (about A.D. 95) rather than one 25 years earlier. Zahn's argument, however, needs to be supported by internal evidence from our apocalyptic letter itself.

The internal evidence that requires a date of origin in the decade or decades after A.D. 70 is found in the label of *Babylon* for Rome. Because Rome, like Babylon of old, had destroyed the temple and devastated Jerusalem, some Jews called Rome Babylon in the decades that followed this disaster. This designation could not have arisen in Judaism prior to the destruction of the temple, when priests offered sacrifices for the well-being of Rome and its emperors. But 2 *Baruch*, 4 Ezra, and the *Sibylline Oracles* (book 5) denounce Rome as Babylon in the light of Jerusalem's destruction. Each of them was composed in the decades after A.D. 70. John's letter as well as 1 Peter adopted this designation from Jewish sources. Thus Irenaeus's date is probably right, and we will use it in this commentary.

Our author was not possessed by a "perfervid and psychotic imagination." More clearly than other Christians, such as the author of Luke-Acts, he saw the inevitability of the conflict between church and state over the issue of worship, and in dramatic pictures he depicted the future conflict, a foretaste of which the churches of Asia had experienced already. But in so doing, he also showed the very nature of the totalitarian state which absolutizes and thus deifies itself. Revelation, as we have argued, was not written in reaction to persecution, but it is a prophetic interpretation of the present condition of the churches (chaps. 2–3) and of the end time (chaps. 4–22) from the perspective of Christ crucified and exalted to the throne of God. He, not Caesar, is God's plenipotentiary over this world, because he, not Caesar, is "worthy" to open the scroll (chap. 5).

There can be no compromise, accommodation, or assimilation with those antagonists of God and his Messiah who are yet to come. John wants his audience to have no doubt about that. Other Christian writers presented Antichrist as a false prophet or as a group of heretical teachers (2 Thess. 2:1-12; 1 John 2:18; 2 John 7). Not so John. He envisioned the Antichrist in terms of the totalitarian, self-deifying, all-embracing power of the state. His letter is meant to clarify the issue that will arise. Those Christians who want to be "with it," whatever the "it" may be, will find that Christ himself shall "war against them" (2:16), "remove" their "lampstand" (2:5), blot their names "out of the book of life" (3:5), strike them dead (2:23), or spit them out like stale water (3:16).

Therefore John called to his churches: persevere and endure (cf. 3:10; 13:10; 14:12) in accordance with Christ (3:10); "worship God!" (14:7; 19:10; 22:9). His victory has already become reality in heaven, and his sovereign saving reign shall be made manifest on earth "soon" (1:1, 3; 2:16; 3:11; 10:6-7; 11:15; 12:12; 22:6, 7, 10, 12, 20). Negatively, John exhorted his people to abstain from heresy and sexual promiscuity, from idolatry, the imperial cult, and food sacrificed to idols (cf. 2:14; 9:20; 21:8; 22:15). But if their zeal for Christ has already waned, they are invited once more to repent (e.g., 2:16), to remember (2:5), to hold fast (2:25; 3:11) what they had received in baptism (1:6), to "take the water of life without price" (22:17), and to become conquerors (21:7), just as their Lord has conquered (3:21; 5:5) and shall conquer (17:14). The conquerors shall be sons of God in the millennium (21:7), kings of Psalm 2 among royal sisters and brothers who have already been designated coregents with Christ and who shall reign with him upon an earth free from sin, death, and the power of the devil, with God himself in the midst of them (20:4-6; 21:1—22:5). It is this all-embracing vision of the sovereignty ("the throne") of God and his Christ which John communicates to his people through his letter.

Who is the author of this prophetic-apocalyptic letter to the seven churches in the province of Asia? John, of course—not the son of Zebedee but the prophet John—not the "elder" John of Papias or of 2 and 3 John, nor the author of the Gospel According to John. The apocalyptic prophet John wrote this magnificent letter. What we know about him comes from his letter (see comments to 1:1-3, 9-10; 19:10; 22:8-9). He was a Jewish-Christian prophet, immersed in the Old Testament within which he walked with idiomatic ease. He may have emigrated from Palestine to Asia Minor in conjunction with the catastrophe of A.D. 70 together with other Jewish Christians bringing a mass of apocalyptic traditions with them. The evangelist Philip, one of the Seven, had also moved there and settled in Hierapolis (Acts 21:8; Eusebius, *C.H.* 3.33.3) together with his four daughters, who were prophetesses. As apocalyptic prophet, John was recognized by his fellow prophets of the province of Asia (22:9; 19:10), and he may have been their leader.

But he had also met opposition from a group identified as Balaamites and Nicolaitans (2:14-15), and their emissaries called themselves "apostles" (2:2). They were probably related to a prophetess to whom John gave the nickname "Jezebel" (2:20-21). The fact that he did not mention deacons, elders, and bishops in the seven messages has raised several hypotheses which we need not discuss. Suffice it to say that he sent his letter not to apocalyptically oriented conventicles within churches but to the churches themselves and beyond them to the whole Christian church on earth. For him, Christ's evaluation of churches in the present and the vision of their eschatological future are subjects for prophets. This does not necessarily imply a downgrading of institutional offices by him.

We should also realize that he, a Jewish-Christian prophet, affirmed Gentile Christianity and with it the Pauline, or rather post-Pauline, tradition (cf. 1:5-6; 5:9-10). On the issue of eating idol meat he agreed with the post-Pauline tradition as enunciated by Luke (cf. Acts 15:20). But on the subject of the Christians' relation to the empire he broke with the Pauline tradition. He could no more affirm that "rulers *are* not a terror to good conduct," because they *are* "God's servant for your good" (Rom. 13:3-4), than he could envision the beast of Revelation 13 to be the companion of the Lamb. In place of the Pauline perspective of a divine order of creation John introduced the apocalyptic perspective of opposing powers. In so doing, he raised the consciousness of his churches to the presence of radical evil within political power structures. To his largely Gentile Christian churches he communicated by letter Christ's appraisal of their present situation and the vision of "what must take place after this" (4:1; cf. 1:19).

His letter reveals him to be the supreme literary artist within the apocalyptic tradition, as it is known to us. With great care and skill he organized his letter down to the last detail. One example of his craftsmanship will have to suffice here. Just as the vision of the Lamb in chap. 5 evolves out of the vision of the throne of God in chap. 4, so the vision of Antichrist (chap. 13) evolves out of the vision of Satan (chap. 12). Both of these contrast scenes become the basis of the grand finale of 19:11—22:5.

About This Commentary

The aim of this series is to produce commentaries not for specialists but for pastors and congregations. The question with which this commentary deals is, What *did* John convey to his hearers/readers in the seven churches to whom he wrote his letter? That question differs from another one, What *does* John's message mean for us today? The answer to this latter question requires that we have struggled to answer the prior one first. When we ask what *did* John communicate to his people, we should be aware that our answers will of necessity be relative. It is what *we* think that John meant that can be found in the following pages. "Our knowledge is imperfect" (1 Cor. 13:9), and so is this commentary. Our listening skills, our perceptions, our abilities to discern and to see connections in the kaleidoscopic sequence of visions are imperfect, and our knowledge of the historical situation of the seven churches is fragmentary. Moreover, this commentary has omitted most discussions of differing points of view.

This commentary is dependent on the works of others. The two great commentaries of our century by Bousset (1906) and Charles (1920) are still basic to the interpretation of the Bible's last book. Bousset's history-of-religions approach focused attention on Jewish apocalypticism and oriental folklore. Charles's standard work emphasized literary criticism, text, grammar, and literary sources. Hanns Lilje's theological interpretation is a welcome alternative to the theologically mute interpretations of Bousset and Charles. The commentaries by Caird, Mounce, Beasley-Murray, Sweet, and others were also consulted together with a host of articles. The books and articles by Adela Yarbro Collins (especially chap. 4 in *Crisis and Catharsis*), J. J. Collins (*The Apocalyptic Imagination*), David L. Barr, David E. Aune, Leonard Thompson, David Hill, and M. Eugene Boring, I found most helpful, even when I disagree with some of their insights. None of them approached Revelation as a letter; some of them rejected such an approach. Their insights have been incorporated without giving credit beyond the bibliography.

Above all I should mention the work of Elisabeth Schüssler Fiorenza, whose interpretation marks a milestone in studies on the Apocalypse. Her thirty pages in the Proclamation Commentaries are probably the best brief summary on this "book" in any language. I appreciate especially her work on the literary unity and the structure of Revelation as well her calling attention untiringly to differences between Jewish apocalypses and John's letter. The fact that several essential items of the apocalyptic genre (such as pseudonymity, the demand for secrecy, the intention to write for the wise or the elite within the community, the division of history into periods on the basis of Daniel 7 or Genesis 1, journeys through heavenly regions, and apocalyptic timetables) are not found in Revelation has prompted Schüssler Fiorenza to question the usefulness of applying a definition of the apocalyptic genre as grid to the interpretation of Revelation. Consequently, she also opposed the alternative that Revelation is either a prophetic or an apocalyptic work, and she shed new light on early Christian prophecy. It is obvious that by calling John's work a prophetic-apocalyptic letter I am indebted to her. I would disagree with her on the structure of the letter (see comments on 1:19 and 4:1) and hold that John's own markers should not be set aside. They are reinforced by his theme (1:7-8) and by the nature of his epistolary communication. The fact that the present time is inseparable from the future and that chaps. 2–3 are linked to chaps. 4–22 should not blur the distinctions in form as well as in content between the two parts of this letter.

More serious is my second objection. Like most modern interpreters, Schüssler Fiorenza holds that Revelation is written in response to an actual crisis situation experienced by the Christians of John's time. Their "experience" of persecution and deprivation "undermined" their belief in God. "Their situation in no way substantiated their faith conviction" (Revelation, 192–199). This is of course true—of all situations at all times involving faith, for example, Abraham's experience of old age and childlessness contradicted God's promise that he would be "the father of many nations" (Romans 4), even as the experience of death contradicts John 11:25 (cf. the beatitudes of the Sermon on the Mount, etc.). But this is not the tension that she pursues. She holds that "the rhetorical situation," that is, the social situation of persecution and deprivation "*generates*" Revelation as a "fitting response" to that situation and therefore Revelation "*cannot* be understood when its 'rhetorical situation' no longer 'persists' " (ibid., 199, italicized for emphasis). We may ask, Could Revelation be understood in Laodicea which by its own admission was rich, lacked nothing, and experienced no tension (3:17)? Moreover, persecution appears as threat of the *future* (cf. 11:7, future tense; chap. 13 refers to the future) rather than as present experience. Therefore Adela Yarbro Collins argued that John responded not to an actual crisis but to an "envisioned" crisis. We should also note that persecution of the true people of God was part of John's tradition, as found in the Synoptic apocalypse and in Daniel. Revelation, like Daniel, connected the end-time persecutions with the appearance of Antichrist. This "dogma" inherited from the tradition, together with the sparsity of references to present persecutions in John's text, and, last but not least, the absence of state-sponsored persecution during Domitian's reign make it unlikely that the actual situation of experienced pressures generated John's visions.

I would like to turn this thesis on its head and argue that Revelation is written in response to the exaltation of the Lamb that was slain. In other words, it was *not* "the rhetorical *situation*" of actual or imagined persecution and deprivation that called forth John's response. On the contrary, it was his response to the exaltation of the slain Lamb that generated his views concerning church and world, present and future. His devastating portrayal of the world in general and the Roman empire in particular is the result of his apocalyptic Christology. Whereas Paul's apocalypticism was softened by his notion of divine orders of creation, John's is not. For Paul, the imperial authority "is God's servant for your good"; for John, it is the realm of idolatry that will turn into the beast. The fact that Rome did bring benefits to Asia Minor, for instance, by stopping intermittent warfare, is of no concern to John. The church according to Paul has no monopoly on moral behavior, truth and virtue are found also in the realm of reason (Phil. 4:8), and Gentiles can "do by nature what the law requires" (Rom. 2:14). For John, "outside" the church are "the dogs and sorcerers and fornicators and murderers and idolaters, and every one who loves and practices falsehood," and that is "every one" (22:15). This apocalyptic black-white portrayal of the world is determined by John's uncompromising commitment to worship of the Creator and the slain Lamb. Where God is not worshiped, the devil takes over and all of culture bears his mark of idolatry. More, the slain Lamb is the supreme symbol of the world's satanic hatred of God and his plenipotentiary (Rev. 12:1-6), and that hatred, manifested in idolatry, is of necessity extended to "those who keep the commandments of God and bear testimony to Jesus" (12:17). John's visions were never meant to alleviate the tension between faith and experience, nor to bring about a "catharsis" of Christian envy and hatred (so Yarbro Collins). Rather, they are meant to heighten the tension, so that there can be no compromise between worship of God and idolatry. Though a state-sponsored persecution did not take place in Asia Minor at John's time, as far as we know, nevertheless his visions were credible, because idolatry and the imperial cult were real and obvious to any Christian with eyes to see and so were the resultant vices, including Roman exploitation and the suffering of the poor. John's portrayal of the world, however, is not generated by social data but by his uncompromising theology which on one hand presents the social data as subject to God's radical judgment and on the other hand bypasses data such as the feeding of the poor by authorities, the modicum of law and order, and other benefits of Roman imperialism. The latter are irrelevant to John because idolatry characterizes the very fabric of culture, society, and the state. Indeed, few historians would deny that polytheistic religion, that is, idolatry from John's perspective, undergirded life in the ancient society of Rome and Asia Minor.

Worship in heaven and on earth is the response that runs like a red thread through Revelation. It is the response to the work of God and the Lamb. But worship also includes our works. They "follow" us into the millennium, or into the final judgment (14:13; 20:4, 12). For the church on earth, worship is to "hear what the Spirit says to the churches," and it includes such items as repent, abstain from eating idol meat, keep the commandments and bear testimony to Jesus, love sisters and brothers, be evaluated, encouraged, admonished, and threatened by the Christ who is present among the lampstands and speaks to his churches in worship. Chapters 4–11 are bracketed by worship in heaven and contain the plagues on earth which cause idolaters to curse their maker. Chapters 12–16 envision the ultimate alternative, worship of the devil and the beast, or worship of God by the community around the Lamb on Mount Zion, followed by the destruction of the beast worshipers through the bowls of wrath. Chapters 17–22 find their high points in the Hallelujah chorus in heaven and on earth (19:1-8) and in the statement that the redeemed reign with Christ and serve as priests of God (20:4-6; 22:1-5) on an earth free from idolatry, death, and the devil. In the church's present worship the reign of God and his Messiah is realized already on earth, though its realization is concealed, hidden, by imperfections within the communities and by tribulations caused by the evil one. Without tribulations a church is but the world on Sunday, under the sway of the evil one, and will be spit out by Christ (3:16).

John wrote a letter, not a treatise on apocalyptic eschatology. Therefore he wrote with a specific audience—or better, audiences—in mind. Martin Karrer was the first to demonstrate that Revelation is a letter and not just a treatise with an epistolary frame. Since his book is not available in English, I limit my critique to three points. First, he did not do justice to John's "encompassing technique" (see above, section 4); second, like most others he thought that Revelation is meant to be John's response to the tension between faith and experienced tribulations; third, his interpretation and criticism of the millennium is inadequate.

The point where I disagree with most modern interpreters is on the subject of John's millennium. It is generally understood that its interpretation in terms of the time of the church is false. However, even the recent German commentaries by Kraft, Müller, Lohse, and Roloff, as well as those in English by Beasley-Murray, Caird, Sweet, Ford, and Mounce, and studies like Karrer's or Rissi's, hold that the millennium (20:4-6) is Christ's interim kingdom on earth. This commentary will try to show that John was probably aware of apocalyptic messianic interim kingdom speculations. However, for him the millennium is, first, the devil's millennium, between his temporary residence beneath the deep blue sea (the abyss, cf. 11:7; 13:1) and his permanent abode in the frying pan (the lake of fire). Second, with respect to the saints, it constitutes their reward and precedence over against "the rest of the dead" (20:5). Third, it is the beginning of their eternal reign with Christ. In short, the millennial reign depicts in the form of a vision what is stated in the tradition: "the dead in Christ will rise first" (1 Thess. 4:16).

John's prophetic-apocalyptic letter moves from the present eschatological time of redemption and encounter with Christ to the future final salvation. This movement would suggest not only that the church is God's eschatological alternative community on earth in which his reign is realized through liberation from idolatry but that the church dare never forget that its final salvation is accomplished only when all idolatrous powers have been destroyed and when the resurrection of the dead in the millennium has occurred. John probably sought to correct an overly realized eschatology which focused upon individualistic spirituality of one sort or another (2:14, 20) and ignored the future resurrection together with the future liberation of the earth. But this correction, like others, such as angel worship (22:9) or a messianic interim (20:4-6), reflects only a secondary aim. What is basic to John's letter is worship of God and of Christ who comes in the present, confronting his churches through the prophet's word, and who shall come as final judge and deliverer. Worship focuses upon the throne of God and the slain Lamb, upon divine omnipotence and divine redemption; it connects heaven and earth, manifests God's reign on earth, celebrates the radiance of his light, encourages the weary, shakes up the lackadaisical, gathers his inclusive people, draws boundaries to idolaters, anticipates the millennium (21:1—22:5), and affirms with "Amen" him who is "the Amen" (3:14) and who has affirmed us. The opening of seals, the blowing of trumpets, the pouring out of the bowls of wrath are connected with worship. And so is the end. Beasts may rave against the people of God, but in the end there will be the Hallelujah chorus sounding forth from heaven and resounding in antiphony from the earth (19:1-8).

John's emphasis on worship may not be transformed into pseudo-pietistic individualism that focuses upon me and my feelings, my aspirations, and my salvation. The Christ of Revelation is the sovereign Lord of the earth who opposes now and in all the future the sundry lords who rape, maim, and destroy the earth (11:18). He reveals that the alternative between "saving souls" or changing unjust social structures is a false alternative. The saints are the representatives of the Creator and of the Lamb, and as such they identify with the oppressed of the earth and denounce the misuse of power. This is the least they can do, even when they are as powerless as the seven churches of Asia had been. Is it not striking that John could expect to get a hearing with his letter in which he reveals that the glorious culture of Roman imperialism is nothing but fornicating, bloodthirsty idolatry? Ostracized Christians manifest their liberation from idolatry and their new status as kings and priests by rejecting the mark of the beast together with the *pax Romana*. Fornication in Revelation has not just a personal but also a social dimension, and the same is true of redemption. The gift of redemption/liberation received and celebrated in worship demands that we manifest it on earth before it is perfected in the millennium.

OUTLINE OF REVELATION

(On the examples of *A-B-A'* structure noted on the right margin in this outline, see the introduction, section 4, pp. 56-61, above.)

I. Prolog (1:1-8)

II. Part One: The Revelation of the Present (1:9—3:22)
   A. Inaugural Audition, Vision, and Commission (1:9-20)
   B. The Messages to the Seven Churches in Asia (2:1—3:22)
      1. To Ephesus (2:1-7)
      2. To Smyrna (2:8-11)
      3. To Pergamum (2:12-17)
      4. To Thyatira (2:18-29)
      5. To Sardis (3:1-6)
      6. To Philadelphia (3:7-13)
      7. To Laodicea (3:14-22)

III. Part Two: The Revelation of the Future (4:1—22:5)
   A. The Revelation of the Sovereignty of God and Christ in Tribulations and Plagues (4:1—11:19)
      1. The Seven Seals (4:1—8:1)
         a. Prelude in Heaven (4:1—5:14)
         b. The First Six Seals (6:1-17)
         Interlude: The preservation of the Faithful (7:1-17)
            (1) Preview: The Sealing of the 144,000 (7:1-8)
            (2) The Conquerors in the Millennium (7:9-17)
         a'. The Seventh Seal (8:1)

2. The Seven Trumpets (8:2—11:19)
   a. Prelude in Heaven (8:2-6)
   b. The First Six Trumpets (8:7—9:21)
      Announcement of Three Woes (8:13)
      Interlude: New Commission; Witness, and Preservation of the Faithful (10:1—11:14)
      (1) Preview: The Open Little Scroll and the Commissioning of John (10:1-11)
      (2) Preview: The Measuring of the Temple and the Two Witnesses (11:1-13)
      Announcement of the Third Woe (11:14)
   a′. The Seventh Trumpet (11:15-19)

B. The Revelation of the Antagonists; Judgment and Salvation (12:1—16:21)
1. The Church at War (12:1—14:20)
   a. The Woman, the Child, and the Dragon (12:1-17)
   b. The Beast from the Sea and the Beast from the Earth (13:1-18)
      Interlude: The Lamb and His Followers on Mount Zion (Preview) (14:1-5)
   a′. The Announcement and Execution of the Final Judgment (14:6-20)
2. The Seven Bowls of Wrath (15:1—16:21)
   a. Prelude in Heaven (15:1-8)
   b. The First Six Bowls (16:1-12)
      Interlude: The Kings of the Earth and Armageddon (Preview) (16:13-16)
         [Exhortation to the Faithful (16:15)]
   a′. The Seventh Bowl; "It Is Done!" (16:17-21)

A′. The Revelation of the Climactic End (17:1—22:5[9])
(A). The Judgment of Babylon and the Triumph of God (17:1—19:10)
   a. The Great Harlot and the Beast (17:1-18)
   b. The Fall of Babylon (18:1-24)
   a′. The Hymn of Triumph (19:1-10)

(B). The Parousia, Final Judgments, and the Final Salvation (19:11—21:8)
- a. Christ's Victory over Beasts and Vassals (19:11-21)
  Satan Removed into the Abyss (20:1-3)
  Interlude 1: The Millennial Reign with Christ (20:4-6)
  Interlude 2: Satan Cast into the Lake of Fire (20:7-10)
- b. The Judgment of the Dead (20:11-15)
- a′. The New Jerusalem and the Final Word of God: "It Is Done!" (21:1-8)

(A′). The New Jerusalem (21:9—22:5[9])
- a. The City (21:9-21)
- b. The People (21:22-27)
- a′. Paradise (22:1-5)

IV. Epilog and Epistolary Conclusion (22:6[10]-21)

The Seven Churches

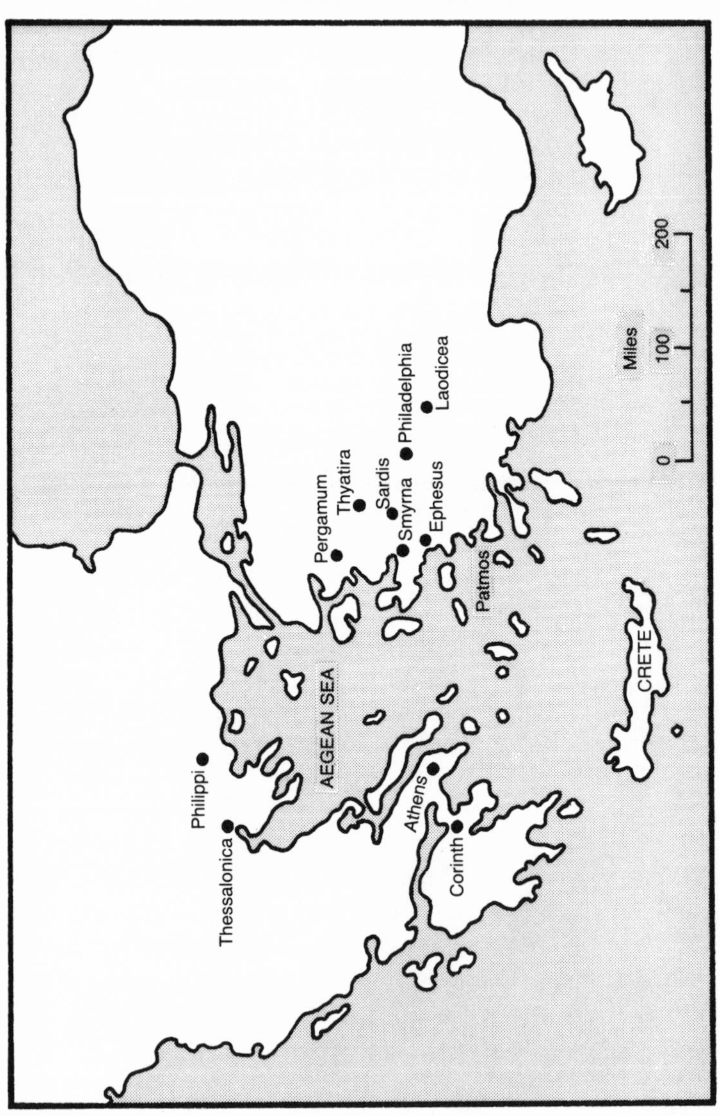

COMMENTARY

■ The Prolog (1:1-8)

The prolog of John's letter functions like the "exordium," also known as *proem,* in Greco-Roman rhetoric. It opens a discourse, establishes rapport with an audience, sets forth the common basis of the discourse (here, vv. 4b-6), and closes with a "proposition" stating the theme, or issue under consideration (here, vv. 7-8). Following the prolog we find a "narration" of relevant events (1:9-20), which displays the author's credibility and his "ethos," indicates the reason for sending this letter, and gives legitimation to it. The narration also introduces the two parts of the "body" of the letter (1:19). Without break the narration continues into Part I (chaps. 2–3). A new vision narrative begins at 4:1 and ends with 22:5(9). In both parts the audience is addressed directly. A "peroration," or closure, forms an epilog and summarizes the substance of the body of the letter (22:6 [10]-21); it contains appeals for the support of the author's viewpoint and for the integrity of his letter together with final admonitions and concluding greetings. According to Stowers's categories, John's writing would be a "protreptic" letter, containing an exhortation to a way of life (cf. pp. 112–114). According to rhetorical classification, it would belong to the genre of deliberative rhetoric (cf. Kennedy). Neither Stowers nor Kennedy treated Revelation as a letter. We will do so, because John himself chose to write a letter.

The prolog and the epilog of this letter are of particular significance in that they disclose the author's intentions, summarize and characterize his literary achievement, and function to aid hearers or readers in their understanding of what follows by putting them on the right track, so to speak. The importance of this prolog can also be seen in that, with the epilog (22:6[9]-21), it forms an inclusion, brackets, around the rest of the book. All the themes of this opening section are taken up in the epilog, as we shall observe. The prolog consists of six units: (1) the preface (vv. 1-2); (2) the first of seven beatitudes (v. 3); (3) the epistolary prescript (v. 4a); (4) the salutation (vv. 4b-5a); (5) the doxology (vv. 5b-6); and (6) the theme, indicated by two oracles (vv. 7-8).

Preface (1:1-2)

The Preface is more than a title, although it fulfills that function too. The present superscription, The Revelation *of* St. John (KJV) or The Revelation *to* John (RSV), was added when this book became part of the New Testament canon, but originally the book began with the preface, vv. 1-2. The only other New Testament book with a preface is Luke's Gospel. In early Christian literature outside the New Testament we occasionally find prefaces in such writings as the *Epistula Apostolorum* (cf. Schneemelcher, 1:191), the *Apocryphon of John*, the *Gospel of Thomas*, and the *Didache*. It is surprising that a book which claims to be a circular letter, addressed to seven churches (1:4, 11), would have a preface, not normal in letters within or outside the New Testament, indicating that our writing is meant to be a peculiar letter, peculiar because of its length, subject matter, and preface.

Before John begins his letter he wants to make it clear to his hearers and readers that he did not write the following letter on his own initiative. Strictly speaking, he did not function as author of this letter but as scribe, as instrument of Jesus. He did not write the revelation of John, or even to John—he wrote **the**

revelation of Jesus Christ. That means the revelation given *by* Jesus Christ and ultimately by God. In his preface John carefully noted five links in a communication chain: One, the ultimate source of the revelation is *God.* Two, God "gave" the revelation to *Jesus.* Three, Jesus made his revelation known through an *angel* as his heavenly agent. Four, the angel communicated it to *John,* his earthly agent and "servant." Five, John "bore witness to the word of God and to the testimony of Jesus Christ, even to all that he saw" by communicating the revelation to Jesus' *servants.* These are the members of the churches addressed (1:4), and John is but one servant among the servants of Jesus. Simultaneously the servant-prophet plays a special role among and over against the community of servants (cf. Amos 3:7) because he is the instrument of Christ's revelation to them. At the very outset, as well as at the end of his letter, John wished to underscore that the revelation comes from God and Christ. Therefore **the words of the prophecy** (1:3; 22:18), which are the content of this letter, lay an absolute claim on Jesus' servants and may not be altered.

A theme of John's prophecy is the expectation of the imminent judgment and salvation. The revelation by Jesus Christ therefore communicates **what must soon take place; . . . for the time** of the eschatological judgment and of Christ's parousia in glory **is near.** This theme also appears in the messages to the seven churches (2:16; 3:11). Later on we hear that there should be "no more delay" (10:6), that the dragon's time on earth "is short" (12:12), and that "the time for the dead to be judged" and "for rewarding" the faithful people of God has come (11:18), and in the epilog Jesus promises three times "I am coming soon" (22:7, 12, 20). The expectation of the imminent end underlines the urgency to gain a new all-embracing perspective on God, Christ, the world, the church, the present, and the future—to allow oneself to be drawn by Christ into the revelation which John seeks to mediate to the churches that they may be strengthened or changed by it.

Beatitude (1:3)

A beatitude is attached to the preface and discloses John's intention. He proposed his letter to be read aloud during the worship of the communities. Therefore the blessing is directed to the lector (singular) and the hearers (plural). Christian prophets gave instruction and encouragement to the assembled congregation, and since John could not be present with them, his letter, like those of Paul before him, could function as substitute for his presence and his oral proclamation (cf. 1 Thess. 5:27). Implicit in this beatitude is the hope that his message will be read by the lector without additions, subtractions, or alterations (cf. 22:18-19). It is the first of seven beatitudes (14:13; 16:15; 19:9; 20:6; 22:7, 14), and it is the only one spoken by John himself instead of by an angel or by Jesus. **Blessed is he who reads aloud the words of the prophecy, and blessed are those who hear, and who keep what is written therein; for the time is near** (cf. 22:7). The gathered community, the audience, is blessed if it not just politely listens but is able to **keep** the **words of prophecy.** His hearers must be grounded in the revelation given by Christ if they are to persevere in the turmoils that are imminent (cf. 22:7).

The preface relates "the revelation of Jesus Christ" to "all that he (John) saw," to "the word of God," to "the testimony of Jesus," to "the words of the prophecy," and finally to "what is written" in John's letter. These different expressions are almost synonymous, but we should note that John never speaks of revelations (plural) when he narrates his visions and auditions. They are the revelation given by Jesus only in their totality. Since God is the ultimate source of this revelation, what John wrote is "word of God" or "words of prophecy." **The testimony of Jesus Christ** (genitive subject, because of the parallel to "word of God") is part of Christ's revelation. Jesus is the faithful witness (1:5) who sealed his testimony, his witness (Greek, *martyria*), through his death. When John claimed that he "bore witness to . . . the testimony of Jesus," he is saying that Jesus' life, death, resurrection, and promise of his parousia determine his life. Moreover, John's own witness communicates the testimony of Jesus, his redeeming death, his loving presence (v. 6), and his glorious future. His witness includes following Jesus "wherever he goes" (14:4). Finally, John's message, written in this letter, is the testimony of Jesus because Christ himself testifies to it (22:20a).

John was the first to use the word **revelation** (Greek, *apokalypsis;* literally, unveiling of what is otherwise hidden) as the title of his letter. With this designation he did not refer to a literary genre, as though he wished to indicate that he was writing another apocalypse, but he referred to a revelatory experience, as the narration in 1:9-20 will clarify. The noun "revelation" occurs only in his preface; otherwise it is found in the New Testament only in letters bearing Paul's or Peter's name. In Gal. 1:12, 16 Paul stated that he received the gospel "through a revelation of Jesus Christ," which means the same as: God chose "to reveal his Son to me, in order that I might preach him [as good news] among the Gentiles." "Revelation" in Galatians 1 as well as in our preface denotes a revelatory, visionary experience, not a literary genre. It refers to the self-disclosure of Jesus Christ to John which he in turn communicated in a letter to the churches. The revelation of Jesus Christ includes all visions and auditions narrated by him and constitutes the content of his "prophecy" in this letter (1:3; 19:10; 22:7, 10, 18). As such, it is an authoritative "word of God" (1:2).

Epistolary Prescript, Salutation, and Doxology (1:4-6)

John's literary achievement has the form of a letter, of a personal communication, addressed **to the seven churches that are in Asia.** It is the longest letter in the New Testament. In the next section each of the seven churches will receive its own message, but the prolog designates the whole book as a letter from **John** (see the introduction, sections 3 and 4). Our author does not claim apostolic authority; in 21:14 the apostles appear only as figures of the past and foundations of the new Jerusalem (cf. Eph. 2:20; 3:5). He does not even explicitly use the title "prophet" of himself in order to legitimate his "prophecy" written in this letter (1:3). But undoubtedly he was acknowledged as a prophet by the churches and their leaders in the Roman province of Asia, though obviously he was not the incumbent of an institutionalized office, whether bishop or elder (cf. 2 John; 3 John; cf. Acts 20:28).

A Hellenistic letter began, "A to B, greetings." In agreement with prior Christian custom, John expanded the salutation into a solemn wish for **grace** and **peace,** and he attached a doxology in response to the gift of grace and peace. In its worship, the community gives **glory** for its delivery from the bondage of sin, affirms Christ's **dominion** over principalities and powers, rejoices in its place in the **kingdom,** and celebrates its new status as **priests** of God. Grace and peace recall the priestly blessing of Num. 6:24-26. In the Christian tradition, **grace** expressed the good news that God's favor reaches out to the undeserving, the lost and the least. **Peace** in the Hebrew tradition is more than the absence of war. It is a state of total well-being resulting from God's saving action and presence within Israel. In John's Christian tradition the peace of God is established through Christ in the power of the Spirit among God's redeemed people. Grace and peace, which are promised to the worshiping community, have a threefold source.

First, grace and peace come **from him who is and who was and who is to come.** Grace and peace are not the Roman emperor's benefactions, as his propagandists claimed, but gifts granted by God. His divine name, the tetragrammaton YHWH of Exod. 3:14, is reinterpreted in accordance with the three dimensions of time. Similar triadic formulas are also present in Hellenistic religion. Yet John's future reference is not the Hellenistic "who will be," which in Hellenism indicates that the future is the persistence of the past and the present. The Hellenistic gods, as well as the emperor worship, were meant to function as guarantors of the status quo. For John, God is the one *who is to come.* He will be doing a new thing, overturning the status quo. He shall make all things new (21:5-6). All that is and has been will therefore be open to a radical transformation by the Coming One. The note of the future, heard already in the preface ("soon," v. 1; "the time is near," v. 3), is struck again and prepares the audience for the theme in vv. 7-8.

Second, grace and peace have their source in **the seven spirits who are before his throne.** The idea of **seven spirits** before God's **throne** had its origin in Babylonian astral religion. There the sun, the moon, and the five then-known planets were worshiped as deities who controlled time in terms of weeks, months, and years. The calendar, in the possession of the priests, controlled life on earth. During the Babylonian captivity Judaism became aware of astral religion and reinterpreted it. In Gen. 1:14-19 the stars are not deities but lamps, created by God and hung from the firmament. In some traditions of intertestamental Judaism, the seven stars are viewed as archangels (cf. Tob. 12:15). John and his churches apparently shared this tradition, but he modified it (cf. 3:1). Seven symbolizes completeness, and the seven spirits are theologically identical with the fullness of the Holy Spirit (cf. 3:1; 4:5; 5:6). The Holy Spirit is pictured here as seven spirit-angels who stand before God's throne (cf. Tob. 12:15; *1 Enoch* 20:1-3). They inspire the church as it listens to the prophetic word and grant grace and peace in the midst of the hardship and carnage that is to come.

Third, the source of grace and peace is **Jesus Christ.** Three designations characterize his identity, and a threefold salvific effect proceeds from him. With respect to his past, he is the **faithful witness,** who has completed his witness on behalf of God by his death on the cross. Our witness to Christ, therefore, must be determined by Jesus' own uncompromising faithfulness, a faithfulness that may include suffering obedience (cf. 2:13). With respect to the future, he is the **first-born of the dead** (cf. Rom. 8:29; Col. 1:18). His resurrection is the world's best news, for it signals the beginning of a new creation in which death shall be no more (21:4).

Finally, with respect to this present world, Jesus Christ is **the ruler of kings on earth.** The hope of Ps. 89:27 has found its realization in him ("I will make him the first-born, the highest of the kings of the earth"). As the resurrected and exalted One, he already now holds in his hands the fate of all humans, including those who had condemned him in the past and who oppose him in the present. In the present his lordship over demonic powers and their earthly royal representatives is hidden and the **kings on earth** are drunk with the illusion of their might (cf. Rev. 16:14, 16; 19:19). Nevertheless the worshiping church already now confesses Christ as ruler and king. To him belongs all power in heaven and on earth (Matt. 28:18; Phil. 2:10; Rev. 5:6-14). The basic issue in this writing turns around the question, Who is **the ruler** of the **earth** and whom should humans worship?

A doxology immediately after an epistolary prescript is found only in Galatians and here. This, together with his use of "revelation of Jesus Christ," would suggest that John was familiar with this Pauline letter. Through his expanded salutation and his doxology John established the common ground between himself and his audience in the seven churches. In all probability he cited a doxology that was familiar to them from the baptismal liturgy. The doxology is the response to the threefold declaration of Christ's sovereignty in the salutation. The faithful witness loves us; the firstborn of the dead has liberated us by his blood; the ruler of the kings on earth has made us a kingdom, an alternative to Caesar's kingdom. In its doxology the worshiping community renders praise to Christ for his threefold saving activity. First, **he loves us** (present tense). His love, extended to his people in the past in their baptism, upholds them in the present (cf. Gal. 2:20). Because **he** loves us in the present, eschatology is realized eschatology and not the subject of future predictions and apocalyptic timetables. His love in the present is also expressed through John's commission to write to the seven churches (cf. 3:19). His love for **us** implies that John, together with his sisters and brothers in the seven churches, is never lost or forsaken, no matter what may befall them.

Second, he has **freed us from our sins by his blood** (past tense). While some manuscripts have "washed" (Greek, *lousanti*) instead of **freed** (Greek, *lysanti*), the latter reading has better attestation, and the former would seem to be a case of mishearing or misreading by a later copyist. Through his **blood,** his death, Christ has redeemed, liberated, the baptized from their past sins (cf. Col. 1:13; Eph. 1:7, 13). The allusion to Israel's deliverance in the exodus is as obvious as the allusion to Lev. 17:11. Blood is the symbol of life. Freedom from sin and guilt means to be rightly related to God and enfolded by the love of Christ (realized eschatology!). The doxological affirmation focuses, not on isolated individuals, but on **us,** the communities of Jesus' liberated servants.

Third, baptism also signaled their installation to kingship and priesthood. He **made us a kingdom, priests to his God and Father.** Again we have an allusion to the exodus story (Exod. 19:6; cf. 1 Peter 2:9). In Exod. 19:6 we read, "You shall be a royal people of priests" (Greek, *hierateuma*), which is a promise for the future. John translated it into the past, changed the adjective *royal* to the noun *kingdom* or *kingship*, and changed "people of priests" into priests. The baptized constitute the realm of God's reign on earth, and they have been installed to reign with Christ in the millennium (20:4-6), provided that they are conquerors in the present (2:26; 3:21, etc.; 21:6-7, 22:5). Their present kingship and priesthood are hidden by tribulations, yet the hour will come when they shall reign with Christ (20:4-6). The new Jerusalem will have no temple and no special caste of priests functioning as intermediaries between God and the people. For the Lord God the Almighty and the Lamb shall be its temple and his people shall worship him (21:22—22:5). Just as Israel's exodus resulted in the promise of a kingdom for Yahweh and a priesthood of the whole people unto God, so Christ's death has already resulted in a kingdom on earth over which God and Christ reign and a kingship of those who are priests.

Already now the church is a priestly community and an alternative kingdom to Caesar's idolatrous empire. The challenge to hold fast what is granted through baptism is implicit. In doxological language, John praised Christ (vv. 5b-6) and reaffirmed the salvation in which he and his hearers share. Christ's love envelops us in the present. His death has achieved deliverance, forgiveness of sins, and he has installed us into the eschatological office of kingship and priesthood. This threefold bond of solidarity unites the prophet with his people and serves as basis for his letter. All baptized persons are beloved, redeemed, and royal priests, with direct access to God, challenged to worship God in priestly purity and to participate already now in Christ's royal power. John did not elaborate on the royal and priestly functions of the Christians except briefly in 7:15 and 8:3-4, because the full realization of these functions lies in the future (20:4-6; 22:5).

Thus in his prolog John set forth the common ground that exists between himself and the worshiping communities in which his letter is to be read. This common ground can be identified in terms of "realized eschatology." What Christ is doing now and what he has already accomplished not only unite John in solidarity with his hearers but also express the conviction that salvation is present already and is therefore not just a matter of hope for the future. Already in the present there is a new experience (Christ's love), a new relationship (redemption), and a new and equal status before God and among the people of God (kingdom and priesthood). All of this has already been realized, and John fully agrees that this is so. Before he unfolds his futuristic, apocalyptic eschatology, he has articulated the present eschatological existence of his hearers, an existence that contradicts the claims of the world and therefore must be affirmed ever anew in faith and perseverance, in trials and tribulations, in worship and in praise.

To him be glory and dominion for ever and ever. In its doxology, the worshiping community resounds with exuberance to the love, the forgiveness, and the new status received from its king. He acts in unity with the **Father** and he is therefore the Son. Not only to God, but also to Christ, belong **glory and dominion** now and in all the future (5:13; 7:10, 12). **Amen:** This Hebrew word was used as a liturgical response in the psalms or doxologies and means, "it is certain, it is true, so be it."

Theme and Summary (1:7-8)

These verses state the theme, or proposition, of the letter and summarize the content of "the revelation of Jesus Christ" (v. 1) with respect to the future. There shall be a future revelation, because Christ shall come and God shall come. John used two originally separate prophetic oracles. The first, v. 7, is a prophetic oracle of judgment, and it is introduced with **Behold.** This interjection is always placed strategically at important points (27 times in Revelation). It is meant to function as an attention-getter, like "Now, pay attention!" (cf. 1:18; 4:1; 21:5). Here the response **Amen** forms an inclusion around v. 7 and highlights its importance. In the second oracle, God speaks directly to the worshipers, the first of only two times in Revelation where God himself speaks (cf. 21:5-8). It amplifies the designation of God in the salutation (v. 4b) and functions as confirmation of the first oracle in v. 7.

7—The doxology had praised Christ's *present* lordship and introduced his future dominion with the phrase "for ever and ever" (vv. 5b-6). Now John takes another step and summarizes Christ's future lordship by fusing two Old Testament texts, Dan. 7:13 and Zech. 12:10-12. These two texts were also connected with each other in Matt. 24:30 and applied to Christ's parousia. **Behold, he is coming with the clouds** soon. The coming of the Danielic son of man on, or with, the clouds of heaven signals the final salvation of the elect. Here Christ's future coming precipitates the universal judgment. **Every eye will see him,** including those **who pierced him,** be they Jew or Gentile. All of humanity will recognize that the crucified one is to be their judge. **All tribes of the earth will wail on account of him.** They will lament, not in godly repentance, but in fear and guilt because they must face their judge (cf. 6:16-17; 14:9-11; 19:11-16). This oracle expands v. 5 by showing the reaction of rebellious humans to "the ruler of kings" on the last day. The first part of v. 7 also discloses that for John the eschatological time begins with the crucifixion and ends with the final judgment. **Even so** (Greek, *nai*) **Amen** is the response of the community to Christ's parousia and judgment, and it finds its echo in Jesus' response in 22:20: "Even so (Greek, *nai*), I am coming soon." Verse 7 serves as transition from realized eschatology to the main theme of Revelation, the future judgment and future salvation as cosmic events. The prophetic oracle of v. 7 recalled Scripture and hence is legitimated by it. In addition, a second word (v. 8) offers confirmation by God himself.

8—"I am the Alpha and the Omega." Alpha and omega are the first and the last letters of the Greek alphabet and thus comprise all letters. This divine predication did not originate from the Old Testament, but, as David Aune has shown, it came from Hellenistic magic. There it abbreviated the seven Greek vowels which were thought to be the name of the supreme God. The oracle adopted and adapted this notion. It could do so because the "I am" style of God's self-disclosure is also found in the Old Testament (Isa. 41:4; 44:6; 48:12). There God revealed himself as the one who was in the beginning and who shall be at the end. The predication, Alpha and Omega, is applied again, not only to God (21:6), but in the epilog also to Christ (22:13; cf. 1:17; 2:8).

The second designation, **who is and who was and who is to come,** forms brackets with 1:4b. The self-predication has its high point in the title **the Almighty** (Greek, *pantokratōr,* which in the LXX translates the Hebrew for "Lord of Hosts"). This is John's favorite title for God (cf. 4:8; 11:17; 15:3; 16:7, 14; 19:6, 15; 21:22) and discloses that God controls the world, its history and its goal. His is the first and the final word, because he is the creator who *was* at the beginning, who *is* the sustainer of the present, and who will *come* to make a new heaven and a new earth (21:1, 5).

Hellenistic magic and astrology sought to figure out *what* will happen in the future; the imperial ideology prattled about Caesar's omnipotence in the present. John's letter will deal with *who* is coming, the Almighty and his plenipotentiary. His coming will reveal the phoniness of earthly potentates, as expressed in Seneca's soliloquy for Nero: "I am the arbiter of life and death for the nations. . . . By my lips fortune proclaims what gift she [the goddess fortune] would bestow. . . . From my utterances peoples and cities gather reasons for rejoicing; without my favor and grace no part of the whole world can prosper" (*De Clementia* 1.1.2). With the announcement of the theme—Christ shall come, God shall come—the stage is set for the body of the letter.

Part I: The Revelation of the Present (1:9—3:22)

The first words of the preface (1:1-3) announced "the revelation of Jesus Christ" and thereby raised the question concerning his identity. Who is this Christ who gave the revelation to John through an angel? The prescript and doxology (1:4-6) gave a first answer by using a tradition common to John and his audience. They have heard by now that Christ is "the faithful witness," "the first-born of the dead," and "the ruler of kings on earth." He is extending his love to "us," his people gathered for worship, in the present; he has delivered "us" from our past sins and established us as his kingdom, the realm of his rule on earth, granting us the status of priests. Moreover, he shall come in glory in the future as judge of all. This is the one who gave the revelation to John.

At once new questions arise. Did this Christ reveal himself to John, and if so, what was he like? If Christ extends his love to us in the present (1:5), what does he think about us? What is his evaluative point of view concerning us, the churches addressed in 1:4? And what about "the angel," this agent of revelation, mentioned in 1:1? How did John meet him? The first part of John's letter (1:9—3:22) deals with these questions. John's situation on Patmos (1:9) leads to an audition on the Lord's day (1:10-11) in which "a loud voice" commissioned him to write to the seven churches. This loud voice will reappear in 4:1 as an angel mediating the revelation given by Christ through John to the churches. Moreover, John's vision of Christ himself (1:12-20) will show to the gathered audience an appearance of the resurrected and exalted Lord in his divine majesty. This visionary encounter along with a second commission to write (1:19; cf. 1:11) not only undergirds the authority and legitimacy of John's letter, as well as his credibility, his "ethos," but it also leads directly into Christ's messages to the churches in Asia. In these seven messages the churches hear Christ's evaluation of their present life and actions, followed by admonitions and concluded with promises about their future. These promises and other issues raised in the seven messages will be taken up in the second part of John's letter (4:1—22:5).

The thanksgiving sections of Paul's letters pointed obliquely to themes discussed in the body of his letters. Similarly, John connected the main theme, the future coming of Christ and God (1:7-8), with a doxology (1:5b-6). His major theme will also appear in this first part, because Christ not only evaluates and admonishes but also issues threats and makes promises which shall be fulfilled in the future. But the focus of Part I lies on the present situation of the churches. In 1:19 John is commissioned to "write what you see [beginning with his "inaugural" vision], what is and what is to take place hereafter." Since the clause "what is to take place hereafter" is taken up in 4:1, it would appear that the body of John's letter has two main parts: 1:9—3:22 deals with "what is," the present situation, and 4:1—22:5 deals with the future. The two parts are interrelated, as we shall discover.

■ Inaugural Audition, Vision, and Commission (1:9-20)

At the beginning of prophetic writings we sometimes find narratives that are connected with a vision (Ezekiel 1–3; Isaiah 6; Jeremiah 1). John too introduced his prophetic message with a vision narrative and commission. Yet unlike the Old Testament prophets, John did not become a prophet through this vision—he had already been one. But he is commissioned twice to **write what you see in a book** (vv. 11 and 19). Not by his own authority does John send his book in letter form to the seven churches but by the authority of the angel (1:10-11; cf. 4:1) and of Christ himself. The vision narrative serves as introduction to the series of seven messages. Verses 9-11 also serve as introduction to all subsequent visions. When John is commanded to **write what you see** (v. 11), then this commission cannot be restricted to the first three chapters but includes all the visions found in Revelation.

John's description of his vision of Christ is almost unimaginable. It is the product of drawing together images from diverse traditions, from Exodus, Daniel, imperial Roman propaganda, astrology, and Hellenistic folk religion. John undoubtedly had ecstatic experiences, but when he narrated them he presented a carefully structured literary pastiche that incorporated and changed diverse traditions and images. In its present form our letter contains literary visions; John's own experiences are no longer accessible to us, except as literary constructions.

John's Situation (1:9)

Emphatically, the author presented himself at the beginning and at the end of his letter (22:8): **I John.** No title of an office is used. Instead, he again declares his solidarity with his readers. He is their **brother,** united with them **in Jesus** (14:13). He shares with them **the tribulation and the kingdom and the patient endurance.** Tribulations are a sign of the end, according to apocalyptic thought. They include a variety of pressures ranging from ridicule, slander, social ostracism, and harassment, to poverty, violence, imprisonment, and possible martyrdom. John is their partner in tribulation, because he himself had probably suffered exile. Moreover, he, like they, has a share in the kingdom. They are partners in the eschatological reign of God and Christ already now (1:6). But because their present kingship is subject to tribulation, endurance is demanded from him and them. Endurance was praised as a virtue among the Greeks. It is the stamina that does not give up in the face of adversity. Later on we hear that endurance also involves waiting for Jesus' coming (3:10-11) and keeping the commandments of God under duress (14:12). Only if they persevere in faith will they be coregents with Christ in the end (20:4-6). As members of God's alternative kingdom they must endure as they face Caesar's kingdom as well as other pressures.

John was **on the island called Patmos.** The past tense **was** may indicate that by the time he finished his book he was no longer there. But the past tense here may simply be due to his narration of the past experience. He was on Patmos, an island about 65 miles south of Ephesus, not because he was seeking solitude or doing missionary work, but **on account of the word of God and the testimony of Jesus.** In the light of 6:9 and 20:4, where the same Greek preposition and the phrases "word of God" and "testimony of Jesus" appear, we may conclude that John was on Patmos because he was being punished. His ministry of proclamation had probably led to his exile. Roman law distinguished between lifelong exile (*deportatio*) and temporary exile (*relegatio*). We do not know which of the two was involved. Tertullian, who as a lawyer knew Roman law, pointed to temporary exile (*De Praescr. Haeret.* 36), though generally this form of punishment was employed against persons of rank.

Audition and Commission (1:10-11)

In unadorned, straightforward language, John recounts: **I was in the Spirit on the Lord's day.** He did not refer to a heavenly journey of his soul (cf. 4:1-2; 2 Cor. 12:1-3) but to an ecstatic experience that took place on a Sunday, the day of the resurrection, when the communities gathered for worship. Absent in body, John is present with them in the Spirit. Impelled by the Spirit, he heard a **loud voice like a trumpet** behind him. In 4:1 the reader will learn that this is not Christ's voice but the voice of his angel who mediated the visions (cf. 1:1; 22:16). Angels as mediators and occasionally as interpreters of revelation also appear in 10:1-3; 17:1, 7, 15-18; 19:9-10; 21:9, 15; 22:8, 16. Since human language can only approximate heavenly reality, we find an abundance of comparisons in Jewish and Christian apocalypses. A voice **like a trumpet** points to a divine epiphany (Exod. 19:16; cf. 1 Thess. 4:16). The heavenly voice commissioned him to **write** a book and send it to **the seven churches.** On one hand, his book is a round-robin letter addressed to specific churches. On the other hand, the number **seven** symbolizes fullness and suggests that John is to write a catholic letter to be heard by all churches. Besides the "seven churches," we find seven spirits (1:4; 4:5; 5:6), seven lampstands (1:12), seven stars (1:16), seven seals (5:1), a lamb with seven horns and seven eyes (5:6), seven trumpets blown by seven angels (8:2), seven thunders (10:3), and seven plagues in seven bowls of wrath (15:1; 16:1).

The background of this number lies in Babylonian astral religion in which the sun, the moon, and the five known planets were worshiped as deities that determined the times and the course of the world. Hence seven became the number for fullness and completion and the seven churches also symbolize the one church. The question why this book was sent to the particular churches mentioned in v. 11 rather than to the churches in Miletus, Troas, Magnesia, Tralles, Colossae, and Hierapolis cannot be answered satisfactorily. The suggestion made by Ramsay is as good as any: The churches lie on the road that led from Ephesus north via Smyrna to Pergamum and from there southeast via Thyatira, Sardis, and Philadelphia to Laodicea. Hence the sequence of the churches in chaps. 1–3.

The Vision (1:12-20)

John turned **to see the voice.** This is a strange way of expressing oneself unless he suggests that the voice is an angel (cf. 4:1; 6:6; 9:13; 10:4, 8; 11:12; 19:5), perhaps an angel whose name is "The Voice." What he saw was not a voice but **seven golden lampstands.** Gold indicates their preciousness. This is not the menorah of Exod. 37:17-24, with a central stand and three pairs of branches, but seven separate lampstands arranged in a circle. Their probable historical background in astral religion is suggested by their relationship to the seven stars (cf. 1:16, 20). Yet astrological notions are undercut by our author. The lamp had already become a Christian symbol (cf. Matt. 5:15), and John's interpretation of the lampstands is found in v. 20. In the midst of the lampstands John saw **one like a son of man.** Note that "son of man" links this vision to the theme of 1:7. The one who shall come on the clouds of heaven is the one who revealed himself to John in a visionary encounter. He did not use "son of man" as a title (cf. Mark 2:10; 8:31, 38) but followed Daniel's usage of a comparison: "like, similar to" a human being (Dan. 7:13). In describing the son of man, he drew details from Dan. 10:5-6 (description of Gabriel), Dan. 7:9 (description of God), and Dan. 7:13 (description of the son of man). The **long robe** and the **golden girdle round his breast** probably symbolize his high-priestly dignity (cf. Exod. 28:4; Dan. 10:5). The description of **his head** and **hair** is borrowed from the picture of the Ancient of Days (Dan. 7:9), and the description of **his voice . . . like the sound of many waters** comes from Ezek. 1:24; 43:2. They reveal characteristic features of God, and with them John indicated that the one like a son of man is like God himself. In this towering overwhelming figure, God himself is present. His **eyes were like a flame of fire** (cf. Dan. 10:6) conveying the impression of absolute truth and perception. He does not just look at us, he looks into us, penetrating the masks and veils behind which we hide our true being. His **voice** echoes his superhuman strength cutting through the fog of phony rhetoric by the self-styled prophets of doom (cf. *Sibylline Oracles* 5, probably from Phrygia, Asia Minor), or the paid propagandists of the status quo (cf. Aelius Aristides, *Eulogy of Rome*). The vision now proceeds from his appearance to his function. In his right hand he holds **seven stars.** His sovereignty extends over prophets and angels (cf. 1:20). The seven stars in his right hand contrast with the pretensions of Roman emperors who asserted their cosmic rule with the symbols of planets surrounding them. Moreover, in astrological magic the stars, or planets, were believed to determine the destiny of people and nations. Christ holding the seven stars in his right hand appears as the one and the only one who controls the fate of each individual and of the cosmos as a whole. Moreover, an ironic interpretation will turn the stars into ecclesiastical angels who are subject to censure and praise (v. 20). The **two-edged sword** that proceeds from his mouth reveals his function as the ultimate judge of the church (cf. 2:16) and the world (19:15; cf. Isa. 11:4; *Pss. Sol.* 17:35; Eph. 6:17). His word divides good from evil and establishes righteousness by his testimony which is his death. **His face was like the sun shining in full strength** (cf. Judg. 5:31). The vision had taken place on the Lord's day, Sunday (*dies solis;* cf. 1:10), and his blazing sunlike face reflects his invincible strength and divine glory (cf. Matt. 17:2). No meek, mild Galilean rabbi appeared to John, not a sweet little Jesus who would not hurt a fly, but attributes of God, angels, high priest, king, and judge have been transferred to the exalted Christ in this vision. His majesty can no longer be visualized clearly, it can only astound. John's visions should be *listened to* rather than visualized. If one lines up the seven items that describe him (head, eyes, feet, voice, hand, mouth, face, vv. 14-16), then what is central is his **voice . . . of many waters,** his word. Whatever the prophets of the old covenant and the apostles and witnesses of the new have said converges in his thundering voice.

John's Reaction (1:17a). Fear and falling down at his feet **as though dead** are part of the style of epiphany accounts. No human being can see the face of God and live (Exod. 33:20; Isa. 6:5; cf. *1 Enoch* 14:14, 24). Also this feature is part of John's credibility.

Consolation, Self-disclosure, Commission, and Interpretation (1:17b-20). The consolation consists of three parts—an act, an admonition, and a threefold reason. **He laid his right hand upon me.** One should not ask how he could do so since he was holding the seven stars in his right hand! John's visions should be heard. The confirming, encouraging touch is a traditional element (cf. Dan. 10:8, 10; 4 Ezra 10:29-31), and the same is true of the admonition, **Fear not** (cf. Dan. 10:12; Mark 16:6). The Lord of the universe, the one who holds the seven stars, touches his frightened servant in love. He gives John a threefold reason not to be afraid.

First, Jesus reveals himself as the one who, like God, is **the first and the last** (Isa. 44:6; 48:12; Rev. 1:8; cf. 22:13), and, like God, he is **the living one** (Josh. 3:10; Ps. 42:2; Rev. 4:9-10; 10:6).

Second, **I died, and behold** (attention!) **I am alive for evermore.** With death behind him, nothing can defeat him. The resurrected One, like God, has life in himself. As such, he transcends Daniel's son of man in two ways. Christ is not just the symbolic representative of the saints of the Most High, like the son of man in Dan. 7:13—14:22, but a real person who actually died. Moreover, he is now alive forever. In contrast to apocalyptic interim kingdom speculations in which the Messiah dies at the end of the messianic interim (4 Ezra 7:28-30), the Christ who appeared to John is "alive for evermore." Third, **I have the keys of Death and Hades.** Like God, he has power over death and the realm of the dead (cf. 20:13; cf. 1 Sam. 2:6; Wis. Sol. 16:13). The keys *of* Death and Hades are keys *to* the realm of the dead (genitive object). The idea of a descent into Hades plays no role in this writing. Nor should Death and Hades be understood as personifications (as in 6:8) but as the region of the underworld. The Christ who holds the keys has the power to unlock the gates that lead to the realm of the dead. He has, in fact, taken the place of the goddess Hecate. In Hellenistic folk religion, she was acknowledged as the one who possessed the keys to the gates of Hades, and her cult was quite popular in Asia Minor (Aune). Christ could take over her role by virtue of his death and resurrection, and John's audience would understand this at once. Only Christ has the power, the keys, to unlock the realm of the dead (cf. 20:13). Therefore John and the Christian people need not fear death.

Christ's self-disclosure functions as the reason not only for the admonition "Fear not" but also for the following commission to write. Thus the threefold self-disclosure gives legitimation to John's book. The reader has taken the first step in hearing the revelation of Jesus Christ (1:1). By now the reader understands that it is a revelation *from* Jesus Christ and *about* him and has also learned that to speak of God is to speak of Jesus and his present godlike power. This vision gives depth, height, and breadth to the statement that he "loves us" (1:5).

1:19—Now write what you see, better, what you have seen (Greek, *eides*), which refers to the vision of vv. 12-18. John is not commissioned to write a history of past empires, their rise and fall, in order to legitimate his work. His legitimation is the vision, the revelation, of Christ and his commission by him. John is to write **what is and what is to take place hereafter.** We have seen that the phrase **what is** refers to the situation of the seven churches (2:1—3:22) and the phrase **what is to take place hereafter** refers to Rev. 4:1—22:5 (9). Of course, John will surprise us by not disclosing an apocalyptic timetable in Part II of his letter. He will not entertain us with a detailed forecast of coming attractions. We shall see what he will tell us.

1:20—Interpretation: **The seven stars** are symbols of the seven **angels** of the seven churches, and the **seven golden lampstands** symbolize these churches as well as the whole church. The metaphorical nature of the vision narrative is now plainly disclosed. The interpretation also serves as transition to the following seven messages. They are addressed to the "angel" of a particular community, and the vision that began in 1:12 continues to the end of chap. 3. But more, if the churches are lamps, then they ought to shine and bear witness (cf. 11:3-4); and since Christ is "in the midst of the lampstands," then he is present with his churches. He is present as the one who loves them, who has redeemed them and appointed them to be God's kingdom and priests (1:5b-6). As the one who is present among them, he will address them through John. The identification of the stars with angels brings about an ironic reversal. Whereas for Hellenistic people, the stars represent fate, chance, and immutable cosmic order, the vision narrative in its interpretation discloses that the stars relate to the church, to those small, insignificant groups of Christians in Asia Minor. They influence the world's fate and destiny because they are in the right hand of Christ. How? Through its worship, as we shall see (8:2-5).

The Messages to the Seven Churches in Asia (2:1—3:22)

"The revelation of Jesus Christ" (1:1) is not just his self-disclosure to John, but now we hear that he discloses his evaluative point of view in the present. The Christ who in the past has redeemed his people through his death (1:5b-6) and who shall soon come in the future for the consummation of judgment and salvation (1:7) is the one who reveals his verdict in the present concerning the present state of his churches. His verdict is not open to question. His admonitions, exhortations, threats, and promises require decisions from his people in the present. The first part of John's letter communicates Christ's evaluative point to the seven churches revealing their strengths and weaknesses, their dangers and opportunities. The form of revelation in the present is written messages, like letters, addressed to specific churches, to their "angels."

With the interpretation of the stars as angels and the lampstands as churches in place (1:20), the stage is set for addressing the present situation of the churches. In this prophetic-apocalyptic letter the seven messages take the place of the fictitious predictions of the past course of history found in Jewish apocalypses. For John, the eschatological time has already begun with Christ's death and exaltation and the time to the end is short (1:1, 3; 2:16; 3:11; 22:6, 7, 10, 12, 20; cf. 12:12). Because of the presence of the eschaton, he had no need for historical surveys. What is needed is the prophetic interpretation of the troubled present in the light of the eschaton.

These seven messages are without prescript and salutation. They do not follow the form of Hellenistic letters. Their closest analogy in the Bible are prophetic letters of the Old Testament, for example, 2 Chron. 21:12-15, which is introduced with the messenger formula, "Thus says the Lord" (Greek, *tade legei,* like Rev. 2:1), followed by a censure of the king's deed and an announcement of divine judgment which begins with "Behold" (cf. Rev. 2:22). The same messenger formula occurs in Jeremiah's letter to the exiles (Jer. 29:1-23; LXX 36:1-23). In Jewish apocalyptic literature we find a letter from Baruch to the nine and a half tribes (*2 Baruch* 78–87), which is to be read "in the assemblies," just like our Apocalypse. John's call to *listen to* (rather than to read) "what the Spirit says to the churches" (2:7, etc.; cf. 1:3) likewise suggests that the gathered communities were meant to hear his written message. These seven "letters," as they are frequently and somewhat incorrectly called, also resemble royal decrees, and we might therefore say that in them Christ, "the ruler of kings," issues his decrees concerning their "works," bestowing praise and blame and announcing his expectations. But the similarity is superficial. The seven messages, however, underline the epistolary character of John's writing. They resemble letters but are distinctive in form and content.

The seven messages were not sent individually to the seven churches named and then collected at some later time and placed at the beginning of Revelation. They were composed as a unit, and their themes are taken up in Part II of this book in letter form. The promises to conquerors (e.g., 2:7) find their fulfillment in 19:11—22:5 (e.g., 22:2). Themes such as "tribulation," "Satan's throne," "endurance," and "false prophet" link the seven messages thematically with Part II (e.g., 2:13 and chap. 13; 2:19 and 14:12; 2:8-11 and 6:3-11; etc.). Though the messages were addressed to individual communities, *all* should hear "what the Spirit says to the churches" (plural). The designations of Christ in the messenger formulae presuppose that his audience has heard John's narration of the inaugural vision (1:12-20). Moreover, the individual messages complement each other and also function as substitute for prophetic proclamation to the whole church on earth, symbolized by the number seven. Their compositional unity is displayed in a common structure.

First, the introductions combine the names of the churches addressed with the commission to **write,** followed by the messenger formula (Greek, *tade legei;* RSV, "the words of him"; better, "Thus says he") and concluded with predications of Christ from the "inaugural" vision. These self-designations of Christ were carefully chosen for their relevance to the particular situation of each church. The messenger formula and the following Christological designations make it clear who it is who speaks through John's writing, that is, who is the authority behind his written word. The functional identity between the glorified *Christ* and the **Spirit** should also be noted: "Let him hear what the *Spirit* says to the churches." Christ comes and speaks to his churches through the Spirit, as his heavenly instrument, and through John, his earthly instrument.

Second, the main section of each message is introduced with **I know** and evaluates each community differently. The basic function of this main section is evaluation and exhortation which, depending on the particular circumstances, may include one or more of the following elements: (*a*) praise (omitted for Laodicea); (*b*) censure, introduced with, "But I have this against you" (omitted for Smyrna and Philadelphia); (*c*) call to repentance, or to wake up, which is occasionally connected with an appeal to "remember" (2:5; 3:3) and with a threat of judgment (cf. 3:2-3); (*d*) a reference to Christ's future coming (found in all, except the message to Smyrna, but see the "ten days" of 2:10); and (*e*) a promise of salvation to encourage perseverance, even as the threat of judgment is meant to lead to repentance and to change in conduct.

Third, the call to listen ("he who has an ear let him hear") is identical in all the messages. It is placed prior to the promise to the conquerors in the first three messages and after this promise in the remaining four. The reason for this switch lies in the fourth "letter." The importance of the call to listen is found in its conditional meaning. Only those who can listen, to whom God has granted the gift of hearing by opening their hearts, minds, and "ears" with his word, only they are able to grasp the message of Christ through his Spirit. And it is only to them that this call is directed, to hear "what the Spirit says to the churches" (plural). The others will hear only words (cf. Mark 4:9-12). The call to listen indicates that there is a problem in the communities. Some members apparently are unwilling to listen to what the Holy Spirit says through his prophets.

Fourth, the promise to the conquerors, or victors, is introduced with "he who conquers," or "to him who conquers." The promises are formulated in the future tense and point to 19:11—22:5 for their fulfillment (e.g., 2:11, second death, and 20:6, 14; 21:8; or 3:21, coregents, and 20:6; 22:5; etc.). The promises are particularized in the light of the distinct situation of each community. Christ, who has become victor through suffering, promises victory to those who persevere.

Finally, we should note that the messages are addressed to **the angel** of each particular church. This is one of many features in this book that is strange to our thinking. How could "letters" containing severe criticism be sent by Christ, who is in heaven, through John, who is on earth, to angels who are also in heaven? Does not the mere fact that the address contains the name of a church on earth require us to understand these angels metaphorically, as referring to church leaders, whether prophets or bishops? Or do these "angels" (Greek, *angellos,* messenger) refer to envoys from the seven churches who had assembled on Patmos and who carried the messages back to their communities?

Elsewhere in Revelation the word "angel" consistently refers to a heavenly being. The angelic interpreter (19:10; 22:9) appears as the heavenly counterpart of a prophet. But even when this angel declared his solidarity with John, with the other prophets, and with all true Christians (22:9) he remained distinct from prophets and communities. John's misguided attempts at angel worship demonstrate that angelic solidarity with prophets is not tantamount to identicalness. After all, it was John, not his angelic counterpart, who is criticized (cf. 22:9). However, in the seven messages it is the churches' *angels* that are subject also to criticism. Hence these community angels are not the heavenly counterparts of John's brothers, the prophets. We conclude that for John each community is represented in heaven by an angel who personifies it.

As far as the background of this strange notion is concerned, we note that Enoch was asked to "*write* a memorial prayer" for the fallen *angels* and he did so (*1 Enoch* 12–14). Moreover, each nation was believed to have its own angelic ruler (*Jub.* 15:31-32; Dan. 10:13; 12:1; *Sir.* 17:17), because a correlation exists between heaven and earth. Thus we also find a heavenly temple with an altar (e.g., 6:9; 8:3; 11:19; 15:5), and actions in heaven manifest themselves on earth (e.g., 8:7). What John wrote to "the angel" he wrote to the whole community, not just to its prophet or bishop. Therefore the second person singular "you" gives way to the second person plural "you," which unfortunately is not obvious in the RSV. We conclude: "the angel" of each of the seven churches is the heavenly counterpart of the whole church in a city and represents it in heaven.

However, the question why the angels are addressed and not the churches themselves requires still another answer, especially since groups within the churches and even individuals, such as Jezebel, are directly identified (cf. 2:15, 20). No other early Christian letter, known to us, is addressed to an angel, nor is the background of Jewish apocalypticism of much help. Its literature contains no letters addressed to the angel of some synagogue. It has been suggested that John invented the fictitious address to angels in order to bypass the official community leadership of bishops and elders (cf. Acts 20:28). This hypothesis seems to be improbable, because John's opponents were not bishops but false prophets and the groups around them (2:2, 15, 20).

But there was still another reason why the messages were addressed to the angels of the churches. Twice we hear that John was ready "to worship" the angel that Jesus sent to him (19:10; 22:8-9) and twice he hears a prohibition, followed by the command, "Worship God." Angel worship did exist in Christian communities of Asia Minor (cf. Col. 2:18) and is attested to in inscriptions from that region (Kraabel). Justin Martyr, who had lived in Ephesus and was converted in that city around A.D. 130, could write, We (Christians) reverence and worship (Greek, *sebometha kai proskynoumen*) the Father and the Son and "also the host of the other good angels . . . and the prophetic Spirit" (*Apol.* 1. 6).

In Rev. 1:16, 20 the angels appear as stars, and stars in John's world were worshiped as deities who controlled the fate of individuals and communities. It is clear that John took a critical position toward angel worship, first, by having the angel which Jesus sent to him prohibit such worship (19:10; 22:9). Second, by showing that the community angels are "stars" in the right hand of Jesus (1:16, 20; 2:1), John's audience hears that it is Jesus who holds the destiny of angels and communities in his hands. Third—and most important—by subjecting the community angels to censure in five of the seven messages, he undercut angel worship. Without engaging in explicit polemics, John revised syncretistic notions about the place and function of angels in the worship and life of his churches.

We have seen his revision with respect to Hecate, the bearer of the keys to the realm of Death and Hades. The Christology of Revelation simply absorbed her function (1:18). With respect to angels who were firmly established in Hellenistic syncretistic traditions John insisted on their subordination to Christ and God. Angels are either God's agents or allies of Satan (cf. 12:7). By addressing the angel of a community, John made it clear that the fate and salvation of the church and its members is not bound to angels but to him who is the first and the last (1:17). Angels are subordinated to him because he holds them in his right hand. If not even the angel who mediated the true testimony of Jesus may be worshiped, how much more does such a prohibition apply to community angels who are subject to severe criticism. Should this interpretation be correct, then we can hear some irony in the address. The heavenly Christ uses John to evaluate and criticize his angel of Ephesus, for instance, reminding him from what he has *fallen* and threatening him with the removal of his lampstand (2:1, 5).

To Ephesus (2:1-7)

Ancient Ephesus was the fourth largest city of the empire after Rome, Alexandria, and Antioch, Syria. It was the cultural and commercial center of the Roman province of Asia, the "temple keeper of the great Artemis" (Acts 19:35), and the most important seaport on the west coast of Asia Minor. Today, its ancient harbor has long been filled with silt from the Caÿster River, and the shoreline now lies eight miles farther away. Since 29 B.C., Ephesus had been a center of the worship of the goddess Roma and of the emperor cult. During Domitian's reign (A.D. 81–96), Ephesus received the honor of "warden" (Greek, *neokoros*) of the imperial cult, and a new temple in honor of the god Domitian was built. The head and arm of Domitian's colossal statue is displayed in the museum of Ephesus. Paul's missionary activity of two to three years (Acts 20:31; about A.D. 52–55) reached its high point in this city, and according to Luke "all the residents of Asia heard the word of the Lord, both Jews and Greeks" (Acts 19:10; cf. 1 Cor. 15:32; 16:9; Acts 20:29-30); Timothy apparently lived there for some time (1 Tim. 1:3), and according to Irenaeus the Fourth Gospel was written in Ephesus, though he may have confused the fourth evangelist with the author of Revelation.

The Christological predication is that the message comes from the one **who holds the seven stars in his right hand, who walks among the seven golden lampstands.** The preeminence of the Ephesian community among the churches of the province of Asia is reflected in this self-designation. Indeed, the Pastoral Epistles and the first and longest letter of Ignatius, together with later traditions, reflect the importance of the church in Ephesus in early Christianity. Some manuscripts even refer to Ephesus in the prescript of Ephesians (Eph. 1:1), though the better manuscripts omit this reference. The prophet John is commissioned to write to the angel of the **church in Ephesus.**

The word **church** (Greek, *ekklēsia*) is synonymous with "the people of God" in the Old Testament. What is peculiar about the church in the New Testament is that it is the people who call upon the name of the Lord Jesus Christ, who confess that "Jesus Christ is Lord" and believe that God raised him from the dead (Rev. 10:9, 13). In Revelation, the church is both the local community and the whole people of God because the fulfillment of

God's promise (1:5-6) is present in both. The seven messages are written for seven local communities and simultaneously for the whole church. In the recurring clause, "what the Spirit says to the churches" (plural), the ecumenical dimension of the individual messages and of the whole letter comes to the fore.

The main section, beginning with **I know** (vv. 2-6), evaluates the situation in Ephesus and offers first praise (vv. 2-3) and then censure (v. 4), followed by the demand to remember and to repent, a demand that is connected with a threat of judgment (v. 5). The main section closes with a repetition of praise (v. 6), found only here. The call to listen (see above) and the promise to victors conclude this message (v. 7).

Christ, who holds in his hand "the seven stars," who "walks among" the communities, is not an absent deity, enthroned in infinite distance beyond the stars. He is present among them in love (1:6), in praise (2:2-3, 6), and in critical judgment (vv. 4-5). Nothing is hidden from him who can say **I know your works.** In contrast to Paul where "works of the law" has the negative connotation of quest for self-righteousness apart from faith in Christ (Rom. 9:31—10:4), our author regards good **works** as the necessary consequence of the status received at baptism. "Works" constitute the conduct of Christians who are delivered from their sins by grace alone (1:4b-6). In this instance, the works consist of **your toil and your patient endurance.** Their toil is apparent in that **you cannot bear evil men but have tested those who call themselves apostles but are not, and found them to be false.** Their endurance under pressure is known to Christ: **you are enduring patiently** (cf. 1:9) **and bearing up for my name's sake, and you have not grown weary** (v. 3). The community has experienced stress, though its form is unknown to us. The Greek past tense, "you bore up" (rather than **bearing up,** RSV), points to difficulties in the past. The confession of the **name** of Christ was the cause of their suffering (cf. 2:13; 3:8; Matt. 10:22; 24:9). Endurance, perseverance (Greek, *hypomonē*), has become the chief Christian virtue in Revelation and presupposes a situation of hardships and perhaps occasional persecution (cf. Heb. 10:36-39; James 1:2-4; 5:11; 2 Tim. 2:12).

Their **toil** is evident in their consistent rejection of itinerant **apostles** who were tested (past tense) and found **to be false** (cf. Acts 20:29-30). In 1 Cor. 12:10 the "discerning" between spirits is the theological charisma of distinguishing true prophets from false ones (cf. 1 John 4:1). "False apostles" had already plagued Paul's ministry (cf. 2 Cor. 11:13-14, 22-28). Here the false apostles are probably emissaries of the Nicolaitans (v. 6). The Ephesian Christians continue to **hate** their **works,** that is, they radically reject the teaching and conduct of this heretical group and their emissaries (v. 6). The nature of their teaching is not indicated here (but see below, 2:14-15; and 2:20-22).

In spite of the high praise, we also hear a sharp censure. **But I have this against you, that you have abandoned the love you had at first.** It has been suggested that in their zeal for orthodoxy, the Ephesian Christians became unloving, inquisitorial, and censorious (Caird). Yet Christ himself can say, **I also hate** the works of the Nicolaitans (v. 6). Love does not exclude hating **the works,** the false teaching and abominable conduct, of heretics. Therefore, the criticism voiced against this church is not the result of an absence of pastoral care and concern toward heretics (cf. 2:20-22). On the contrary, the Ephesians know that tolerance of falsehood is not a charisma, and they are commended twice for their clear stance against heretics. But their first **love** has grown cold, which is one of the first signs of the end (Matt. 24:12). Our text does not specify whether it is love toward God and Christ or love toward sisters and brothers within the community. It probably refers to both. In Jer. 2:2, the Lord says to Jerusalem, "I remember the devotion of your youth, your love as a bride," and the new Jerusalem of the end is "prepared as a bride adorned for her husband" (21:2). The liturgy of the redeemed at the end will reflect reciprocal love between God and his people. But during the interim, their love and enthusiasm for God and their new sisters and brothers which was so obvious at the beginning is being worn down by daily stress and fear. Their patient endurance (v. 3) of ridicule and diverse chicaneries is without love, and thus their good works become worthless (1 Corinthians 13). Love is the first and foremost gift of the Spirit; it is the bond that goes out from Christ (1:5) and should unite the Ephesians with each other in solidarity. As a gift of the Spirit, love should be the light of the Ephesian lampstand, and when that light is not rekindled, then the lampstand itself will be removed (v. 5). Without love toward God, toward brothers and sisters, a church ceases to be a church in spite of its commendable orthodoxy and brave endurance of hardships.

Remember then from what you (singular) **have fallen.** Behind this sentence lies the common apocalyptic idea of the fall of angels (e.g., *1 Enoch* 6–18; 64–69; *Jubilees* 5; etc.). The point here would be that the angel of Ephesus, far from guaranteeing the charisma of love, has himself **fallen.** He is part and parcel of the problem of lovelessness in the Ephesian church. He has fallen, perhaps, because the dragon's "tail swept down" these stars of heaven (12:4). Three imperatives punctuate Christ's exhortation: **remember** your beginnings. The Old Testament emphasis on remembering (cf. Deut. 5:15; 7:18; 8:18-19; Isa. 44:21; 57:11) is taken up in the New Testament. To remember is to make the past come alive, to rediscover the liberation that had propelled the Ephesian Christians out of an idolatrous society and into the kingdom and to recall the love of their Lord who energized their lives; to remember is to **repent.** Repentance is not the same as feeling sorry for oneself, or crying over spilled milk, but it means to turn daily to him who "loves us" (1:5b) and who is therefore able to give us the charisma of love; **do the works you did at first.** Faith is active in love, and the love that was the beacon at their beginnings must shine again in the turmoil of the present. These three imperatives are not to be confused with legalistic injunctions. They are gospel imperatives, spoken by Christ. They demand what the church's Lord offers. Yet they are imperatives, and their urgency is underscored by a threat of judgment.

If not, if the three imperatives do not find realization by the Ephesians, **I will come to you and remove your lampstand from its place, unless you repent.** The threat of exclusion from the one church by the church's Lord underlines the seriousness of his demand for repentance, mentioned twice in v. 5. This demand is also a twofold invitation, to take the opportunity offered and to repent. Repentance is not a right that the church possesses but a privilege granted to it. This becomes clear through texts such as Heb. 6:4-8; 10:26-31. It would be false to conclude that **I will come** does not refer to the parousia (cf. Caird). The meaning is: unless you repent, the parousia will be judgment for you, namely, the removal of your lampstand, the exclusion of your church from the millennium with Christ (cf. 2:16, 25; 3:3, 11; 20:4-6; 21:9—22:5). His coming is not dependent on the community's conduct, but the consequences of his coming are. Furthermore, judgment does not just fall on the world, but the church is also subject to judgment. The threat of judgment in this message to the Ephesians may also have been an answer to the notion that the believer "does not come into judgment, but has passed from death to life" already (John 5:24; cf. Eph. 2:4-10). If so, then an overly realized eschatology was held not just by heretics but also by members of a church that received both praise and criticism.

The call to **hear** what Christ is communicating through **the Spirit** continues the demand to remember and repent. The time to listen and repent is now. Simultaneously, the call to hear introduces the promise to conquerors which concludes the exhortation on a positive note. **To him who conquers** lovelessness and indifference toward sisters and brothers, who every day anew (present participle; continuous action!) overcomes apathy and stoical unperturbed resignation and becomes again fervent in Spirit, **I will grant to eat of the tree of life, which is in the paradise of God.** The tree was one of the symbols of Artemis, whose temple at Ephesus was one of the seven wonders of the ancient world. The Artemision offered asylum within its sacred precinct. For John, the sacred precinct, the paradise of God, will receive the

Christians who are alienated by the idolatry surrounding Artemis. Only victorious Christians share in the life to come. As historical background we read in the *Testament of Levi:* And God "shall open the gates of paradise and he shall remove the sword that has threatened since Adam; and he will grant to the saints to eat of the tree of life" (18:10-11). In the new Jerusalem, with paradise not just restored but created anew, the conquerors shall eat the fruit **of the tree of life** (cf. 22:2). This future eating in the kingdom is anticipated in the sacramental eating, and it has its absolute contradiction in the eating of food sacrificed to idols (2:14).

To Smyrna (2:8-11)

Smyrna, the modern İzmir, is the only one of the seven cities in which the church has continued to exist through the centuries to the present. Together with Philadelphia, it received unqualified commendation from Christ. Both churches faced threats from Jews (2:9; 3:9). Smyrna's community is **rich** in spite of its **tribulation** and **poverty,** the very opposite of Laodicea, which fancied itself to be rich and did not even know that it was "poor, blind, and naked" according to Christ's evaluation (3:17).

In A.D. 26, after several cities requested permission to build a temple to Caesar Tiberius and Livia, Smyrna was chosen because of its loyal relations to Rome (Tacitus, *Annals* 4.55-56). The city had become a center of the imperial cult at John's time. Smyrna's claim to be "first of Asia" is mocked in Christ's self-designation (v. 8). Some decades after John, the orator Aelius Aristides recalled that Smyrna had come to life again and had risen, like a phoenix, from the ashes of its destruction in 600 B.C. For him, Mount Pagos was "the crown of Smyrna." In short, local color is reflected in Christ's self-designation, in the conqueror saying, and above all in the bitter conflict with the local Jewish community.

Rome had granted Jews the privilege of practicing their religion in any part of the empire, thereby exempting them from participation in the emperor cult and from military service. After the war of A.D. 66–70, Jewish self-interest widened the gap between synagogue and church also in the diaspora. From a Jewish point of view, the Christians were messianic troublemakers and their claim to be the true Israel was simply absurd. Apocalyptic ideas, such as those in John's book, would be repugnant to them, especially to emancipated Jews who were involved in civic life but kept in touch with the synagogue. An inscription from this city tells of a Jewess, Rufina, who was the leader of a synagogue. To "progressive" Jews, the Christians appeared to be an antisocial group and their beliefs about an imminent end of the world through a risen Messiah demonstrated the provocative nature of this messianic sect. At any rate, Judaism began to exclude all "heretics" from the synagogue, probably during the decade in which Revelation was written. Finally, Jews were undoubtedly annoyed that the church attracted ever more Gentiles who had been Jewish sympathizers and offered them what, from a Jewish viewpoint, amounted to cheap, cut-rate salvation without circumcision and obedience to the Torah (cf. Acts 13:45). Hence Jews of Smyrna probably threatened Christians with **the second death** after the final judgment.

For John, the immediate threat to the church in Smyrna came from public authorities who had the power **to throw some of you into prison.** But he saw the Jews and their defamation as instigators of hostile actions against members of the church. Thus there will be a repeat of the passion of Jesus, who through his death became **the first and the last, who died and came to life** (v. 8; cf. 1:17-18).

In this message of four verses the words **death, died, tribulation, suffer, prison, slander,** and **poverty** appear nine times. It is the contrast between death and tribulation on one hand, and the promise of life on the other, which determines the tone of this "letter." The theological reason for the opposition by Jews is found in the Christological predication of v. 8. By raising Jesus to **life,** God has acted eschatologically for the salvation of all humans (cf. Rom. 10:9; Acts 2:35; 4:10-12). This Christological affirmation is the cause of the alienation between church and synagogue.

Some interpreters hold that the Jews of v. 9 were Jewish Christians who belonged to the circle of the Nicolaitans. This seems improbable. These messages warn against Nicolaitan infiltration of the churches, not persecution by them. The Jews of Smyrna may have called themselves the **synagogue** of God. John denounced them with bitter irony as a synagogue **of Satan,** because Satan, the devil, in the form of the Roman authorities, uses Jewish **slander** to throw some Christians of Smyrna **into prison.** John, who was himself a Jew, regarded those Jews who would cooperate with Gentile magistrates in the imprisonment of Christians as allies **of Satan.** An apocalyptic point of view sees history as a battleground between God and the forces of the devil, who was a slanderer from the beginning. There is no neutral middle ground in this ultimate struggle (cf. 1 Peter 4:12-16; 5:8-9). An example of the hostility of some Jews against Christians is found in the *Martyrdom* of Polycarp, bishop of Smyrna (about A.D. 150; cf. 12:2; 13:1; 17:2). The words of the 86-year-old bishop of that city, before he was burned alive, are memorable (Eusebius, *C.H.* 4.15.20):

> Eighty-six years I have served Christ and he has never done me wrong. How can I blaspheme my king who saved me?

Imprisonment, which this message predicted for some of the members, was not a punishment under Roman law but functioned as detention prior to trial and after sentencing until execution. Imprisonment was also used to enforce obedience to a magistrate's order, but no one was sentenced to some years in prison. If the procedures that John envisioned for the future were identical with those followed by Pliny, governor of Pontus and Bithynia in A.D. 111, then imprisorment would lead to capital punishment unless the Christians apostatized, "cursed" Christ, and worshiped the emperor. In such a situation, the imperative, **Do not fear what you are about to suffer,** is sheer madness unless faith in the God who has raised Christ from the dead opens up a new vision of truth and reality. The **tribulation** that lies ahead will last but a short time, symbolized by **ten days** (cf. Dan. 1:12-14), in comparison with the millennium and the life of the world to come (20:4-6; 21:1-8). Moreover, the tribulation is the time in which believers will **be tested** by God to remain faithful and tempted by the devil to apostatize. Every temptation and trial has this dual nature. The conditional promise, **Be faithful unto death, and I will give you the crown of life** (v. 10), contains the same life/death contrast as the messenger formula (v. 8). Christ's fate remains both a source of undefeatable fortitude in Christian women and men as well as an example, an exhortation to the faithful practice of the confession of faith until life's end, **unto death** and even unto martyrdom. The crown was a wreath of leaves which was valuable only as a symbol. It was used to honor victors in athletic games, benefactors of a city, and others. Here, **the crown of life** is the wreath of the conquerors whose faith had triumphed under duress. It symbolizes the gift of final salvation. **He who conquers,** the victors, **shall not be hurt by the second death.** This is the only conqueror saying that is formulated negatively, probably in response to Jewish threats. It will not be the faithful Christians who will be subject to the second death after the final judgment. The expression **second death** has its origins in Judaism, and in Revelation John uses it to point to the final fate of the wicked (20:14-15; 21:8).

To Pergamum (2:12-17)

Pergamum probably was the official seat of the Roman government in the province of Asia at John's time and a center of the imperial cult. Its temple to the goddess Roma and Augustus was the oldest in the region, having been built in 29 B.C. Moreover, the city boasted an imposing temple to Zeus Savior, with an immense altar, on a plateau 900 feet above the city. Another temple was dedicated to Aesclepius, the god of healing. Both deities were symbolized by a serpent. For John, "that ancient serpent" is Satan (12:9). Through the cult of Aesclepius and through reports of miraculous healings Pergamum became the "Lourdes of Asia Minor" (Lohmeyer), with pilgrims flocking there from near and far. The threat to the church did not come from this popular cult but from the patriotic religion of the emperor worship. Participation in emperor worship was viewed as an expression of political loyalty; rejection of it was synonymous with godlessness and subversion, in the eyes of magistrates and the people. In general, Christians in Domitian's time were accused of "hatred against the human race," "atheism," and of advocating a "mischievous superstition" (cf. Dio, *Hist.* 67.14; Tacitus, *Annals* 15.44; Suetonius, *Nero* 16; Pliny, *Epistles* 10.96). The cry "Away with the atheists" showed the contempt in which Christians were held by the pagan populace (*Martyrdom of Polycarp* 3.2; 9.2).

Since the middle of the 60s, Roman magistrates as well as the common people had learned to distinguish between Christians and Jews, for only Christians were executed in Rome in Nero's time. What appeared to the populace as obnoxious standoffishness (cf. 1 Peter 4:3-4), lack of patriotism, and atheism were all the more scandalous because the Christians were not an ancient nation, like the Jews, to whom Rome was bound by treaty and decrees. The unique offense of Christianity was its radical rejection of polytheism and of the imperial cult which undergirded the whole life of the empire. The Jewish religion could be tolerated because it was the national religion of a particular people which by its very nature could never permeate the empire. The supranational "superstition" of Christianity, however, which sought to win the world for Christ (Acts 1:8) was another matter. Even though Rome was tolerant of foreign religions, as long as they did not cause social unrest, a unique situation became apparent at the time of the emperor Trajan (about A.D. 111). Christians were executed by Pliny, Trajan's representative in Pontus and Bithynia, simply because they were Christians.

The prophet John, writing some 15 years earlier, perceived more clearly than any other New Testament writer the inevitability of a conflict between church and state in the immediate future. Roundly he denounced Pergamum's temple of the imperial cult as **Satan's throne,** the home **where Satan dwells,** thus linking the seven messages to Part II, chaps. 12–13. For him, the emperor cult was the pinnacle of pagan idolatry, and the community of Pergamum is commended for its perseverance in the face of the danger emanating from it. For the church in Pergamum it was good to know how their Lord evaluated their social context. In a city like Pergamum, it was not easy to be a confessing Christian. But daily pressure, ridicule, and ostracism did not wear down the community of Christ, not even when **Antipas,** one of its members, met a martyr's death. To be sure, this was just one death, not a general persecution beyond the daily chicaneries. The great test was yet to come. In order for them to be ready for it, Jesus reveals the weaknesses of his church in Pergamum.

Within the community there are followers of Balaam's teaching. In Jewish tradition **Balaam** (Numbers 22–24) had become the instigator of idolatry within Israel (Num. 31:16). He was believed to bear the responsibility for the fornication of Israelites with Moabite women (Num. 25:1-5). With biting irony John suggests that this Balaam had become the example that **some** church members of Pergamum imitate. The followers of Balaam and the **Nicolaitans** do not appear to be two different groups but one and the same. Just as Balaam misled the Israelites into committing idolatry and fornication, so now the Nicolaitans were misleading **some** members with their false teaching. They represented the view that the church is society on Sunday, that church and culture can live together harmoniously, that the Christian's true spiritual self cannot be influenced by **eating food sacrificed to idols,** by emperor worship, or fornication (RSV, **immorality**). All such things belong to the sphere of the body, the earth, the flesh, and hence cannot impinge upon a Christian's true spiritual self.

The structure of the message: After the commission and the messenger formula (v. 12) comes the main section, introduced with **I know,** which has two parts. First, the community is praised for its resistance against the external threat of the imperial cult (v. 13). Second, it is called to repentance because of the presence of an internal threat in the form of heretics (vv. 14-16). The call to listen and the promise to victors (vv. 17-18) conclude the message.

The formula, thus says the one **who has the sharp two-edged sword** (cf. 1:16; Greek, *romphaia*), applies to both parts of the main section. The Roman proconsul holds the *imperium.* His legal power included the right to inflict capital punishment. The sword (Greek, *macheira*) was its symbol (cf. Rom. 13:4). Pergamum was one of the few cities to which Rome had given "the right of the sword" (Latin, *ius gladii*), the power to inflict capital punishment. Because this kind of sword was now used in the service of Satan, it has become a symbol of evil (6:4; 13:10, 14). Therefore another sword, the two-edged sword (*romphaia;* cf. Gen. 3:24 LXX) of the ultimate judge, shall bring justice at last. But he shall also **war against** the heretics within the church.

The first part of the main section (v. 13) is framed by two references to Satan's dwelling in Pergamum. Instead of the evaluative introduction, "I know your works," we hear **I know where you dwell.** It is a consolation to know that the ultimate judge is aware of the hostile environment in which his community must live. His evaluation, **you hold fast my name and you did not deny my faith** (better: "your faith in me"; cf. 14:12), is praise indeed. More: **even in the days of Antipas my witness, my faithful one, who was killed among you** there was no apostasy among the members of this church. Pliny gave accused Christians who were brought before him the opportunity to curse Christ and offer incense upon the emperor's altar (cf. *Martyrdom of Polycarp* 9.2-3). Pergamum's church persevered in faith during the crisis of **Antipas**'s martyrdom. He is not called a **witness** of Christ (Greek, *martys*) because he was a martyr. He became a martyr because he was a faithful witness (cf. 1:5). We hear of only this one martyrdom in Revelation, though others are presupposed (6:9-11). The two references to **Satan** would suggest that Antipas died as a result of judicial procedures perhaps in conjunction with mob action. The community that had withstood external dangers in the past and the present had become vulnerable to the internal danger of heresy.

With **but I have a few things against you,** the second part of the main section begins, containing censure, a call to repentance, and threat of judgment (vv. 14-16). In contrast to the Ephesian church, the church at Pergamum tolerated those who **hold the teaching of Balaam** which seems to be identical with the **teaching of the Nicolaitans.** John did not describe their doctrine (Greek, *didachē*). There was no need to give space to their propaganda! Instead, he focused on their conduct. They **eat food sacrificed to idols and practice immorality** (literally, fornication). The same accusation is leveled at the prophetess Jezebel (v. 20), and we are probably safe in assuming that the false "apostles" of Ephesus (v. 2), the Nicolaitans and followers of Balaam of vv. 6 and 14-15, together with the circle around the prophetess of Thyatira, belong to the same group of heretical Christians. They had sent emissaries, called "apostles," to different churches and found a foothold in Pergamum and Thyatira.

A literal understanding of immorality in terms of sexual promiscuity, fornication, is supported by the preceding offense of eating meat sacrificed to idols (which is meant literally) and by the "rogues catalogs" of 9:21; 21:8 and 22:15 which clearly distinguish between fornicators and idolaters. However, a metaphorical understanding of "fornication" is demanded by texts like 17:2; 18:3, 9. The background of this metaphor lies in the Old Testament (cf. Isa. 57:3; Jer. 7:9; 23:10). For John, idolatry was equal to fornication, metaphorically speaking, and it also leads to sexual promiscuity. Eating meat sacrificed to idols had been forbidden in the Apostles' Decree (see ACNT: *Acts*, on Acts 15:28-29). Yet at banquets, at feasts of trade guilds, and on other festive occasions, this was the only meat offered. Moreover, most meat that could be purchased in the marketplace had been offered symbolically to some god or goddess by the butcher. Who were these Nicolaitans who advocated practices that were harshly condemned?

Nicolaus, a Gentile who had become a proselyte and was chosen to be one of the Seven (Acts 6:5), was the founder of the Nicolaitans, according to Irenaeus (*Adv. Haer.* 1.23.3). Balaam was a Gentile prophet, and Jezebel of old was a Gentile princess of Sidon (1 Kings 16:31). The names Nicolaus and Balaam mean "Conqueror of a people." The members of this group were probably aware of this meaning. Whether John knew this we do not know. If he did, he formulated the conqueror promises also in opposition to them. At any rate, the Gentile background of these heretical Christians is expressed in their names. It is possible that they called themselves Balaamites. Like the later gnostic Cainites and Sethians, they may have taken their self-designation from the Old Testament and regarded Balaam as prototype of Gentile prophecy and Nicolaus of Acts 6:5 as founder of their group. If this is right, then it was John who added the clause **who taught Balak to put a stumbling block before the sons of Israel** (cf. 2 Peter 2:15-16; Num. 31:16; 22:1—25:3). Moreover, John pinned the name Jezebel on the prophetess of Thyatira. She would no more call herself by that name than the Jews of Smyrna would identify themselves as a synagogue of Satan (cf. 1 Kings 21:23).

We receive only one brief glimpse of their teaching, namely, their claim to know "the deep things of Satan" (v. 24). This may mean that they know the mysterious depths of Satan and therefore feel free to indulge in fornication and to eat idol meat. Or John, with biting irony, may turn their own claim to know "the depths of God" (1 Cor. 2:10) into the very opposite, holding that their claim to know God's mysteries is, in fact, a knowledge of satanic realities which they express in their behavior.

Since they were able to gain access even to faithful churches, we can be certain they did not deny Christ, his resurrection, and salvation through him. They may have developed gnosticizing tendencies which drew on prior Christian traditions. They may have argued that John's position against the empire and the imperial cult amounted to fanaticism, which was contrary to Rom. 13:1-7 and traditions such as 1 Peter 2:13 and Titus 3:11, and even to Jesus' advice to "render to Caesar the things that are Caesar's." They may have concluded: Let the emperor do his thing in the earthly sphere and if he wants a little incense on top of our taxes, let him have it; it does not matter. Is it not verbal overkill on John's part to denounce this as fornication—idolatry? Jesus rules in the spiritual sphere where no emperor can touch us. Finally, they may have repeated Paul's declaration, "We know that an idol has no real existence" (1 Cor. 8:4) and concluded that there is no need to abstain from meat sacrificed to idols, which also belongs to the earthly sphere. How could anyone abstain from it anyway, without withdrawing from all social contacts? The meat served at banquets of guilds or bought in the market, as well as the coins with images of emperors dressed like deities, should be used without fear of defilement. Perhaps they went even so far as to advocate sexual libertinism, teaching that sex can no more defile a person than meat or money. All of these three items pertain merely to the body, to the sphere of the earth, but not to the spirit, in which salvation is realized. If not even Satan can interfere with the salvation of the baptized, how much less can meat or sex? Of course, our reconstruction of their teaching remains hypothetical, since they do not speak directly to us. But their teaching must have appeared quite reasonable to some church members, and its reasonableness probably provoked John's harsh ironic language.

For John, the issue is, Who is your God? Whom do you worship? is the ultimate question. It is of such importance that if it were possible for someone to give a wrong answer to every other question that life puts before him or her, but a right one to this supreme question, that person's life would be crowned with glory. And vice versa, if a person is an idolater, his or her life will be revealed as failure no matter how successful he or she or others may think it to be. There may be no compromise with and accommodation to this idolatrous culture, no matter what the cost may be. Accommodation leads to assimilation, which is merely another word for idolatry-fornication. It is sheer unfaithfulness to God and his Christ who has liberated us if we now eat meat sacrificed to idols. For John, a government that absolutizes itself by deifying its emperors is no longer God's good order but a Satanic perversion, and its idolatrous demands must be resisted. A body/soul dualism is a denial of God, who is the creator of both. As God's alternative community on earth, the church lives in perpetual struggle with pagan values and mores until the end; and sexual promiscuity is no charisma, no matter how cleverly or stupidly it is disguised!

Although only **some** members belong to this heretical group, the whole church is requested to **repent** for allowing this heresy to be present in their community. Again, the call to repentance is undergirded by a threat of judgment. Christ's parousia will be **soon.** If business continues as usual, then his coming will mean **war,** not against the church, but **against them,** the heretics within the community. His weapon will be **the sword of my mouth,** the word of God. His eschatological coming is **to you** (singular), the whole community represented by the angel. His judgment falls only on **them.** Only the Nicolaitans will feel the cutting edge of his word against them. The promise to victors is twofold (v. 17). First, conquerors are people who do not deny their faith in Jesus even under duress, nor eat food sacrificed to idols (vv. 13-14). They shall therefore receive **some of the hidden manna** in the life of the world to come. The background of this promise can be found in various Jewish traditions: "It will happen at that time that the treasury of manna will come down again from on high and they will eat of it in those years because these are they who will have arrived at the *consummation* of time" (2 *Bar.* 29:8). In Revelation, **manna** will be the heavenly food in the new paradise (22:1-5). The conquerors had forgone eating food sacrificed to idols, but they will be recompensed with heavenly food at the eschatological meal (cf. 19:7, 9). For Christians, manna is a type of the Eucharist, and, in turn, the Eucharist anticipates the heavenly meal in the future kingdom. In the present the manna is **hidden,** like all eschatological salvation benefits. Thus far we interpreted the manna on the background of Exod. 16:32 and the Jewish expectation of this gift in the future. However, in Greek the word **manna** could also refer to the granules of frankincense that were used in the emperor cult and a sign of loyalty to the emperor. Thus we have a double entendre here. Those who resist worship before Satan's throne, refusing to offer granules of manna, frankincense, to him in the censer on his altar, to them Christ will **give some of the hidden manna,** heavenly frankincense, when they begin their reign with him as kings and priests unto God (1:6; 3:26; 5:10; 20:4-6; 22:5).

Second, the conquerors shall receive **a white stone, with a new name written on the stone.** The background of the notion of a "new name" is found in texts like Isa. 62:2; 65:15. Israel's old name was "The Forsaken," and the land was called "Desolate." But when God will bring about Israel's vindication, then land and people will receive a new name (Isa. 62:2-5). The conquerors are those who **hold fast my name** (v. 13), and therefore they will receive new names which no one at present knows. The meaning of the **white stone,** on which the new name is written, is unknown to us. Stones without inscriptions were used for diverse purposes, including for voting at trials or as tokens for admission to feasts. In neither case did they have to be white, nor were they inscribed.

In Revelation, **white** is the color of purity and perfection, of the victory of Christ, and of the victor's garments washed in the blood of the Lamb (1:14; 3:4-5, 18; 4:4; 6:11; 7:14; 19:14). It would seem that John adopted and adapted the notion of magical stones, of amulets with magical "secret" inscriptions. They were meant to give their bearers protection from demonic forces (so Bousset) or reveal secret truths. The stone that the victor receives is white, the color of purity, victory, and perfection. And the **name** inscribed is either the secret name of Jesus, "which no one knows but himself" (19;12), or it is the new name of the conqueror. The meaning would be that what magical amulets with secret inscriptions seek to accomplish in the present, this will be granted to conquerors only in the future. Other suggestions are that these stones with inscriptions are the entrance ticket to the future kingdom, or paradise; or that the hardness of stones is contrasted with parchment (from Pergamum the word "parchment" is derived).

To Thyatira (2:18-29)

The longest message is written to the church in the least important city. Thyatira was located inland, halfway between Pergamum and Sardis. The city had a temple of Tyrimnos, who, during Hellenistic times, became identified with Apollo, son of Zeus, and the sun-god Hellios. Hence the title **Son of God** (v. 18), which is not found otherwise in Revelation, has been chosen to contrast with the religious atmosphere of the town. If the emperor was also worshiped there, the title "Son of God" would reject the imperial pretensions of Caesars as sons of Apollo. Moreover, the contrast to the sun-god Hellios is brought out in the description of Christ's eyes as **like a flame of fire.** Nothing is hidden from his searching, penetrating rays (v. 23). Finally, Thyatira produced **burnished bronze,** which is likened to Christ's **feet** (cf. 1:15). The word translated as "burnished bronze" is found in Greek only in Rev. 1:15; 2:18 and was probably a trademark or a special product of the town (Hemer). At any rate, the self-predications of v. 18 reflect knowledge of locale. As an aside we may note that the church of Thyatira followed the Montanist prophets in the second century (cf. Zahn, *Forschungen,* 5:35-36; see above, introduction, section 1).

Thyatira was a city of craftsmen and merchants. Lydia, the seller of purple cloth (Acts 16:14), came from there. Artisans and merchants, dyers of wool, and tanners and metalworkers belonged to diverse guilds, as we know from inscriptions. Membership and participation in the activities of merchants' associations or guilds of craftsmen and workers were not mandatory, but they were the natural result of engaging in commerce and trade, of retaining a job and having some social life. Periodic meetings and occasional festivities were specified in the guild's constitution and held under the auspices of some deity, the guild's patron god(s). The meals, of course, consisted of "food sacrificed to idols." Such feasts may have occasionally degenerated into immorality, but licentious behavior was neither inherent nor generally accepted by these associations (cf. 3:7).

So, then, what was a Christian to do? If he withdrew from his guild or consistently avoided its meetings, he was eventually ostracized and became a social outcast. And when the reasons for his disavowal of his association membership became known, then the accusation of "hatred against the human race" was raised against the followers of Jesus. For this dilemma a dynamic woman in Thyatira had a ready-made answer.

18—The predications in the commission formula link up with the inaugural vision (1:14-15), pick up local verbiage (see above), and connect with the main themes of this message. The **eyes like a flame of fire** anticipate Christ's omniscient evaluation of his church, of Jezebel and her followers. His **feet . . . like burnished bronze** manifest omnipotence in judgment (vv. 22-23). The title **Son of God,** which alludes to Ps. 2:7, connects with the promise to conquerors and its allusion to Ps. 2:8-9. Moreover, the predicate **my Father** (v. 27) is the reverse of "my son" of Ps. 2:7, and even **the morning star** (v. 28) must be seen in relation to divine sonship which the conquerors as sons of God shall share with Christ (cf. 21:7; 22:16).

The main section (vv. 19-25) is structured thus:

A. Praise of the community (v. 19)
B. Censure of the community (vv. 20-23)
 1. Accusation (vv. 20-21)
 2. Announcement of judgment in three parts (vv. 22-23a)
 3. Recognition formula (v. 23b)
A′ Admonition of the community (vv. 24-25)

The focus of the main section clearly lies in its center, B (vv. 20-23). Subsection A′ (vv. 24-25) does not contain a call to repentance, nor a threat of judgment, because the community's **works** in the present show progress from those of its beginnings

(19b). The promise to the victors and the call to listen (vv. 26-29) conclude the writing. For the first time the call to listen is placed at the end of the message (v. 29) and thereby functions as brackets with the opening command to "write."

19—The church receives high commendation for its **works,** a word that occurs five times in this message. The works that deserve praise are **love,** which according to Paul is the highest gift of the Spirit (1 Corinthians 13); **faith,** probably in the sense of faithfulness (cf. 13:10); **service** (Greek, *diakonia*), the support of the poor, the old, the sick within the community, in distinction from almsgiving, which was directed to those outside the community of faith; and **patient endurance,** or perseverance (Greek, *hypomonē*), refers to the fortitude that bears daily pressures in a pagan society. Also significant is the evaluation that **your latter works exceed the first** in quality and quantity. In contrast to the Ephesian Christians who had regressed from their beginnings (2:4-5), the believers at Thyatira had shown spiritual growth in their good works. The praise of him whose critical **eyes like a flame of fire** pierce behind fraudulent religious facades and phony piety and perceive the depths of human hearts (v. 23b) prepares the hearer to listen for more.

20-23a—But what he is going to hear the hearer may not like. Thyatira, in contrast to Ephesus, had not excluded the heretics (cf. 2:2, 6), and therefore it is criticized like the church in Pergamum (2:14-15). In evaluating his church, Christ accuses it: **you tolerate the woman Jezebel, who calls herself a prophetess.** The pronoun **you** is singular; the angel is addressed. Many manuscripts read: "**your** woman," that is, "your wife." In that case, "the angel" of Thyatira is either the bishop, whose wife is now being characterized as prophetess and harlot, or else Jezebel claimed a special relationship to Thyatira's angelic representative in heaven. The latter would seem more likely. While the manuscript evidence is equally divided, the omission of the pronoun ("your") is more easily explained than its later addition. Married bishops, or married angels, seemed highly objectionable, and hence, it would seem, the pronoun was omitted by later copyists.

The Old Testament is used to shed light on the present (cf. 2:14). The Gentile queen Jezebel who introduced idolatry and sorcery, magic, into Israel (cf. 2 Kings 9:22; 1 Kings 16:31) found her successor in the prophetess of Thyatira who introduced eating of **food sacrificed to idols** and the practice of **immorality** (literally, fornication), thereby **beguiling** the servants of Jesus. Even though the church as a whole did not succumb to Jezebel's teaching and life-style, the angel, that is, the whole church, is censured for **tolerating** her in its midst. Because the church is Christ's kingdom on earth (1:6), it may not become a religious replica of the prevailing culture. The purity of the church demands the exclusion of heretics. Like a sorceress, she is beguiling **my** servants, who are enamored of her and consort with her. Her success within the community is indicated in the reference to **those who commit adultery with her.** Her **teaching** met a need of Christians in Thyatira who, as members of guilds, found it disadvantageous to separate themselves from the city's economic, political, and social life. They were relieved to hear by the authority of the Spirit speaking through the prophetess (the spouse of Thyatira's angel?) that they were free to participate in the activities of their guilds. They may eat food that had been sacrificed to idols without fear (cf. 1 Cor. 8:4). Situational ethics, first-century style, is what Jezebel represented.

I gave her time to repent, said the ultimate judge through his scribe. John had probably met her on a previous occasion. In that encounter he had requested that she mend her teachings and her ways; but to no avail. **She refuses to repent of her immorality.** She did not acknowledge John's authority (cf. 3 John 9). Therefore, only the announcement of judgment is left—in contrast to a mere threat which has the form: If, or unless, you do xyz, I shall. . . . The judgment is announced with **Behold.**

First, **I will throw her on a sickbed.** If we were to understand the fornication literally, then the double entendre would be: Her bed of sexual depravity will become a bed of bodily infirmity.

Second, those members of the church, **my** servants (v. 20), who committed **adultery with her** (Greek, *moicheuo*) **I will throw into great tribulation.** Christ will inflict suffering on them before the end (cf. 6:5-8) **unless they repent of her doings,** literally, "of her works." This is a threat, not an announcement of judgment as in the case of Jezebel. One would have expected to hear that they should repent of *their own* adultery with Jezebel rather than of *her* adultery. The text therefore requires a metaphorical understanding of **adultery** (v. 22) and of **immorality** (v. 21). It was not sexual pleasures, but her teaching, which attracted part of the church membership. These church members should repent of, turn away from, **her** teaching. It should be obvious that Jezebel was not attacked because she was a woman and acknowledged as a prophet. The polemics against her are not the result of her gender but of her heresy.

Third, the final chilling announcement of judgment is directed against Jezebel's children: and **I will strike her children dead.** These are hardly her physical children, but, metaphorically, her devoted followers around her. Thus we can distinguish the following groups within the community of Thyatira: In the first place, there are Jezebel and John, two antagonistic prophets, neither of whom acknowledges the other's authority. In the second place, there are the majority whose spiritual growth is noted, who are chided for tolerating Jezebel and her clique in their midst and who are admonished to "hold fast what you have" (v. 25). In the third place, there are Jezebel's "children," her disciples, who are the product of her teaching and conduct. To them the announcement of judgment guarantees an awful death. **I will strike her children dead.** A more literal, better translation would be, "I will kill her children with the plague" (cf. Ezek. 33:27 LXX; Rev. 6:8b). In the fourth place, we find a group of sympathizers who are not yet Jezebel's disciples but who are impressed by her. They are still called **my** servants. Christ's judgment is not announced to them, even though they are threatened with "great tribulation." But a threat is not an announcement of judgment. In contrast to the followers of Jezebel, her sympathizers still have time to repent, and repentance is indeed demanded of them (v. 22b). For Jezebel and her circle, the time for repentance has passed.

23b—And all the churches shall know that I am he who searches mind and heart. The purpose of his judgment on Jezebel and her followers is the recognition by **all the churches** (plural) of Christ's sovereignty. This implies that Jezebel had established her reputation beyond Thyatira. Her and her disciples' death will become known among the churches of the region of Asia, and this judgment will lead the communities to recognize that Jesus Christ, like God himself, perceives the innermost being of his people (cf. Jer. 11:20; 17:10; Ps. 7:9). He judges **each of you** (plural) **as your** (plural) **works deserve** (v. 23c). Judgment according to works is not an outmoded idea in the New Testament but is present from Matthew 7 to Revelation 22; nor is judgment according to works in tension with redemption by grace (Rev. 1:4-6; see comments on 20:12-15).

With this sentence, **I will give to each of you as your works deserve,** the focus has shifted from Jezebel and her devotees to the majority of Thyatira's community. The "angel" is no longer addressed but the members themselves, as the second person plural of the verbs shows (vv. 23c-25). The sequence of accusation (vv. 20-21), announcement of judgment (vv. 22-23a), and recognition formula, introduced with "You shall know that I am he who . . . ," is derived from Old Testament prophetic speech (e.g., Ezek. 25:3b-5, 6-7, 8-11, etc.).

Admonition (2:24-29). **But to the rest of you in Thyatira . . . I do not lay upon you any other burden.** This **rest,** which we identified as the majority, had been praised in v. 19 but criticized for their toleration of Jezebel and her circle in their midst. This "rest" are not asked to repent but to draw the logical conclusion from this message and excommunicate Jezebel. No additional **burden** will be laid on them. This may refer to the Apostles' Decree—"It seemed good to the Holy Spirit and to us to lay upon you no greater **burden** than these necessary things; that you abstain from what has been sacrificed to idols . . . and from unchastity" (Greek, *porneia*). Perhaps more generally, it may also refer to traditions that they received in baptism. Or perhaps no additional "burden" simply means no additional threats beyond those made already against the sympathizers. Be that as it may, the majority are admonished: **only hold fast what you have,** persevere in your redemption "by his blood," and in your status as "a kingdom, priests to" his God (1:6). Moreover, **hold fast** the traditions concerning Christian conduct, concerning the works that ought to be done, **until I come.**

The rest are now identified as those who **do not hold this teaching** (Jezebel's), **who have not learned** (Greek, *ouk egnōsan*) **what some call the deep things of Satan.** It is possible that the claim of Jezebel's group to know the **deep things** of *God* has been turned sarcastically into the very opposite (cf. 2:9). But it is equally possible that Jezebel is actually quoted here. If so, her claim was to know the depth of Satan. This would not imply Satan worship but would express her belief that Christians are immune to Satan no matter what they do, because *they know* all there is to know about him by intuition or inspiration. Their salvation is realized, accomplished, and therefore eating idol meat is a manifestation of their freedom in the Spirit (and in agreement, perhaps, with Jezebel's angelic spouse).

26-28—The promise to victors begins with a definition. The conqueror is one who **keeps my works until the end,** whether his or her own end or the end of the age. As important as our works are, what is all-important is keeping the **works** of Christ. Ultimately our works of love, faithfulness, service, and fortitude (v. 19) are the works of Christ performed through us. The same holds true for "the testimony of Jesus" which, according to 19:19, is "the spirit of prophecy." Jesus bears witness through his faithful prophets. And what John—or better, what Jesus, speaking through John—found lacking in Jezebel were the works of Jesus and the testimony of Jesus. Her teaching, "her works" (RSV, **her**

doings, v. 22) were not Christ's works. Though she was certainly not a religious whore in a literal sense, John labeled her as successor of the idolatrous princess of Sidon and as predecessor and prototype of the great harlot to come (cf. Revelation 17). Her views on the permissibility of participation in the imperial cult amounted to fornication from John's perspective, and her endorsement of eating idol meat was no better. In contrast to her, the conquerors keep **my works** and Jesus promises them **power over nations** in the age to come.

The image of ruling nations is borrowed from the Old Testament, from the messianically understood Psalm 2. The title "Son of God" in v. 18 has already alluded to Ps. 2:7. Now Jesus promises to the conquerors that they shall be coregents with him, and he uses language from this same Psalm 2 in order to articulate this promise (cf. 1:6; 5:10; 20:4, 6; 22:5; and also 12:5; 19:15). What is said of his own future rule over nations (12:5; 19:15), he will share with the conquerors (2:26-27). In ancient Near Eastern coronation rituals, **earthen pots** with the names of enemies inscribed on them were smashed to symbolize the future victory of the king. Yet in the vision of the slaughter of Armageddon (16:16; 19:11-21) the Christian conquerors are not present as participants. There is no vision in this letter that deals with Christians exercising **power over nations,** ruling them **with a rod of iron** and smashing them **in pieces** like **earthen pots.** Here too we find a reversal of a traditional image. The "power over nations" will be shown in this letter to consist on one hand in the perseverance of the saints in the face of the nations' idolatry, especially the imperial cult, and on the other hand in the solidarity of the millennial people of God which will not tolerate "abominations and falsehoods" (Rev. 13:1—14:5; 21:27).

The emphasis in Christ's promise to the conquerers of Thyatira does not lie on the fate of the nations but on the privilege granted the conquerers to be coregents with Christ (20:4-6). This privilege is repeated throughout Revelation to its very end (22:5), and it is also present in the second part of the promise to the victors: **I will give him the morning star.** The morning star is Venus, herald of the day after the darkness of night and symbol of victory and symbol of imperial authority in Roman legions. In 22:16 Jesus identifies himself as "the bright morning star," for he is King of kings and Lord of lords (19:16), "the Son of God" (2:18). And just as God promises the conquerors that they will be sons of God (21:7), so Jesus, the Son and morning star, promises to **give** them **the morning star.** The conquerors of Thyatira are assured that Christ's victory will be theirs, that nothing can defeat him or them, provided they keep his works.

To Sardis (3:1-6)

Sardis was the capital of the ancient kingdom of Lydia. In the sixth century B.C. the fabulously wealthy king Croesus was its most famous ruler. Two demands to be "vigilant" (3:2-3; RSV, "awake") allude to the fact that Sardis was captured twice, in 546 B.C. by Cyrus and in 214 B.C. by Antiochus III. Imposing as its citadel was, the lack of vigilance and preparedness resulted in its fall. Christ's statement that he will come "like a thief, and you will not know at what hour" (v. 3) also refers to Sardis's unpreparedness at the time of its seizure. Moreover, the city was greatly damaged by an earthquake in A.D. 17. Although it was rebuilt, it had the reputation of having been "alive" in the past, but was now a dreary, "dead" place in John's present (3:1b). Sardis had had a large Jewish population from the end of the third century B.C. (Josephus, *Ant.* 12.147-153). Its magnificent synagogue dating from the second century A.D. is being excavated and restored by a U.S. archaeological team. A second-century Christian chiliast was Melito, the bishop of Sardis (about A.D. 170).

1—The commission with messenger formula links this message to the prolog, to the "inaugural" vision of chap. 1, and to the throne room vision which introduces Part II. The **seven spirits** of God (cf. 1:4; 4:5) can be imaged as blazing lamps or stars, suggesting the seven archangels who stand before God's throne (4:5), or as the seven eyes of the Lamb (5:6). They are the symbol of the Holy Spirit in the fullness of his gifts. He proceeds from the Father through Christ into the world. Therefore Christ **has the seven spirits of God,** just as he holds **the seven stars,** the angelic representatives of the churches, in his hand (1:20). The angel of Sardis at once receives a stern rebuke introduced with **I know your works** (v. 2). For the first time we hear no word of praise. The angel represents a church in the doldrums, which has the reputation for being **alive,** a lively church, when in fact it is **dead** from Christ's viewpoint. A living church is a community fervent in the gifts of the *Spirit,* in love and faith, in hope and endurance (cf. 2:19). A dead church may parade activities, but its **works** prove it to be without that Spirit who comes from Christ.

2-3—Admonitions (awake and strengthen . . . remember . . . keep . . . repent) are intertwined with accusations, **You have the name of being alive, and you are dead. . . . I have not found your works perfect,** and concluded with a threat of judgment which harks back to the opening admonition: **Awake.** His negative evaluation of the Sardians reveals why their church is dead, or near death, and gives urgency to his admonition and serves as basis for his threat of judgment (v. 3b).

Awake (better, be vigilant) **and strengthen** what is **on the point of death.** If we were to ask who should do this strengthening in a dead church, we would be referred to those **few names** of individuals (v. 4) **who have not soiled their garments.** The verb "to soil" (Greek, *molynein*) is frequently used of cultic or sexual defilement (cf. 14:4; Jude 23). The soiled garments are an image of sexual promiscuity. Here we meet a church that has been brought to the point of death by pagan sexual mores. We hear nothing of persecution or hostility of Jews, nor of false teachers corrupting the community. But the church is infected with immorality, and **what remains** of the community's spiritual life is at the **point of death.** Its **works,** which had given it the reputation of a lively church among the Asian communities, are not acceptable to Christ. He unmasks their activities as pseudospirituality. **Awake.** To awaken, to be vigilant, is to live; to continue in the stupor of promiscuity is to die. Not only the memory of Sardis's past but also the Christian tradition accentuates the necessity of alertness in view of the imminent end (cf. 1 Thess. 5:6; Rom. 13:11; 1 Peter 5:8; Mark 13:32-36). Spiritual alertness not only contradicts ecclesiastical sleepwalking, it also belies the indifference toward the parousia and refutes the belief that the eschaton is realized without a future consummation.

The absence of **works** that are **perfect** (better: whole, complete) **in the sight of God** reveals the state of the church in Sardis. Even today quite a few unfinished, incomplete, columns are still lying around. Perhaps the Christians of Sardis believed they were **perfect** already through the mediation of salvation in baptism, and therefore they may have felt free to let their **works** reflect the conduct of the general public. Quite a few pagan penitential inscriptions from an area a little east of Sardis express a sensitivity toward wrongdoing which apparently was absent among the church membership of Sardis. Obviously John represented an early Christian moral rigorism which is far removed from the moral mediocrity of present-day Protestant mainline Christianity. But was he also a perfectionist who maintained the illusion that the conduct of Christians is in no need of forgiveness? Hardly, even though this is not the question he faces in this message. For him, love, the highest gift of the Spirit, is either real love, and thus "perfect," or not love at all, and thus dead. Love is not just an emotion and a feeling but a deed exhibited in thought, word, and actions. Without the gift of the Spirit their works are not perfect, not complete, in the sight of God. In short, their works are not an embodiment of love, faith, service, and patient endurance (cf. 2:19), but signs of busybodyness and phony piety.

The awakening is described in two parts. First, the community should **remember** (not only Sardis's sordid past) the redemption **received** in baptism (cf. 1:5-6). The awakening is in fact a return to baptism, to their appointment as kings and priests unto God. The community should also **remember** the traditions concerning Christian conduct **heard** in baptismal instruction. The community is exhorted to **keep** them in faithful obedience. Second, in view of their present sorry state, the members of the church at Sardis are admonished to **repent,** to turn at once to the God of promise and the giver of obligations (cf. 2:25a).

The threat of judgment is connected with the admonitions through the catchword **awake.** If the church does not wake up, then Christ will come **like a thief, and you will not know at what hour I will come upon you** (cf. Matt. 24:42; 1 Thess. 5:2; 2 Peter 3:10; Rev. 16:15). The use of this tradition may have been suggested by Sardis's conquest by night. At any rate, the unexpected coming of Christ signals their eschatological judgment, not his coming in a historical crisis (thus Caird). It is not Jesus' coming that is in doubt in this message. What is in doubt is whether or not he will find then asleep in a state of acculturated stupor. Like the Ephesians (2:5), so the Sardians may discover that his coming will result in their condemnation. Not the community as such, but only the victorious believers will share in the life of the world to come. Those found asleep will share the fate of Sardis of old.

4—Actually, the main part of the writing could have ended at this point. John, however, added a promise to **a few** individuals **who have not soiled their garments.** In Pergamum, a few had become intoxicated with heresy. Here only a few have remained faithful. The **white** robes that are promised to them symbolize the forgiveness and purity received from Christ. This may allude to the custom of wearing white robes at baptism. If so, the few believers who have not soiled their baptismal garments through promiscuous behavior are promised that in the present they shall **walk with** Christ **in white.** Their present unsoiled garments (v. 4) are metaphors of the gift of redemption which was received in baptism and retained in conduct. On account of their conduct, Christ judges them to be **worthy** to walk with him **in white,** both now and in the ultimate future.

5-6—The promise to victors here implies that the conquerors are not limited to the martyrs, even though martyrs most pointedly exemplify the Christological principle of victory through apparent defeat. **He** or she **who conquers** is the one who has not soiled his or her garments through immoral conduct. The victors **shall be clad thus in white garments,** which are the garments "of glory" (*1 Enoch* 62:15-16), the new resurrection body, the gift and reward for victory achieved on earth (7:9-14). Eternal life shall be theirs.

Second, **I will not blot his** or her **name out of the book of life.** A city register contained the names of its citizens. The book of life contains the names of the citizens of the kingdom, of the new Jerusalem (21:27; cf. Dan. 12:1; *1 Enoch* 47:3; Luke 10:20; Heb. 12:23). Their names are inscribed in it "from [or before] the foundation of the world" (Rev. 17:8; 13:8). God's saving eschatological action has logical and theological priority over our decisions and our faith. Citizenship in the kingdom is not earned by us but is dependent on God's election. Christ's love and redemption with his own blood (1:5-6) fulfills God's eternal purpose. Yet while no human being can earn inscription in the book of life, it can be forfeited through immoral conduct. Christ may blot out one's name from the book of life, according to his message to Sardis's church. The baptized are not magically insured but are challenged to respond to the gift of redemption received in baptism with faith, endurance, and love, with "works," in their daily conduct. In short, the promise is conditional. Only the names of the victors shall remain in the book of life in which all the baptized are registered (cf. 20:15).

Third, the scene changes to a court of law. At the final judgment, Christ himself will function as witness and advocate before God on behalf of the victors. John again alluded to a Synoptic tradition (Luke 12:8; Mark 8:38). **I will confess his name before my Father and before his angels.** His testimony will be decisive in the final judgment, even as now their conduct in Sardis is decisive for Christ's evaluation of their present lives. Jesus promises to testify in God's final court that the Sardian conquerors did not just have the reputation of being alive while in reality they were dead (3:1) but that their baptism resulted in "works." They have "kept" the faith and the tradition they received. They are conquerors who swam against the currents of their culture. John's dialectic between "works" and election will be the subject of the final judgment vision (20:11-15). Then *many* books containing the "works" of people will be opened (20:12). But there also will be the *one* book of life which is "the Lamb's book of life" (21:27b), containing the names of all for whom he will make intercession, confessing them before his Father and before his angels of judgment (cf. Rom. 5:9; 8:34). Let the churches listen to the message of the Spirit to Sardis through John.

To Philadelphia (3:7-13)

Philadelphia, established in the middle of the second century B.C., was destroyed by an earthquake in A.D. 17 and rebuilt with aid from Emperor Tiberius. For some time after the earthquake, part of the population preferred to live in the surrounding countryside or left the city at dusk. Probably the reference to the permanence of residence in the temple of God (3:12b: "never shall he go out of it") draws a contrast to life in Philadelphia. Moreover, its name had been changed, first to Neocaesarea and, in Vespasian's time, to Philadelphia Flavia. The promise to conquerors includes the giving of new names.

No mention is made of immoral behavior within Philadelphia's Christian community. Such moral conduct was by no means unique in Hellenistic society. To be sure, there was prostitution, abortion, the exposure of children, keeping of concubines, the hiring of slaves, and the installing of boys for sexual gratification, as well as adultery and divorce. Juvenal, who sighed that corruption reigns supreme in Rome, gives a devastating (and one-sided) picture of the depravity of Roman aristocracy, exemplified in the insatiable harlotry of Messalina, the wife of Emperor Claudius (*Satire* 6). However, on the other side there were moralists who clearly set forth the ideal of marital fidelity and advocated general virtuous conduct (e.g., Plutarch and Musonius Rufus). But what is more important for our letter than the principles of philosopher-moralists are the voices of common people in matters of morals and religion.

We have an inscription from Philadelphia (first century B.C. or late second century) which contains the ordinances of a private religious association that met regularly in the house of a certain Dionysius for sacrifices to Zeus and other Greek gods. The association was under the guardianship of the Phrygian goddess Agdistis, who was a manifestation of the Great Mother goddess. The ordinances given by Zeus were, in part:

> Those who enter this house (i.e., the association and its private shrine), men and women, free persons and slaves, must swear before all the gods that they are conscious of no deceit toward (any) man or woman, that they will not use drugs (or poison) . . . nor evil charms (magic) . . . abortive or contraceptive drug. . . . Apart from his own wife a man may not take another woman for sexual relations, regardless whether she is a free woman or a slave, nor may he corrupt a boy, or a virgin, nor suggest it to another person. . . . Mighty are the gods who dwell in (this cult-room). They watch over these things and punish the transgressors of their ordinances. A free woman is to be pure and may not know the bed or intercourse with another man, except her husband. (Barton and Horsley, 8-10)

In short, according to the ordinances of this private religious association in Philadelphia, which was inclusive in terms of gender and social status, the immoral conduct of a member rendered him or her "unworthy to worship this god" (Zeus) and resulted in a threat of divine retribution. Before performing their ceremonies, the members had to touch the stone with the inscription of the ordinances of Zeus, thereby expressing their compliance with the moral code of their god.

The Christian community in **Philadelphia** had **but little power,** but it has **kept** the ordinances of **the holy one** and **the true one.** Therefore it is a holy and true community (3:7-8). Like Smyrna, it experienced conflict with Jews, and, like Smyrna, it received only praise and encouragement from its Lord. There is no call for repentance in either message. Similar as they are, they contain distinct emphases. Whereas the Jews of Smyrna apparently used political clout against the Christians, the conflict in Philadelphia is primarily theological.

7—The messenger formula alludes to the Christological issue of this conflict. The One who speaks through John is **the holy one, the true one.** With these predications Jesus claims attributes for himself which the Old Testament reserved for God (Isa. 6:3; 65:16; cf. Rev. 6:10). God is the Holy One in Israel. "True" in the Old Testament means the same as "trustworthy"; among Greeks it means "real." These Christological predications also legitimate the church's confession and life-style which is the cause of the conflict between synagogue and church. The same thrust is found in the declaration that Jesus **has the key of David, who opens** the entrance into the city of God, the new Jerusalem (cf. 3:12), **and no one shall shut, who shuts and no one opens.** Jesus Christ decides the identity and membership of the people of God, both now and in the future. The **key of David** is a reinterpretation of Isa. 22:22: "I will place on his shoulder the key of the house of David; he shall open, and none shall shut; and he shall shut, and none shall open." In Isaiah, it referred to the authority of the new steward to grant or to bar access to the royal palace. Here it means that Jesus alone has the authority to determine who *now* belongs to the house of David, the people of God, and who *shall* belong to the future city of David, the heavenly Jerusalem (3:12; 21:1—22:5), and who is to be shut out (21:8, 27; 22:15). The key of David links with and supplements the image of the keys to Hades and Death (1:18). Accordingly, Jesus holds not only the keys to the realm of death but also to the realm of God's eschatological salvation.

8-9—The picture of the **open door** has a meaning that differs from Acts 14:27; 2 Cor. 2:12. There it refers to mission opportunities. Here it conveys reassurance to the community. **Behold, I have set before you** (past tense) **an open door, which no one is able to shut.** Because he has already opened the door of God's kingdom to them (cf. 1:6), their membership among God's eschatological people is assured. Simultaneously, the claim of Jews to be the synagogue, the gathering of the people of God, is identified as falsehood (cf. 2:9). By closing their hearts against Jesus, by rejecting him, they have aligned themselves with Satan, the deceiver and false accuser; 12:10 will introduce a new aspect on this matter.

Three times in two verses (vv. 8-9) we hear the call **Behold** introducing prophetic promises. Jews who harass the church of Philadelphia will experience a most surprising reversal of an Old Testament promise. They will have to pay homage to Christians, most of whom are Gentiles, even though as Jews they had expected that it would be Gentiles who would **bow down** and pay homage to Israel at the end (cf. Isa. 45:14; 49:23; 60:14). Verse 9 envisions the vindication of Christians rather than the conversion of Jews. It speaks of the recognition by Jews at the end that they were wrong in rejecting Jesus and the church. In retrospect, at the end, they will realize that Jesus, the bearer of the key of David, has **loved** the Christian community of Philadelphia (cf. 1:5) and has opened the door to the kingdom for them. **I will make them** (the Jews) **bow down before your feet** implies that the Christian community will participate in Christ's future reign (cf. 3:21) and their present opponents will acknowledge their reign. Does not this reversal from hostility to acknowledgment at least imply the future salvation of Jews? John is silent on this theme (cf. Phil. 2:10: "every knee shall bow"). When we read this message today, we do well to substitute terms like "Lutherans" for "Jews" and remember that (1) John was a Jew, like Jesus; (2) there is a great difference between criticism arising from within the family and criticism voiced from outside the family; and (3) polemics voiced by the oppressed or socially weaker groups must be distinguished from the polemics of oppressors. Beyond doubt, the Christian communities at John's time and the following two centuries were the socially weaker and more vulnerable groups in comparison to Judaism. This, however, requires that John's language of polemics against the synagogue (e.g., "synagogue of Satan") may not be used by *us*. Conversely, white Americans did poorly when they told Black Americans during the civil rights struggles not to protest too loudly and offensively for white sensitivities.

10-11—The community of Philadelphia has not denied Christ's name (3:8), which is synonymous with confessing him before people, including magistrates (cf. Luke 12:8-9). They **kept** his **word** (cf. v. 8), which challenged it to **patient endurance** under pressure. Therefore they receive the promise that Christ will preserve the community from the coming apocalyptic upheavals (**Because you have kept my word . . . I will keep you). The hour of trial** (Greek, *peirasmos*) is not a period in this letter that can be calculated according to an apocalyptic timetable. It denotes the trial itself which is a testing by God to persevere and a tempting by the devil to apostatize (cf. 2:10; Mark 14:35).

The church of Smyrna had been told to expect a short, 10-day period of "tribulation" (2:10), which apparently embraced only their local situation. Now, for the first time, we hear of a cosmic trial that will involve the **whole world** and all **who dwell upon the earth.** Part II of John's book will deal with this trial from different perspectives. Hence the call to listen at the end of the message includes the demand to listen to the rest of the letter-book. The Christians of Philadelphia are promised that Christ will **keep** them safe from God's apocalyptic tests and trials. Will they be exempt from them? The message to the Philadelphians does not answer this question. Hence we should continue to listen to the rest of John's letter (cf. 7:1-17; 13:4-8). **I am coming soon.** Christ's parousia is imminent. Therefore **hold fast what you have, so that no one may seize your crown.** Here the crown is a metaphor for the redemption already received (cf. 1:5-6) in distinction from the future crown of 2:10.

12-13—The promise to victors is filled with salvation predicates. They shall become pillars **in the temple of my God.** Just as James, Peter, and John had been "pillars" of the Jerusalem community (Gal. 2:9), so likewise the victors will serve as pillars of the new Jerusalem. Although it has no special sanctuary, the new Jerusalem itself will be one great heavenly temple with God in the midst of his people (21:1-4, 22-27). Further, the victor receives the **name of my God, and the name of the city of my God** and Christ's **own new name** which is hidden (cf. 19:12; 2:17). These names signify to whom the victors belong. They are God's property (cf. 14:1), citizens of the new Jerusalem and coheirs and regents with Christ, whose new name, unknown today, they will bear.

The promise of the new Jerusalem coming out of heaven was understood in literalistic fashion by the Montanists, a charismatic movement that arose in the middle of the second century and was eventually excluded from the church (see above, introduction, section 1).

To Laodicea (3:14-22)

14—Affluent Laodicea was located at the junction of three important trade roads and was known as one of the three sisters of the Lykos valley, the others being Colossae, a few miles east, and Hierapolis, famous for its thermal baths, a few miles north. Laodicea established a reputation as a commercial and industrial center. Its wool and linen industry manufactured black cloth, and its medical school produced an eye ointment (made from alum) that was famous around the Mediterranean world. These items are in view in vv. 17-18 (i.e., rich, garments, eye salve). Affluent Laodicea was so "rich" (cf. v. 17) that it could afford to refuse financial aid from Rome when an earthquake destroyed most of it in A.D. 60 or 61 (Tacitus, *Annals* 14.27). The disadvantage of the city lay in its water supply. Since local water tasted putrid, water was channeled from five miles away via an aqueduct and tended to be lukewarm in contrast to the hot springs of Hierapolis and the cool wells of Colossae.

The Christian community was established in this city by a coworker of Paul, probably by Epaphras. It met in the house of Nympha at the time when the letter to the Colossians was written. A letter by Paul (or by one of his coworkers) was sent to the church in Laodicea. Unfortunately it has been lost, like Paul's "previous" letter to the Corinthians (1 Cor. 5:9). The letters to the Colossians and Laodiceans were to be exchanged, so that Colossians would be "read also in the church of Laodicea" (Col. 2:1; 4:12-16).

Christ's message to his church in Laodicea contains not one word of commendation. Not even a few individuals are singled out for praise, as in Sardis (cf. 3:4). His evaluation of the present state of the Laodicean church is summarized in the startling declaration, **I will spew you out of my mouth** (v. 16). This pronouncement is the most severe verdict on any of the seven churches and seems to leave no room except for total condemnation. However, the **love** of Christ (1:5) does not give up on his lukewarm church, and Jesus issues an invitation to **repent** in words of appealing love. Thereby his apodictic pronouncement of judgment is transformed into a conditional announcement. The promise to victors summarizes all prior promises and discloses once again that it is not just martyrs who can be conquerors. The call to **hear** at the very end of this last message, as well as the symbol of the throne, forms a linkage to the beginning of Part II. Now to some details.

The commission formula contains the credentials of the risen Christ. He is **the Amen.** Jesus transfers a predication of God to himself. Isaiah 65:16-17 speaks of "God whose name is Amen" (so NEB; RSV, "God of truth"). He will create a new heaven and a new earth (cf. Rev. 21:1, 5). Even as God's integrity stands behind his word, just so Jesus' guarantees this message. He can do so, because he is the **faithful and true witness** (1:5), who discloses God's purpose in a dependable, trustworthy communication. He alone is **the beginning of God's creation.** This does not mean that he is the first of the created beings. The word "beginning" (Greek, *archē*) also means source, cause, or principle. Hence the NEB translates: He is "the prime source of all of God's creation." This self-predication may allude to Colossians, the letter that was also read in the Laodicean community. In Col. 1:15-20, Christ is hailed as "the first-born of all creation . . . the beginning. . . . He is before all things and in him all things hold together." Christ precedes creation. Like the divine wisdom of Prov. 8:22; Sirach 24; Wis. Sol. 7:22-25, Christ has priority over the world. He is the source of all creation, and therefore he has a legitimate claim on it. Like God, he is "the first and the last, the beginning and the end" with reference to both creation and new creation (Rev. 22:13; cf. 1:5, 8; 2:8). In conclusion, Jesus is **the Amen** of God because he is the trustworthy witness to and source of God's creation and redemption. The latter has already been inaugurated through his death and resurrection (1:17-18). If the Laodicean Christians want to be involved in the world, then Christ should be their approach to the world as God meant it to be.

15-18—I know your works: you are neither cold nor hot. This is his evaluation of their present condition. They are "limping" with two different opinions, like the Israelites of old (1 Kings 18:21; cf. Matt. 6:24; 12:30). To be **hot** may mean to be "aglow with the Spirit" (Rom. 12:11; Acts 18:25), committed to God's purpose and Christ's testimony. Such commitment would result in a dynamic witness. To be **cold** means to be a pagan, unwilling to listen to the gospel. The Laodiceans are neither. They do not indulge in pagan idolatry and vices, nor do they express their redemption through Christ in Spirit-empowered conduct. They are complacent, "wishy-washy" Christians, as insipid as their water supply, and Jesus will have none of it. **Would that you were cold or hot!** Here Jesus is saying something that no preacher would dare to say if the Lord had not spoken it first, namely, that ice-cold atheists and pagans are preferable to him than lukewarm Christians. For them, the gospel has degenerated into "opium for the people." The living faith has shrunk to liturgical incantations and recitals of formulas without conviction. Their "works" show that their church is in a **wretched** state (3:17).

Christ's evaluation is followed by an announcement of judgment with no "if" or "but" attached. **So, because you are lukewarm, and neither cold nor hot, I will spew you out of my mouth.** The metaphor of lukewarm, stale water, which makes a person vomit, would have been easily understood by the Laodiceans. No one could drink the lukewarm water that ran down from the cliffs of Hierapolis, nor was the city's own water, brought in by an aqueduct, refreshing. Rejection therefore is their lot. In v. 17, we hear the Laodiceans speak for themselves: **I am rich, I have prospered, and I need nothing.** Materially as well as spiritually, we are well off (cf. Luke 12:16-18; Hos. 12:8). Obviously, we have here a reference to the social stability of this city. The Christians of Laodicea would also claim that they are blessed with "spiritual" riches (cf. 1 Cor. 4:8), not just material ones. From Christ's perspective there is indeed a relationship between their brand of spirituality and their material prosperity. They are materially well off because they have been unwilling to draw the radical consequences from the gospel for their conduct, works, and lives. They avoid conflict with the surrounding culture by means of a privatistic piety, which reveals itself in their speech (**I am**. . . , **I have**. . . , **I need** . . .). But Christ, who is the beginning, the source and goal of creation, impinges upon social relations and economic dealings. The Laodiceans, however, preferred an individualistic savior of souls who makes no demands but undergirds their quest for self-sufficiency. The Greek ideal of self-sufficiency, **I need nothing,** has in Laodicea been fused to bourgeois piety, complacency and cultural accommodation.

Their self-evaluation is interrupted by Christ. You Laodiceans, wrapped up in your myopic, insipid piety, are lacking in self-criticism. You are unaware of your reality, **not knowing that you are wretched, pitiable, poor, blind, and naked.** These five attributes reveal their true situation as perceived by the Amen, the faithful and true witness. Those Christians are like beggars with the illusion that they are rich (by contrast, Smyrna, which is poor, is called "rich"). Actually, the main part of the message could have ended here. The judgment has been announced and the reasons for it have been given (3:15-16). But the surprise is that the message does not end—that Jesus gives an admonition, the goal of which is not condemnation but transformation.

The last three attributes, **poor, blind, and naked,** are taken into a threefold admonition and allude to Laodicea's importance as a banking center, pharmaceutical producer, and manufacturer of linen and clothing. **I counsel you to buy from me gold refined by fire, that you may be rich.** Acquire genuine wealth which Christ alone can give. Such a purchase is "without money" (Isa. 55:1) and constitutes an exercise in faith. His gold is refined by fire, by the cross, and it retains its value in the heavenly city which is "pure gold, clear as crystal." The **white garments,** instead of the city's black clothing, should **keep the shame of your nakedness** from being seen. This is a double entendre, alluding to nakedness as a symbol of judgment (cf. Ezek. 16:35; 2 Cor. 5:3) and to the nakedness in Greek gymnasiums and baths. Sexual promiscuity in bathing establishments (Juvenal, *Satire* 6.419–425) is not an issue here. From John's Jewish point of view, the **shame** of these naked Laodicean Christians is paraded around by them (cf. *Jub.* 3:31). Their nakedness will be put to shame by God at the end—unless they buy **white garments** from Christ, returning to their baptismal gift (cf. 3:4; 1:5-6), and **salve to anoint your eyes, that you may see.** Overcome your myopic vision, Christ calls to them, with the salve of my vision. Learning to **see** through his eyes means to recognize the illusion of self-sufficiency, to accept his stern verdict, and to act upon it, so that in the end "they shall see the face" of God himself (22:4).

19-20—The admonition finds its high point in the call to repent. A community that by its lukewarmness has made its Lord so sick that he can only spit it out is granted another opportunity. Christ's **love** is the reason for his stern admonition and unexpected invitation to repentance. His love finds a way to hold off his judgment. Alluding to Prov. 3:11-12, he characterizes his message as bringing to light and correcting sins (cf. Sir. 18:13). The chastening or disciplining (Greek, *paideuein*) includes trials and suffering (Heb. 12:7; James 1:12). Its goal is restoration and salvation. Simultaneously, one must recognize one's true state. **So be zealous.** Not momentary but ongoing zeal is demanded; **and repent.**

A call for decision is issued, a call to turn away from their complacency and self-sufficiency. The invitation to repentance is an act of grace, not a right, nor a foregone conclusion. This becomes obvious when we compare 3:18-20 with Heb. 6:4-8 which precludes a "second" repentance after baptism (cf. Heb. 10:26-31; 12:16-17). The Shepherd of Hermas received a special divine authorization for offering a second repentance to Christians who sinned after baptism (*Vis.* 2.2.4-8). In Hebrews, the Shepherd, and Revelation repentance is never a privilege which the believer possesses, it is God's gracious and sovereign offer, granted in the present.

With **behold,** a prophetic announcement is introduced and given prominence. Instead of the expected threat of judgment, we hear the promise, **Behold, I stand at the door and knock; if any one hears my voice and opens the door, I will come in to him and eat with him, and he with me.** This promise does not take up specific features peculiar to Laodicea. Rather, it is placed at the end of the message septet because it applies to all Christian communities. Hence the promise does not use the second person pronoun, singular or plural, but speaks of **any one.** Anyone who listens to Jesus is promised participation in the messianic feast to come (cf. 19:7-9; Mark 14:25; Luke 22:29-30). Since Jesus is already **at the door** knocking with admonitions and promises, we meet again the imminent-end expectation which is characteristic of this letter (cf. Luke 12:35-38). But more, every celebration of the Eucharist is also a joyful anticipation of the messianic feast to come.

21-22—The call to listen to **what the Spirit says to the churches** connects this section of seven messages with the following visions of Part II. The promise to victors refers to Christ's **throne** and his Father's **throne,** thus making a transition to the opening vision of Part II. The issue of who rules the world, who sits on the throne (4:2), whom we should worship—this is the basic question of the rest of this book. Moreover, this last promise to conquerors summarizes all prior promises. Christians who through baptism have been designated for kingship (1:6) shall in the end be coregents with Christ and God (cf. Luke 22:30; Rev. 5:6; 20:6; 22:5). Just as Jesus by his conquest became the victorious coregent with his Father, just so Christians who persevere in faith shall participate in the messianic reign and share in Christ's sovereignty. No greater privilege, no destiny more triumphant than this one, can be imagined. It is "the crown of the promises" in the seven "letters" (Lohmeyer), and it is found at the conclusion of the message addressed to the worst church.

It is also the last word that Jesus speaks through John. The next time that Jesus speaks directly to him will be in the epilog (22:7). The message to Laodicea should make it clear to us that John's circular letter was *not* written in response to present persecution, and its purpose is *not* consolation of Christians who are persecuted by the state. Jesus hardly consoles when he threatens to spit the Laodiceans out like stale water or to throw away the lampstand of the Ephesians. The difficulties that are present in each of the seven churches differ according to cause and makeup.

First: there were pressures from Gentiles, social pressures resulting in ostracism and in the temptation to deny Jesus. Second: Jews exerted political and theological pressure on two churches. The synagogue rejected the claim that Christ holds "the key of David" and threatened Christians with "the second death." Third: heretical teachers had gained entrance into communities and attracted followers. Fourth: immoral, pagan behavior was eroding Christian substance without pressures from outside, and false prophets were agitating for such conduct from within. Fifth: lack of "love" leads to regression and jeopardizes the very reason for the community's existence. Sixth: compromise and accommodation resulted in a lackadaisical form of Christianity, one that enjoys its peace and prosperity within its social setting. Seventh, and naturally last: at least one church did experience hostile action in which "Satan's throne," the Roman government, was involved. But one martyrdom does not amount to a general persecution by the state in John's view or ours. It is not persecution by the state that concerns Christ as he evaluates the present state of his churches. The danger comes from the opposite direction. Peaceful coexistence with society without and heresy within constitutes the chief threat to the churches in John's present.

Christ's exhortation to his churches commands them to persevere, to hold on to the gift of redemption already received, to keep the status granted to them, to avoid idolatry and cut out immorality. Their enemies are not just outside but among them and within them. There is no forgiveness without repentance, no grace without discipline, no communion with Christ without resistance to idolatry (Bonhoeffer). The severe evaluation given by Christ to his churches is undergirded by the vision of Christ himself, who he is, what he has, and what he does.

Who is he? He *is* the First and the Last, who died and is alive forever (1:17). He *is* the Holy One, the True One, the Amen, the source of all creation, the Son of God. He *is* in short, one with God. And what does he have? He *has* the seven stars and a two-edged sword, and the seven spirits of God, and the key of David, and eyes like a flame of fire. He *has* what God has. And what does he *do?*

He loves his churches, even the one that makes him sick (3:16, 19). He rebukes them and commends them. He reveals to them their true state. He knows them and is present with them (2:1-2), and he pledges his integrity, that they shall reign with him, if they but persevere. In short, Part I sets forth a Christological reinterpretation of the first commandment: I am the Lord, your God, who loves you and has redeemed you. You may not indulge in those things for which I have censured you. You must persevere in the struggle between God and Satan. There is a dualism which is structured into this world and its history and you are a part of it. You are either on one side or on the other, irrespective of whether you are aware of it.

The dualism between God, Christ, the Spirit, and the saints on one side, and Satan, his minions, and "the earth dwellers" on the other, has been touched upon already in Part I (e.g., 2:9, 13, 20; 3:9-10), but this dualism will be unfolded broadly in Part II.

From Part I we know that the line of demarcation between God and Satan runs right through the communities. Only two of the seven churches received commendations, untarnished by rebukes. This means that churches as such are not automatically on the side of God, as ecclesiastical pomposity and illusion have believed from John's time to the present.

Moreover, John's dualism is not absolute but modified dualism in that neither Satan nor his beasts can operate outside God's control. It is an eschatological dualism in that the future of humans will find their end and goal either in the "second death" (2:11; 20:14) or in the new Jerusalem (3:12; 21:2). It is a soteriological dualism in that those who are saved are saved by grace, because their names were written in the book of life "before the foundation of the world" (13:9; 20:15). And it is an ethical dualism in that those who are shut out from God's future are "the dogs," namely, "the cowardly, the faithless, the polluted, . . . murderers, fornicators, sorcerers, idolaters, and all liars" (21:8; 22:15). They and the beast worshipers will have "no rest," while the saints who persevered will "rest from their labors" in the life of the world to come (14:11, 13b).

It is time for us to turn back to John's audience who had listened to his letter. They know that the series of messages, addressed to the seven churches, has now been completed. They have also gained an understanding of the meaning of "the revelation of Jesus Christ" (1:1) which formed the title of this letter. Revelation is not just John's experience of an encounter with Jesus; it became the hearers' experience also as the letter was read. They themselves experienced the revelation as confrontation with the risen Christ. It was not interesting information that satisfied their curiosity which they heard as the messages were read. They themselves were addressed and confronted by the Living One who revealed their shortcomings as well as his love which had not given up on them. This revelation of Jesus Christ in the present was communicated through his word, mediated by John in his letter. Will there be more?

Part II: The Revelation of the Future (4:1—22:5)

The new stage in the vision narrative is clearly marked in 4:1 ("after these things"; "Behold, in heaven an open door." Up to now, Jesus had appeared to John on earth, but now he is bidden by the angel, "Come up hither," to heaven). John is promised that he will see "what must take place after this." This promise refers back to 1:19, and the divine "must" clearly indicates that the revelation of the future will be the content of Part II of his letter. Again it will become clear to the hearers that revelation does not consist of information about apocalyptic timetables, or heavenly topography, but of the encounter with him who has the power to open the sealed scroll and bring the end-time events to their consummation. Moreover, the future is viewed from a particular perspective, namely, from the perspective of worship, which is the response to the "throne" and power of God and his plenipotentiary.

The first section of Part II (A), 4:1—11:19, is bracketed by worship in heaven. The heavenly liturgy of chaps. 4 and 5, interrupted by the seal and trumpet visions, continues in 11:16 with "loud voices in heaven" proclaiming that "the kingdom of the world has become the kingdom of our Lord and of his Christ and he shall reign for ever and ever." The worship in heaven will reach its climax in the Hallelujah chorus of 19:1-8: "Hallelujah! Salvation and glory and power belong to our God." However, the acclamations, offered to God and the Lamb in the throne room vision (chaps. 4–5), are challenged by the worship of the satanic trinity (chaps. 12–13).

Hence there is and will be a radical conflict between two opposing power groups, symbolized by the throne of God and the Lamb on one side (4:2-10; 11:16; 12:5; 14:3; etc.) and the throne of the dragon, shared by the beast, on the other (13:2; 16:10). This conflict is carried out in the center section (B), 12:1—16:21, and it leads to the grand finale of the third and last section (A′),

17:1—22:5. The basic issue in John's circular letter is: Whom do you worship? Who is your God? This issue is unfolded with respect to the future in Part II in three sections: 4:1—11:19 (A); 12:1—16:21 (B); and 17:1—22:5 (A′). At the conclusion we hear that God, the creator and center of all power, dwells among his servants. They "shall worship him; they shall see his face . . . and reign for ever" with him, sharing his throne (22:4-5).

By narrating his visions, John drew his audience into the supreme alternative that life sets before us: the worship of God or of the forces allied with anti-God. Through the narration of his lengthy vision (4:1—22:5), John sought to entice his audience to participate in this struggle of cosmic dimensions, to persevere in the worship of the one true God, and to endure the pressures which will intensify in the future. Thus, the purpose of John's book is not to console the afflicted but to attract the comfortable but endangered Christians to embrace an alternative vision of God's triumph in judgment and salvation. His vision may also function as consolation in distress, but that is not its primary purpose, which is summarized in the demand: Worship God, give him glory (14:7).

■ The Revelation of the Sovereignty of God and Christ in Tribulations and Plagues (4:1—11:19)

The demand to worship God is already realized in heaven. But more, the authority over the world is already transferred to Christ at the very beginning of this vision (chap. 5), not at its conclusion, as in other apocalyptic texts. This means that the victory in the conflict has already been won through the Lamb that was slain, and the whole company of heaven rejoices in celebration (cf. 5:9-14; 11:15-19). He has the power to unseal the scroll and put into effect the end-time events, symbolized by the opening of the seals and the blowing of the seven trumpets.

While the seal septet (6:1-17) is modeled according to the Synoptic apocalypse (Mark 13; Matthew 24; Luke 21), the trumpet cycle (8:6—9:20), which evolves out of the seventh seal (8:1), projects a new version of the Egyptian plagues on a cosmic scale. The blowing of the trumpets signals not only local and regional disasters, like the first four seals, but universal catastrophes which fall upon nature and humankind. The seal and the trumpet septets of the first section reveal the incomparable majesty and sovereignty of God and of his Messiah, and simultaneously they function as call to repentance, like the Egyptian plagues (cf. 9:20-21). The bowls of wrath in the center section (12:1—16:21) also have the Egyptian plagues as their model. Their peculiar emphases are (1) they are "the last" plagues and "with them the wrath of God is ended" (15:1); (2) the destruction described in the bowl visions is intensified in comparison to the trumpet septet; and (3) the bowls are poured out as judgment upon the beast worshipers and their city, Babylon (16:2, 6, 10, 19). Their specific function is the punishment of idolaters. From the seventh bowl (16:17-21) with its destruction of Babylon evolves the final section, 17:1—22:5, which elaborates the doom of Babylon concluding with the great Hallelujah in heaven (19:1-10). Then follow Christ's parousia (19:11-16), a series of judgments, and the vision of the new Jerusalem (21:9—22:5). John leads his hearers to envision that there is but one power that controls the future and that even the ugliness and perversity of the future is part of God's grand design.

One would have expected that John, in agreement with the apocalyptic tradition, would present an apocalyptic timetable after narrating the throne room vision (chap. 4). But, surprise! John has none of it. Instead of telling us that God, or the Lamb, read the contents of the scroll and disclosed apocalyptic secrets to John that had been hidden until now, we hear of the transfer of power and authority to the Lamb and of the acclamation by the heavenly court. There are no revelations concerning a time schedule of end-time events. The sequence of visions cannot be translated into a chronological sequence as the end of section one (11:15-19) and the beginning of section two (12:1-6) clearly demonstrate. What is revealed is not an apocalyptic timetable but the sovereign reign of God and of his Messiah (11:16). The seal and trumpet septets demonstrate his majesty, the bowl septet reveals his judgment upon idolaters.

In short, John uses apocalyptic traditions to drive home the point: Worship God (14:7). Just as he reinterpreted the significance of the community angels by taking from them any salvific role, so he reinterpreted apocalyptic traditions by throwing out disclosure scenes that were meant to convey hidden information. Revelation for him is not the communication of hitherto secret information about the hierarchies of angels, the furniture of hell, or the chronology of the end. Rather, revelation is the confrontation with the hidden God, whose ways are not our ways and who meets his creatures in judgment and salvation.

His reinterpretation also involved a recasting of basic images, mentioned already in the introduction. In the throne room vision John heard about the conquering Lion of the tribe of Judah (5:5), a traditional image of the Messiah who will slay his enemies. But what John saw was not a lion but a Lamb that was slain. The conqueror *is* the Crucified One; the victim *is* the victor. Hence future tribulations in the churches of Asia constitute their victory, already now, and will be revealed as such in the end. And just as John reinterpreted particular focal images, so he also reinterpreted certain apocalyptic ideas that were current at his time, such as the idea of a messianic interim kingdom (20:4-6). For him, the millennium is not reserved for the generation living at the time of the Messiah's appearance (4 Ezra 7:28) but for the victors, the martyrs, who are raised from the dead.

The Seven Seals (4:1—8:1)

Prelude in Heaven (4:1—5:14)

The prelude to Part II consists of a double vision which discloses the control center on which all reality is dependent and from which all actions of judgment and salvation emanate. The vision of the **throne** and the heavenly court around it (4:1-11) is followed by the vision of the sealed **scroll** and **the Lamb** who is worthy to open the scroll (5:1-14). The opening of the seals is interrupted by an *interlude* (7:1-17) between the sixth and the seventh seal. This interlude shifts our attention from the catastrophes that befall the world through seals one to six, to the preservation and salvation of the saints. The interludes also forestall the translation of the sequence of his visions into a chronological sequence. From the opening of the seventh seal, a new cycle evolves—the trumpet septet (8:2—11:19). An interlude (10:1—11:13) between the sixth and the seventh trumpet connects the first section (A) with the second (B) (12:1—16:21).

The messages to the seven churches evaluated their conditions from the point of view of Christ, who appeared to John on the island of Patmos, on earth. The prelude of 4:1—5:14 focuses our attention on heaven, where the central symbols are the **throne** of God and **the Lamb.** John used images from many traditions and integrated them into a new magnificent picture. Parallels to his report (which should not be confused with sources) reflect the complex social setting in which oriental astral mythology and Hellenistic and Greco-Roman traditions were operative alongside Old Testament and apocalyptic traditions. David Aune detected some influence of the ceremonial of the imperial court on John's description of the throne room. The acclamations and hymns, the acts of prostration, the surrender of crowns, the claim to represent cosmic order, and the cosmic symbolism of numbers were as much a part of the imperial ceremonial as were the officials surrounding the emperor who saw to it that appropriate honors and accolades were offered to him. By using some features of the imperial court ceremonial, John was able to reveal that the pomp and circumstance surrounding the emperor and his worship are but a demonic parody of worship in heaven.

The Throne (4:1-11). **1-4**—John connected the throne room vision (4:1-11) with the "inaugural" audition (1:9-11) through the **voice** of the revealer angel which sounded **like a trumpet** (1:10; 4:1). **And lo, in heaven an open door!** We have already heard that Jesus stands at the *door* seeking entrance and that he holds "the key of David" and opens the door to the new Jerusalem (3:7,

12). Thus the images of the throne and the door link this vision to the message septet. Now John is permitted to look through an "open door" into heaven (cf. Acts 7:56) so that he can write to his people about the future. The angel promises to show him **what must take place after this.** This promise refers back to 1:1 because his new visions will be mediated by an angel. And the promise refers back to John's commission (1:19) to "write . . . what is to take place hereafter." **After this** (4:2) does not imply that the remainder of the book will deal *only* with the future (12:1-6 refers to the past). **After this** points to further visions and auditions after the commission to write the seven messages has been completed. But more, what *must* take place **after this** is the future judgment and the future salvation promised in the seven messages and envisioned in chaps. 6–22. Revelation 1:19 as well as 4:1 is dependent on Dan. 2:28, 45. Revelation 1:19 introduces the seven messages; 4:1 introduces Part II, which will focus specifically on the future manifestation of God, who is to come (1:8; cf. 21:5-8), and of Christ, who is to come (1:7; cf. 19:11-16; 20:4-6). In so doing, John extended the realized eschatology which he shares with his audience (cf. 1:5-6) into the future, for it is out of the future that God and Christ will come in judgment and salvation.

A heavenly voice bids John to **come up hither,** to heaven. **In the Spirit,** that is, in a state of ecstasy, John was translated into heaven. Strange as this may sound to us, such heavenly journeys were part of the apocalyptic tradition that was at John's disposal (cf. 17:3; 21:10; 2 Cor. 12:2; *1 Enoch* 70:1—71:3; 81:5). Generally an apocalyptic seer would receive insight into God's secret plans for the future. Yet what John sees and what he discloses in this book is not an apocalyptic schedule of events, but **lo, a throne stood in heaven, with one seated on the throne!** He is the Alpha and the Omega, the One who is and who was and who is to come (1:8). In distinction from the detailed description of Christ in the inaugural vision, there is no parallel description of God here. The awe-inspiring sight is the **throne,** symbol of God's majesty and omnipotence. While John's narration of his vision made use of

Ezek. 1:26-28, unlike Ezekiel he did not draw God's contours in terms of "a likeness, as it were, of a human form." Only the impression of brilliant awe-inspiring splendor is conveyed. Heaven is not pictured as a temple or a synagogue but as the throne room of a great king. Dazzling light of brilliant colors radiates from him, translucent **like jasper and** glowing red like **carnelian, and round the throne was a rainbow** with the soft green colors **that looked like an emerald.** God dwells in light unapproachable to humans (1 Tim. 6:16). But, surprise! God remains silent throughout the vision. No friendly consolation is uttered, such as: The future won't be as bad as you think; every cloud has a silver lining and the sun shines again after a hurricane. No inane comments, only total majestic silence.

In concentric circles around the throne, John saw a brilliant rainbow and around it a circle of **twenty-four thrones, and seated on the thrones were twenty-four elders.** Are they the twelve patriarchs and the twelve apostles whose names are found on the gates and the foundation of the new Jerusalem (21:12-14)? Perhaps. But these **elders** are not human beings who have been exalted to heaven. John clearly distinguished between the elders seated on the thrones and the believers who stand before the throne (7:9, 13-14). Hence it would appear that the elders are angelic beings (cf. Isa. 24:23; 1 Kings 22:19; Ps. 89:8; *1 Enoch* 39–40; *2 Enoch* 20:22). They may be the heavenly angelic counterparts of patriarchs and apostles, representing the true people of God. As such, they would be quite different from the seven angels of the seven churches who were subject to censure. The 24 angelic representatives of faithful Israel and of the victorious church are part of the heavenly council that surrounds the throne of God. Their **white garments** symbolize their holiness, even as white garments symbolize "the righteous deeds of the saints" (19:8). Their **thrones** and **golden crowns** indicate their *royal* functions. In 5:8 we hear of their *priestly* task of bringing "the prayers of the saints" before the throne. Moreover, they glorify God and the Lamb in heavenly worship (4:11; 5:9-10, 14). Finally, they also interpret some visions to John (5:5; 7:13-14).

5-8—The space between God's throne and the elders is filled with **flashes of lightning, and voices and peals of thunder** issuing from the throne. These are traditional signs of theophanies, of appearances of God in the Old Testament (cf. Exod. 19:16-18; Ezek. 1:13). These manifestations emanate from the throne at the end of each judgment cycle in which God's glory made its appearance (8:5; 11:19; 16:18). **Before the throne burn seven torches of fire, which are the seven spirits of God** (1:4). This symbol of the Holy Spirit in his sevenfold activity can also be found in Christ's possession (3:1), or be depicted as the "eyes" of the Lamb (5:6). Here the **torches of fire** should probably be envisioned as seven burning stars. (For fire as metaphor of the Spirit, see Matt. 3:11; Acts 2:3.) Farther out in front of the throne and the torches there is a **sea of glass, like crystal** (cf. 15:2; 22:1). An old idea of water above the firmament (Gen. 1:7) is used in a new way. Unlike *2 Enoch* 3:3, John does not say that there is a great lake in heaven. What is in front of the throne looked to him **as it were** like a sea of glass, like crystal, symbolizing the transcendent purity of God's realm which constitutes a threat to all that is impure. Hence in 15:2-4 we hear that the sea of glass is "mingled with fire," a symbol of threat and judgment.

On each side of the throne are four living creatures, the symbols of creation, as it ought to be. They are God's pets within the heavenly court. Just as the number twelve symbolizes the people of God, so the number four is a cosmic number (e.g., the four corners of the earth, 7:1), and here it is a symbol of the new creation. Again John modified a traditional image. Ezekiel's cherubim are "four living creatures," who carry the throne-chariot of God. Each of then has multiple faces—of a man, a lion, an ox, and an eagle. For John, each of the living creatures has its own distinct features (lion, ox, man, and eagle). Creatures with human and animal faces surround the throne in harmony, attentive and ready to serve. For creation is God's pet project and hence these four creatures are nearest to his throne. They do not carry the throne, as in Ezekiel, but they encircle it. John's vision also omitted the "wheels" of Ezekiel's throne, the rims of which, we are told, were "full of eyes round about" (Ezek. 1:18). This distinctive trait is transferred to the four creatures themselves who now are **full of eyes in front and behind.** If we tried to picture them, they would look rather bizarre. John's images are meant to be heard rather than imagined as pictures. John mentioned their eyes twice, "in front and behind" (v. 6) and, with a slight variation, **all round and within** (v. 8). The hearer would understand that nothing is hidden from these all-seeing omniscient creatures, whose attention is focused on God, their Master. Moreover, John endowed each of these four creatures with the **six wings** of Isaiah's seraphim (Isa. 6:2), to be ready for service at once. Like the seraphim, the living creatures lead the liturgy in heaven and that distinguishes them most from Ezekiel's cherubim. Since the time of Irenaeus these four creatures have come to symbolize the four Gospels (Matthew, the man; Mark, the lion; Luke, the ox; and John, the eagle; *Adv. Haer.* 3.11.8), but that was not John's meaning.

Readers of this commentary should not be upset that I speak of God's pets. They should remember their own faithful dogs and cats whose joy it is to live in their presence, to please them and adore them. Worship ought to be just that—not a dreary hour on Sunday morning with a boring sermon, not another responsibility to be fulfilled. But worship should and *shall be* as natural as exhaling and inhaling, comprising the sum total of our work, time, and existence—the adoration of God, whose presence is life, joy, and peace. God's pets in John's vision are the symbol of harmony and worship yet to come, when God shall dwell among his people (21:1—22:5).

And day and night they never cease to sing, "Holy, holy, holy, is the Lord God Almighty, who was and is and is to come!" (cf. Isa. 6:3). The four living creatures not only demonstrate the future harmony of animals and humans, they also serve as leaders in the liturgy and the obeisance of the heavenly court. God's pets fulfill the highest task of creation, worship. Their thrice holy acclamation, called the trisagion, is the high point of the first part of the throne vision. The three times most Holy One is set apart as the Wholly Other from everyone else in heaven and on earth, in the present and the future. In Isaiah's trisagion the seraphim proclaim: "The whole earth is full of his [God's] glory" (Isa. 6:3). Not so in John's Apocalypse where the earth is full of abominations. God is the **Almighty** One, the Pantocrator, John's favorite title. He is the sovereign Lord of past, present, and future, the One who **is to come.** The Lord of history is one who not only exists in the beginning (Gen. 1:1) but whose glorious all-transforming presence shall be revealed in the end in harmonious new paradisiacal creation (21:1—22:5). His coming in judgment and salvation is the theme of the rest of John's book.

9-11—The focus of the throne vision shifts to the future, from the unceasing praise and worship day and night to one particular future event. Unfortunately, the RSV misses the point by failing to translate the verbs with future tense. The Greek conjunction *(hotan)*, with future tense, does not denote a continuous process in the present. The 24 elders do not perpetually cast down their crowns before the throne, but they *shall* surrender them when God has come to establish his power on earth. When the events of 6:1—22:5 happen, then the eschatological praise and **thanks** (Greek, *eucharistia;* cf. 11:17-18) shall be offered by the four creatures and the eschatological homage and worship by the elders will take place, and they shall lay down their **crowns before the throne** of the Almighty King, prostrating themselves before him. The surrender of their crowns not only illustrates that their rule is subordinate to and derived from God, as is every other legitimate rule and authority, but also indicates that in the end there will be no need for subordinate authorities of angelic or earthly princes; for God will be all in all (cf. 1 Cor. 15:28), and all earthly servants shall be a democracy of kings and priests unto God. Rome's imperial ceremonial which requires rulers to surrender their crowns before Caesar is but a sham parody of heaven (cf. Tacitus, *Annals* 15.29).

The acclamation **Worthy art thou** was not derived from the biblical tradition. It probably was shouted by the populace of the provinces at the triumphal entry of emperors or their representatives into cities. The acclamation "Worthy art thou" expresses a value judgment that includes the consensus of the governed subjects regarding the moral excellence of their ruler. The ideal king should reign and sit in judgment not just by right of legitimate succession but by his superior virtue. God's moral excellence finds an echo in the consensus of his entourage in heaven who acclaim him with, "Worthy art thou." The 24 angelic rulers pay homage to him who alone is **Lord and God** in opposition to the pretensions of Roman emperors who assumed divine status in the eastern part of the empire and appropriated unto themselves titles and powers that belong to God. He shall come in judgment and salvation, and he alone is worthy **to receive glory and honor and power.** His eschatological deeds are grounded in his work as creator; **for thou didst create all things,** and whatever exists owes its being to his **will.** This acclamation of the future reign of God forms a transition to the second part of the double vision which initiates the apocalyptic events at the end time.

Two concluding comments: one, this introductory vision deals with worship, rather than with consolation, because worship will be the issue John's churches will have to face in the future (Revelation 12–13); two, the liturgy of John's churches in Asia is not projected into heaven, as some interpreters have thought. The hymns and acclamations in this book are creations by John, appropriate for their literary context. Yet their literary function is to connect the worship of the churches on earth with the liturgy in heaven. It is the same God who is worshiped on earth as well as in heaven, and many individual words and phrases, like the trisagion, the Amen and Hallelujah, are the same on earth as in heaven.

The Scroll and the Lamb (5:1-14). The second part of the double vision brings new movement into the picture of the heavenly worship by introducing the decisive event, the transfer of the scroll to the Lamb. The vision of the **scroll** in God's **right hand** is interrupted by John's weeping (v. 4) and the reply of one of the elders (v. 5). Verses 6 and 7 describe the acceptance of the scroll by the Lamb. Verses 8-14 bring antiphonal acclamations of the Lamb by the heavenly court, followed by the doxology of all of creation concluded with the Amen of the four creatures and the worship of the elders. While chap. 4 was influenced primarily by Ezekiel 1, this chapter is dependent on Dan. 7:10-18, 27; 12:4, 9.

Some interpreters thought that John made use of an oriental enthronement ritual, in which a person is adopted (by a god), enthroned, and acclaimed by the court and the people. If John had such a ritual in mind, he changed it drastically. The exaltation and enthronement of Christ are presupposed not only here but already in chaps. 1–3 (cf. 3:21). There is no real enthronement, except that Christ takes the scroll from God (v. 7). John did not even narrate that the Lamb, after taking the scroll, sat down on his throne. The emphasis in this vision does not lie on the Lamb's enthronement but on his authority to open the scroll and initiate the end-time events. Yet the acclamation and the homage of the heavenly court (vv. 8-14) disclose that a new stage in the eschatological drama has been reached, a drama that began with Christ's death and resurrection. In short, John modified individual features of the enthronement ritual.

1-5—Behind these verses lies a traditional pattern in which a search is made to find someone who is able to perform a most difficult task. In the pattern, the perplexity of the gathered people is resolved when an able person, or a god, is discovered who can do the job. Traces of this pattern are found in the question; "Whom shall I send, and who will go for us?" (Isa. 6:89). John modified this pattern. It is not Christ himself who answers, "I will open the scroll," but the elder reveals it to John in order to console him.

The image of a sealed **scroll** is also a traditional symbol. Apocalyptic literature knows of heavenly books or tablets (*1 Enoch* 81:1-2; 93:1-14; 106:19—107:1) and of sealed books (Dan. 8:26; 12:4, 9). But again, John modified the tradition. Instead of bringing a disclosure scene in which an apocalyptic timetable that stretches from the remote past to the final end is read, John tells us that the Lamb takes the scroll and his authority to enact the end-time events is acknowledged by the heavenly court. What follows in the rest of the book is not the revelation of heavenly secrets, but in ever new visions and auditions the Lamb enacts the end-time events. Not even after the opening of the seventh seal (8:1) does Christ sit down and read from the scroll. This means that John deliberately broke with the tradition that had endeavored to "predict" consecutive events from the remote past to the ultimate future. For him, this type of apocalypticism is irrelevant. What is relevant to faith is God and the Lamb forever! The content of the scroll is put into effect in three cycles (seals, trumpets, and bowls) which are not consecutive along a time line. They are three parallel accounts, like three one-act plays, with new emphases, intensities, and perspectives. They make one point, that it is God and the Lamb who execute judgment and bring about salvation. Judgment is necessary because of Satan on one hand and idolatry on the other. Salvation is the rectification of all that is wrong. God shall establish his rightful claim upon the world by vindicating his people and destroying idolatry, death, and the devil.

1-3—John **saw in the right hand** of God **a scroll written within and on the back, sealed with seven seals.** The phrase "written within and on the back" (Greek, *esōthen kai opisthen*) has elicited quite a few interpretations. Some copyists changed this to written "on the front and on the back" in agreement with Ezek. 2:10. Another variant reading is: written "within and on the outside." In the latter case John would have envisioned a doubly written document (Latin, *diploma*), which had a summary of its contents written on the outside. Such documents were used for marriage contracts, purchases, loans, and similar social contracts. However, this kind of doubly written document was not used for testaments, which were supposed to be secret and therefore sealed with seven seals by seven witnesses.

It would seem that John's scroll was not a sealed, doubly written deed, but an opisthograph, that is, a papyrus scroll with writing on both sides. Generally one would write only on the side where the papyrus fibers run horizontally (called recto). It was more difficult to write on the **back** side of a papyrus leaf (verso), because its fibers run vertically. That this scroll had writing on both sides may point to the completeness of God's plan or to his acts of judgment which are the reverse side of his acts of salvation. Moreover, this scroll combines features of Ezekiel's unsealed scroll (Ezek. 2:9-10) with Daniel's sealed scroll (Dan. 12:4) and perhaps also with Isa. 29:11. But the type of scroll envisioned is unimportant. The Greek word *biblion* (and *biblos*) can refer to a scroll, a letter, a book in codex form, or other documents with different shapes. What is important are three things. First, the scroll is never read. Second, it is sealed. The **seals** may be meant to keep the contents of the scroll secret or to protect the contents from illegal appropriation and fraud. Third, whoever breaks the seals brings about the enactment of the scroll's content.

The number **seven** indicates completion, and a heavenly scroll with seven seals would suggest that it contains all of God's plan for the end, an end which, according to John, begins with Christ's death and resurrection. Since God never speaks directly in Revelation (except at its beginning, 1:8, and at its end, 21:5-8), an **angel** asks the heavenly assembly, **"Who is worthy to open the scroll and break its seals?"** Will someone from among the angels or archangels, or the four pets, volunteer for this job? If anyone did, John does not tell us, except that **no one in heaven or on earth or under the earth was able to open the scroll or to look into it.** No one was fit, "worthy," to execute the end-time events. Again we note that John modified the apocalyptic tradition. Secret revelations gained from heavenly books are irrelevant for him. Not Ezra or Baruch, not Enoch or Daniel, none of them have opened, or can open, the scroll in God's right hand. None of the prior apocalypses have unlocked the purposes of God.

4—The vision is interrupted by John's weeping. **I wept much** indicates a problem for John and for the church on earth. For if no one is found to open the seals and enact the end-time events, then indeed the church's situation on earth is hopeless. Chicanery, deprivation, and death will continue without end, ad infinitum. The weeping prophet has a parallel in the cry of the martyrs, "How long before thou wilt judge?" (6:10). The church on earth should look forward to the establishment of God's justice on earth. It is indeed reason for weeping if there were no one to initiate the end-time drama, if the ambiguity of history were all that is left forever. If that were to be the case, then indeed Christian believers "are of all human beings most to be pitied" (1 Cor. 15:19). Then the call for perseverance, heard in the message septet, would be quite beside the point.

5—One of the elders, functioning as an interpreting angel (cf. Luke 24:4-7; Acts 1:10-11), consoled the prophet by pointing to him who is worthy to open the scroll. **Lo, the Lion of the tribe of Judah, the Root of David, has conquered.** He can open the scroll because he fulfills the messianic expectation of the Old Testament (Gen. 49:9-10; 4QPatrBl; *Test. Judah* 24:5). In 1 Macc. 3:4 we read that Judas Maccabeus "was like a lion in his deeds, like a lion's cub roaring for prey." The Messiah, pictured as a lion, destroys the enemies of God and of his people. In 4 Ezra the Messiah appears as a roaring lion who devastates the eagle, which represents the Roman empire, "so that the whole earth, freed from your [Rome's] violence, may be refreshed and relieved" (4 Ezra 11:1—12:35; 11:46). The **root of David** alludes to Isa. 11:1, 10, where we hear of "a shoot from the stump of Jesse [David's father], and a branch" that will "grow out of his roots." A glorious Messiah, descendant of David, shall restore David's kingdom. "The Spirit of the Lord shall rest upon him. . . . With righteousness he shall judge the poor. . . . He shall smite the earth with the rod of his mouth, and with the breath of his lips he shall slay the wicked" (Isa. 11:2, 4).

6-7—The elder had spoken to John of a Lion, but what John actually **saw** was **a Lamb standing, as though it had been slain.** Its appearance in this vision is sudden and unexpected. It does not even sit on a throne, like the elders (4:4), but stands **between**

the throne and the four living creatures, next to God, and yet it also stands, or walks, "among the elders." The Lamb shows the cut of the knife on his throat **as though** it had been slain. This conjunction "as though" is due to the context of the vision. Later it is omitted (5:12; 13:8). The reference to his death discloses how Christ has **conquered** (v. 5). "Like a lamb that is led to the slaughter" (Isa. 53:7), Christ bears forever the mark of his suffering, dying obedience on the cross. And as such, he is the victorious One, the Lion, because he persevered unto death. He, the victim, is the conqueror. His victory through death radically alters, reinterprets, and modifies all messianic hopes of the Old Testament and of Judaism concerning a nationalistic conquering Messiah. Simultaneously the slain Lamb fulfills all hopes. The apocalyptic tradition used different animals as symbols for its warrior king. In *1 Enoch* 90:37, for instance, he is imaged as a "white bull" with large horns. In *1 Enoch* 90:9 the Maccabees appear as a sheep with one great horn battling ravens, vultures, and eagles (cf. *1 Enoch* 89:45-48; *Test. Jos.* 19:8-9), but nowhere does the Messiah appear as a defenseless, slain lamb.

This slain Lamb has complete power, for it has **seven horns.** The **horn** is a traditional image for power in war or peace (cf. Num. 23:22; Deut. 33:17), and **seven** signifies completion, perfection. He is the risen one whose omnipotence, symbolized by seven horns, lies in his death, his self-sacrifice. Moreover, it has **seven eyes, which are the seven spirits of God** (cf. Zech. 4:10). The Lamb is omniscient. It is empowered to **send out** the Holy Spirit so that believers can hear "what the Spirit says to the churches" (1:4; 4:5; 2:7, 11, 17; etc.). Of course, this picture of the Lamb is not a realistic one, but it presents Christ's victory, omnipotence, and omniscience as the powerless One who was slain. His power lies in his self-sacrifice, which is in total contrast to the beasts of chap. 13. There the second beast looks "like a lamb" but speaks "like a dragon" (13:11).

The Lamb represents in his person the solution to the two fundamental problems of human existence—the problem of sin in the form of idolatry and the problem of power. By his sacrificial death, he brought about God's solution to both. God looks upon his death as a proper sacrifice that removes sin. His death not only redeems as a sacrifice but it conquers. It is his victory. The slain Lamb is the Lion of Judah, and God has granted to him the execution of judgment over all who misuse power and revel in sin, idolatry, and other vices. Just as the blood of the Passover lambs saved Israel from death at the exodus (Exod. 12:13), so Jesus' death accomplished redemption for God's eschatological people. Hence, he is **the Lamb,** a title found 28 times in Revelation.

The slain but victorious Lamb went to the throne and **took the scroll.** The Greek verb can also mean "received." Its perfect tense indicates the present state of possessing the scroll. He took, or received, the scroll, the symbol of lordship over time and space, and he retains it irrevocably. John avoided portraying this as an enthronement because, since the resurrection, Jesus was for him the enthroned One (cf. 12:5). Instead, he pictured here what he meant in his preface (1:1): God "**gave**" Christ the revelation. It means Christ received, or took, the scroll from his right hand. By taking the scroll he received a new function, namely, to execute God's end-time plan of judgment and salvation. This end-time plan does not consist of an apocalyptic timetable. It will reveal who God is and who Christ is and what the powerful potentates who ravage the world are all about.

8-14—The response to the Lamb taking the scroll begins with antiphonal acclamations in heaven and expands into a doxology that includes all of creation and concludes with the "Amen" of the four creatures and the worship of the elders. This liturgy anticipates the renewal of creation and celebrates the Lamb who has begun his reign as executor of the end time. The four creatures and the 24 elders render him the same adoration as they do to God. They can do so, because he is God's plenipotentiary and, as such, one with God in terms of attributes and purpose. **With golden bowls full of incense** they bring the **prayers of the saints,** the faithful church, before the Lamb. These prayers relate to

John's weeping (v. 4), to the cries of the martyrs in 6:10, to the liturgical action of the angel in 8:3-5, and to the prayer that Jesus taught his church: "Your kingdom come, your will be done on earth, as in heaven." And the **new song** which the four creatures and the elders sing corresponds to the consolation which John received (v. 5). A **new** song is needed because a new deed has been done (cf. Ps. 33:3; Isa. 42:10; Rev. 14:3; 15:3-4). The Lamb has taken the sealed scroll and with it the authorization to realize God's will for the end time. Though the world may remain blind and ignorant in idolatry, the church already knows through John that a new song has sounded forth in heaven.

Worthy art thou to take the scroll and to open its seals. The angel's question of v. 2 has also been answered. The Lamb who is **worthy** has the power to put into effect the decrees of the scroll. The destiny of all lies in his hands. The reason why he has such power is **for thou wast slain,** "led to the slaughter" like Isaiah's suffering servant, sacrificed, like a powerless Passover lamb. But God saw to it that **by thy blood didst ransom,** liberate, women and men, old and young, **for God.** To "ransom" means to purchase something or someone, such as a slave, for freedom. His death accomplished a new deliverance of people from the slavery of idolatry (cf. Rom. 3:25; 1 Cor. 5:7; 6:20; 7:23; Gal. 3:13; 4:4-5; 1 Peter 1:18; Mark 10:45). As the exodus resulted in Israel's nationhood, so Christ's ransom resulted in a new people of God **from every tribe and tongue and people and nation.** Moreover, the ransomed became **a kingdom and priests to our God** (cf. 1:6). Christ **made,** that is, he created a kingdom of priestly people in which the promise of Exod. 19:5-6 is fulfilled. Moses had told the Israelites to "wash their garments" in anticipation of God's epiphany (Exod. 19:10), and thus the new priestly people of God have "washed their robes and made them white in the blood of the Lamb" (7:14; cf. Exod. 29:21). The church is the realm in which God's kingship, his rule, finds realization on earth, among those who persevere in faith and love. As **priests** they have access to God and the Lamb and their petitions and intercessions are brought before his throne (v. 8). **They shall reign on earth** in the future (3:21; 20:4-6; 22:5), but they have already been appointed for this task (1:6).

However, quite a few Greek manuscripts have the present tense: "they reign on earth" already. This reading should probably be preferred, because the new song speaks of Christ's present authority (to open the seals) and his past accomplishment (he ransomed a new people). The ransomed are a kingdom (1:6; 5:10a); they share in his reign under tribulation, through faithful witness, and in patient endurance (1:9). To be sure, their kingship and priesthood shall be made manifest in their future reign with Christ (20:4-6), but they have already been installed in it. In short, the present tense, "they reign," also includes the future. Thus the **new song** spans the time from Calvary to the consummation. The one who through his death in powerlessness brought about deliverance from sin and the gathering of God's universal eschatological people is the agent who will inaugurate and carry out God's purpose for the end time.

The response to the new song is the antiphon sung by an ever-increasing multitude of angels **numbering myriads of myriads** (the Greek *myriades* is 10,000; cf. Dan. 7:10). Their response begins with **Worthy is the Lamb who was slain,** and it continues by assigning to him all the attributes offered to God in the celestial worship of 7:12: **power and wealth and wisdom and might and honor and glory and blessing** are his. The first four attributes express the Lamb's sovereignty as the supreme agent of God. The last three reflect the proper recognition and respect of the Lamb by the angelic court. Acclamations beginning with "Worthy art thou" were probably rendered to Caesar by the populace as he entered a city.

The doxology expands still more as the whole creation joins in giving honor and glory to the Lamb. Up to this point, God's sovereignty had been acknowledged only in heaven. Now **every creature in heaven and on earth and under the earth and in the sea** joins the eschatological chorus of the end. It is the doxology of the renewed creation in which God's will is done on earth as it is in heaven. When his kingdom has come with the finality of the resurrection of the dead, then no segment of creation is excluded from this praise: **to him who sits upon the throne and to the Lamb be blessing and honor and glory and might for ever and ever!** (cf. Phil. 2:9-11). This doxology is a fitting counterpart to the awkward silence of v. 3. The universal homage discloses the future revelation of the sovereignty and the unity of God and Christ. Creation and redemption come together in the end. A cosmic Christology is articulated which is not based on Christ's preexistence and mediation in creation but which grows out of his redeeming work in the past, determines the present status of the church, and encompasses his apocalyptic work of the future. The homage of creation of v. 13 is itself the anticipation of the praise of the world to come (21:22—22:5). It is *not* an evaluation of the world's *present state.* But "in the Spirit" (4:2) John sees and hears in heaven that cosmic praise which on earth is yet to come. The final **Amen,** which means "So be it, this is certainly true," is fittingly given by the four living creatures who had started the worship in chap. 4. The worship by the **elders** takes us back to 4:10. John's churches hear not only that the agent for God's end-time events is already in power, but they also hear the joy and praise of angels, yes, even of the whole creation, in anticipation of the world to come.

The importance of the double vision for the second part of John's letter cannot be overestimated. On one hand it is a prelude, an introduction, but on the other hand it is more than that. It is the focal vision from which everything else flows. It is also the theological center which expresses John's basic convictions: (1) God is the radiant transcendent One on whom all things in heaven and on earth are dependent because he is the creator (4:11), pulsating with brilliance, light, life and glory, infinite calm and absolute power. The three times holy God controls history and will lead it to its triumphant goal when he shall *come* (4:8). (2) The decisive victory has been won already. The Lamb, slain yet exalted, has taken the sealed scroll. His future triumph is not just a matter of hope and expectation, but it is realized already in heaven (5:9-12). This conviction constitutes the common ground on which John and his churches stand (5:9-10; cf. 1:5-6). Simultaneously a realized eschatology without a future dimension would be an occasion for weeping. Without future action by God and the Lamb, in judgment and salvation, the realized eschatology would turn out to be a pious illusion. (3) Worship is the response to God's glory and his future coming and to the Lamb's accomplishment, past, present, and future. Worship in heaven and on earth has a center, God and the Lamb; it is inclusive, rendered by women and men from every tribe, tongue, and nation; it unites the churches on earth with the heavenly liturgy, and thus it is a foretaste of the things to come.

The First Six Seals (6:1-17)

One would have expected that the opening of the seals would lead to a disclosure of the scroll's secret content. But the content is never disclosed, and for good reasons! The scroll is the document that transfers to the Lamb the authority to execute God's end-time plan. The opening of the seals pictures how the Lamb initiates and carries out the end-time events manifesting his sovereignty. War, bloodshed, famine, plagues, and cosmic upheavals are under his control. It is he who leads history through innerworldly turmoils and through cosmic catastrophes to its God-intended goal.

The tribulations and cosmic convulsions caused by the opening of the seals raise the question concerning the fate of God's faithful people on earth. John gives three answers in this septet. First, the cry of the martyrs for justice receives assurance (6:9-11). Second, the question of who will survive the great day of wrath (6:17) receives its answer in the sealing of the 144,000 (7:1-8). And third, a picture of the redeemed after the day of wrath shows them clothed in the white garments of conquerors, worshiping before the throne and the Lamb with the host of heaven (7:9-17). These are the people "who have come out of the great tribulation."

The seal visions are meditations about the end-time tribulations based on the apocalyptic discourse of our Synoptic Gospels, or their underlying traditions (Mark 13: Matthew 24; Luke 21). In Revelation 6, as well as in Luke 21, we hear of wars, earthquakes, famines, pestilence, and persecution, followed by cosmic upheavals, signs in the sun, moon, and stars, resulting in the shaking of the powers of heaven and the distress of nations on earth. John omitted all references to the fall of Jerusalem, since that event lay in the past. But in agreement with the Synoptic apocalypse he alluded to the figure of Antichrist in the first seal (6:1-2), and, for obvious reasons, he moved the "great earthquake" to the end of the septet (6:12-17), even though earthquakes are mentioned prior to the famines in the Synoptic apocalypse. The cosmic catastrophes of the sixth seal make warfare impossible.

SEALS (6:1-17)	**SYNOPTIC APOCALYPSE**
1. White horse Bow, Crown, Conquest	False Christ(s): "Many will come in my name," Mark 13:6; wars, Mark 13:7
2. Red horse Sword	Nation against nation, Mark 13:8
3. Black horse Scales (famine)	Famines, Mark 13:8
4. Pale horse Death and Hades	Pestilence, Luke 21:11
5. Martyrs "How long?"	Persecution and witness, Mark 13:9-13, 20; shorten the days
6. Great earthquake	Great earthquakes, Luke 21:11 (Mark 13:8)
sun, moon, stars,	sun, moon, stars, Mark 13:24-25
like "the fig tree"	Fig tree, Mark 13:28-29
"The sky [heaven] vanished"	"The powers in the heavens will be shaken," Mark 13:25

John's apocalypticism raises problems for modern readers who are accustomed to hearing a "gospel" in which tribulations and judgments are not precursors of salvation. The God of wrath finds no place in segments of Protestantism today. The result is that we create a god in our own image and likeness. The God of John's prophetic-apocalyptic vision is the One who effects both salvation and disaster, good and evil. Through Amos he had asked, "Does evil befall a city unless the Lord has done it?" (Amos 3:6). Through Isaiah he announced, "I form light and create darkness, I make weal [that is, welfare, security] and I create woe [that is, peril and distress]." Both are his doing (Isa. 45:7). "The Lord kills and brings to life; he brings down to Sheol and raises up" (1 Sam. 2:6). Such a God who brings about death and life, evil and good, destruction and deliverance, judgment and salvation, is the One who effects everything and is active in everything. He is the "hidden God," the Deus absconditus, of Luther. And it is God who challenges us to believe that in all tribulations and in all catastrophes that may befall us he is working out his purpose which is life and salvation (cf. Rom. 8:28-39). Apart from his revelation he can be perceived only as sheer terror and moral enigma, or else he becomes the occasion for humans to create their gods in their own likeness, thus indulging in the game of ancient or modern idolatry. Contrary to our natural feelings, the disasters of the seal visions are not proof of God's absence, but paradoxically they disclose his involvement in human affairs within the "short" time before the end. If God and the Lamb are at work in all miseries that befall us, then indeed our myopic visions need stretching.

The Four Horsemen (6:1-8). The first four seals belong together because they have the same structure. The opening of a seal is followed by the command **Come,** which causes the appearance of a horse with a distinctive color. The rider is briefly characterized, and he is commissioned to perform a task (Greek, *edothē,* "he/it was given," 6:2, 4, 8; RSV, "was permitted" in 6:4).

The same commission is found in 9:1-11 (RSV, "they were allowed," 9:1,5). The horsemen execute their deeds at Christ's commission, who opens the seal. A command "Come," given by the four living creatures around the throne, ushers in their appearance. The horses of different colors seem to be an adaptation from Zech. 1:7-15; 6:1-8. There they draw four chariots symbolizing "the four winds of heaven" and report back to the Lord. In Revelation 6, the chariots have disappeared and the four riders do not patrol the earth but bring tribulations upon all "who dwell upon the earth" (3:10; 6:10; 8:13; 11:10; 13:8, 12, 14; 17:8). In John's letter the phrase "those who dwell upon the earth" signifies idolaters, opponents of God and the Lamb and of his faithful people.

It is the Lamb who opens the seals (6:1) and thereby sets in motion "the beginning of the birth pangs" of the end time (Mark 13:8). To open the seals means to put into effect the end time events through which the Lamb establishes his sovereign reign on earth. Moreover, to open the seals means to reveal that the end time consists of birth pangs, tribulations (seals one to four), persecution (seal five), and cosmic catastrophes (seal six). These birth pangs are of two kinds, representing two stages. First come innerworldly tribulations in the form of wars, bloodshed, civil strife, famine, pestilence, and death symbolized by the first four horsemen. These tribulations also lead to persecution and martyrdom (the fifth seal), which are also "signs" that the last days before the end have come. Second, the cosmic upheavals of the sixth seal are Christ's vindication of his suffering people in response to their question, Lord, how long? (6:10). The opening of the sixth seal leads up to the punishment of all who are not "sealed" (cf. 7:3). The great day of wrath "has come" (6:16-17).

1-2—The first rider, on a **white horse,** had a **bow; and a crown was given to him.** He is commissioned to exercise regal power. **And he went out conquering and to conquer.** Albrecht Dürer's famous picture of the four apocalyptic horsemen (A.D. 1498) rightly grouped the first rider together with the other three as conveyers of calamities. Dürer's interpretation contradicted the notion that the rider on the white horse symbolizes Christ (cf. 19:11).

That notion can be traced back to Irenaeus (*Adv. Haer.* 4.21.3), and it still appears occasionally even today (e.g., Bornkamm). A similar interpretation sees the victorious progress of the gospel in the first horseman (so Cullmann; cf. Mark 13:10). On the other hand, many interpreters simply identified the first rider with the Antichrist (e.g., Rissi). It would be better to speak of an allusion rather than an identification. An identification of the first rider with Antichrist would not be apparent to the hearer who listened to John's message during the worship service. Only the interpreter who reads the whole book will perceive this identification in retrospect. At any rate, since Christ opens all seven seals, he can hardly be the first rider, nor would he be subject to the command of the four heavenly pets.

John's hearers would at once understand that the horseman with the bow refers to the Parthians. The biting irony and parody of the first seal would be perceived only in retrospect. The only mounted archers within John's purview were the Parthians, Rome's archenemies who threatened the eastern frontier in Asia Minor. The Parthian cavalry had inflicted a humiliating defeat on the Roman legions at Carrhae, Mesopotamia, in 53 B.C. Then the mounted archers unfurled brilliantly colored banners of silk, imported from China, attacked with ruthlessness and skill ("the parting shot" was one of their specialties), dazzled and terrified the legionnaires, put them to flight, captured and executed the proconsul Crassus, who was a member of the triumvirate with Julius Caesar and Pompey. Less than twenty years later, in 35 B.C., Mark Antony lost more than one-third of his army of 200,000 through Parthian attacks during his retreat through Armenia. In A.D. 62 the Parthian king Vologeses I defeated the Romans again, and the Parthians continued to threaten the eastern frontier for the next two centuries. In short, the hearer would readily connect the mounted conquering archer with the victorious Parthian cavalry and their king. After they heard the second and third section (16:12-16, 19; 17:8-18; 19:19-21), they could perceive the parody.

The Parthians had also conquered Babylon, and in John's apocalypse Babylon is Rome. The portrayal of the first horseman as a Parthian conqueror on a white horse with the royal insignia of a crown and a bow allowed John's audience, after reading the whole book, to make the connection: Babylon equals Rome. The Antichrist, who represents Roman imperial totalitarianism and emperor worship (13:4, 8, 12), will also appear as a conquering Parthian and he will destroy Rome (16:12; 17:12-17). The parody is perceived only when the hearer recognizes that the

Antichrist represents both the glory of conquering Rome and a Parthian conqueror who will "devour the flesh" of "the harlot" Rome and "burn her up with fire" (17:16).

3-4—The second rider, on a **horse, bright red,** is given authority **to take peace from the earth, so that men should slay one another; and he was given a great sword.** While the first rider represents triumphant conquest, the second represents one aspect of conquest, which is war, bloodshed, and civil strife.

There is again irony. Rome was so proud of its *pax Romana* and its role as benefactor bringing **peace** to the nations. A half century after John, the rhetorician Aelius Aristides, in his panegyric *To Rome,* boasts: "No envy sets foot in the empire. You [the emperors] have set an example in being free from envy yourselves. . . . Cities shine in radiance and beauty. . . . Prior to your rule, things were all mixed up, topsy turvey. . . . But with you in charge turmoil and strife have ceased, universal order and the bright light of life and government have come." Of course, not all would agree with such extravagent praise of Rome's achievement of peace. At the other extreme there is the voice of the Celtic chieftain Galgacus, who, in Tacitus's words, bitterly denounced Roman imperialism: "[The Romans are] robbers of the world, having by their universal plunder exhausted the land, they rifle the deep. . . . To robbery, slaughter and plunder they give the lying name of empire. *They create a desert and call it peace*" (*Agricola* 30). John projected harsh experiences of past and present into the future with the opening of the second seal signaling the end of **peace** on **earth** in the turmoils of eschatological bloodshed. People slaying **one another** may also point to future civil strife. In *1 Enoch* 10:9 the Lord commands Gabriel: "Proceed against the bastards and the reprobates. . . . Send then against one another so that they may be destroyed in the fight."

5-6—The third horseman, sitting on a **black horse,** holds **a balance in his hand.** The balance suggests that food will be rationed, a famine will hit the poor the worst. Prices will be driven up. **"A quart of wheat for a denarius"** (one denarius was the daily wage of a laborer). Normally, according to Cicero, the denarius bought twelve quarts of wheat. One quart of wheat can feed one person, but what of his family? **"Three quarts of barley for a denarius,"** again an exorbitant price. **"But do not harm oil and wine!"** The meaning of this prohibition is not certain. Contrary to some interpreters, oil and wine were not luxury goods. They are singled out here probably because they had a larger profit margin than wheat or barley. Moreover, whereas wheat and barley would be scarce during famine time, wine and oil would be available, but people cannot survive on them. Asia Minor produced enough wine and oil, but the region was dependent on Egypt for imports of wheat. When a regional famine occurred around Antioch, Pisidia, in A.D. 92–93, the legate of the emperor Domitian took responsible emergency measures. He fixed a maximum price for grain and stated: "It is most unjust that hunger of one's own fellow-citizens should be the basis for profit to anyone" (Ramsay). It would seem that John projected the experience of famine on a grand scale into the future. In case of wars, the army would use up the wheat imports, thereby causing inflationary prices. When civil strife disrupted the country, imports would cease.

7-8—The fourth horseman sits on a **pale horse,** the color of a corpse. **Death** was its rider, **and Hades,** the personification of the underworld, **followed him** on foot collecting the corpses. **They were given power over a fourth of the earth, to kill with sword and with famine and with pestilence** (Greek, *thanatos;* cf. 2:23) **and by wild beasts** (alluding to Ezek. 14:21; 33:27). This fourth rider reaps the results of the previous three. There is logic in the sequence of the horsemen: Conqueror—war and bloodshed—famine—Death and Hades. Undoubtedly the churches of Asia had already experienced some previews of the tribulations represented by the four horsemen. Their appearance, however, lies in the future, from John's point of view. What he has described thus far is "the beginning of the birth pangs" of the age to come (Mark 13:8), not a timeless repetition of the evils of militarism. But more important: This time before the end, filled with inhumanities, does not demonstrate that God is dead, even though it would seen so. On the contrary, this time will be under the control of God and Christ. Through innerworldly turmoils Christ will lead the world to its destined goal. But then these tribulations also affect the church, especially in the form of persecution.

The Fifth Seal, the Cry and Consolation of the Martyrs (6:9-11). In agreement with the traditional pattern of end-time tribulations, John deals with the subject of persecution after the subjects of war, famine, and pestilence (cf. Mark 13:8, 9-13). Through its most illustrious members, the martyrs, the church under severe pressure asks the troubled question, "**Lord,** . . . **how long?**" This is, first, a question arising from faith that clings to God's promise and power, even though his power is no longer self-evident. It is, second, a question about God's own vindication. When will you vindicate your righteousness and establish your will, your rule, on earth as it is established already in heaven? In short, the question is, When will you vindicate your people who are oppressed and slaughtered by your enemies who despise you and kill us? What makes persecution so difficult to bear is not just the loss of freedom and even the loss of life but the apparent inertia of God for whose sake persecutions are endured. Nothing happens. God does not seem to care. **How long,** Lord?

Academicians and writers as D. H. Lawrence who never experienced the terror of persecution and who lack the imagination to put themselves in the place of the oppressed have labeled John's theology of judgment and the cry of the martyrs for justice as being sub-Christian and contrary to the gospel's demand for love toward enemies, persecutors, and slanderers. In answer to such views we ought to remember that, first, the Synoptic tradition which contains the injunction of love toward the enemies also contains the pronouncement of "woes" and of judgments (e.g., Luke 6:20-26, 27-36; 10:13; 11:42-44, 47-52; 17:1-2, 26-30). Second, the apocalypse does not champion vindictiveness but the vindication of the oppressed. Their vindication indeed means that God's judgment shall fall on the oppressors who spilled innocent blood. Jesus taught his disciples that they themselves should not seek revenge on their own behalf. They should not enter the vicious circle of retaliating with cruelty to cruelty experienced, but they should wait *and pray* for the establishment of God's eschatological vindication (Luke 18:1-8). It is God's will, his rule, his purposes which are at stake. If the tears of the oppressed and the blood of the martyrs are not avenged in all eternity, then not just the apocalypse but the whole New Testament and its precursor, the prophetic-apocalyptic tradition of the Old Testament, are wrong. The same Paul who wrote 1 Corinthians 13, the hymn of Christian love, admonished the Romans, "Beloved, never avenge yourselves, but leave it to the wrath of God; for it is written, 'Vengeance is mine, I will repay,' says the Lord" (Rom. 12:19). John's commitment is the same.

When he opened the fifth seal, I saw under the altar the souls of those who had been slain for the word of God and for the witness they had borne. Why are the souls of the martyrs **under the altar?** Several traditions converge at this point. One, John used an apocalyptic tradition that had its origin in Ezekiel's temple vision (Ezek. 40:1—44:3). In this tradition there is a temple in heaven (cf. Rev. 7:15; 11:19; 14:15; 15:6) which is the heavenly counterpart and prototype of the earthly temple. This heavenly temple also has altars, an altar of incense (8:3) and an altar of burnt offerings (6:9). Two, John used the Old Testament tradition that the blood is the seat of life, that is, of "the soul" (Lev. 17:11, 14). Three, John presupposed the tradition of an interim state in which "the souls of the righteous are in the hand of God" (Wis. Sol. 3:1; cf. Luke 16:22-26; Phil. 1:23; 2 Cor. 5:2-4) and not in Hades. Four, just as the blood of sacrificial animals was poured out at the base of the altar (Lev. 4:7), so the martyrs' souls, residing in their blood that was spilled, are **under** the heavenly **altar,** that is, at its base. They are near to God, but not yet vindicated in the sight of their tormentors. Their urgent plea, **How long?** asks God to intervene and to reverse the judgments of the oppressors. This plea also reflects an apocalyptic tradition. In 4 Ezra we read: "Did not the *souls* of the righteous in their chambers ask about these matters, saying, '*How long* are we to remain here? And when will come the harvest of our reward?' An archangel answered them, 'When the *number* of those like yourselves is *completed*' " (4 Ezra 4:35-36).

Then the judgment will fall on **those who dwell upon the earth.** In John's book these are the oppressors of God's people—idolaters, thieves, and murderers—who are unwilling and unable to repent (cf. 9:20-21). In the end, God will declare war on them. In the meantime the souls of the martyrs **were each given a white robe** as consolation and as pledge of their future vindication (cf. 20:4) and of their participation in the marriage feast of the Lamb (19:7-8). The white robes symbolize both the salvation accomplished by Jesus *and* the perseverance in faith accomplished by the martyrs (cf. 7:14). Moreover, the martyrs are consoled and told to wait, **to rest a little longer.** Only a short time is left for God's enemies (cf. 2:10; 12:12). In Luke 18:7-8a, we probably hear the voice of a Christian prophet who asked a question similar to Rev. 6:10. "Will not God vindicate his elect, who cry to him day and night? Will he delay long over them?" And his answer is similar to Rev. 6:11, "I tell you he will vindicate them speedily." Only **a little longer** . . . then God's just judgment will come upon them (cf. 18:20). This short time is needed to complete **the number of their fellow servants,** sisters and brothers, **who were to be killed as they themselves had been.**

Since John mentioned only one martyr in Asia by name, Antipas (2:13), he probably also included in 6:9 the Christians of Rome who, under Nero, were condemned to death in A.D. 64 for a disastrous fire that destroyed almost one-fourth of the city. "Covered with skins of beasts, they were torn by dogs and perished or were nailed to crosses or were doomed to the flames and burned to serve as nightly illumination" in Nero's gardens (Tacitus, *Annals* 15.44). In A.D. 62, James the brother of Jesus was stoned to death in Jerusalem at the instigation of the high priest (Josephus, *Ant.* 20.9,1). Paul and Pater were executed in Rome in the 60s. Thus within five years the church lost its three great leaders through martyrdom. Though the fifth seal, like the prior ones, reflects the church's experience, it clearly envisions *future* martyrdoms (cf. 3:10). Rome will be "drunk with the blood of the saints" (17:6).

The Sixth Seal (6:12-17). The sixth seal brings us to **the great day** of **wrath** (v. 17), the day of judgment. In contrast to the tribulations and persecutions of the first five seals, these cosmic, cataclysmic upheavals, initiated by the opening of the sixth seal, are wholly future. These catastrophes signal the end of history and the end of the world. Moreover, and quite surprisingly, they answer the plea of the martyrs for justice and judgment of God's enemies. With their world disintegrating, the earth dwellers and murderers of the saints would like to hide "from the face" of God and "from the wrath of the Lamb." This cosmic judgment scene uses hyperbolic rather than descriptive language and leads up to the parousia of Christ. John, however, postponed the vision of the parousia until 19:11-21, and between chaps. 6 and 19 he brought several cycles of judgment visions, interspersed with previews of the salvation to come.

The stars of the sky which hang like lamps on the firmament **fell to the earth.** The firmament itself, **the sky vanished like a scroll that is rolled up** (cf. Isa. 34:4). When the sky is rolled up, then the throne of the Almighty appears and his judgment occurs (cf. 20:11-15). **Every mountain and island was removed** as the foundations of the earth are shaken. The reaction of humanity is sheer terror and the futile attempt to hide from the eyes of **him who is seated on the throne, and from the wrath of the Lamb** (cf. Isa. 2:10, 19, 21). Jesus, like God, is both savior and judge and therefore John can refer to it as **their wrath** (6:17), which terrifies sinful people. The representatives of all societal strata encounter their judge in the same way. The present distinctions between **king** and **slave, rich** and **poor** will be meaningless. All wish to escape and no one can. They would prefer **the mountains** to fall on them rather than to meet their maker (cf. Hos. 10:8; Luke 23:29-30). Then, on the **great day** of judgment, the idolaters and murderers, the earth dwellers, will realize their sin and guilt. Their question, **"Who can stand before it?"** who can survive the day of judgment, has but one answer: None of them (cf. Joel 2:11; Nah. 1:6; Mal. 3:2).

Interlude: The Preservation of the Faithful (7:1-17)

This chapter is an intercalation sandwiched between the opening of the sixth and the seventh seal. It can also be viewed as a digression from the theme of the seals. We have already heard what God had told the church's martyrs prior to the day of wrath (6:11). The opening of the sixth seal brought a preview of the final judgment which will fulfill the promise given to the martyrs. But it also raised the anxious question, "Who can stand before" the judgment throne and survive "the great day of their wrath" (6:17)? The interlude gives an answer in two visions. The first shows the church on earth *before the last day.* It is being sealed. Note the pun on the word "seal." While the fate of the earth dwellers is sealed, so to speak, by the opening of the sixth seal, the fate of the saints is sealed for salvation "with the seal of the living God." The second vision shows the church at worship before the throne *after the last day.* By using interludes, John focused the hearer's attention on the church's situation within and after the cosmic apocalyptic drama, thereby stimulating his audience to identify with his alternative vision.

The Christians, who will be despised, oppressed, and even martyred before the end, shall be protected from the plagues to come (9:4) and from the wrath of God and the Lamb at the end. They will be gathered around the throne of God in worship with joyful thanksgiving (7:10). The gates of Hades shall not prevail against the church of God, redeemed with the blood of the Lamb (7:14). The church's tribulations and martyrdoms yet to come do not herald the church's end. The church has a future, but the world's future will be judgment and destruction.

The Sealing of the 144,000 (7:1-8)

It would seem that John made use of an earlier Jewish prophetic tradition in which the end signals the gathering of the twelve tribes of Israel (cf. Ezekiel 47–48). Indeed, the description of the church in vv. 4-8 is most unusual, especially since 10 of the 12 tribes had ceased to exist. Moreover, the picture of the church in this first vision is strikingly different from that in the second (vv. 9-17). Finally, the reference to the destructive **winds,** which does not reappear in the rest of John's letter, also points to the use of tradition. Thus we concur that John adopted and adapted a Jewish tradition in vv. 1-8 (so Bousset and Charles).

1-3—After this I saw expresses the sequence of John's visions. It does not disclose a chronological sequence of apocalyptic events. The past tenses of verbs indicate his narration of prior visions. He **saw** the visions before he wrote about them in his letter. The **earth** and **any tree** are as yet untouched by the cataclysmic upheavals of the sixth seal. We are taken back to the dawn of the day of wrath when the cosmic catastrophes have not yet been unleashed through the opening of the sixth seal, when **four angels standing at the four corners of the earth** are **holding back the four winds** that will wreak havoc on the earth (cf. Hos. 13:15; Dan. 7:2; *1 Enoch* 76:4). A great stillness prevails. No ripple on the **sea** and no stirring of the leaves of **any tree**! The apocalyptic terrors are being restrained until an ordinance of God is completed (cf. *1 Enoch* 66; *2 Bar.* 6:4-5). From **the rising of the sun,** that is, from the east (cf. Ezek. 43:2; *Sib. Or.* 3:652) **another angel** will **ascend** to fulfill a special command of God. Carrying **the seal of the living God,** he will command the four angels, **Do not harm the earth or the sea or the trees, till we have sealed the servants of our God upon their foreheads.** What is meant by this? Sealing is a mark of property, of protection, and of authentication. Ancient kings, for instance, placed a seal of authentication on documents with their signet rings. In 14:1, we hear that the mark is the name of the Lamb and his Father. The followers of the beast likewise bear a mark, the name or number of the beast (13:16-17; 16:2; 19:20).

In the vision of Ezek. 9:4-6, God commanded an angel to "put a mark upon the foreheads" of those Jerusalemites who lament over Jerusalem's abominations. The people who are thus marked will be spared in the judgment of the city. The mark in Ezekiel is the last letter of the Hebrew alphabet, *tau*, which in archaic writing appeared as + or X. To Greek Christians this sign would suggest the first letter of the name of Christ (the letter *chi*) or his cross. The seal would be a sign of God's property, of his protection and authentication. But from what would the seal protect? In the tradition that John used, it would protect from the four destructive winds. In John's composition the seal protects from the wrath of God and the Lamb (6:16-17), and it protects from the plagues aimed at the idolatrous earth dwellers. Just as the plagues in Egypt were directed not against the Israelites but against their oppressors, so likewise the trumpet and bowl plagues in this letter fall upon those who refuse to worship God (9:4, 20; cf. Exod. 8:20-22; 9:1-7, 26; 10:3, 23; etc.). However, the sealing of God's servants does *not* symbolize protection from physical danger or death (cf. the fifth seal, 6:9-11), even though it may symbolize divine protection in spite of and *within* persecution and death. Does this sealing refer to baptism? Not directly, for two reasons: One, the sealing as an eschatological mark of protection was taken over by John from a Jewish text. Two, we can hardly imagine that at the dawn of judgment day, with the angels holding back the winds of destruction, Christians would quickly be rebaptized. From John's point of view, the symbol of sealing did not include just a reference to Ezekiel 9 but probably also to the blood sign of the exodus (Exod. 12:1-13; 13:9) and therefore to the blood of Jesus (5:9; 7:14). The eschatological sealing would seem to suggest *God's* reaffirmation of their baptisms. What is important to John is that all true Christians are marked and protected from the judgment of God. All faithful Christians are **servants of . . . God** (cf. 1:1) together with prophets and angels (22:9; 19:10). *All* receive the seal, not just a select few.

4-8—The **number** of **a hundred and forty-four thousand** symbolizes the totality of believers who are on the side of God and have been redeemed by the Lamb (1:5; 5:9; 7:14). The number should not be understood in blind literalism; it symbolizes the perfect number of God's people, the square of twelve by the cube of ten (12 x 12 x 1000). The church militant (11:3-10; 14:1-5) is pictured in this number. Nor may the number be identified as the martyrs who have gone before into heaven; the people of God in vv. 1-8 are still on **earth** (vv. 1 and 3). Nor are they Jewish Christians in distinction from Gentile believers. Nor are they simply Jews. The people of God are presented on the last day as being in continuity with the Old Testament people. Paul also could speak of the church as *"the Israel of God"* (Gal. 6:16), and James wrote to "the twelve tribes in the dispersion" (James 1:1; cf. 1 Peter 1:1). When John enumerated those who were sealed **out of every tribe of the sons of Israel,** he was not referring to Jewish Christians only, and certainly not to Jews who rejected the Messiah Jesus. He portrayed the church as the Israel of God. More exactly, he was referring to the church before the last day, sealed from the wrath to come. John did not give a description of the act of sealing. What was important to him was not a precise identification of the sealing, be it in the form of a cross or an X. For him, the sealing is the symbol of the authentication and protection of the true Israel of the last days. The church is God's authentic property, and the eschatological judgment (cf. 6:17; 3:10) is one tribulation that Christians need not worry about.

The list of tribes contains two peculiarities. First, **Judah,** rather than Jacob's eldest son **Reuben,** heads the list, because the Messiah comes from the tribe of Judah (cf. Gen. 49:10; Heb. 7:14). He is the Lion of the tribe of Judah (5:5). Second, the tribe of Dan is absent, because of its idolatry (Judges 17–18). In the *Testament of Dan* (5:6), Satan is identified as prince of this tribe and, according to a later tradition, Antichrist was to arise from the tribe of Dan (Irenaeus, *Adv. Haer.* 5.30, 2). In order to complete the number 12, **Manasseh,** the firstborn son of Joseph (Gen. 41:50-51), was substituted for Dan in this list, even though the tribe of **Joseph** is also listed (7:8).

The Conquerors in the Millennium (7:9-17)

9—A new vision pictures **a great multitude which no man could number.** The previous vision contained the symbolic number of

144,000 and presented the church militant on earth as the true Israel. The new vision gives us a preview of the church triumphant in the millennium (cf. 15:2-4; 20:4-6). While the 144,000 are still on earth, this multitude stands **before the throne and before the Lamb.** These are the victors who have overcome and are **clothed in white robes,** the symbol of Christ's righteousness and of their own perseverance in faith (v. 14). **With palm branches in their hands,** holding the symbols of victory and happiness (1 Macc. 13:51; 2 Macc. 10:7), they celebrate the consummation of salvation in *worship.* The innumerable multitude cannot be limited to the martyrs, because martyrs are not the only ones who will be clothed in white robes (3:4-5, 18; cf. 6:11). The multitude are the conquerors "who have come out of the great tribulation" (v. 14). They are probably identical with the 144,000, that is, with all who have been sealed. There is disagreement on this point. If the 144,000 were to be limited to the people of God who are alive on the last day, then, of course the great multitude which no one can number (7:9) would have to be larger and include all who died in faith. But either way, this multitude **from every nation** includes all believers who have "washed their robes" in the "blood of the Lamb" (v. 14) and who are now celebrating the consummation, the beginning of the unimpeded life with God in the millennium (20:4-6). Hence individual items of this vision link up with John's millennial vision (e.g., vv. 15a-b = 22:3; 15c = 21:3; 17a = 21:4; 17b = 22:1-2).

10—After the "great day of . . . wrath," they stand before the throne of God and the Lamb, not praising their own accomplishments of faithful perseverance, but praising God and the Lamb. **Salvation belongs to our God who sits upon the throne, and to the Lamb!** This salvation (Greek, *sōtēria* with article) denotes total well-being. Its source is God and the Lamb, and salvation is to be ascribed to them alone. This is the meaning of **belongs to** (cf. Jonah 2:9, "Deliverance belongs to the Lord"). This praise acclaims the final salvation which God and the Lamb have accomplished. The multitude celebrates its total deliverance from everything that could limit life (cf. vv. 15-17). Fear and tears, hunger and thirst, sin and death are past. We owe our salvation to God and the Lamb. Salvation is not just deliverance from diverse evils, but wholeness of life in God's presence and participation in his life and reign (cf. 1:6; 5:10; 7:15-17; 20:4-6; 21:7; 22:1-5). Implicit in this acclamation is the rejection of idolatrous claims made by, or on behalf of, imperial powers and other religions.

11-12—The response to the acclamation of the multitude is the doxology of the worshiping host of **angels,** . . . **elders, and the four living creatures.** With **Amen** they confirm the acclamation of the multitude and then add their own doxology (cf. 4:9, 11; 5:12-13). **Blessing and glory and wisdom and thanksgiving and honor and power and might be to our God for ever and ever! Amen.** The ascription of "wealth" in 5:12 is replaced here by **thanksgiving,** because this doxology refers back to the thanksgiving of 4:9 (see comments there). Now with the salvation completed, the elders, who are the angelic counterpart of the people of God, cast their crowns before the throne in **thanksgiving** and offer their sevenfold doxology. The salvation of his people is the ultimate purpose of God, the creator, and it has been accomplished at last. The concluding **Amen** reinforces the praise.

13-17—John assisted his audience by providing an explicit interpretation. He had already provided interpretations in 1:8 (the Alpha and Omega is the One who is and who was and who is to come) and in 1:20, and he will continue to do so whenever in his view his symbols need clarification (e.g., 8:3, the angel with the golden censer refers to the "prayers of all the saints"; 11:17; 17:7-18; etc.). The great multitude, we hear from one of the elders, are **they who have come out of the great tribulation** which precedes the great day of wrath. The great tribulation includes all the trials and pressures to which Christians have been and will be subjected and views them from the perspective of the climactic end. Some Asian churches already experienced eschatological tribulations in their initial stages (1:9; 2:3, 9, 10, 13).

Tribulations are the pressures of the world against those who witness to the Word of God. While God, through the word of his witnesses, makes his assault upon the world, the world does not simply collapse. It strikes back, and, using diverse means, creates tribulations for the church. These tribulations, in turn, are signs of the church's faithfulness and signs of the "birth pangs" (Mark 13:8) of the new age, an age free from all tribulations and from death—free for life with God in worship.

The reason for the salvation of the white-robed multitude is twofold: **they have washed their robes and made them white in the blood of the Lamb.** The basis of salvation is Christ's saving death. His blood "freed us from our sins" (1:15; cf. 1 John 1:7; Heb. 9:24). "Though your sins are like scarlet, they shall be as white as snow," Isaiah (1:18) had promised to those whose "righteous deeds are like a polluted garment" (Isa. 64:6; cf. Rev. 3:4). The idea of washing garments may also allude to Exod. 19:10, 14, where the people of Israel must wash their garments in order to be ready for God's manifestation on Mount Sinai. Above all, this strikingly paradoxical image of washing and making their robes white in the blood of the Lamb refers to baptism, to the forgiveness received in baptism.

Yet there is still more to it. In contrast to 1:5, which focuses exclusively on the saving deed of Christ, we should notice the additional emphasis upon the activity of Christians in 7:14. **They have washed their robes and made them white.** They experienced suffering because of their witness to Christ, and thereby they participated in the suffering of the Lamb. Through their perseverance they retained the redemption bought by his blood and received in baptism. In their conduct, they remained faithful to Jesus Christ. Dirty, soiled clothes of Christians reveal unbelief expressed in immoral behavior (3:4). Their washing has not become a meritorious work, but it is the consequence of the redemption received. The Christ who redeems is also the Christ who empowers to faithful witness and obedience (cf. 12:11). In short, the slogan "Once saved, always saved," will not do justice to John's letter. The gift of redemption received must be ratified with one's life. Only those clothed in white garments can stand **before the throne** and **serve** as priests in God's **temple** (cf. 1:6; 5:10). The visions of the royal throne room of Rev. 4:5 and of the heavenly temple coalesce here. The victors in white garments serve God as priests **day and night within his temple.** This does not contradict 21:22, 25, because "day and night" is an idiom meaning always; and the "temple" here is not a separate building in heaven but the presence of God among his ecumenical people (cf. 7:9). Thus the new Jerusalem needs no separate temple building, because God will be in the midst of his people, who are his temple, even as he and the Lamb will be their temple (see comments on 21:9—22:5).

The service which the victor-priests shall perform is not a Levitical ritual but worship performed in unity with angels and archangels and all the company of heaven. The conquerors, gathered before the throne, know that the blessings of salvation are theirs. (Note, John switched from the past tense of the narration of his vision to the future tense.) God **will shelter them with his presence.** This alludes to the glory and presence (*shekinah*) of God which had led Israel in the form of a pillar of cloud by day and a pillar of fire by night (cf. Exod. 13:21-22) and which filled the tabernacle (Exod. 40:34-36; cf. Isa. 4:5-6). In John's preview, the chief characteristics of the ultimate future are worship, God's presence, the absence of **hunger, thirst, scorching heat** (cf. Isa. 49:10), and the **Lamb** as **their shepherd.** The picture of a lamb as a shepherd may strike us at first as being an incongruous exchange of roles. But certain domestic animals, as well as wild ones, such as wild horses and wolves, do lead their respective herds or packs. Sheep, however, in contrast to cows, do *not* lead their flocks to pasture. The fourth evangelist had already identified Jesus as Lamb of God *and* as the Good Shepherd. Our author brings both images together. The Lamb, who by his death has redeemed his flock, leads them **to springs of living water** (cf. Ezek. 34:11-16; Psalm 23; Rev. 21:6; 22:1-2, 17b), and in so doing, the Lamb plays the role of God himself (Psalm 23; Ezekiel 34).

Thus there will be no pain, no grief, no hardship, and no tears in the life of the world to come.

John's preview of the consummation sharply contrasts with the hopes for a golden age, envisioned by Roman poet-prophets such as Virgil. "Remember, O Roman, to rule the nations . . . to crown peace with law, to spare the humbled, to tame the proud" (*Aeneid* 6.851–853). John's millennial vision contemplates a community free from active or passive subjugation, free in equality, free from all forms of want and sorrow, free to worship God and the Lamb. In its light, Caesar's present domain appears as tyranny, marked by idolatry (cf. chap. 13). In conclusion, John's interlude portrays the security of God's people in spite of the destruction that is to come, and it depicts the life of his people in the millennium after the present order.

The Seventh Seal (8:1)

The opening of the seventh seal results in an anticlimactic **silence.** Instead of the expected culmination of all that had gone before, there is no action at all, but **silence in heaven for about half an hour.** How should we understand that? First, note the importance of silence in the Old Testament. "Be silent, all flesh, before the Lord" (Zech. 2:13); "Be still, and know that I am God" (Ps. 46:10); "The Lord is in his holy temple; let all the earth keep silence before him" (Hab. 2:20); "Commune with your own hearts . . . and be silent" (Ps. 4:4). However, here the **silence** is not in human hearts or on earth but **in heaven.** God reveals his glory not only with lightning, thunder, and earthquake (cf. 8:5) but also in "a still small voice" (1 Kings 19:12). Thus the silence *may* indicate that nothing can supersede the glory of the last vision (7:9-17).

Second, the silence certainly serves as a dramatic contrast to the cosmic upheavals of the sixth seal (6:12-17) as well as to the subsequent blowing of trumpets. Moreover, the seventh seal indicates that the two visions that follow the opening of the sixth seal are an interlude (7:1-17) offering prophetic previews of the church before, and after, the day of wrath.

Third, the silence following the opening of the seventh seal also indicates that the seal visions are now complete. In 4 Ezra 7:30 a cosmic silence of seven days signals the return of the world to its primeval state. John may have used this motif and, as usual, changed it. The interval of seven days of silence enveloping the whole world becomes a brief half-hour period and it is enjoined **in heaven** only. At any rate, the silence in heaven rounds off the seal visions. Finally, out of the silence of the seventh seal vision evolves the trumpet cycle which expands the seal visions. The half-hour silence in heaven therefore also serves as preparation for and transition to the trumpet septet.

Still, the silence in heaven is startling! It is the counterpart to the throne room vision. God is listening to us (cf. 8:3; 5:8)! Thus far he has not spoken one word in the body of this letter. In John's noisy world where everybody is talking and no one is listening, where ears get filled with state propaganda, phony advertisements, whining gossip, self-serving rhetoric, ideologies from religious hucksters, words and more words and lies, the **silence** in heaven is extraordinary. God is listening to us, to our prayers, groans, and helpless cries: Lord, how long (6:10)? Out of the silence of the listening God, listening to the prayers of the saints, the blasts of the seven trumpets evolve.

With the seventh seal, the scroll has now been fully opened. But, surprise! The content of the scroll is never read. It is enacted in such a way that the seal visions may be regarded as introduction to and summary of what is to come.

The Seven Trumpets (8:2—11:19)

John's vision of the end time which was told in the seal septet is now retold in the cycle of the blowing of the seven trumpets and will be retold several times more. If we interpret these cycles as recapitulations, we may conclude that John followed the educational principle that repetition is a means of learning (*repetitio est mater studiorum*). Still more important was John's insight that the end-time events cannot be expressed within one definitive sequentially organized timetable of events (contrary to Charles). The attempt to express the ultimate future deals with what is inexpressible in terms of a timetable. Therefore John used ever new cycles of visions which interpret each other and view God's future from different perspectives, with different images and symbols and different emphases. The relationship of the trumpet septet to the seal cycle on one hand and the bowl cycle on the other is not a chronological but a thematic relationship in spite of the fact that the bowl plagues are "the last" plagues (15:1).

Thus, for instance, the *sixth seal* signals the arrival of the day of judgment with stars falling down from heaven and the sun becoming black and the sky vanishing (6:12-14). However, the *fourth trumpet* and the *fourth bowl* visions presuppose that the heavenly bodies are still in place (8:12; 16:8). The relationship between the three cycles therefore is thematic, not chronological! One other example: The *seventh trumpet* signals the arrival of the consummated kingdom (11:15-19), and thus it corresponds thematically to the interlude of 7:9-17. However, the *bowl* visions of chap. 16 presuppose that the kingdom has not yet arrived on earth. The sequence of the narration of John's visions may therefore not be interpreted chronologically but spirally. The cycles subsequent to the seal septet elaborate and expand particular details, for example, chaps. 12–13 expand the vision of the first horseman (6:2); the trumpet septet elaborates the seal tribulations with plagues on nature and on humans, using new images and making new emphases.

John's artistic structure should forestall the construction of apocalyptic timetables and facilitate our perception of thematic relationships within his letter. We ought to recognize that the cosmic destruction wrought by the opening of the sixth seal (6:12-17) is recapitulated in the seventh bowl vision (16:18) and in the vision of the great white throne (20:11). Recapitulation does not imply mechanical repetition of content, but recapitulation becomes the occasion for *new emphases*. The sixth seal focuses on the inescapable "wrath of the Lamb" (6:16). The seventh bowl has its point in the destruction of Babylon (16:19), and 20:11 serves as introduction to the general judgment of the dead and as counterpart to the new creation of 21:1-8. Moreover, the *reactions* of the people exhibit distinct emphases. In the sixth seal it is sheer terror that the day of wrath has come. Their reaction is the very opposite of the martyrs' question, "Lord, how long?" (cf. 6:10, 17). The reaction of the people to the trumpet septet is found in 9:20: They "did not repent" and therefore their reaction to the bowls of wrath expresses their hardness of heart—they cursed God (16:11, 21). But there will be no reaction from those who face their judge and receive his final verdict (20:12-15). In short, the new emphases also indicate thematic development and progress in the vision narrative.

The intensification of destruction in the three septets (seals, trumpets, and bowls) reflects progression within the thematic structure of recapitulation. While one-fourth of all humans are killed after the opening of the fourth seal (6:8), this percentage is heightened to one-third at the sixth trumpet (9:15), and the annihilation appears to be total after the last bowl (16:17-21). The question that we should seek to answer deals with the relationships and distinct emphases of the three septets of Part II (seals, trumpets, and bowls).

The seal septet is modeled on the Synoptic apocalypse, as we have seen. The trumpet and bowl cycles will project the Egyptian plagues onto a cosmic screen, as we shall see. Apparently *seals one to five* may be viewed as eschatological tribulations to which also Christians are subjected. *Trumpets one to six* are directed against the idolaters, not against the sealed people of God. They function as God's final warning. *Bowls one through seven* signal the end of the wrath of God (cf. 15:1) and interconnect thematically with the "wrath" of the sixth seal (6:16-17) and of the seventh trumpet (11:18). Yet the main thrust of the seventh trumpet is not "wrath" but salvation, or the presence of "the kingdom of our Lord and of his Christ" (11:15), which is the dialectical counterpart to the sixth seal and the seventh bowl.

Thus we may discover peculiar emphases that distinguish the trumpet septet from the bowl septet, such as: First, the intensification of destruction (cf. 8:7, 9, 11, 15 and 16:4, 8-10, 17-21).

Second, while the trumpet plagues affect idolatrous humans in general, the bowls are poured out upon the worshipers of the beast specifically (16:2, 6, 10, 19). Third, the trumpet plagues are manifestations of the sovereignty of God and the Lamb and final warnings to repent; the bowls of wrath, on the other hand, manifest divine judgment upon the beast worshipers and their world. With the bowls, "the wrath of God [anticipated in the sixth seal, 6:17] is ended" (15:1). In short, the theme of judgment, absent in seals one to four and trumpets one to six, is unfolded in the bowl septet and focused upon the worshipers of the beast.

Looking back to the beginning of Part II, we can see that the double vision of chaps. 4 and 5 portrayed the sovereignty and majesty of God and the Lamb as the ultimate reality *in heaven*. In the seal, trumpet, and bowl septets, we see that sovereignty is being brought to bear upon *the world* in three ways, as tribulation, as final warning, and as judgment. All three septets reveal that catastrophes are not proofs of God's absence. On the contrary, they are signs of his coming in judgment and in salvation.

We can also recognize that the trumpet and bowl septets are modeled after the Egyptian plagues. This would suggest that both cycles have something in common. What is it? The plagues in Egypt, the hearers may recall, were unleashed not because the Egyptians were unusually immoral and evil people but because they prevented Israel from worshiping God. (Exod. 5:31; 7:16; 8:11, 20; 9:1, 13; 10:3). The trumpet visions take the connection between worship and plagues one step farther. The plagues reveal the futility of idolatry, of "worshiping demons and idols." They unmask and destroy the illusion of humans that "the works of their hands" (9:20) guarantee safety. Therefore the plagues should lead to repentance, that is, to worship, not the worship of our work but of God. The bowl plagues are directed against those who worshiped the beast's image (9:20; 16:2; cf. 16:9, 11). Through both plague cycles God and the Lamb establish their sovereignty over an earth that perishes through its idolatry.

Structure of the Trumpet Septet: A brief preparatory scene in heaven (8:2-5) is introduced with "then I saw," distinguishing it from the half-hour of silence of the seventh seal. Simultaneously, the appearance of the seven angels with trumpets evolves out of the silence of the seventh seal, so that the whole new trumpet cycle becomes a series of events initiated by the opening of the seventh seal. This procedure gave John the opportunity to retell the end-time story from a new perspective and with new images. The high point of the trumpet visions is reached with the blowing of the seventh trumpet (11:15-19) which presents the vision of the final salvation and interlocks with its thematic parallel in 7:9-17.

Unexpectedly John introduced **three woes** into the trumpet septet (8:13; 9:12; 11:14) in such a way that the third woe is not completed within the trumpet cycle but only in chaps. 12–16 (cf. 12:12, "woe to you, O earth"). By means of the "woes," John interlocked the trumpet cycle with the bowl cycle of chap. 16. Hence the significance of the seventh trumpet, like the seventh seal, is twofold. On one hand the seventh trumpet rounds off the trumpet cycle. The hymn of thanks looks back at the final salvation which has been accomplished. "The mystery of God" has been fulfilled (10:7; 11:15-19). God's wrath has come, and he has established his eschatological kingdom on earth (11:15, 18). But on the other hand the third woe is announced (11:14) immediately prior to the blowing of the seventh trumpet, and the visions of Revelation 12–16 are the realization of the third woe. Therefore the seventh trumpet, like the seventh seal, encompasses the visions that are to come.

As in the seal septet, so here an *interlude* (10:1—11:14) is placed between the sixth and the seventh trumpet vision. Like the interlude of chap. 7, so this new interlude deals with God's faithful people. Moreover, it also connects the trumpet septet with chaps. 12–16 for two reasons: first, because John is once more commissioned to prophesy "again" (10:11), which he does beginning with chap. 12; and second, because a new actor is introduced in the interlude, "the beast that ascends from the bottomless pit" (11:7). The action of this beast and its allies will be the theme of the center section (B), 12:1—16:21, and will be recapitulated in the climactic section (A′), 17:1—22:5.

As in the seal cycle, so here the first four trumpets belong together because they exhibit the same pattern. The fifth and sixth trumpet visions are greatly expanded, like the fifth and sixth seals. In contrast to the seal cycle, the first four plagues of the trumpet vision inflict destruction on the natural *world* and thus they elaborate the sixth seal, while the last two trumpets bring plagues upon *humans,* like the first four seals which unleashed the horsemen (6:1-8).

Prelude in Heaven (8:2-6)

Each of the three septets is introduced by a preparatory vision (chaps. 4–5; 8:2-6; chap. 15) that interlocks with the following vision narrative. The structure of this preview is *A-B-A′*. Two references to **seven angels** with **seven trumpets** (vv. 2 and 6) enclose scene B, in which **another angel** is standing **at the altar with a golden censer** (vv. 3-5). The use of the article shows that "the seven angels" are a definite group (cf. Tob. 12:15). They are probably the seven archangels **who stand before God** in distinction from the myriads of angels (cf. 5:11). Their names are given in *1 Enoch* 20:2-8. Gabriel and Michael also appear in the New Testament (Luke 1:19, 26; Jude 9; Rev. 12:7). The passive voice ("were given," v. 2) is a circumlocution for divine activity. God, or the Lamb, assigned a trumpet to each angel. Therefore the following plagues serve his purposes. Trumpets are sounded in the Old Testament on different occasions—among them to signal the day of the Lord (Joel 2:1; Zeph. 1:16; 4 Ezra 6:23). Also, the trumpets of Revelation are eschatological trumpets (cf. 1 Thess. 4:16-17; 1 Cor. 15:51-52; Matt. 24:31) which reveal God's sovereignty through plagues.

3-5—The royal throne room of Revelation 4 has changed into the heavenly temple, the counterpart of the earthly temple. A priestly **angel** standing **at the altar** adds **incense** to the **prayers of all the saints** so that the prayers of the church and the martyrs, supported by the angelic incense, rise **before the throne; and the smoke of the incense rose with the prayers of the saints** (cf. Tob. 12:12). This liturgical action connects the trumpet cycle with the vision of the throne room (5:8) and with the cry of the martyrs in the seal cycle (6:9-11). The prayers of the church, "Thy kingdom come, thy will be done on earth as it is in heaven, deliver us from evil" (cf. 11:15-17), and the cry of the martyrs for justice, "How long?" (6:10), ask God to intervene and to make short shrift of all ruthlessness and deceit, of idolatry and oppression, and to establish his reign. **The saints** are not limited to martyrs but include all of God's faithful people. The church on earth prays for God's manifestation in judgment and in salvation. Human words of prayer have tremendous power, this vision tells us, because angels bring the prayers into God's presence. More, in response to the prayers of the church, the plagues are unleashed as final warning to the world.

Then the angel took the censer and filled it with fire from the altar and threw it on the earth; and there were peals of thunder, loud voices, flashes of lightning, and an earthquake. The effect of the prayers of the saints is a spectacular preview of the plagues that follow. God is ready to demonstrate his power against a self-sufficient world, and in so doing he answers the prayers of the church in his own way. Just as 6:12-17 and 7:9-17 are a twofold fulfillment of the request of the martyrs of 6:10, so 8:7—9:20 and 11:15-19 fulfill the prayers of the saints of 8:3-4. Throwing **fire** from heaven upon the **earth** symbolizes destruction, caused by God (cf. Ezek. 10:2), and anticipates the first four plagues which fell from heaven causing cosmic catastrophes.

The **peals of thunder, loud voices, flashes of lightning, and an earthquake** also display the majesty of God, who is ready to confront an idolatrous world. This series of divine manifestations serves as a formula that appears at important literary junctions (4:5; 8:5; 11:19; 16:18) and is always related to God's "throne," or his "temple." Moreover, the formula in 8:5 connects this preparatory vision with the previous one of chaps. 4–5 (cf. 4:5). It also forms an inclusion around the trumpet cycle (cf. 8:5 and

11:19), and finally it links the conclusion of the trumpet visions with the conclusion of the bowl visions (16:18). Naturally the formula varies. For obvious reasons there can be no earthquake or hail in the throne room vision (4:5), because it is confined to heaven. In the seventh bowl vision, the earthquake is highlighted and causes Babylon's doom (16:18). It functions there as instrument of God's sovereign judgment.

The First Six Trumpets (8:7—9:21)

A series of cosmic plagues pictures the absolute dependence of the world upon the sovereignty of God. There is nothing that the world can do to defend itself against the plagues sent by God and the Lamb—nothing, except to pray, worship, and repent. But this is precisely what idolatrous humanity does not want to do. This may seem terribly naive to us modern "sophisticated Protestants." For John, the plagues dispel the myth of human self-sufficiency. They are signs, warnings to repent, even as the Egyptian plagues were meant to manifest the sovereignty of Yahweh vis-à-vis an idolatrous people which prohibited Israel from worshiping God. Moreover, just as the plagues at Moses' time did not fall upon Israel, so the end-time plagues shall not fall upon the church, the Israel of God, that has been sealed "with the seal of the living God" (7:2-4; 9:4). We will avoid using the language of judgment in the interpretation of the trumpet cycle, because John avoided it. For him, God's judgment is expressed through the bowl cycle.

The first four trumpet visions are linked together by the motif of fire from heaven, or the fire (light) of celestial bodies. They were anticipated in the prelude (8:3-5) by the action of the angel throwing fire upon the earth. In terms of content, they differ greatly from the first four seals. Whereas the tribulations of the first four seals were directed against human beings, the trumpets bring destruction on the elements of the world, as did the sixth seal. In short, the first four trumpet visions are elaborations of the cosmic catastrophes of the sixth seal vision.

John used the Egyptian plagues here and in the bowl cycle, *not* because his church faced oppression, as did Israel in Egypt, but because the plagues on the Egyptians were the first act of Israel's deliverance from Egypt. John wanted all Christians to know, especially those whose realized eschatology did not include a future dimension, that there will be no final salvation without preceding plagues. He reinterpreted the Egyptian plagues by scaling down their number from ten to seven, by changing their sequence, and, above all, by giving them a cosmic dimension. Thus they are clearly identified as future events. The destruction unleashed by the first four trumpets is not total, even as the harm done to the Egyptians was limited. The reader also remembers that God's sealed servants are excluded from the plagues (7:1-8; cf. 9:4, 20-21), like Israel of old. The form of the first four trumpet visions is identical: (1) The angel blows his trumpet; (2) the effect is stated; and (3) the damage is noted. The motif of fire (light) is present in all four.

The First Trumpet (8:7). **The first angel blew his trumpet,** and its effect is reminiscent of the seventh Egyptian plague (Exod. 9:22-26) but now with worldwide dimensions. **Hail and fire, mixed with blood . . . fell on the earth.** The reference to the blood probably comes from Joel's picture of the last day (Joel 2:31; cf. Acts 2:19). **A third of the earth was burnt up,** together with a third of the trees, **and all green grass was burnt up.** In view of John's use of Old Testament imagery, it is unlikely that he was thinking of the red rain that occasionally falls on Mediterranean countries as a result of sandstorms in the Sahara. The damage in John's vision is different. The discrepancy concerning the **grass** between 8:7 and 9:4 did not bother John. He is describing his visions, not giving us a journalist's report.

The Second Trumpet (8:8-9). The **second** trumpet damages the sea, **and a third of the sea became blood** (cf. Exod. 7:20-21), **a third** of the sea animals and **of the ships** perished, because **something like a great mountain, burning with fire, was thrown**

into the sea. One should not ask how large this mountain-like mass would have to be in order to result in such devastation (e.g., meteorite, star-angel, cf. *1 Enoch* 18:13-14). John's point is that the disasters come from heaven and fall upon the elements in a world that can do nothing about them. Moreover, these plagues are warnings to the world to repent. They precede the church's exodus into the new promised land. The fraction one-third indicates that God's judgment has not yet begun.

The Third Trumpet (8:10-11). The **third** plague has no parallel in Exodus. Once more **a great star fell from heaven, blazing like a torch. A third** of the earth's sweet water supply in rivers and springs became **bitter** and **many** people **died.** The star's name is **Wormwood,** which is also the star's effect on the water. **A third of the waters became wormwood.** Wormwood is the name of a shrublike plant that has a bitter taste. In the Old Testament it is often used as a metaphor for sorrow, bitterness, and perverted justice (cf. Prov. 5:4; Amos 5:7; 6:12). In Jer. 9:15 and 23:15, God threatened to feed false prophets with wormwood. John apparently borrowed the metaphor from Jeremiah. This third plague is the miracle of Marah in reverse. At Marah, Moses threw a tree into the bitter waters and they became sweet (Exod. 15:25). Here the sweet waters of streams and springs become bitter and many die.

The Fourth Trumpet (8:12). With the **fourth** trumpet, **a third of the sun was struck, and a third of the moon, and a third of the stars, so that a third of their light was darkened.** This plague alludes to and reinterprets Exod. 10:21-23 and indicates the total absence of light, that is, total darkness for one-third of both day and night (cf. Mark 13:24; Isa. 13:10). The reader remembers that the plagues are the beginning of the deliverance of God's people. Finally, a comparison with the sixth seal (6:12-13) demonstrates that John's narrative sequence may not be translated into a chronological sequence.

Announcement of Three Woes (8:13). **Then I looked,** and suddenly an **eagle** appeared, **crying** a threefold "woe" **with a loud voice.** The eagle serves as transition from the first four plagues to the fifth and sixth. The catastrophes of the first four trumpet blasts affected primarily the elements of earth, water, and the celestial bodies. These plagues added details to the sixth seal vision. The reaction of humanity is omitted in the first four trumpet visions because it had already been given in the sixth seal vision 6:15-17 and it will be found after the sixth trumpet (9:20-21).

The Greek word for eagle can also mean vulture. This bird of prey hovered in **midheaven,** so that he could be seen by all, and cried out **with a loud voice,** . . . **"Woe, woe, woe** (Greek, *ouai*) **to those who dwell on the earth, at the blasts of the other trumpets."** The "first woe" is fulfilled through the fifth trumpet blast (9:12). The "second woe" is not mentioned until after the interlude (11:14), even though it must be identified with the sixth trumpet (cf. 9:13-19). No clear indication is given concerning the fulfillment of the "third woe." The seventh trumpet (11:15-19) cannot be its fulfillment, because that last trumpet announces salvation and not new additional disasters (11:15). Therefore the third woe, mentioned prior to the seventh trumpet (11:14), links the trumpet cycle with the bowl cycle through which the wrath of God comes to an end (cf. 12:12; 15:1; 16:1-21—"It is done!" 16:17).

An **eagle,** or vulture, is a bird of prey, unclean according to the Old Testament. In apocalyptic literature the eagle appears as symbol of the Roman empire (4 Ezra 11:1-12:11; *Test. Moses* 10:8). An eagle is used as a letter carrier in 2 Bar. 77:17-26, but nowhere does it turn up as a messenger sounding a warning. On the contrary, in Hos. 8:1, trumpets warn against the vulture representing the enemies: "Set the trumpet to your lips, for a vulture is over the house of the Lord" (cf. Hab. 1:8). In Rev. 8:13, however, it is the vulture who warns with a piercing cry of new disasters. Caird's solution, that our text recalls Luke 17:37 ("where the body is, there the eagles will be gathered together"), perhaps points in the right direction. But it is also possible that we have here an ironic reversal of an Exodus image. Yahweh bore the Israelites "on eagles' wings" (Exod. 19:4). Instead of symbolizing deliverance, the eagle flying in midheaven announces disasters. Hovering over prey that will soon be dead, the eagle is an ironic symbol of the inevitability of calamities to come. The eagle is also related to "the wild beasts of the earth" in the fourth seal vision (6:7) as well as to "the birds" that are called to feast on the corpses of the army of the beast (19:17-18). Of course, this eagle cannot be identified with the one "like" an eagle in the throne room vision (4:7). Rather, it links up with the animals of prey of 6:7 and 19:17. Here, however, it announces a threefold solemn warning.

The Fifth Trumpet (9:1-12). The fifth and sixth trumpet visions could be compared to horror movies or to performances of the theater of the absurd. One could also dismiss these visions as creations of a deranged mind that is fascinated with painting monstrosities, heaping the grotesque upon the ugly—"without religious value," as one commentator said. John indeed revealed the bizarre, spiritual dimension of the world, a dimension that is present, though still hidden, under a veneer of culture. The demonic locusts, we hear, cannot torment the saints who bear **the seal of God** (9:4). The message of trumpets five and six is quite simple and traditional. With an eschatological twist they visualize the truth that "a person is punished by the very things by which he or she sins" (Wis. Sol. 11:16). Moreover, both trumpets presuppose the traditional view that idolatry is the worship of demons (1 Cor. 10:20; Deut. 32:17).

The locust-demons seem to reappear in new disguises and torment in forms such as alcohol and drug abuse, insatiable yearning for sexual promiscuity, sexually transmitted diseases, collective hysteria and subgroup temper tantrums, neurotic drives in diverse forms, driving passions for power, prestige, and wealth at the expense of one's own humanity, torments of psychic disorders, debilitating inability to maintain personal relationships, and other "locusts." One can only wish them to go away—and they do—after a while (**five months,** 9:10). In contrast to the demonic cavalry of the sixth trumpet, "the locusts" do not kill. Yet their torment is bad enough for people to wish they were dead (9:5-6). These "locusts" arise out of the abyss, which is the counterimage to the heavenly temple, the place of worship. They can attack only those who do not worship God and the Lamb. Moreover, while locusts are always around, like idolatry, this fifth trumpet plague is not an everyday occurrence but an eschatological assault. It is God and the Lamb who unleash this end-time plague, who hand over the key to the abyss. At the end, God shall reveal idolatry and immorality in all their ugliness and perversity.

1-2—When **the fifth angel blew his trumpet** John saw **a star fallen from heaven to earth, and he was given the key of the shaft of the bottomless pit** (Greek, *abyssos*). In contrast to the star of 8:10, the one here is an angel (cf. *1 Enoch* 21:6; 86:1-3; 88:1). for he is commissioned (Greek, *edothē*) to unlock the shaft that leads into the abyss. The statement that he **has fallen** from heaven should probably not be pressed. To be sure, the idea of "the fall of Satan" and his angels is known to John (cf. 12:7-9; Luke 10:18), but he probably did not use it here. This star/angel acts by divine decree and exercises God's will. He is perhaps identical with the angel of 20:1, who also descends from heaven with the key to the abyss. In short, "to fall" probably means here "to descend." **The bottomless pit,** or the abyss, occurs in the Bible in two senses; one, as the place of the dead (Ps. 70:21 LXX; Rom. 10:7); two, as a jail for evil spirits (*Jub.* 5:6-8; *1 Enoch* 10:4-6; 18:11-13; 21:1-7; Luke 8:31). Behind this second meaning lies the Babylonian creation myth in which the abyss is the waters of the deep, the source of chaotic powers. Echoes of this myth are found in texts such as Isa. 27:1 and Amos 9:3. At any rate, here the abyss is thought to be the place of demonic beings beneath the earth (cf. 2 Peter 2:4) and connected with the earth by a **shaft. Smoke** arises from the shaft and darkens **the sun** (cf. Joel 2:10).

3-6—Then from the smoke came locusts on the earth, and they were given (Greek, *edothē*) **power like the power of scorpions of the earth.** Just as the fifth angel blowing his trumpet acts by divine decree and just as the star/angel who opens the shaft fulfills God's will, so likewise this demonic host of locusts remains an instrument for the execution of God's purposes. The irony should not escape us. Even the demons must do God's bidding when he is ready to manifest his glory on earth. The plague of locusts is derived from Exodus 12–20 and from the eschatological interpretation of this plague in Joel 1:2—2:11. In Joel, the day of the Lord dawns with an attack by a mighty army of locusts. Here in Revelation the locusts **were told not to harm the grass . . . or any green growth or any tree** but to **torture** the people. These locusts do not belong to the natural species which can devastate the vegetation of a region by feeding on it. The locusts here have been prohibited from doing what natural locusts do. Instead, they have received a scorpion-like power for tormenting all humans **who have not the seal of God upon their foreheads** (7:1-8). In short, these locusts are demonic beings that nevertheless remain under God's sovereign control. Their power is limited in three ways: (1) They may not harm the people of God; (2) they may not **kill,** but only torture; and (3) their torment is limited to **five months,** the life span of locusts.

In v. 6 John addressed his audience directly, changing to prophetic speech and using the future tense: **And in those days men will seek death and will not find it; they will long to die, and death will fly from them.** It is ironic that death will be desired by those who will inflict death on Christians in the near future. Yet their desire will be as futile as their exclamations in 6:15-17. Their self-destructive point of view connects the fifth trumpet with the sixth seal. In contrast, "the seal of God" (9:4) protects the saints from the plagues and links up with the sealing of 7:1-8. In short, the locust plague is related to the "Day of the Lord," and that "day" has now been stretched into a period of "five months" (9:5).

7-11—The detailed and quite grotesque description of the locusts strikes us as being the result of uncontrolled fantasy. But we should remember that John used and fused traditions, namely, Exod. 10:12-20 and Joel 1–2, and apocalyptic traditions about demonic hordes. The locusts are **like horses** with **wings,** and with **human faces** and **crowns of gold** on their heads, symbolizing their irresistible onslaughts. They **have tails like scorpions** to sting with, **hair like women's hair,** and the teeth in their human-like faces are **like lions' teeth.** Their scales **like iron breastplates** make them invulnerable to human defenses, and as this army of locusts flies across the land it sounds **like the noise of many chariots with horses rushing into battle.** Most important of all, they have a **king,** contrary to normal locusts (Prov. 30:27). The **king** of this demonic army is **the angel of the bottomless pit.** He is to be distinguished from the angel of v. 1 who descended from heaven. The king of the demonic locust army ascended with his host from the abyss. **His name** is given twice. In Hebrew he is called **Abaddon.** This Hebrew word means "destruction," and it was used for the realm of the dead (Job 26:6; Ps. 88:2), as a synonym for Sheol. When death became personified (cf. Job 28:22; Rev. 6:8), Abaddon could be used as the name for the prince of destruction presiding over Sheol. **In Greek he is called Apollyon,** which is not an exact translation of the Hebrew Abaddon. The Greek equivalent would be *Apoleia,* a word that John used in 17:8. *Apollyon* is the participle of *apollymi* (I destroy) and means the destroyer.

Since John knew the difference between *Apoleia* and *Apollyon,* it would seem probable that he used the latter because it sounded like the name of the Greek god Apollo, a name that Greek writers also derived from *apollymi* (I destroy). Moreover, one of the many symbols of Apollo was the locust, and he was also known as the god of plagues. Thus there is irony in the name of the king of the locust plague whom pagans worshiped with great zeal. Their idol will reward them by tormenting them (Jeremias). Some interpreters have gone one step farther and suggested that John's irony has an additional sting. In the imperial cult in Asia Minor the emperor Domitian was regarded as Apollo incarnate at John's time. Thus the king of the demonic host would be none other than Domitian, their god (Schüssler Fiorenza). But this conclusion is uncertain. At any rate, this personified demonic power, called Apollyon, must do God's bidding and execute his purpose, which constitutes the supreme irony. John will later return to this subject, unfold it, and give it a new twist in Revelation 13 and 17. Finally, there are some plagues to which Christians are not subjected. "One is punished by the very things by which one sins" (Wis. Sol. 11:6).

12—The first woe has passed; behold, two woes are still to come (cf. 8:13; 9:12; 11:14; 12:12; 16:17: "It is done!").

The Sixth Trumpet (9:13-21). While the sixth *seal* initiated the total destruction of nature, the sixth trumpet brings death to one-third of humanity. It recapitulates the destructive powers of the first four seals, which are also directed against people (6:1-8), and does so from a new perspective, in new images, with greater intensity and new direction. There might not even be a discrepancy between the casualty figure of 6:8 (one-fourth of humanity is killed) and the casualty figure of 9:18 (one-third are killed), if the death toll from *all four* horsemen (seals one to four), and not just from the fourth rider (6:8), were to be counted. The apocalyptic horsemen reappear in new forms as demonic angels of death and direct their onslaught indiscriminately against idolatrous humanity.

13-16—Introduction: After the sounding of the **sixth** trumpet, **a voice** is heard **from the four horns of the golden altar** (cf. Exod. 27:2; 30:2-3). Whose **voice** is it? It is probably the voice of an angel. His name might even be "Voice." It may be the priestly angel who offered incense with the prayers of the saints and who threw fire upon the earth (8:3-5). The voice comes from the **altar,** from the place where the church's prayers for the coming of the kingdom rise to God's throne. Once again, John reminds his hearers of the power of prayer (cf. 5:8; 6:10-11; 8:3-5). The sixth trumpet vision is therefore God's surprising response to the church's prayer for the manifestation of his sovereignty which will rectify all wrongs (cf. 6:9-11). The sixth angel, who has just blown his trumpet, is ordered by the voice, "**Release the four angels who are bound at the great river Euphrates.**" Once again, the introduction indicates the direction of the action which is initiated in heaven and causes destruction on earth, here to humans. The **Euphrates** marked the eastern boundary of the Roman empire in Asia Minor. On the other side of the river lay the Parthian empire which had inflicted humiliating defeats on the Roman legions in 53 B.C. and A.D. 62. So it is not surprising that the Romans were quite neurotic about the Parthian menace. *1 Enoch* 56 envisions Parthians and Medes being stirred up by evil angels and invading Palestine like hungry wolves. John may allude to this widespread fear (cf. 6:2). However, as always, he reinterpreted it. He was not interested in *historical* manifestations of this plague but only in its *eschatological* dimension. Therefore he explicitly noted that these four demonic angels **had been held ready for the hour, the day, the month, and the year.** Only when God's eschatological "hour" strikes, only then will they be released. The past tense of John's narration of what he saw should not be confused with the future content of his visions. The reference to the hour, day, and month clearly points to a *future* action and so does the casualty figure of 9:15. "A third" of humanity was not killed in John's own present, or past.

The **four angels** of this vision may remind us of the four angels of 7:1. Though a common tradition about destructive angels may lie behind both texts, nevertheless these two groups of angels are not identical. These four **were released** in order **to kill a third of** humanity. Unexpectedly we hear that these four angels are the leaders of a **cavalry** of two hundred million troops, **twice ten thousand times ten thousand.** Equally unique are John's additions here and in the following verse: **I heard their number. I saw . . . in my vision.** The size of this army of cavalry is unimaginable. It is twice the size of the myriads of angels in 5:11. It is the army of the host of hell, and it is not without irony that it too must serve the "strange work" of God. No kingdom without judgment and no judgment without prior warnings and plagues.

17-19—Appearance and effect of the demonic horde: The picture that John gives of these mythical monstrosities and their riders is as grotesque as their number. **The heads of the horses were like lions' heads, and fire and smoke and sulphur issued from their mouths,** which killed **a third** of humanity. **For the power of the horses is in their mouths and in their tails** which are **like serpents, with heads. By means** of their tails, **they wound.** Fire and sulphur characterize their hellish nature (cf. 14:10; 19:20; 21:8). Fire and smoke come out of the monster Leviathan (Job 41:1, 19-21). Sulphur and fire destroyed the godless cities of Sodom and Gomorrah (Gen. 19:24, 28). The fifth and sixth trumpets employ military images but never refer to actual battles (cf. 12:7; 16:12, 16; 17:14; 19:19). There is a reason for this omission. In our section (4:1—11:19) all demonic powers, beginning with Antichrist (6:2), serve as minions of God, doing his bidding. He manifests his sovereign majesty by using even them! In the following sections these powers will function as opponents of God and his people. Then the image of battle and the theme of judgment over all anti-God forces will be prominent. While the second woe is completed with this plague, the announcement of its completion is postponed until 11:14.

20-21—These verses constitute the climactic conclusion of the first six trumpets. They, together with 8:2-6, form one set of brackets around the trumpet vision. And the brackets deal with the issue of worship—the prayers and worship of the saints on one side and the idolatry of "the rest of humanity" on the other. In magnitude beyond the Egyptian plagues, the trumpet plagues manifest God's incomparable sovereignty. Simultaneously, they are his final call for repentance. But just as the reaction had been in the Egyptian past, so shall it be in the eschatological future. **The rest of mankind . . . did not repent of the works of their hands nor give up worshiping demons and idols.** Polemics against idol worship is a common topic of the Old Testament and of Hellenistic Judaism (cf. Isa. 2:8. 20; 44:9-11; Jer. 1:16; Mic. 5:12; Ps. 115:4-7; Dan. 5:4, 23; *1 Enoch* 99:7; *Sib. Or.* 5:77-79). The relationship between idolatry and worship of demons is found in Deut. 32:17; Ps. 106:37; 1 Cor. 10:20. Paul knew that an idol has no real existence (1 Cor. 8:4), but demons operate in idol worship. What is not God (whether race, land, beauty, or what not) becomes demonic, if worshiped. John's irony here is that the demons are viewed from the perspective of having to function as God's executors and that they will pay back their devotees in ways their worshipers never dreamed of. Finally, the consequences of idolatry are stated in a catalog of vices (cf. Rom. 1:23-31), prohibited by the fifth, sixth, and seventh commandments of the decalog. **Immorality** (Greek, *porneia*) here means fornication and should not be understood metaphorically in terms of idolatry, because it is distinguished from idolatry within this list of vices. It includes all sins against the sixth commandment. It is interesting that our letter frequently referred to **sorceries,** or magic (18:23; 21:8; 22:15; cf. Acts 19:13-19). Idolatry, which from a Jewish point of view is demon worship, found its most popular expression in the broad subculture of magic.

In conclusion: The trumpet cycle expands the universal dimensions, present in the seal cycle, and reflects John's deep-seated alienation from his contemporary culture. He offers an alternative vision to the glorification of Greco-Roman cultural achievements which were lauded by many of his contemporaries. In John's vision those achievements will be brought low and the people will not be able to do one thing about it—unless they repent. God will utilize the world's own spiritual-demonic forces and resources and thereby reveal the world's absurdity. He, the Pantocrator, has fixed the time for the manifestation of his sovereign reign on earth, and then he will employ those demonic forces which undergird the world's culture in John's present, a culture that bears the indelible mark of idolatry. The demons which undergird the culture will turn against that culture. Thus will be disclosed the absurdity of a world that has turned away from and against its creator. However, the gates of hell shall not prevail against his faithful people whose prayers will be answered in ways beyond their imagination. The seventh trumpet introduces the heavenly liturgy of God's total victory (11:15-19).

Since the trumpet plagues will not lead idolatrous humanity to repentance (9:20-21), the drama of the end time will continue with an emphasis on judgment (Revelation 12–20). The military images in the fifth and sixth trumpet visions will also reappear in new forms. Above all, the role and fate of Satan and of his minions need further clarification. Last but not least, questions concerning the earth after the cosmic judgments and questions concerning the death of the faithful need elaboration and clarification.

It should have become obvious by now that John did not want his hearers and readers to understand his visions in these two cycles as predated predictions of events that have already happened at his time. He did not "predict" in 8:8 the eruption of Mount Vesuvius in A.D. 79, because that event lies in the past, from his point of view. Though the destruction of Pompeii and Herculaneum caused great consternation among the people of the empire, it did not form the content of the second trumpet. Equally false would be to see in 8:10 a prediction about acid rain and the contamination of rivers and lakes through industrial pollution; or to find in 9:17-19 predictions about atomic explosions, napalm bombs (8:7), and similar modern military fireworks. It would be wrong to identify the locusts with Islam or other tormentors of Christianity (see 9:4b) or to equate the demonic cavalry of 9:13-19 and/or the rider on "the red horse" with the Soviet or Chinese army, and so forth, as has been done and is still being done. In each case, the presupposition is false. It is wrongly assumed that John wished to convey predictions of future historical events that might be relevant to the interpreter's own time. But John did not predict the course of world history or of the church's history, and to use Revelation in this way is to misuse it.

John wrote for *his* churches, not for us, and his message is prophecy, not an apocalyptic timetable. His prophecy is not primarily a critical analysis of his world and of his church's situation within the Roman empire. His prophecy is, at its core, the proclamation of the exaltation of Jesus Christ. The Lamb that was slain receives the scroll and the worship of heaven's court. The authority over the end time is his. The end will come with Christ's parousia and the worship of his people "before the throne and before the Lamb" (7:9). Then "the kingdom of the world has become the kingdom of our Lord and of his Christ and he shall reign for ever and ever" (11:15). John's visions describe in ever new images and symbols the struggle that is determined by Christ's taking the sealed scroll on one hand and by humanity's idolatry and immorality on the other. However, this struggle has already been decided in heaven, and John's churches are part of this decision because they worship God and the Lamb.

Revelation does not portray the future course of history but the encounter with the end, present in Christ's exaltation. Its theme is "the revelation of Jesus Christ" (1:1), not revelations (plural) about him, but the revelation of the final judgment and of the final salvation. It also pictures in ever new images the revelation of the world in its absurdity and of the church as God's alternative community in which God's reign is present already (1:6; 5:9). Christ's exaltation assures his final victory over demonic forces, and it assures the church's final salvation. His reign on earth cannot be completed unless and until all demonic forces are destroyed, so that all can join the heavenly liturgy: "Worthy art thou, our Lord and God, to receive glory and honor and power, for thou didst create all things" (4:11); "Hallelujah! For the Lord our God the Almighty reigns" (19:6). The world will collapse into the nonexistence from which it came. A humanity that refuses to worship its creator will be subjected to plagues, some of which are of its own making, and to judgments that will reveal who God is and what humans are about.

Interlude: New Commission; Witness and Preservation of the Faithful (10:1—11:14)

This interlude is a digression that delays the blowing of the seventh trumpet. It plays a pivotal role in the structure of Revelation by connecting section A (4:1—11:19) with the center section B (12:1—16:21). We shall take a closer look at John's artistic structure. In the first place, the seer is commissioned a second time through a vision (10:11), which is a parallel to the "inaugural" vision of chap. 1. There he was told to write what he saw, "what is, and what is to take place hereafter" (1:19). Since the last clause of his first commission is repeated in 4:1, it would seem obvious that the inaugural vision was meant to serve as the introduction not only to the seven messages of chaps. 2–3 but also to Part II. Now in 10:8-11 John is commissioned to **again prophesy** (10:11). His prophetic role will not be completed with the vision of the blowing of the seventh trumpet which announces the end, the presence of God's reign on earth (11:15-19). Thus far the *seal* visions have shown us the essential aspects of the end time (Antichrist, war, famine, death, persecution, cosmic upheavals), and the *trumpet* visions have disclosed cosmic catastrophes and demonic plagues. Both septets have been presented from the perspective of heaven. The new commission directs our focus from heaven to earth. In the interlude John himself is presented as being on earth, not in heaven in the Spirit (cf. 4:1-2). In new visions the seer will present the fate of the church on earth before the final end and therefore he is commissioned to prophesy again. New actors will be introduced in chaps. 12 and 13. The question of idolatry, evil, and antagonism against the Messiah and his people will be unfolded thematically and John has to prophesy again.

In the second place, this interlude is thematically connected with chap. 5 through the **mighty angel** of 10:1 and 5:2. Both are introduced as *angelos ischyros*, and both visions involve a heavenly scroll. The one scroll is sealed sevenfold, the other, a **little scroll,** is **open.** By taking the sealed scroll, the Lamb that was slain was found worthy, qualified, and authorized to enact the end-time events. By taking the little open scroll and eating it (10:10), John is authorized to continue to prophesy. Moreover, the "mighty angel" reappears once more in 18:21, executing a symbolic action against Babylon and pronouncing the final verdict against "the great city" (18:24). Through the "mighty angel" of the interlude the first section (A) is interlocked with the second (B) and the third section (A′, 17:1—22:5). Through the mighty angel, the Lamb executes judgment on earth, putting into effect God's plan for the end time, as symbolized by the sealed scroll.

In the third place, the interlude links up with the cry of the martyrs under the altar (Lord, how long? 6:9-11). When the fifth seal had been opened, the martyrs were told to wait "a little longer." Now, in the interlude, we hear that there shall be **no more delay** (10:6).

In the fourth place, we have heard thus far that the people of God are "sealed," protected from the wrath of God (7:1-8) and from the demonic onslaughts of the end time (9:4). The impression could arise that they would have smooth sailing through the apocalyptic storms which will engulf the world. The second part of the interlude will clarify such misconceptions. The community which has already experienced tribulation because of its witness (1:9; 2:9-10, 13) will be subjected to "the great tribulation" (7:14), exemplified in the fate of the two witnesses (11:4-13) and narrated in the visions of chaps. 12–14. Thus the interlude serves as introduction to chaps. 12–14 and simultaneously connects with and elaborates 7:14. There the redeemed are identified as those "who have come out of the great tribulation." In short, the interlude discloses that the faithful are not protected from death, but *in* death, like the two witnesses of 11:3-13.

In the fifth place, the interlude is thematically connected with the seventh trumpet (11:15-19), because at its call **the mystery of God** shall be fulfilled (10:6-7). The word "mystery" in apocalypticism means divine but concealed information about heaven and/or the end time, which is revealed to the apocalypticist. Just so, *1 Enoch* 103:2 reads: "I know this mystery; I have read the tablets [in heaven]. . . . I have understood the writing in them." For John, this mystery is an open message. It is "the revelation of Jesus Christ" (1:1), who shall reign with the Lord God on earth (11:15) in the days of the seventh trumpet blast. Then "the mystery" is fulfilled.

In the sixth place, the interlude refers to the same time span and situation as do chaps. 12–14. The 42 months of 11:2, or 1,260 days of 11:3, are repeated in 12:6 and 12:14 ("a time, and times, and half a time" = 3½ years, or 42 months). Likewise, the time for the beast to exercise its blasphemous power lasts 42 months (13:5). Through identical time references the center section (chaps. 12–16) is tied to the interlude and thereby to the first section (chaps. 4–11) of Part II.

Finally, **the beast** mentioned for the first time in the interlude (11:7) reappears in chap. 13, together with its worshipers (cf. 14:9-11; 16:2, 6, 10). The climactic conclusion of John's letter (17:1—22:5) will deal with the destruction of the beast, his two colleagues, and his minions. This beast "that ascends from the bottomless pit" (11:7) is the counterimage of the Lamb even as **the great city, Sodom and Egypt,** is Babylon, the counterimage of the new Jerusalem. In summary, the interlude connects important prior and subsequent topics and functions as introduction to chaps. 12–16. The announcement of **the third woe** (11:14) is placed strategically between the interlude and the seventh trumpet. Thereby it joins the interlude as well as the last trumpet vision via 12:12 with the bowl visions (15:1—16:21) which complete the third woe.

After we appreciate the bridge position of this interlude in terms of structure and themes we should also take cognizance that this subsection has an integrity of its own. It consists of one single vision in several parts, dealing with the theme of prophecy (explicitly in 10:7-11; 11:3, 11 and implicitly also in 10:3-4; 11:1-2). Without ever calling himself a prophet, John treated the subject of his own prophetic task at the beginning (1:3), at the center (10:8-11), and at the end of his letter (22:9, 18-19).

Preview: The Open Little Scroll and the Commissioning of John (10:1-11)

The Angel and the Seven Thunders (10:1-4). The **mighty angel** that John saw **coming down from heaven** has characteristics similar to those of Christ in the inaugural vision (1:12-20). He is

wrapped in a cloud like the Son of man (Dan. 7:13; cf. Rev. 1:13; 14:14) with a **rainbow over his head** (cf. 4:3), **and his face was like the sun** (cf. 1:16), **and his legs like pillars of fire** (cf. 1:15). He spoke **with a loud voice, like a lion roaring** (1:15b; 5:5). The cloud also recalls God's revelation on Mount Sinai, and the rainbow which surrounded God in the throne room vision (4:3) recalls his covenant with Noah. The angel's appearance is appropriate for his task as representative of God and the Lamb, and his gigantic size is equal to his loud roaring voice. **His right foot on the sea, and his left foot on the land** marks him as representative of God and his Messiah who have authority over land and sea. He held in his hand **a little scroll** that was **open.** The reader would now like to know the content of the little scroll, but our text does not tell us. The most we can perceive is a contrast between the sealed scroll and the little **open** scroll. The content of the latter was accessible to all, because the scroll was open, even though it needed prophetic interpretation. Instead of hearing about the content, an interruption occurs in the vision narrative.

When the angel **called out, the seven thunders sounded** (Psalm 29), and John understood what they said. When he **was about to write** what he had just heard, **a voice from heaven**—perhaps from an angel, named Voice—called out, "**Seal up what the seven thunders have said, and do not write it down.**" This prohibition is surprising in view of the twofold command to write in the inaugural vision (1:11, 19; cf. 22:10). In contrast to the usage of Dan. 12:4, to **seal** here means not to write at all. It is obvious that what the seven thunders had spoken is not contained in John's apocalypse, so there is no way for us to know what the seven thunders actually said. Yet we must ask, Why did John narrate this episode which interrupts the flow of the narration of his new commission? Why tease the reader or hearer and tell of the prohibition against divulging this particular message? Two suggestions may be in order. One, by narrating this prohibition John tells us that his book does not contain all there is to know about the end. It is not an all-embracing prophecy. Two, with this teaser John *may* have marked the difference between his own prophecy and that of other apocalyptic prophets. They tried to predict apocalyptic timetables and figure out the date of the day of the Lord and the date of the parousia. John's book of prophecy, from the first to the last chapter, is a testimony that it is not for us "to know the times and seasons which the Father has fixed by his own authority" (Acts 1:7). God knows the day and the hour of Christ's parousia (Mark 13:22). All that true prophets and the church need to know is that he is coming "soon" (Mark 13:30; Rev. 1:1; 22:6, 12, 20). The transmission of calculations is prohibited because it would constitute false prophecy. Incidentally, the reference to 2 Cor. 12:3-4 as background to this prohibition is beside the point, since John is pictured as being on earth and not involved in a heavenly journey.

The Oath of the Angel (10:5-7). Then **the angel . . . lifted up his right hand to heaven.** Standing "on sea and land" and raising his hand "to heaven" the angel is touching the basic elements of creation. And he **swore by him** who is the creator of **heaven . . . the earth and . . . the sea** and all that exists within them **that there should be no more delay.** The background of this oath is Dan. 12:4-9. After Daniel had sealed his book "until the time of the end," an angel swore "by him who lives for ever that it would be for a time, two times, and half a time" (= 3½ years) until the end arrives and the oppression of God's people ceases. In contrast to Daniel's prediction, God's strong angel swore that there shall be **no more delay** (cf. 6:10), but when the trumpet call of the **seventh angel** is sounded (11:15-19), then **the mystery of God, as he announced to his servants the prophets, should be fulfilled.** The combination of the imminent-end expectation and the prohibition against calculating the dates of the end is typical of early Christian prophecy (cf. Mark 13:26-33; 1 Thess. 5:1-3). The **mystery of God** is not identical with mysterious calculations or reading heavenly tables or scrolls about the end. It is "the revelation of Jesus Christ" (1:1) in judgment and in salvation. This "open" mystery is announced by the loud voices in heaven after the blowing of the seventh trumpet: "The kingdom of the world has become the kingdom of our Lord and of his Christ, and he shall reign for ever and ever" (11:15). This mystery of God's purpose with his creation comes to full realization only at the end. God's purpose in creation and the redemption made possible by the blood of Christ will be brought to fulfillment, and that purpose is the kingdom of God on *earth* (cf. Matt. 6:10: "Thy will be done on *earth*"; Matt. 5:5: "Blessed are the meek, for they shall inherit the *earth*"). God's saving purpose, his reign over his creation as king, was **announced** by him as good news (Greek, *euengelisen*) to his **prophets.** According to Amos, "the Lord God does nothing, without revealing his secret to his servants the prophets" (Amos 3:7). John saw himself in continuity with Old Testament and New Testament prophets, even though he never explicitly applied this title to himself. It is the prophets' all-consuming task to communicate a vision of God's kingdom and to inspire trust in the certainty of its future coming. The next verses will attend to this task.

John's Commission (10:8-10). **Then the voice . . . from heaven,** the voice that had prohibited him from writing down the message of the seven thunders (v. 4), spoke to him **again,** commanding him to **take the scroll which is open in the hand of the angel.** In turn, the mighty angel commanded him: **"Take it and eat; it will be bitter to your stomach, but sweet as honey in your mouth."** And John **took the little scroll from the hand of the angel and ate it** and found it to be **sweet** and **bitter.** The background to this commissioning in the form of a prophetic symbolic action is found in Ezek. 2:8—3:3. There the prophet is asked "to eat a scroll" which tasted in his mouth "as sweet as honey." Ezekiel 2 and John's subsequent interpretation of this symbolic action make it clear that the point is prophesying rather than eating books (10:11). The prophet's task is to appropriate and internalize God's message entrusted to him. This message, symbolized by the little scroll, does not originate with him but comes from God. The prophet's mission is, first of all, to make that message his own, to assimilate it. The word of God has to become his or her own word. John's commission, in contrast to Ezekiel's, will also be a **bitter** experience because as a prophet he will be subject to opposition. The two prophetic witnesses (11:7-10) suffer death in the war with the beast. He too will encounter the world's opposition. He himself will be involved in suffering that precedes the salvation of Christ's followers. Trials and even martyrdom are the road into the kingdom of the last day. Hence the scroll is bitter. Yet the prophetic task of representing God and proclaiming salvation and victory is also **sweet** like honey (cf. Jer. 15:16). It is God who preserves his church through trials and even death, and hence the scroll tastes sweet. The cruciform church will share in the glory of the new day with the Lamb that has conquered through death.

Commission (10:11). **And I was told** (literally, "and *they* say"; Greek, *kai legousin,* the angel-voice *and* the mighty angel), **"You must again prophesy about many peoples and nations and tongues and kings."** After the prophet internalizes God's word, his mission is to announce it. **He must again prophesy about many peoples** and **kings.** And so he does in the visions following the trumpet cycle. But there is a small problem with the identification of the "peoples" and the "kings." Also, the translation of the Greek preposition *epi* (with dative) is uncertain. If its meaning is "against" (e.g., Acts 11:19, "against Stephen"), then the "peoples" and the "kings" are pagans. In favor of this meaning is the prophetic activity of the two witnesses in 11:3-11 which infuriates the beast (king) to the point of killing them. And "the peoples . . . gaze at their dead bodies" and rejoice. If the meaning of the preposition is "to" or "about" (so RSV; e.g., John 12:16, "about him"), then there are two possibilities. One, John's task may be to prophesy about the future destiny of (pagan) kings and peoples, as he does in the rest of the letter. Two, the "peoples" and "kings" may refer to Christ's inclusive, royal community, consisting of many tongues and peoples (cf. 5:9) in which all are equal, kings and queens before God. It is "about" the church that John must prophesy, about the church's immediate future under persecution by beasts and its ultimate future in the presence of God and the Lamb (cf. 21:1—22:5). Of the three options, I would prefer the first because it ties in with the last part of the interlude.

Considerable discussion has taken place also concerning the content of the little scroll and its relation to the sealed scroll of Revelation 5 on one hand and to the rest of John's letter on the other. The sealed scroll, some argued, extends only from 6:1 to 11:19, while the little scroll covers chaps. 12 to 22. In that case, the little scroll (Greek, *biblaridion*) would be "longer" than the sealed scroll (Greek, *biblion,* 5:1). This is improbable. Hence other interpreters proposed that since the little scroll with its bitter-sweet taste has to be shorter than the sealed scroll, its content is found in 11:1-13. Hardly—because 11:1-13 is part of the same vision. Still another approach would see the content of the little scroll in "the mystery of God" (10:7) which includes the "bitter" ordeal for the church, chaps. 12–16, as well as the "sweet" reversal of the conquerors in 15:2-4. Finally, one could see the content of the little scroll in the authorization of John to prophesy again (10:11).

We should keep in mind that John did not specify the content of either scroll. Therefore it would seem to be a questionable undertaking to try to refine his writing and specify what he had left open-ended. When he used difficult symbols he always provided an interpretation, for example, eating the little scroll means to prophesy. All we can say with certainty is that the little scroll is **open.** John's commission and message are open for each and all to hear and scrutinize. Moreover, the **sweet** and **bitter** taste expresses the theme of victory through tribulations (cf. 11:4-13), and John's new commission entails his existential participation in this theme.

Preview: The Measuring of the Temple and the Two Witnesses (11:1-13)

The Measuring of the Temple (11:1-2). Chapter 11 continues the same vision that began in 10:1. The symbolic action of eating the little scroll, A (10:8-11), is followed by the commission, B (10:11), and by the new prophetic action of measuring the temple, A′ (11:1-2). It concludes with the commission and fate of the two witnesses, B′ (11:3-13). The action has moved from heaven to earth. Up to the interlude, John had been a spectator in heaven of the drama which originated from heaven. With his new commission he is placed on earth, and with the command to measure the temple he becomes actively involved in one brief episode. He was given a measuring rod and commanded to **measure the temple of God and the altar and those who worship there,** but not the outer court, because it has been given over to **the nations** who will **trample over the holy city for forty-two months.**

Measuring the *sanctuary* rather than the **temple** (so RSV, but Greek, *naos*) is done either in order to rebuild it (e.g., Ezek. 40:3-5; 41:3), or in order to destroy it (e.g., Amos 7:7-9), or in order to protect and preserve it (Zech. 2:1-5). Here, obviously, only the last meaning applies, for a contrast is drawn between the sanctuary and the altar on one hand and the court outside the sanctuary on the other. The latter will be given over to the nations. From Wellhausen's time on, interpreters have suggested that John here used a Jewish prophetic oracle from the Zealot party which promised God's protection for Jerusalem's temple during the rebellion of A.D. 66–70. The difficulty with this suggestion becomes apparent when we ask, Why would John incorporate an oracle that was plainly contradicted by the subsequent events that led to the temple's destruction? Moreover, why would he use a prophetic prediction from the Zealots, who started the war against Rome with false messianic hopes and who caused grief to the church of Jerusalem because it would not participate in the war hysteria? Josephus clearly identified messianism as the cause for the war (*War* 6.312).

More realistic would be the hypothesis that these two verses are the oracle of a Jewish-Christian prophet at the time of the war against Rome. This Jewish-Christian prophet understood the **temple of God** metaphorically, as the Jewish-Christian community. The Qumran community, which denounced the temple in

Jerusalem as being polluted and in need of an eschatological cleansing, also regarded itself as the temple of God. Thus, a metaphorical understanding of the temple of God was known in the first century, prior to John, and was also taken over by other New Testament writers (e.g., 1 Cor. 3:16; 6:19; 2 Cor. 6:16; Eph. 2:21). In this Jewish-Christian oracle the temple of God (better: God's sanctuary) consists not of stones but of people who **worship** God by calling upon the name of Jesus (cf. Acts 2:21). God's temple, the Jewish-Christian community, will be protected even though God's judgment will fall on Jerusalem, the holy city. A tradition such as this may have been available to John. According to it, the **court outside the temple** sanctuary and the **holy city** (Jerusalem) are not to be "measured," that is, God will not protect them. Unrepentant, unbelieving Judaism will be **given over to the nations.** The Gentiles, Romans, will **trample over** Jerusalem for **forty-two months.** A parallel to this hypothetical oracle is found in Luke 21:24: "Jerusalem will be trodden down by the Gentiles, until the times of the Gentiles are fulfilled."

How did John use this tradition? First, for him the **temple of God** is no longer Jewish Christianity but the Christian worldwide community.

Second, for him Jerusalem is no longer the **holy city,** but it is symbolic of the world hostile to God and therefore equal to **Sodom and Egypt** (v. 8).

Third, just as the interlude of 7:1-8 speaks of the preservation of the church during the apocalyptic tribulations, so 11:1-2 conveys the same promise but with a new emphasis. The temple of God, the true worshipers in all countries and among all tongues and tribes, are promised protection *from* God's wrath and preservation *in* the end-time tribulations which last but a short time, only **forty-two months.**

Fourth, in John's reinterpretation **the holy city** has also become the symbol of the Christian community, like the temple of God, the altar, and the worshipers at the altar (cf. 5:10a). The holy city, the Christian community, will be trampled over by the nations for a limited time (cf. 13:5-7). John's reinterpretation focuses on the apparent paradox that on one hand the community (the temple) will be protected (measured) and on the other hand the community (the holy city) will be trampled upon and experience suffering without protection. This point of view is determined by the cross of Christ. The crucified, defenseless one is the protected one and vice versa. The temple of God and the holy city, the faithful church on earth, will share his fate, his suffering and death, which are at the same time victory and preservation from eternal death.

Fifth, the newly commissioned John is commanded to **measure** the sanctuary, the altar and those who worship there. It is the prophet's task to determine who belongs to God's people and who does not (cf. 2:14-15; 2:20-23; 3:16). Therefore the measuring here symbolizes not only divine protection but also "prophetic action" that marks off the area that belongs to God. The instrument for his prophetic task is **given** to him. This measuring rod is none other than "the word of God" and "the testimony of Jesus" (1:2, 9; 19:10). The "area" to be marked off by John is God's people who **worship** him. It is a rather small area in comparison to the vastness of space outside the sanctuary. Yet, however small the area may be in which God is worshiped, it is filled with dynamic witnesses (11:3-13).

Sixth, the measuring of the sanctuary is also a prophetic anticipation of the measuring of the new Jerusalem (21:15-21). The community, preserved by God, will appear as new creation, a perfect foursquare city, with no separate temple building, because "its sanctuary [Greek, *naos*] is the Lord God the Almighty and the Lamb." And "nothing unclean shall enter" this city of perfect measurements, "nor any one who practices abomination or falsehood" shall be found in it (21:22, 27).

The suffering of the church lasts but **forty-two months.** This period of three and a half years has its origin in Daniel (7:25; 12:7). It was the time from the persecution and abomination by Antiochus Epiphanes (167 B.C.) to the rededication of the temple (164 B.C.). However, the number 42 also has a symbolic significance in that it is a messianic number. Three times fourteen equals forty-two. Fourteen is the sum of the letters of David in Hebrew (*daled* = 4; *waw* = 6; *daled* = 4: *dwd* = David; cf. Matt. 1:17). In this context the 42 months indicate the period of the messianic woes, to which the community will be subjected and in which it will be protected. This period is also the time of the church's witness (11:3) and the time during which the beast can exercise his bloody authority (13:5). While the church's future is assured, the *trampling* of the church (cf. Dan. 8:13-14) will hardly bring cheap consolation to troubled Christians.

There is a striking difference between this interlude and 2 Thess. 2:1-12. There, Christians are indeed consoled, because the future manifestation of Antichrist, of "the man of lawlessness," will not bring new oppression, persecution, and martyrdom. Rather, the Antichrist will appear as a false prophet with "wicked deception" who, through signs and wonders, will seek to lead astray "those who did not believe the truth." For John, eschatology is not just the consolation of the orthodoxy of all who "love the truth," but it is the call for a new vision in the face of the forthcoming "trampling" of the church by the pagans. In short, the purpose of Revelation is not consolation but a new vision.

The Two Witnesses (11:3-13). Without a new introduction, this section expands and unfolds the commission of 10:11 and it also interprets aspects of the two symbolic actions. By eating the little scroll, John received a foretaste of the things to come. Now he will show us why the little scroll tasted not only sweet but bitter and why the community, in spite of divine protection, is subject to being trampled down by the nations (11:2). This is the most difficult section in Revelation. We can safely assume that John used and reinterpreted a Jewish-Christian tradition, but its original form is no longer accessible to us. Hence we must try to understand its meaning within John's composition and be aware that not every detail of this picture may have an equivalency in meaning. The section has two parts: vv. 3-6 describe the two witnesses ("these are . . . ," "these have . . . ," vv. 4 and 6); and vv. 7-13 narrate their fate and its effects.

3-6—Once again a heavenly voice is heard, just as in 10:4, 8, 11. Here it is the voice of Christ who speaks of **my two witnesses.** He calls and empowers his witnesses. That there are **two** may express the law of Deut. 19:15 or the two functions of the church as priests and kings, pictured in the olive trees and the lampstands of v. 4. Moreover, these two priests-kings-witnesses are also prophets. They have the **power to prophesy.** "Prophesy" in Revelation means to bear witness to the word of God and to the testimony of Jesus Christ (1:2, 9). Hence the designations of witness and prophet are interchangeable in this section (cf. vv. 3 and 10). The exalted Christ himself is "the faithful witness" (1:5), who enacts God's purpose for the end time, and the prophet John bears witness to the revelation of Jesus Christ (1:1-2). The two witnesses of this section are prophets who announce God's judgment and salvation even though the content of their message is not specified. What is specified is the duration of their witness, during 1,260 days, which equals 42 months (v. 2). This means that their prophetic witness takes place during the period of the church's persecution, when the church, "the holy city," is being trampled over by the nations. Finally, their appearance is specified. They are **clothed in sackcloth,** which pictures them as preachers of repentance in view of the impending doom (cf. Isa. 22:12; Jer. 4:8; Matt. 11:21). During the time of the church's tribulation, Jesus Christ will raise up powerful prophetic witnesses that call for repentance.

Who are these two witnesses? **These are the two olive trees and the two lampstands which stand before the Lord of the earth.** Attempts to identify the two witnesses with historical persons such as Peter and Paul or James the Lord's brother, and John the apostle or John the Baptist (as Elijah) and Jesus (as Moses), or Enoch and Elijah (cf. *1 Enoch* 90:31; *Coptic Apocalypse of Elijah*), or Jeremiah and Elijah (thus Victorinus of Pettau), or Moses and Elijah (Deut. 18:15, 18; Mal. 3:23) are doomed to failure. John clearly shows that he employs symbolic language. It is the symbols that communicate his message if we recognize their connections and relationships within John's book. The olive trees and the lampstands are symbols of the witnessing, royal, priestly, prophetic church during the time of the church's trials before the end. These symbols are a reinterpretation of Zech. 4:2-3; 6:11-13. In Zechariah, the two olive trees referred to *the king*, Zerubbabel, and to *the high priest*, Joshua. For John, the two olive trees represent priesthood and kingship which God has given to the church. "He made *us* a kingdom, priests to his God and Father" (1:6; 5:10; 20:6). In Zechariah the two olive trees stand on the right and the left of the single lampstand which is the temple menorah. John reinterpreted the text of Zechariah. The one lampstand of Zechariah now becomes two, so that the **two olive trees** are the **two lampstands.** This identification recalls the churches as lampstands in the inaugural vision (1:12, 20; 2:5). In short, John clearly indicated that the "two witnesses" are not two individual persons but symbols representing the Christian community. Moreover, as lampstands, the community is empowered with the Holy Spirit for its prophetic witness (4:5; 5:6). "Not by might, nor by power, but *by my Spirit*, says the Lord of hosts," according to Zech. 4:6. As olive trees and lampstands the community fulfills the functions of kings and priests in the power of the Spirit (1:6; 5:10). The number **two,** like the number seven, symbolizes the whole community and recalls the principle of two witnesses (Deut. 19:15) as well as two functions of the church, priesthood and kingship.

The witnesses are under God's special protection, so that no one can **harm** them. This recalls the prophetic action of 11:1, the sealing of 7:1-8, and the protection of 9:4. It *may* also recall the promise of Luke 10:19, where the same Greek verb occurs that is translated here with to "harm" and where the context speaks of disciples being sent "two by two" (Luke 10:1). The community, pictured as Spirit-empowered, royal and priestly prophetic witnesses, not only stands under divine protection but also is empowered like Elijah and Moses of old. The passage from Zechariah finds its fulfillment, not in two Messiahs as in Qumran (1QS 9:11), but in the church's dynamic witness. The **fire** that **pours from their mouth** recalls Elijah's destruction of the messengers of their idolatrous king (2 Kings 1:2-17, modified in the light of Jer. 5:14; cf. also Sir. 48:1-3). The **power to shut the sky** refers to the drought, through Elijah's word, of 1 Kings 17:1 (cf. Luke 4:25; note its reference to time, absent in 1 Kings). The **power over the waters to turn them into blood, and to smite the earth with every plague** recalls Moses' miracles in Egypt and points forward to the plagues of the bowl cycle (Exod. 7:14-19, etc.; Revelation 16). The Spirit-endowed community of the end time is the successor to Moses' rod and to Elijah's mantle. John pictured the church's powerful witnesses according to the pattern of correspondence between primal time and final time. As in old times Elijah and Moses heaped plagues upon their godless opponents, so during the end time will the witnesses of God do. During the final struggle between the church and the world there will be a powerful call to repentance. Just as the plagues of the first six trumpets come in response to the church's prayers (8:2-5; cf. 5:8) and just as cosmic upheavals followed the cry of the martyrs (6:10), so the prophetic witness of the community and of its dynamic preachers will call forth the eschatological law of retribution: "if any one would harm them . . . he is doomed to be killed" (v. 5).

7-13—The Fate of the Two Witnesses: The style changes from description ("these are . . . ," "these have . . . ," vv. 4 and 6) to narration. A time limit is set for their prophetic witness. **When they have finished** (Greek, *teleō*) **their testimony, the beast that ascends from the bottomless pit will make war upon them and conquer them and kill them.** Abruptly the major opponent of the church in the last days is introduced. Demonic powers from **the bottomless pit** had already appeared in 9:1. But there ironically they functioned as executors of God's wrath and therefore they could not harm the faithful (9:4). Now the eschatological antagonist makes his first appearance. His activity will be elaborated later. Through the presence of the beast in the interlude, John connected the first section (4:1—11:19) with the second and third sections. The **beast** from the bottomless pit corresponds to the beast that rises out of the sea (13:1; cf. 17:8), modeled after Dan.

7:3, 7-8. It is the anti-image of the Lamb that carries the mark of his slaughter. The fate of the prophetic witnesses parallels that of their Lord.

Against them the beast **will make war . . . and conquer them and kill them** (cf. Dan. 7:21). Again we can see that the two witnesses are not two individuals but symbols of the Christian community and its preaching. One can hardly **make war** against only two persons. The witnesses represent the church and its prophetic preachers. The word "witness" (Greek, *martys*) begins to approach the meaning of martyr. Again John links the interlude with the following section (cf. 12:17; 13:7) in which the theme of the church's eschatological struggle and apparent defeat is further developed. But the interlude also points back. The fate of **my two witnesses** (11:13) corresponds to the fate of Antipas, whom the exalted Christ called "my" faithful witness (2:13). The end-time trials of the church are prefigured and anticipated in the pressures experienced in John's present (cf. 2:3, 9, 13, 19; 3:8, 10). The question arises of whether John sought to convey that the whole church of his day with all its members will suffer martyrdom. Hardly. Even though the impression of total martyrdom could be gotten from 11:7, there are other pictures that clearly show that martyrdom is not the fate of all the faithful contemporaries of John (2:24-25; 3:3-5, 10-11, 18-20). John's point here is that the martyrs are the church's foremost witnesses and therefore they are the church's representatives. Dynamic prophets, preachers, and witnesses will experience not only protection but also death and resurrection, like their Lord. Their witness leads to the apparent triumph of evil, just as it did on Calvary's hill. Whoever bears witness as God's prophet has to deal with the satanic opponents of God's purpose and perhaps suffer visible bodily defeat. Though God equips his prophets, he does not exclude them from suffering, death, and execution. There is no room in John's book for ecclesial triumphalism which characterized much of the post-Constantinian history of the church.

8—The **dead bodies** of the witnesses lie **in the street of the great city which is allegorically called Sodom and Egypt, where**

their Lord was crucified—a picture of utter degradation. To lie unburied is the height of indignity and impiety toward the dead (cf. Tob. 1:18-20; 2:3-7). The **great city** in which they lie unburied for **three days and a half** is, first, historic Jerusalem, **where their Lord was crucified.** Also the reference to the number of its inhabitants in v. 13 (70,000, of which one-tenth, 7,000, were killed) points to Jerusalem rather than to Rome. Moreover, in Isa. 1:9-10; 3:9 and Ezek. 16:46-50 Jerusalem's inhabitants are compared to Sodom. However, in Revelation, **the great city** always refers to Babylon/Rome (14:8; 16:19; 17:18; 18:2, 10, 16, 18-19; 21:24). Therefore the great city in Revelation is, second, not a geographic location but a symbolic place. Its essential characteristic lies in the allegorical label of **Sodom and Egypt.** Sodom was the city of fornication that rejected the commandments of God and was therefore rejected by God (Isa. 1:16; Jer. 23:24). Egypt was the place of the oppression of the people of God. In short, Jerusalem, Babylon, and Rome, together with the fornicating, idolatrous, and oppressive world, are fused by John into one single entity, **the great city.** The presupposition of this fusion is that for John the historic Jerusalem has ceased to be the holy city (cf. 11:2; 20:9; 21:2, 10-23). But the beast from the abyss who brought death to Christ's witnesses is not limited to Jerusalem, for it operates through Babylon/Rome, as we shall see. The "great city" is every city that embodies self-sufficiency in place of dependence on the creator, achievement in place of repentance, oppression in place of faith, the beast in place of the Lamb, and murder in place of witness to God.

Therefore **men from the peoples and tribes and tongues and nations gaze at their dead bodies** for **three days and a half,** refusing permission for their burial. Instead of **bodies** (plural), the Greek text has the singular in vv. 8 and 9 (Greek, *ptōma*). It views the witnesses as one corporate entity. Clearly, the "great city" consists of the people of the world, that is, **of those who dwell on earth** (3:10; 6:10; 8:13; 10:11; 13:7-8; etc.). From John's point of view they are idolaters, fornicators, and oppressors of God's elect. Not only do they refuse burial for the two witnesses but they **rejoice** over their death, **make merry,** and **exchange presents** as was customary on happy occasions in antiquity. In the Fourth Gospel, we hear that people will "rejoice" at Jesus' death (John 16:20). The Lord's fate is extended to his witnesses.

But after the three and a half days a great reversal takes place. Into the two witnesses a **breath of life from God entered** (cf. Ezekiel 37) and the rejoicing of the idolaters turned into **great fear.** The **three and a half days** correspond to the 42 months, or 1,260 days, of 11:2-3 and Dan. 7:25; 12:7. They also correspond to the resurrection of Jesus "after" three days (Mark 8:31; 9:31; 10:34), indicating a brief span of time. Their resurrection and ascension **in a cloud** take place before the eyes of the world that opposed God. Our author distinguishes between "the first resurrection" of the faithful (20:4-6) and the resurrection of the rest of humanity (20:11-15). The resurrection/ascension of the witnesses in 11:12 introduces the notion of the "*first* resurrection" which is unfolded in 20:4-6. *John never tells all at once* but presents different aspects in succeeding cycles. Here he shows the apocalyptic reversal of the fate of the witnesses, raised and exalted from death and disgrace to new life (cf. 1 Thess. 4:16-17: "The dead in Christ will rise *first* . . . and we will be caught up together with them in the clouds to meet the Lord in the air"). Then he turns to the reaction of humanity that had been hostile to God's witnesses. Thereby he connected the interlude with the preceding six trumpet visions and with their climax through the seventh trumpet. On one hand, the resurrection of the witnesses unleashes **a great earthquake** in which **a tenth of the city,** that is, **seven thousand people,** perish (cf. 8:7, 9, 10, 12; 9:5, 15). But on the other hand something new occurs. While the plagues of 6:12-17; 8:7—9:19 did not lead to repentance (cf. 9:20-21), the reversal of the fate of the prophetic witnesses, their resurrection/exaltation, does make an impact. The **rest were** not only **terrified** but they **gave glory to the God of heaven.** That means that nine-tenths of humanity, or of the citizens of the Roman empire, turn to God and give him glory! Frequently, interpreters argue that the reaction of the world in 11:13 does not imply repentance and turning away from their idolatry but merely the fear of unbelieving humanity in the face of the unambiguous manifestation of God's power. However, John's statement that they **gave glory** to **God** may not be watered down. To give glory to God is the proper response to the gospel (14:7). Furthermore, to give glory to God anticipates 15:3-4 and 21:24, and it certainly precludes the damnation of those who render glory to God. In short, with 11:13c John leads us beyond the vision of 6:15-16 and 9:20-21. God's triumph in the resurrection of his faithful witnesses brings about the salvation of **the rest** of humanity. In conclusion, the interlude introduced us to the dialectic of the church's existence, to its witness and its opposition, to its protection and vulnerability, to its success (for a time) and its defeat (for a time), to its death and triumph. God is full of surprises. Through his tiny faithful church, with the measurements of the sanctuary only, he saves nine-tenths of the city in ways beyond the city's present imagination (11:1-2, 13).

The Announcement of the Third Woe (11:14)

The second woe has passed (cf. 8:13; 9:12); **behold, the third woe is soon to come.** Some interpreters are puzzled by the position of this **second woe.** Why was it not placed after 9:19? The answer is quite simple. The three woes are a literary device that serve as horizontal connections between the cycles of visions. The cycles describe different aspects of the same endtime period. The second woe connects the plagues of the trumpet visions (8:7—9:21) with the activity of the beast from the bottomless pit (11:7-10) as well as with the bitter taste of the small scroll (10:9-11). We should note that the events of the second woe are twofold. On one hand they are directed against the godless world (8:7—9:21); on the other hand they are directed against the faithful church, its prophetic preachers and martyrs. Likewise the onslaught of the demonic powers is twofold. They plague not only godless humanity, but in the beast's action they seek to destroy the church.

The announcement of **the third woe** connects the trumpet visions and the interlude with the following chapters. One would expect that the third woe would occur through the seventh trumpet (11:15-19). But, surprise! The seventh trumpet, like the seventh seal, does not contain *plagues*. Instead, it introduces the theme of *judgment*, of God's wrath "destroying the destroyers of the earth" (11:18). The theme of judgment, present in the sixth seal (6:16-17) but absent in the trumpet cycle thus far, will be elaborated in chaps. 12–20. The bowl visions of chap. 16 complete "the wrath of God" (15:1), and therefore they complete "the third woe," anticipated in 11:18.

The Seventh Trumpet (11:15-19). The oath of the angel in 10:6-7, that "there shall be no more delay," finds its fulfillment. "The mystery of God," which is his and the Lamb's eschatological reign over the world, is to be "fulfilled" in "the days of the trumpet call" by the seventh angel. Therefore the seventh trumpet announces the accomplished final judgment (11:18) and the final salvation (11:15-17, 18c). It describes the same final end events in new variations and from the perspective of the consummation of the kingdom of God. The seventh trumpet call therefore corresponds to the visions of 4:9-11; 7:1—8:1; 11:11-13; 15:2-4; 19:1—22:5. Each of John's cycles climaxes in the triumph of God in judgment and salvation. Just as the opening of the seventh seal (8:1) did not result in further destruction, so likewise the sound of the seventh trumpet did not unleash new plagues. Yet in contrast to the silence of the seventh seal, we now hear **loud voices in heaven** proclaiming the reign of God and of his Messiah on earth.

15—The proclamation in heaven of salvation on earth (v. 15) is followed by a thanksgiving (vv. 16-18) and concluded with a theophany (v. 19). The **loud voices in heaven** (cf. 19:1) are the voices of the redeemed people of God together with angels and archangels and all the company of heaven. They proclaim the final salvation. **The kingdom of the world has become the kingdom of our Lord and of his Christ** (cf. Ps. 2:2), **and he shall reign**

for ever and ever. The millennium commences (20:4-6). The manifestation of the eschatological reign of God constitutes salvation with cosmic dimensions. The worship in heaven, interrupted by seals and trumpets, resumes. As in 7:9-12, so here a heavenly liturgy in two parts proclaims salvation and responds in thanksgiving to it. The struggle of God's people on earth has ended in their victory (11:11-13), which is the consequence of God's triumph (11:15). The Messiah who has the power to open the seals by virtue of his death and exaltation reigns in unity with God forever (cf. 21:22—22:4).

16-18—Thanksgiving: As in 7:11, so here **the twenty-four elders,** the heavenly representatives of the one people of God, **who sit on their thrones before God** (cf. 4:4) **fell on their faces and worshiped God** (cf. 4:10). In chap. 4 they praise the creator. Here they give thanks that God has established his reign with finality over his creation. He did not surrender it to demonic forces and rebellious nations. Thus the vision of the heavenly worship of chap. 4 finds its conclusion in the heavenly liturgy of thanksgiving of the seventh trumpet vision. **"We give thanks to thee, Lord God Almighty, who art and who wast."** No longer is God the One "who is to come" (as in 1:4, 8; 4:8)—he has come. God is not the immutable, changeless, eternally static being that guarantees the world's status quo. At the end of time he will do a new thing. He will come and establish his kingdom with finality. In this vision of the end, he *has* come and therefore it can no longer be said of God that "he is to come." By taking his **great power,** which was his from the beginning, and putting it into operation against his rebellious creatures, God has come and **begun to reign.** His coming signals the final judgment of the **nations** who raged against him and his people (Ps. 2:1-5; Rev. 11:1-13). Their rage will be further developed in chaps. 13; 17; and 19–20, and then we will hear that God himself will declare war on them. **The time for the dead to be judged** links the seventh trumpet with 20:11-15 as well as with 11:11-13 and 20:4-6. The judgment of the **destroyers of the earth** includes not just godless people but also

Death and Hades (20:14) and the satanic trinity (16:13; 19:19—20:10) as well as Babylon (chaps. 17–18). Note the *A-B-A′* structure of v. 18. Two references to God's judgments (A and A′) enclose the main point, the thanksgiving **for rewarding thy servants, the prophets and saints, and those who fear thy name, both small and great.** To **reward** does not mean to recompense for merits achieved but to fulfill the promise of salvation to his faithful servants. Salvation in this letter is not a gift that can no longer be lost, according to the slogan, "Once saved, always saved." Rather, salvation, received in baptism (cf. 1:5-6), must be proved in life and conduct, in tribulations, the rejecting of idolatry, and in faithful perseverance unto the end. The **servants** of God that are rewarded in the end are not just the **prophets** (cf. 10:7; 11:10; Amos 3:7), but they include the **saints** and the God-fearers who "gave glory to the God of heaven" (11:13c), **both small and great.** This inclusive meaning of **servants** of God, referring to the whole people of God, also occurs in 19:5. Their *reward* is their participation in the first resurrection and the millennial reign with Christ, as we shall see (20:4-6).

19—The events initiated by the seventh trumpet conclude with a scene that contains elements of Old Testament theophanies. **God's temple in heaven** (6:9; 8:3) **was opened** so that the Holy of Holies becomes visible and **the ark of his covenant,** the symbol of God's presence and faithfulness toward his people, **was seen.** According to a Jewish tradition, the ark was hidden by Jeremiah or by an angel prior to the destruction of the temple in 586 B.C., and it will remain hidden until the final salvation has come (2 Macc. 2:5-8; *2 Bar.* 6:7-9). Now the heavenly counterpart of the hidden earthly ark becomes visible to Gentile and Jewish believers for whom the earthly ark had always been inaccessible. This disclosure of God's heavenly temple is accompanied by **flashes of lightning** (cf. Exod. 19:16ff.; Hab. 3:3ff.), **loud voices** (cf. Ps. 47:5-6), **thunder** (Ps. 104:7), **an earthquake** (Pss. 46:6; 68:8), and **heavy hail** (Isa. 30:30; Ps. 18:13). A series of theophany motifs was found also in the introduction of the throne room vision (4:5; of course, without the earthquake and hail). It occurs again as introduction and as conclusion of the trumpet cycle (8:5; 11:19); and we will encounter it once more as the high point of the seventh bowl vision (16:18). In short, the series of theophany motifs is a literary device that aids the structure of Revelation 4–16 and signals the importance of the eschatological events and their heavenly origin. On each occasion the theophany motifs are connected with the throne of God and/or the temple of God.

■ The Revelation of the Antagonists; Judgment and Salvation (12:1—16:21)

After the seventh trumpet, the hearer expected the conclusion of the letter—perhaps with a description of God's kingdom on earth (11:15-19). But John's story does not end. Instead, we now hear of the dragon's attack and the church's perils brought on by beasts. With the center section before us (B of Part II), we have arrived at the heart of John's letter which is the presence of evil, the struggle of satanic powers against God, and the place of the church in this struggle. The concluding section (A′, 17:1—22:5) will evolve out of the last episode, the seventh bowl vision (16:17-21).

The literary sequence from the seventh trumpet in chap. 11 to the visions of the woman, the dragon, and the beast in chaps. 12–13 demonstrates the basic correctness of the recapitulation theory, provided it leaves room for thematic development. As we move from the seventh trumpet vision to the vision of war in heaven we realize that the sequence of John's visions cannot be translated into an apocalyptic timetable. Rather, in kaleidoscopic fashion he now pictures the same end time in a new section with new images and emphases and from new perspectives. Obviously, in terms of time, the birth of the child in 12:5 did *not* follow the sound of the seventh trumpet (11:15-19). This child, however, is part of a new section that begins with the Messiah's birth and ends with the final judgment (16:17-21). This center section had already been introduced in 10:1—11:14, and it refers to the same time as the interlude (cf. time references in 11:2-3; 12:6, 14; 13:5). We should also keep in mind that the final judgment had already been reached in the sixth *seal* (6:16-17) and in the seventh *trumpet* (11:18; cf. 10:6-7). With the seventh *bowl* "the wrath of God is *ended*" (15:1; 16:17-21). Yet we note that 19:11—20:15 contains a new series of judgment visions. Once more, the sequence of John's visions is meant to preclude an understanding in terms of a temporal sequence of historical or eschatological events.

One could compare the three sections of Part II with three one-act plays. Each one-act drama is complete in itself, and each reaches a climactic conclusion (11:15-19; 16:17-21; 21:1-8). Yet these three sections of Part II are also interrelated and they do exhibit thematic development. Thus far we have seen that the *seal* septet, modeled on the Synoptic apocalypse, contains the birth pangs and preliminary signs of the end leading up to the final judgment. *Trumpets* one to six are the last stern warnings before the end. They are not meant to be understood as judgments. They are plagues that reveal the world's impotence when confronted with God's sovereign majesty. They are also surprising answers to the church's prayers for vindication and for the coming of the kingdom and final calls to repent, warnings issued to the world hostile to God and his people. Because humankind in its perverse stupidity refuses to repent and turn to him on whom it is totally dependent (9:20-21), a new section (chaps. 12–16) begins which will deal with the reality and experience of evil.

John's letter will now focus on those forces which challenge the sovereignty of God and the Lamb. In so doing, he responds to an obvious objection that his hearers would raise on the basis of his visions narrated thus far. It is all well and good to envision God's sovereignty (chaps. 4–11), but it is also quite irrelevant, they would argue. Where in our world is his sovereignty, except in our individual hearts that have been reborn and experienced "the first resurrection"? This center section is not concerned with theoretical questions such as: Where does evil come from? How can there be anti-God forces if God is the Almighty, the Pantocrator? It is not the satisfaction of our curiosity that John sought to meet, but the development of an in-depth vision which is able to perceive the existential experience of evil as being part of one gigantic end-time battle. This battle has already been won in heaven! (12:7-8) and the end will demonstrate it. *The bowls of wrath* will be poured out upon the worshipers of the beast. While the trumpet plagues were directed against non-Christian humanity as such, the bowl plagues are judgments that focus specifically on the followers of the demonic trinity. With them "the wrath of God is ended" (15:1; 16:17-21). We noted already, however, that a new climactic section will follow that will include new judgment visions (17:1—22:5).

The center section (chaps. 12–16) introduces new characters: the *woman* clothed with the sun (12:1), who is the counterimage to the great harlot of chap. 17; the great *dragon,* who would like to devour the woman's child but fails three times in chap. 12; *Michael* and his angels, who expel the dragon from heaven; the first *beast,* rising out of the *sea* and receiving the dragon's throne, who is the Antichrist and who, like the Lamb, also bears a mortal wound (13:1-3); the second *beast,* rising out of the *earth,* who is his ally and the counterimage of God's prophets (13:11; 19:20). The triumvirate of beasts performs "*signs*" (Greek, *sēmeion*). This noun, which is also translated as "portent," occurs exclusively in the center section of Part II (12:1, 3; 13:13-14; 15:1; 16:14; and 19:20, which refers back to 13:13). Of all these signs and portents only the heavenly woman, clothed with the sun, is a good sign (12:1).

In addition to new actors we find new verbs that did not occur in the first section (chaps. 4–11), namely, to *deceive*, to *blaspheme* and the corresponding noun "blashemy," to *accuse*, to *make war.* These verbs indicate the new theme of conflict between two contrasting power groups, between God, the Lamb, and his people on one side, and the dragon, the beasts, and their followers on the other. Moreover, *beatitudes,* absent in chaps. 4–11, reappear in this center section (14:13; 16:5) and so does the theme of *judgment*, which was absent in the first section with the exception of 6:10, 16-17, and 11:18. It now moves to the foreground and determines the bowl cycle. Just as judgment on the Egyptians at the Red Sea accompanied Israel's deliverance and its song (Exodus 14–15), so judgment is poured out upon the beast worshipers and "a new song," "the song of Moses . . . and of the Lamb," is heard (14:3; 15:3-4).

With these new characters, John changed the perspective in this one-act drama. No longer is the action of chaps. 12–13 determined exclusively by God or his angels, but the dragon and the beasts appear as antagonists on earth. The perspective of heaven that prevailed in the seal and trumpet septets has shifted to the earth, to the dragon's warfare against the woman and her offspring.

The saints had been spared the plagues of the trumpet cycle (8:3-5; 9:4). Yet God's people will not be immune to suffering. The cry of the martyrs in the fifth seal (6:9-11) and the murder of the two witnesses in the interlude (11:3-13) provided a "bitter" foretaste of chaps. 12–13. John's new visions interpret the coming struggle so that his churches can perceive the nature and underlying cause of the persecution that awaits them. He endeavored to provide an alternative, all-embracing vision for his people. Therefore the vision of the victory of God and his people provides a powerful contrast to the warfare of the dragon and his two allies that is soon to come (12:7-12; 14:1-5; 15:2-4).

In interpreting this center section, we should also be sensitive to the literary relationships between the visions, for example, (1) between the visions of the *Lamb* in chap. 5 and of the *beast* in chap. 13. Both texts follow the same pattern: presentation (13:1; cf. 5:6); authorization (13:2b; cf. 5:7); and worship and acclamation (13:4, 8; cf. 5:8-14). Individual features, such as the "mortal wound," the "horns," the description of the feet and the mouth (13:2; cf. 1:15, 16), and the "throne," show that the beast-Antichrist is an imitation of Jesus, the Lamb. (2) Note the relationship between 7:1-8 and 14:1-5. Both visions deal with the *144,000* servants of God from different perspectives. (3) We have already learned that the trumpet and bowl plagues allude to the *plagues in Egypt* with distinct emphases. The same is true of the *reaction* of the earth dwellers. Unwillingness to repent (9:20-21) leads to hardness of heart which can only curse God (16:11, 21). However, note the opposite reaction of "the rest" in 11:13. (4) The thanksgiving of the 24 elders in heaven after the seventh trumpet (11:16-18) is related to *"the new song"* of the redeemed from the earth 15:3-4. (5) The *"third woe,"* announced at 11:14, connects the trumpet septet with the bowl septet, even as the *three angels,* flying in midheaven (14:6-9), connect the center section with the climactic final section: first angel, cf. 19:10 (worship God!); second angel, cf. chap. 18; and third angel, cf. chap. 17. Note the chiastic structure! The same reverse order is found with respect to the judgments: Rev. 14:14-20 = the general judgment (A) which is followed by the judgment on the beast worshipers (cf. 14:9), chap. 16 (B); The destruction of Babylon (14:8), 18:1—19:10 (C); The destruction of the beasts and their followers, 19:11—20:10 (B′); The general judgment (A′), 20:11-15. In short, what at first glance seems to be a confusing sequence of visions turns out to be a carefully structured narration.

It should therefore not be surprising that besides the general structure found after the introduction we can detect *many other* relationships. For instance ("A" designates persecutions and judgments; "B" refers to salvation):

A	10:1—11:14	B	11:15-19
A′	12:1—13:18	B′	14:1-5
A″	14:6—20	B″	15:1-4
A‴	15:5—16:21	("It is done!" 16:17)	

The Church at War (12:1—14:20)

The Woman, the Dragon, and the Child (12:1-17)

The narrative consists of three scenes: A, vv. 1-6; B, vv. 7-12; A′, vv. 13-17. The first two scenes begin in heaven but end on earth. The last scene (vv. 13-17) expands v. 6. The high point lies in the center subsection (B) which narrates Satan's expulsion from heaven and the subsequent proclamation of victory in heaven (vv.

7-12). This proclamation also discloses the beginning of the third woe over the earth and the sea (v. 12; cf. 8:13; 9:12; 11:14). The third woe, announced in 11:14, is completed through the seventh bowl of wrath and the announcement, "It is done!" (16:17). In this way the woes connect the bowl cycle with the trumpet cycle (11:14).

The Woman, the Dragon, and the Endangered Messiah (12:1-6). The **woman** in this vision is a complex symbol because of its background and its utilization in this chapter. **A woman clothed with the sun, with the moon under her feet, and on her head a crown of twelve stars** suggests the description of Joseph's dream in Gen. 37:9, where the sun represents Israel/Jacob, the moon Rachel, and the stars the twelve patriarchs. The figure of the woman crying **out in her pangs of birth** recalls the idea of Israel/Zion as a mother in labor, awaiting the delivery of a new age in the midst of times of distress (cf. Isa. 26:16-27; LXX 26:14; 54:1; 66:7-9; Mic. 4:9-10). The woman in the "wilderness," "nourished" by God, suggests Israel's journeys during her desert years, even as the "wings" of the "eagle" in v. 14 echo the words of Exod. 19:4: "I bore you on eagles' wings."

However, the primary background of the woman in this chapter is a popular Greek or Egyptian story which John borrowed. In Greek mythology, the pregnant goddess Leto is pursued by the dragon Python, who wants to kill the goddess lest her child destroy him. But Poseidon rescues Leto, and her child Apollo does indeed slay the dragon. In Egyptian mythology the dragon's name is Typhon and his color is red. Again the mother was rescued and her child eventually killed the dragon.

In none of these stories is the woman's child separated from the mother and snatched up securely to heaven while the mother remains endangered on the earth (12:5-6). Either John has modified the Greek or Egyptian version of this myth or the modification had already been made when he adopted the story (A. Y. Collins). At any rate, he did not create vv. 1-6 out of nothing, because in that case he would have mentioned the Messiah's death.

How did John use the symbol of the mother and her child? Does the **child** refer to the Messiah? Could it not be the symbol of God's promises (so Corsini)? To answer this question we note the reference to Psalm 2 which was understood messianically in Judaism and in the New Testament. The woman's child **is to rule all the nations with a rod of iron** (v. 5). The eschatological function of the Messiah is reiterated in 19:15.

But if the child represents an individual, the Messiah, why should not the **woman** who gave birth to him also be an individual, Mary the mother of the Messiah? Would any Christian at the end of the first century not think of Mary, Jesus' mother, when hearing about the Messiah's birth? Yet there are quite a few obstacles to such an interpretation. One, the flight of the woman into the desert *after* the child's exaltation does not square with our knowledge about Mary after Jesus' ascension (Acts 1:14). Two, the New Testament does not speak of a persecution of the "rest of her offspring" (v. 17). According to the interpretation of the woman as Mary, v. 17 would single out Mary's other children, the sisters and brothers of Jesus (cf. Mark 8:31-35) as special objects of persecution. Third, while John identified the dragon as a serpent, devil, or Satan (v. 9), no such identification of the woman occurs in the text. Finally, the early church fathers did not give a Mariological interpretation of the woman of Revelation 12. Only since the late Middle Ages has Mary been pictured as the queen of heaven of 12:1.

Whom, then, does the woman represent? She represents the true people of God—more precisely, the true Israel from whom the Messiah came and the faithful church which, after his exaltation, bears witness to him (v. 17).

A woman, clothed with the sun, adorned with **a crown of twelve stars** and with **the moon under her feet,** appears as a **great portent** (Greek, *sēmeion*) in the sky (RSV, *in heaven*). John probably interpreted the constellation Virgo when the moon is at the feet of Virgo and stars surround her head. He saw in this constellation a portent, a sign, of the heavenly splendor, of the origin and destiny of the people of God on earth. This woman is the anti-image of the great harlot Babylon/Rome (Revelation 17–18). In radical contrast to the imperial cult which depicted the goddess Roma as queen of heaven, the prophet John will reveal her as a whore. He presented God's people in the image of a glorious woman arrayed with the brilliance of the sun, with moon and stars at her bidding. John had pictured the leaders of the churches as stars (e.g., 1:20), so he can depict the whole people of God in terms of the queen of heaven. **Sun, moon,** and **twelve stars** (cf. 21:14) adorn her and symbolize the promise of victory over the powers of darkness, the promise that God's people shall reign with God in the end (1:6; 5:10; 22:5).

In sharp contrast to the majestic woman in the sky is the picture of the same woman crying out **in her pangs of birth, in anguish for delivery.** John's focus has shifted to the earth, to God's people in history who, like women in labor, are wracked with pain and filled with distress. For John, the woman in childbirth can only be the true people of God prior to Jesus' birth, even as the majestic portent in the sky symbolizes the origin and destiny of God's people.

3-4—Another portent appears in the sky. Again we may think of a constellation such as the water snake, Hydrus or Typhon. **A great red dragon** appeared in the sky, **with seven heads and ten horns, and seven diadems upon his heads.** They symbolize the dragon's awesome power. In the Old Testament, such a monster served to depict Israel's oppressors (e.g., Ps. 74:14; Ezek. 32:2-4; Isa. 27:1). John's description of the beast with its **ten horns** (cf. 13:1; 17:3) recalls the fourth beast of Daniel (Dan. 7:8, 20, 24). Unlike Daniel, Revelation does not deal with a succession of empires but seeks to disclose the nature of the Roman empire and its "war" against the church. The dragon's color is **red,** like Typhon's, the color of blood and murder. His claim to rule the world is manifested in his **seven heads.** The **ten horns** show his seemingly limitless power, and **seven diadems** reflect his wealth, arrogance, and claim to world domination. The dragon is also hostile to God's creation. With **his tail** he **swept down a third of the stars** (cf. Dan. 8:10). But the primary objects of his hatred are the woman and her child. **The dragon stood before the woman who was about to bear a child, that he might devour her child.** Her situation appears hopeless.

5—Her child is to be the promised Messiah whom a young woman (LXX, a virgin) shall bear (Isa. 7:14), a male child to whom the daughter of Zion shall give life (Isa. 66:7). His destiny is to **rule all the nations with a rod of iron** (Ps. 2:9), subjecting Gentile nations to his judgment and bringing them under his lordship, paradoxically, through his word alone (19:15). His destiny discloses the reason for the dragon's enmity: this child will scuttle the dragon's plans, overthrow his power, and smash his haughtiness. The child was born **and caught up to God and to his throne.** Nothing is said about Jesus' ministry, passion, and death, which may indicate that John used a Jewish version of the popular myth (A. Y. Collins). In it Messiah designate, born of Israel, is already present in heaven, having been rescued by God from the dragon, while Israel, pursued by the dragon, awaits his coming from heaven.

John's hearers would understand the child to be Jesus. His birth in v. 5 probably refers to his death and resurrection as "the first-born of the dead" (1:5) rather than to his birth in Bethlehem. His being **caught up** to the throne of God would be understood as his exaltation (cf. Acts 2:33-35). There is another possibility. A hearer could interpret v. 5 upon the background of a hymn such as 1 Tim. 3:16: "He was manifested in the flesh" (i.e., he was born of a woman); he was "vindicated in the Spirit" (i.e., he was taken up to God's throne). In this hymn the earthly birth and the exaltation are the two foci of the Christ event. But in either case, John's main point remains the same. The dragon's attempt to **devour the child** has been foiled by an action of God, who placed Jesus on his throne in heaven (5:6). The passive voice indicates God's action; the Greek verb (*harpazō*) suggests a sudden, vehement action.

6—The child is now safe, but it is also separated from the woman who becomes the object of the dragon's murderous intent. She remains vulnerable on earth to the dragon's attacks and therefore she **fled into the wilderness.** Her flight into the desert will be the theme of the scene in vv. 13-17. The desert is the place into which God's exodus people were led. It is a place for refugees fleeing persecution. Thus Elijah fled into the desert. At the same time, the desert is the place where God nourished Elijah (1 Kings 17:2-6) and where God kept faith with his people on their journey to the promised land (Exodus 16). The desert is the opposite of "the great city" (11:8; 16:19). Just so, the **woman,** saved from the dragon, was **nourished** by God in the desert. The duration of her refuge in the wilderness was short, **one thousand two hundred and sixty days.** This is the same period as the "time, and times, and half a time" of v. 14, which has its origin in Dan. 7:25. It is the period of the persecution (11:2; 13:5), a period between John's present and the final judgment. It is also the time to bear witness (11:3) and to endure (13:10). John's picture of the woman in the wilderness is also meant to give encouragement to his churches in their faith. They must know that the dragon shall not accomplish his goal, and they must act accordingly.

The Defeat of the Dragon in Heaven (12:7-12). A new scene begins in heaven. We are not told how the dragon, who in the previous verse pursued the woman into the desert, returned to heaven. The reason for this omission is quite simple. John's story is not organized in terms of chronological sequences. Rather, our author is interested in showing the underlying causes of Satan's hatred of the church. Because he has been thrown out of heaven, he rails against the church on earth and pursues the woman into the wilderness. His wrath is great **because he knows that his time is short!** (v. 12). On the literary level we can see that John used two traditional stories, sandwiching the story of the dragon's expulsion into the story of the woman, the child, and the dragon. Hence the oddity resulted that in v. 7 the dragon is in heaven, while in the prior verses he is on earth.

7-9—The dragon is identified with **the Devil and Satan** and the **serpent** of Genesis 3. The word "devil" comes from the LXX, where it translates the Hebrew word "Satan." While Satan in the book of Job (1:6-11) was one of the sons (angels) of God and functioned as prosecutor in heaven's court, he became the opponent of God in Jewish apocalyptic traditions. This view of Satan was adopted by New Testament writers (cf. Ron. 16:20), and, like others before him, John identified Satan with the serpent of Genesis 3, who tricked Adam and Eve into disobedience and mistrust of God's word. As such, the serpent, Satan, is **the deceiver of the whole world.** Finally, John also retained Satan's Old Testament function as **accuser** before God (v. 10). As accuser, Satan is disbarred from heaven's court; as opponent, he and his angels are defeated in battle by **Michael** and expelled from heaven.

Contrary to Milton's *Paradise Lost,* Satan's expulsion from heaven is an end-time event, not one that occurred in primordial times. According to John, the dragon's expulsion takes place after, that is, in consequence of, Christ's exaltation. In contrast to the Greek and Egyptian myth, it is not the woman's child, the Messiah, who wages war in heaven against the dragon and his host, but the archangel **Michael,** Israel's guardian (Jude 9; Dan. 10:13, 21; 12:1; 1QM 13:10; 17:6-8). His name means "Who is like God?" He and his angels defeated the dragon and cast him down to earth. We can only guess why John did not substitute Christ for Michael. Perhaps the reason for the retention of Michael as leader in this heavenly war lies in the fact that this battle is not the final battle. It will be then and only then that Christ himself will wage war (19:11-21). Decisive as Satan's defeat in heaven is, his downfall is only a stage in the apocalyptic drama from the perspective of the church on earth.

10-12—The victory song in heaven is the prophetic interpretation of Satan's expulsion. The **loud voice in heaven** which John **heard** is the voice of the heavenly court (cf. 4:10-11; 5:8-9; 11:15; 19:10; 22:9). John does not know of a church triumphant in heaven before the end (cf. 6:9-11). **Now,** that is, in the time between Christ's exaltation and parousia, **the salvation and the power and the kingdom of our God and the authority of his Christ have come.** They are established **in heaven,** once and for all. In this new version of the throne room vision (chaps. 4–5) the salvation of our God consists in his victory through Michael. The **accuser of our** sisters and brothers on earth has been disbarred from heaven's court. "Who shall bring any charge against God's elect? It is God who justifies; who is to condemn? Is it Christ Jesus, who died, yes, who was raised from the dead, who is at the right hand of God, who indeed intercedes for us?" (Rom. 8:33-34).

But more—the church on earth not only lives with the assurance of God's victory over Satan in heaven, but the church itself is already victorious over its foe through **the blood of the Lamb** and **their** own **testimony.** Now it becomes clear that the ultimate cause for Satan's defeat is not Michael but Christ, his death and exaltation. The redemptive act of Christ freed believers from their sins (1:5; 5:9) and is the reason for their victory over Satan. But their victory is also inseparable from **their** own **testimony** to Christ even unto their own death (cf. the conqueror saying, 2:10). To lose one's life for the sake of Christ (Mark 8:34-35) is not defeat but victory, even as the cross of Christ is the symbol of his victory. A church that ceases to be merely a religious organization and becomes a witnessing community is a sign of Christ's eschatological reign in the present on earth. Such a church, however, inevitably becomes a suffering community, because Satan's wrath will lash out against it. The voice that John heard admonished the inhabitants of **heaven to rejoice** (cf. Isa. 49:13; Ps. 96:11). But Satan's expulsion means **woe** to the **earth.** This woe announces God's judgment not only over the anti-Christian world (14:6-20); it also anticipates persecution, sorrow, and distress for the believers, because **the devil has come down to you in great wrath,** knowing full well that **his time is short.** Yet his final perdition is a foregone conclusion because he has already been expelled from heaven. Thus the church on earth is challenged to persevere through the atoning power of Christ's death and their own testimony to his power. In summary, the hymn corrects the impression that it is Michael rather than the Messiah who will win the final battle over the foes on earth.

The Persecution of the Woman (12:13-18). John continued his mythological narrative of v. 6 and expanded it. The **dragon . . . thrown down to the earth . . . pursued the woman.** Having failed to devour the child and having been expelled from heaven, he now turns against the child's mother and fails a third time. This vision the church must appropriate as it faces the future. Before the child's birth the mother clearly represented the true Israel, and after the child's exaltation (v. 5) the woman represents the faithful church. In short, the woman here is a complex symbol. It would be false simply to identify her with the church, because the church did not bring forth the Messiah. On the contrary, Christ brought forth the church! Yet the church is in essential continuity with the true Israel of the Old Testament, not with the empirical Israel of John's day which also contains the "synagogue of Satan" (2:9; 3:9). This essential unity of the one people of God is symbolized by the twelve stars in the woman's crown which allude both to Israel's tribes and to the church's apostles (cf. 21:12, 14). In 7:1-8 we hear of those who were "sealed out of every tribe of the sons of Israel." There the sealed persons are the eschatological Israel of God before the last day. Here the woman symbolizes first the people of God in their divine destiny, second, the Old Testament people who brought forth the Messiah, and finally, after Christ's exaltation, she represents the church, the true Israel of the last days.

In her persecution by Satan the church is sustained by God. **The woman was given,** that is, God gave her, **the two wings of the great eagle** to fly **into the wilderness** and there **to be nourished** by God. The eagle's wings evoke the declaration of Exod. 19:4; Deut. 32:11; Isa. 40:30. God brought Israel on eagles' wings from Egypt, the land of idolatry and oppression (11:8), into the desert. For John, **the wilderness** in this story is not the place of demons and wild beasts (cf. 18:2-3; Mark 1:13; Luke 11:24), of nettles and thistles, jackals and hyenas (Isa. 34:13-14); here it is a place of safety and asylum from the ravages of the "great city," called "Sodom and Egypt" (11:18), where their Lord was crucified. The "great city" represents the idolatrous culture of those who oppose Christ. The desert, then, is the place where the city's influence comes to a halt.

Seeing the woman's flight into the desert, **the serpent** spit out **water like a river** to drown her in a **flood.** The sentence evokes a multitude of pictures: the sudden flash floods in the desert; Pharaoh's scheme to drown Israel at the Red Sea; the dragon's persistence and his impotence in the desert (having failed twice, vv. 5 and 9, he now fails a third time); the church's existence separate from the dominant culture. The dragon here is pictured as a sea monster and is called the **serpent.** As such, it functions as "the deceiver of the whole world" (v. 9).

The flood that was meant to drown the woman also suggests the deceptions and lies spread by Satan's apostles, whether Christians (2:2, 6, 13, 14, 20), Jews (2:9; 3:9), or imperial propagandists (13:11-17; 16:13). Their lies will seek to drown the church with falsehoods. This flood of water, spit out by the dragon, is the counterimage to "the river of the water of life" that flows from the throne of God and of the Lamb through the city of God, the new Jerusalem (22:1). The **earth** comes to the woman's rescue by swallowing the flood that had poured from the dragon's mouth. It is not easy to locate an Old Testament parallel to a personified earth rescuing the people of God from water. Perhaps John thought of Noah's **flood** in reverse, or of God's promise: "When you pass through the waters I will be with you; and through the rivers, they shall not overwhelm you" (Isa. 43:2). And we also hear of the rebellious men of Korah that "the ground opens its mouth, and swallows them up" (Num. 16:30). At any rate, the earth as God's good creation is pictured here as a helper of his people. It **swallowed** the dragon's spit, even as "the earth swallowed" the Egyptians (Exod. 15:12).

17-18—Though the dragon has failed again, he does not give up but makes **war on the rest of her offspring** (literally, on "the rest of her seed"; cf. Gen. 3:15). Once again John's letter explains to the reader/hearer what is meant by an image. The woman's offspring are **those who keep the commandments of God and bear testimony to Jesus.** This explanation is at the same time a challenge for hearers and readers to remain her offspring. The distinction between the **woman** and the rest of her **offspring** is surprising and has led interpreters to identify the woman with the Palestinian church and her offspring with the Gentile church. But elsewhere such a distinction plays no role in John's book. It would therefore seem that John viewed the church not only from the perspective of her unity, as woman, but also from the perspective of individual believers and their struggles. The individual believers are then the woman's offspring. The church has theological priority over individual Christians. Her one offspring is the Messiah (v. 5); her other offspring are those women and men who obey God's commandments and witness to Jesus who as offspring of the woman is also their brother.

The concluding statement that the dragon **stood on the sand of the sea** serves as transition to the next vision of the beast rising out of the sea. It also forms an inclusion with the scene of the Lamb standing on Mount Zion (14:1-5). Thus the intervening section deals with the dragon's war against the woman's offspring.

The Beast from the Sea and the Beast from the Earth (13:1-18)

The dragon standing by the sea was awaiting the arrival of his helper from the abyss below the sea in order to wage war more effectively against the church. In Revelation 12–14 we reach the high point of John's letter. These chapters expand Satan's struggle against the church to which the interlude (11:7) briefly referred. In the quest for world dominion Satan is aided by two demonic allies—the beast from the sea, representing Antichrist, and the beast from the earth, representing the empire's propagandists, magistrates, priests, philosophers, and others. Nowhere in Revelation do its symbols and images become so transparent for the historical situation of John's present and his envisioned future as in chaps. 13 and 17.

In order to interpret the present and the envisioned future John used parody and contrasts. His purpose was to disclose the nature of the self-deifying power, its rules and cult. The sea from which the first beast arises is the abyss, the bottomless pit (11:7), the symbol of chaos. In Near Eastern mythology the chaos monster had been bound there when creation began, but according to John it will emerge again in the last days. The counterimage to the sea as symbol of chaos is the sea of glass, brilliant like crystal, before God's throne. The beast's power and throne are a parody of Christ's authority to open the seals (5:7), as are the worship offered to the beast and its efforts to unify humanity (cf. 13:4, 7b and 5:9-10). His blasphemous name contrasts with the name of the Messiah, who is called The Word of God (19:13). Like the Lamb, the beast has "a mortal wound" (5:6; 13:3, 12). The second beast from the earth is later identified as a false prophet, and thus he functions as parody of the spirit of true prophecy (19:10). The beast's mark on his followers is a parody of baptism.

The Beast from the Sea (13:1-8). John constructed this beast on the basis of different traditions. First, the rising of the seven-headed monster **out of the sea** echoes the old story of the struggle of a god with a sea monster. In Babylonian mythology, Marduk slays Tiamat, a sea serpent, and thus becomes king. Some Babylonian and Canaanite myths tell stories of conflict between chaos and life, between destruction and creation. The Old Testament also refers to Israel's God subduing sea monsters: "Thou didst break the heads of the dragons on the waters. Thou didst crush the heads [plural] of Leviathan" (Ps. 74:13-14). According to Canaanite mythology, Leviathan had seven heads. Isaiah transferred the myth of Leviathan's destruction to the future. "In that day the Lord with his . . . strong sword will punish Leviathan the fleeing serpent, Leviathan the twisting serpent, and he will slay the dragon that is in the sea" (Isa. 27:1). This struggle will take place at the end of time. Also, the four great beasts of Daniel "came up out of the sea" (Dan. 7:3), the symbol of chaos. This chaos monster which had been defeated by the Creator in the beginning is about to return from the bottomless pit (11:7) of the sea (13:1).

Second, John's seven-headed beast has **ten horns,** speaks **blasphemies against God** (v. 6), and makes **war on the saints** (v. 7). In appearance it seems like a composite picture of Daniel's four beasts (v. 2; cf. Dan. 7:2—8:14). Indeed, the prophet John updated Daniel's apocalypse. As in Daniel, so in Revelation, the beast is used as the symbol for the godless, idolatrous empire as well as for an individual particular king who fulfills the role of Antichrist. But this role is no longer taken by Antiochus IV Epiphanes, who desecrated Jerusalem's temple in 167 B.C. by sacrificing a pig to Zeus/Baal upon its altar. For John, the envisioned Antichrist is yet to come. As a corporate entity, the beast from the sea represents the Roman empire and no longer the Seleucid kingdom of Syria.

Third, the **mortal wound** of one of the beast's heads, which **was healed** (v. 3), or the mortal wound of the beast itself (vv. 12 and 14), alludes to the Nero legend. The 32-year-old Nero had committed suicide in A.D. 68, but the circumstances of his death were apparently not widely known at that time. At any rate, the rumor arose that he had not really died but had fled to the Parthians, the great enemy on Rome's eastern frontier. Some versions of the rumor said that he would return at the head of a Parthian army and take revenge on Rome. This rumor even prompted some people to pretend to be Nero, and at least one was welcomed by the Parthians (Suetonius, *Nero* 57; Tacitus, *History* 2.8; *Sibylline Oracles,* sections in books 4 and 5). John made use of this legend when he wished to present the beast as an individual, as Antichrist, and he gave the legend a new twist. His wound was mortal (v. 12), he had really died. The Greek words of v. 3, *esphagmenēn eis thanaton* (literally, "slain unto death"), require that we recognize the parallel to the slain Lamb (5:6, 12; 13:8) where the same Greek verb is used. This beast, therefore, represents a parody of the Lamb that was slain. The fact that John avoided speaking of the beast's resurrection should not mislead us into thinking that he was merely talking about the empire's vitality (so Mounce). The beast was "healed" from the wound that brought it death. It came to life again (v. 14; see comments there). The Nero legends that circulated toward the end of the first century did not refer to his death and resurrection or to his return from Hades (A. Y. Collins, 176–83). Therefore it will rise out of the sea, or the abyss (11:7; 13:1), in contrast to the Lamb, who shall come from heaven. The beast in Revelation 13 and 17 represents not only the Roman empire (17:3) but also an individual person in whom all evil and idolatry are concentrated (13:14-15; 17:8-16). To portray this individual, John made use of the Nero legend. Thus the beast is a complex symbol suggesting that the chaos monster shall return like a reincarnated Nero and wage war against God's people like the Syrian oppressor. But he also shall destroy Rome, the great harlot (17:16), in accordance with God's supreme irony.

1-4—The beast **rising out of the sea** is the same one as in 11:7. It has **ten horns** with **ten diadems** and **seven heads,** and a **blasphemous name** written **upon its heads.** For John, the titles applied to Roman emperors in the imperial cult of his region express their blasphemous intent: Augustus, "The Venerable One"; its Greek form, *Sebastos,* "The Revered One," the one worthy of reverence; divine (Latin, *divus*); Lord and God—all of these expressions of deification are blasphemies against the one true God. These names are a parody of the King of kings and Lord of lords whose name is "The Word of God" (19:13, 16). The beast from the sea combines the shape and the features of the four beasts of Daniel 7. There the lion, the bear, a four-headed leopard, and a fourth beast with ten horns represent four world empires in succession. John was not interested in portraying the sequence of oppressive empires from the Babylonians to the Hellenistic states, but in evocative images he presented the nature of the empire of the last days in its opposition to God and his people. As the beast, this empire has assumed all the bestial features of the four animals in Daniel. Its form is like a **leopard, its feet**

were like a bear's, and its mouth was like a lion's mouth. It has **ten horns,** like Daniel's last beast. Moreover, it has **seven heads,** the sum total of the heads of Daniel's beasts. The **diadems,** insignia of royal messianic authority (19:11), are not worn on its heads but on its horns, suggesting the glorification of the beast's brute power. Though it has seven heads, it seems to have but one **mouth** with which it utters **blasphemies** (vv. 5-6). John expressed individual ideas in pictures, and he was not bothered that the resulting picture as a whole would look rather bizarre.

The dragon invested the beast with his **power** and **throne** and **authority** in a parody of the Lamb (3:21; 5:8, 13). Moreover, one of the beast's **heads seemed to have a mortal wound** (literally, one head was "like slain unto death"). The words "like" and "seemed" (Greek, *hōs*) do *not* indicate that death had not occurred (cf. 5:6 with respect to the Lamb). Later on, John will simply speak of the beast's mortal wound (vv. 13, 14; cf. 5:12; 13:13 with respect to the Lamb). The beast at this point represents the empire and is distinguished from the head, which represents an individual, an emperor. Later, in vv. 13 and 14, however, the beast becomes the symbol of an individual whose image is to be worshiped on pain of death. The idea of Antichrist emerges in this chapter and is further developed in chap. 17.

This idea can be traced back to Dan. 9:27; 11:31; 12:11. The Qumran community also expected the appearance of a cursed one, "one of Belial," who would make Jerusalem a "bulwark of godlessness" (4QTest 22-26). The Marcan apocalypse referred to false Christs who appear before the end (Mark 13:21-22) and to the desolating sacrilege (Mark 13:14), which in the language of Daniel recalls the infamous deed of Antiochus IV, the prototype of the Antichrist (cf. 2 Thess. 2:3-8). In contrast to the Johannine epistles, where the Antichrists are heretical teachers (1 John 2:18, 22; 4:3; 2 John 7), our prophet John modeled Antichrist on Daniel's portrait of Antiochus, with features from other beasts and from the Nero legend.

The humanity of the inhabited world **worshiped the dragon and the beast.** The issue in the coming struggle of the church will be worship. People will either worship God and the Lamb or they will hail and render obeisance to the beast and to its master, the dragon. Their cry, **"Who is like the beast?"** is a parody of "Who is a God like you?" (Mic. 7:18; cf. Exod. 15:11; Isa. 44:7; Ps. 89:8; etc.). The second rhetorical question, **"Who can fight against it?"** parallels the question, "Who is worthy to open the scroll?" (5:2). The rhetorical questions of the beast worshipers are implicit affirmations of its assumed omnipotence and its universal claim.

5-8—The beast's omnipotence had been presented as a gift from the dragon (v. 2), but now we hear that it is God who tolerates its blasphemous activity and limits its authority to **forty-two months** (11:2-3; 12:6, 14; Dan. 7:25). The dragon and the beast remain minions under God's supreme control, and they can function only by his permission. The Greek verb *edothē* (it was given; it was allowed) is repeated four times in vv. 5-7. John's hearers may not lose their proper perspective in the distress that is to come. Not even Antichrist can escape God's plan and time frame. "One little word subdues him" (Luther, "A Mighty Fortress Is Our God").

The beast **was allowed to make war on the saints** (v. 7). It was for this purpose that the dragon/Satan had waited for his ally's arrival (12:18—13:1). In this war, which for John lies in the near future, the beast will be victorious and will be able to **conquer them** (cf. Dan. 7:21, 25). Against the onslaught of the beast, the church on earth is no match. It will suffer the fate of its Lord. There is an apparent tension between 13:7 and 12:14 which promises God's nourishing care during the time of the eschatological persecution. This tension can be maintained only if we keep in mind that for John, as well as for other New Testament writers (e.g., Mark 8:34-35), martyrdom equals victory and vindication because God raised the Messiah Jesus from the dead. Furthermore, it is improbable that John envisioned that the whole church would be martyred in the end, even though the whole church will have to face the martyrdom of many of its members. For

John, the martyrs represent the church, even as Antichrist, slain but alive, represents the empire.

The worship of the beast has unifying power. **Every tribe and people and tongue and nation,** all are united in the patriotic worship of Antichrist. Their unity is a parody of the inclusive nature of the people of God (5:9-10) and its worship (19:6-8; 22:1-5). Everyone is fascinated by the beast, except the church, which John now defines from the perspective of predestination. The church is those people whose names are **written . . . in the book of life.** These are the elect, predestined for salvation since **before the foundation of the world** (Eph. 1:4). Simultaneously, John would insist that the mere presence of one's name in the book of life does not guarantee that Christ himself "will not blot his name out of the book of life" (3:5; cf. 2:5; 3:16).

The Call for Endurance (13:9-10). Because the elect can fall away, John interrupts the vision narrative with a call for attention to his hearers (cf. 2:7; etc.). This call consists of two couplets. The Greek text of the second couplet is uncertain. The RSV translates, **If any one slays with the sword, with the sword must he be slain.** This is a prophetic oracle which introduces the principle of retributive justice as a warning to persecutors and Christians alike. The latter may not retaliate with violence. This version of the oracle was probably produced by an early copyist under the influence of a saying such as "all who take the sword shall perish by the sword" (Matt. 26:52). Our best manuscript for Revelation, Codex Alexandrinus, contains a different version which reads: "If anyone is to be slain with the sword, she/he will be slain with the sword" (cf. Jer. 15:2 as background for this oracle). The first couplet reads: **If any one is to be taken captive, to captivity he goes.** John prophetically admonished his people to acknowledge God's will in whatever befalls them, even captivity, even martyrdom. Those believers who accept what God has ordained are the conquerors of the beast (cf. 12:11) and followers of their Lord whose victory was sealed in his death (3:21). No lukewarm coexistence with the beast is possible for those who have **an ear** to **hear. Here is a call for the endurance and faith of the saints** (cf. 14:12). This call contains the reason why John told his vision about the beast. His people must know what will be coming upon them, and they must persevere in the worship of God. In the assurance that their names are already written in the book of life, Christians can withstand the attacks of the beast and endure unjust suffering.

The Beast from the Earth (13:11-18). In contrast to the beast from the sea which is a composite of diverse traditions, the **beast** from the **earth** was John's own creation. The hippopotamus-like land monster Behemoth of Job 40 (cf. *1 Enoch* 60:7-10) did not lend any features to John's earth beast. The Synoptic apocalypse, however, referred not only to "false Christs but also to false prophets" (Mark 13:22). Therefore after the pseudo-messianic sea monster, John presents the pseudo-prophetic land monster whose propaganda glorifies the beast and whose signs and wonders legitimize his message and fascinate the people. With the dragon and the two beasts, John depicted a "Satanic trinity," as J. H. Jung Stilling (died 1817) called this triumvirate of evil. The parody is now complete. As Jesus Christ received his power and authority from God the Father, so the countermessianic beast receives his "power and his throne and great authority" from Satan, the dragon (13:2). And just as the Holy Spirit bears witness to Christ through the testimony and signs (cf. 11:4-6) of prophets and witnesses (19:10), so the second beast is identified as a false prophet (19:20; 20:10) who proclaims the dragon's message and performs "signs" (13:11, 14). The prophetic beast's goal is to establish the worship of Antichrist within a worldwide cultic community under Satan, the dragon. Some details are as follows:

11-14—The second beast **rose out of the earth.** This does not just mean that the false prophet is indigenous to Asia Minor, whereas the first beast arrives from Rome via the sea, representing the empire. The phrase also alludes to 12:12, to the "woe" over the **earth** and the **sea.** The dragon assures his control over both regions through his allies from the sea and the earth. The second beast **had two horns like a lamb.** Not the beast's whole appearance but only its **horns,** the signs of its power, are likened to the Lamb. The power of the false prophet is impressive, like the power of the Lamb. But **it spoke like a dragon,** like the serpent (12:9) in the Garden of Eden, deceiving, deluding, and seducing women and men. We are reminded of the warning against false prophets who are wolves but appear in sheep's clothing (Matt. 7:15). In Revelation, however, the false prophet does not claim to speak in the name of Jesus. He is the dragon's mouthpiece. Yet he imitates the activity of Jesus' prophetic witnesses.

Just as their authority is totally derived from their Lord, so the second beast's **authority** is derived from the **first beast.** And just as the prophetic witness of Jesus proclaims the crucified and risen one to the whole world, so the function of the false prophet is to make the world **worship the first beast, whose mortal wound was healed.** Finally, just as Jesus' prophets perform miracles (11:5-6; cf. 2 Cor. 12:12), so does the pseudo prophet of the beast (cf. Mark 13:22), aping the **great signs** of Elijah (cf. 11:5), **making fire come down from heaven to earth in the sight of men** and with their miracles they **deceive those who dwell on earth** (vv. 13-14). Like the magicians at Pharaoh's court (Exod. 7:11), the false prophet imitates the miracles of God's servants. Miracles in themselves are always ambiguous. The difference lies in their origin, purpose, and goal which are either those of God or the dragon. This second beast represents Roman proconsuls of the province of Asia, the local political authorities, and also the "philosophers," orators, and priests of the emperor cult who function as propaganda organs on behalf of Antichrist. Moreover, worship will be the issue. Just as the Israelites made an image, the golden calf (Exodus 32), so the advocates of the emperor cult are **bidding** the populace to **make an image for the beast which was wounded by the sword and yet lived,** better, "came to life" (Greek, *ezēsen*). John avoided resurrection terminology with respect to the beast and instead used an equivalent: the beast with the fatal wound *came to life* again (cf. 2:8; 20:4-5 for this meaning). The **image** of

Antichrist, with a fatal wound, yet alive, is the ultimate parody of God's Messiah slain, yet enthroned. We should not imagine that cult statues of the slain Nero had already been fashioned at John's time of writing, but he envisioned such for the immediate future.

15-18—The second beast **was allowed** (Greek, *edothē*) **to give breath to the image** of the first **beast** with the fatal wound, **so that the image of the beast should even speak.** God permits religious hucksters to rip off the world's gullible and idolatrous people. There are quite a few references in the literature of that time to magicians who made statues of gods move and talk. Simon Magus (Ps. Clem. *Recog.* 3.47; cf. Acts 8:9-11) is said to have brought statues to life, and, according to Lucian (*De Dea Syra* 10), some statues in the temple of Hierapolis, near Laodicea, were also able to move. John did not deal critically with the tricks employed by pagan priests, the hidden pulleys that made statues move or the ventriloquy by priests that made them speak. For him, it is a given tradition that false prophets perform miracles (cf. Mark 13:22), though undoubtedly his vision reflects contemporary rumors about miraculous images.

The second beast causes **those who would not worship the image of the** (first) **beast to be slain.** In the near future the people of God will have to face the threat that had confronted them at the time of the Babylonian king Nebuchadnezzar. He had set up a golden image and demanded that all nations worship the image on pain of death (Daniel 3). But John did not merely incorporate a tradition about the persecution of God's people because of their rejection of pagan images. He also reflected concrete experiences of his own time (cf. 2:13). Pliny's letter, written only 15 years after John's letter, demonstrates that Christians who were brought before him and refused to sacrifice before the emperor's image were executed (see introduction, section 2).

Moreover, the second beast **causes all . . . to be marked on the right hand or the forehead.** Such a mark is a parody of the sealing of Christians through baptism. The community with the mark of the beast is a satanic counterpart to the community of the Lamb (5:9-10; 7:3; 14:1, 9, 11), and, like the church, it is all-inclusive, containing **both small and great, both rich and poor, both free and slave** (cf. 5:9d). It is a matter of debate to what the beast's mark (Greek, *charagma*) **on the right hand or the forehead** refers. Does it refer to imperial coins that bore the image of the divine emperor and/or the goddess Roma? Indeed, without currency **no one can buy or sell.** However, one does not carry coins **on the forehead** in order to participate in commercial transactions. The background of the mark on the forehead is Ezek. 9:4, where Yahweh commands his messenger to "put a mark upon the foreheads" of all who repent of Jerusalem's sins. This "mark" is the Hebrew letter *tau*, which also means sign, or mark, and which was written in old Hebrew script as + or X. In Ezekiel, this mark was a sign of repentance; it was also a protective sign, an indication that the person so marked was Yahweh's property. In the *Psalms of Solomon* (15:6-9) we hear that "the mark of God is upon the righteous, that they may be saved," while pagans, "the lawless," bear "the mark of destruction on their foreheads." Here the mark is spoken of metaphorically, since the mark of destruction hardly refers to a physical mark on anyone's forehead. The ideas of allegiance and confession, salvation or destruction, are expressed by metaphorically understood marks on the forehead.

Slaves or devotees of a cult were actually branded in rare instances (cf. 3 Macc. 2:29) to indicate that they were someone's property. At any rate, it is unlikely that John envisioned an actual tattooing or branding of all emperor worshipers on their foreheads or right hands. He understood the mark of the beast metaphorically as a parody of the seal of the living God upon the foreheads of his people. The mark or seal expresses whose property the person is and under whose protection he or she stands. To whom do they give allegiance and from whom do they expect salvation? Those who have the name of the Lamb and his Father on their foreheads (14:1) are, during the time of Antichrist, socially ostracized and face economic ruin. Yet they will learn to sing the new song of the redeemed (14:2-5). But those who bear the mark of the beast are his property and are subject to plagues (14:9-11; 16:2-21).

But why a mark **on the right hand?** Is it because a pious Jew wears the phylacteries on the left hand or arm and the head but not on the right hand (Strack-Billerbeck, IV 260–264), or is it because the sacrifice before the emperor was performed by sprinkling incense with the right hand? We do not know. Either suggestion is possible.

The mark of the beast, without which one faces economic boycott, **is a human number;** better, *"the number of a human being,"* **and its number is six hundred and sixty-six, This calls for wisdom.**

This number is a real brain teaser, and the "solutions" to this riddle are many. Two of the recent ones are found in *ZNW* 1986 and *Exp. Times* 1986. One argues that if 666 is written in Hebrew letters, the result is a verb meaning, "you should destroy," alluding to Amos 6:1. The other one transliterates the Greek *ho Nikolaites* (cf. Rev. 2:6, 15) into Hebrew letters and adding up their numerical equivalent totals 666. The first solution is precluded by the text; the second does not fit the context. We shall briefly discuss three approaches to this puzzle.

1. An interesting proposal interprets the number 666 as a *triangular number.* For instance, 10 is the triangular number of 4. If one were to add 1+2+3+4=10, it would look like this:

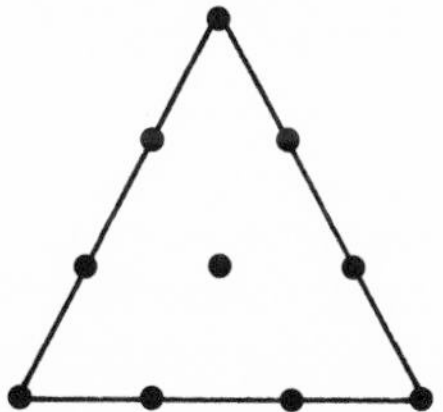

The number 666 is the triangular number of 36, and 36 is the triangular number *of 8* which is the *key to 666*. There is no doubt about the meaning of 8 in Rev. 17:11. The beast "that was and is not, it is an eighth." Thus 666 would merely be a symbolic reference to the Antichrist. However, this solution comes to naught on the text of 13:17-18. The mark, that is the name of the beast or the number of its name . . . is a human number, that is, the number of a man or a human being (Greek, *arithmos anthrōpou*).

2. A symbolic interpretation of this number shares the same weakness in that it fails to do justice to the text and does not come up with the name of a human being. According to the symbolic interpretation, 666 falls three times short of seven, the number of perfection. The 666 means "failure upon failure upon failure." Neither empire, nor emperors, nor imperial policies are perfect or divine. They are merely three sixes, not three sevens.

A similar symbolic interpretation had been advanced already by Irenaeus (*Adv. Haer.* 5.28.2), who saw in that number the recapitulation of all apostasies from the Garden of Eden to the end. A symbolic interpretation, however, may at best yield a secondary meaning, because the text demands that we discover in this number the name of a human being.

3. An interpretation in terms of gematria, using letters as numbers, would seem to be the only other approach that is left. The Greek verb *psephizō*, to calculate, to **reckon** (v. 18), also points in this direction. Hebrew as well as Greek letters of the alphabet also served as numbers, as we still use Roman numerals. (Thus a=1; b=2; i=10; k=20.) By adding the numerical value of the letters of a name, one received "the number of the name." The trouble is that while it is easy to calculate the number of any name, it is next to impossible to discover a name from a number. A graffito in Pompeii reads; "I love her whose number is 545." Apart from the scribe and his beloved lady and perhaps some friends, no one would discover her identity. Latin, Greek, and Jewish writers of antiquity engaged in gematria, and so did common people. After Nero had murdered his mother Agrippina, someone wrote on a wall in Rome, "Count the numerical values of the letters in Nero's name and in 'murdered his own mother' [matricide], and you will find their sum is the same" (Suetonius, *Nero* 39). The numerical value of the letters in Nero's name must, however, be calculated on the basis of the Greek, not the Latin, alphabet to be identical with the aggregate value of the letters in "matricide," namely, 1,005.

One more observation—John did use *Hebrew* words in 9:11; 16:16; 19:1; 20:8, and the Aramaic petition "Maranatha" was also understood in Greek-speaking churches (1 Cor. 16:22). In all probability the number and meaning of 666 was part of an apocalyptic tradition that John thought his churches would understand.

While many answers have been offered to solve this puzzle, the one that seems most plausible is that 666 is the number of

Caesar Nero on the basis of the *Hebrew* alphabet. It would be written *nron qsr* (*nun*=50 + *resh*=200 + *waw*=6 + *nun*=50 + *qoph*=100 + *samekh*=60 + *resh*=200). The spelling *nron qsr* has been found on a document from Murabet, thus eliminating earlier objections to this solution (A. Y. Collins, 175; Basor, 170, 1963, 65; cf. Charles, 1:367).

The advantages of this identification are threefold. First and foremost, it fits into the context of Revelation 13 and 17 which, beyond doubt, made use of the Nero legend. Second, it explains the variant reading of the Western text manuscripts which have 616 in place of 666. In Latin, Nero's name would not be pronounced Neron but Nero. Thus if his Latin name is put into Hebrew, the final N (=50) must be subtracted and the number 616 results. Third, the numerical value in Hebrew letters of the Greek word for beast *(therion)* is also 666. Thus we can understand why the **number of the beast** in v. 18 is the *number of a human being*. For some silly interpretations, see above introduction, section 1.

Paul, as well as the authors of Acts, 1 Peter, and the Pastoral Epistles, saw church-state relationships quite differently from John. His vision of the triumvirate of evil was not the result of an analysis of the empire in general and of the social-political situation of his churches in the province of Asia in particular. Rather, his Christology determined his devastating view of the empire. His vision, that the Lamb that was slain is designated to reign on earth, brought the issue of idolatry and worship into focus. In the near future, idolatry would reach its climax in mandatory imperial cult participation and result in inevitable eschatological tribulations for the faithful church. John's view that Caesar's empire will become Satan's beasts was his theological response to his vision of Christ's all-embracing reign on earth and of worship on earth as the all-embracing response to that reign. The conduct of Caesar's representatives who were contemporaries of John (people like Pliny) was merely grist for his mill but not the catalyst for his vision.

Interlude: The Lamb and His Followers on Mount Zion (14:1-5)

This interlude is the counterpart to the vision of the followers of the beast. Once again we shall see that it is worship which distinguishes both communities. Their antithetical worship finds expression in antithetical life-styles. Simultaneously the Lamb's followers are designated as "first fruits for God," suggesting the image of harvest which is a metaphor for judgment. In this way the vision introduces two new series in which judgment becomes the central theme (vv. 6-11, 14-20). While the images of the first fruits and of the subsequent grain harvest refer to salvation (vv. 14-16), the image of the gathering of grapes (vv. 17-20) is used to express the wrath of God and the Lamb over the worshipers of the beast (cf. 14:8-11, 17-20). Chapters 13 and 14 are linked by the "call for the endurance of the saints" (13:10; 14:12) which forms an inclusion. Within the evolving narration of visions and auditions we can detect the following contrasts:

A	14:1-5	B	14:6-11
A′	14:12-13	B′	14:14-20
A″	15:1-4	B″	15:5—16:21

In antithesis to the forecast of a worldwide persecution and economic ruin of the faithful by the beast, John now presents a preview of their glorious redemption in a vision (v. 1), an audition (vv. 2-3), and an explanatory comment for the reader (vv. 4-5).

The Vision (14:1). **Then I looked, and lo, on Mount Zion stood the Lamb, and with him a hundred and forty-four thousand who had his name and his Father's name written on their foreheads** (cf. 3:12). The saints who have endured (cf. 13:10) are gathered around their Lord, **the Lamb,** on **Mount Zion,** the symbol of God's presence and deliverance. The earthly geographic Jerusalem is, for John, part of the great city "where their Lord was crucified" (11:8) and therefore the faithful are not gathered there on the historical temple mount. Nor is Mount Zion identical with the heavenly Jerusalem, because heaven and earth are still distinguished. In the audition a voice comes "*from* heaven" and clearly distinguishes Mount Zion from heaven. In short, the 144,000 are not in heaven or in the new Jerusalem but "on Mount Zion" which has become the symbol of the persevering, conquering church, the place of Christ's presence on earth. "For in Mount Zion . . . shall be those who escape" God's judgment, Joel proclaimed (Joel 2:32); and "the Lord will reign over them in Mount Zion" (Mic. 4:7; cf. 2 Esdr. 2:42-47; 13:35-40). Mount Zion is wherever the Lamb is with his followers on earth. This vision recalls the sealing of the 144,000 elect before the last day, before the apocalyptic storm of judgment breaks loose (7:1-8), and it anticipates the vision of those who have conquered the beast and who sing the victory song of Moses and of the Lamb (15:2-4). It is the fitting conclusion to the story of the woman pursued by the dragon into the wilderness (12:13-17; cf. outline) and a summary of all the promises granted to conquerors (e.g., 3:12). The vision of the Lamb on Mount Zion also anticipates the marriage of the Lamb (19:9) and his millennial reign (20:4-6). The Lamb, standing on Mount Zion, is God's eschatological agent, the anti-image of the beast rising up out of the sea to do the dragon's work; and the 144,000 are the symbol of God's people during the last days. They have endured the assaults of the beasts and refused to bear the mark 666 of Antichrist. Instead, the **name** of the Lamb and **his Father's name** (thus, the Lamb is "the Son") are **written on their foreheads.** This "seal" shows that they are God's property and are protected by him from the final judgment. They are in fact the "first fruits" of the eschatological harvest that is yet to come (14:4, 14-16). Later we shall hear that they shall reign with Christ for a thousand years and shall not be subjected to the final judgment (20:4-6, 11-15). John never tells everything at once. God's name on their foreheads also symbolizes that they are the new high priests, fit for the divine liturgy in the city-paradise of the new Jerusalem (22:1-5).

The Audition (14:2-3). **A voice from heaven** (Greek, *phōnē;* cf. 1:10; 4:1; etc.) sounded like the rushing of **many waters** and like **loud thunder** (cf. 6:1; 19:6). The heavenly liturgy becomes again audible (cf. chaps. 4–5; 8:3-5; 11:16-19). The **sound of harpers playing on their harps** is part of the worship before God's **throne** (5:9). And **they,** the heavenly host, **sing a new song,** the words of which the reader has already heard in 5:9-10, 12-13. This new song is in praise of the Lamb who is worthy to be the Lord of lords and King of kings. But this new song is heard on earth only by the followers of the Lamb. Only they can **learn** it, because they are a priestly people whom the Lamb, through his death, has **redeemed from the earth** (5:9-10). The other inhabitants of the earth know only the old song of self-glorification, idolatry, and worship of the beast (cf. 13:4, 8, 12, 15). In their worship on earth the redeemed learn to sing a new song. Their song is the absolute opposite of the blasphemies uttered by the beast worshipers.

Interpretive Comment (14:4-5). Writing a letter requires that John also addresses his readers/hearers. He had done so in his call for endurance in 13:9-10 and will do so again in 14:12-13. Here he addresses his audience by means of an interpretive comment (cf. 1:20; 7:14), explaining to them the identity of the **redeemed.** In the first place, he makes it clear that "the redeemed" may not be limited to martyrs, which is contrary to some of his modern interpreters. In the second place, the redeemed **have not defiled themselves with women, for they are chaste;** literally, "they are virgins." Some interpreters take this characterization literally and hold that the 144,000 are unmarried male ascetics. Others hold that John here is promoting his own agenda of advocating the desirability of celibacy in the light of the imminent end. His ideal, it is argued, is to be "eunuchs" for the sake of the kingdom (Matt. 19:12), celibate because of the imminent end and its prior tribulations, unencumbered by wives and children because of the hardships experienced by itinerant prophets. However, John stated a requirement, not an ideal. Membership among the 144,000 demands virginity. The question is, then, what did John mean by virginity here? The notion that in his view only unmarried male ascetics are members of the people of God is unconvincing, to say the least.

Still others have argued that John's requirement of (male) celibacy was inspired by Israel's holy war tradition and the priestly purity regulations found in the Old Testament and in Qumran (e.g., Deut. 23:9-14; 1 Sam. 21:5; Yarbro Collins). Participation in the holy war requires ritual purity and sexual abstention for all (male) soldiers. True enough, but irrelevant here. A *literal* understanding of *defilement with women* caused by sexual relations would imply that John required *lifelong* celibacy for *all* members of the people of God, symbolized by the 144,000. The holy war ideology with its temporary abstention from sexual relations is irrelevant to our text.

Moreover, a *literal* interpretation of v. 4 would not only expose John as being a misogynist and raise the obvious question, Why should all women be excluded from the 144,000? It would also mean that John viewed *marriage as defilement*. This would place him in contradiction to the whole biblical tradition. Above all, a literal approach to v. 4 would demand a literal interpretation of all the other images in this vision, such as "Lamb," "Mount Zion," and "written on their foreheads." This would obviously be absurd. Nor do we need to take recourse to Charles's hypothesis that regarded v. 4 as an interpolation, which came about when a copyist incorporated a marginal comment into the text.

Our v. 4 *may not* be interpreted literally but must be understood metaphorically. It was not in sexual relations *with spouses* that believers **defiled themselves.** The faithful are *virgins* (RSV, **chaste**) because they **have not defiled themselves** with *idolatry*. The prophets of Israel had denounced idolatry in terms of adultery and fornication (Exod. 34:15; Deut. 31:16; Judg. 2:17; Hos. 2:14-21; 9:1; Jer. 3:20; etc.). Babylon/Rome is the "mother of *harlots*" (plural) in Revelation (17:5), and those who participate in the imperial cult commit "fornication" (18:3). In antithesis to the harlots of the imperial cult (who were male priests!), the 144,000 are called *virgins,* whether male or female. They have kept themselves pure and undefiled from idolatry in general and from emperor worship in particular, and also from the kind of immorality advocated by Christian heretics, such as the prophetess of Thyatira (2:20).

The faithful (women and men) are pictured later on as "bride" of Christ (19:7). Paul "betrothed" the Corinthians to Christ "as a pure bride to her one husband" (2 Cor. 11:2). **Virgin** is a title of honor for Zion in the Old Testament (e.g., 2 Kings 19:21; Isa. 23:12; Jer. 14:17). As *virgin,* the church resisted the seductive powers of the emperor cult, as *bride* the church belongs to and is loved by Jesus (cf. 1:5). However, the imperial cult with its festive pageantry exerted a magnetism of its own and was attractive, not merely because objection to it might spell economic ruin (13:17), but because it was the patriotic thing to do. John's hearers are challenged to resist the enchantment of the harlot Babylon/Rome and of her *male* priests who are depicted here with sarcastic irony as **women** who **defile,** that is, as prostitutes. Relations with them would exclude believers from participation in the heavenly liturgy, from learning the new song. John probably spoke of "women" rather than of harlots, lest his hearers quickly nod with approval, thinking that defiling merely involves visiting whorehouses. This verse is meant to jolt their imagination, and it does so still!

In the third place, another characteristic of the 144,000 is that they **follow the Lamb wherever he goes** (Greek, *hypagei*). "If any one is to be taken captive, to captivity he goes" (13:10; *hypagei*). To **follow** the Lamb includes the possibility of suffering and of martyrdom as well as the promise of victory. The tense in the verb "follow" is present tense (cf. 7:14). The faithful have followed him in the past through trials and tribulations (cf. Mark 8:34; Matt. 10:38), and they follow him now and in the future. This verb, which refers to discipleship in the Gospels and Acts, occurs in this sense in the rest of the New Testament only here and in 19:14. The verb reflects John's knowledge of the gospel tradition.

Fourth, the 144,000 are described as **redeemed from,** that is, out of, humanity, **as first fruits for God and the Lamb.** Their redemption through the blood of the Lamb (5:9) *separated* them from the rest of humanity that is ripe for the harvest of judgment (14:6-20). The redeemed are already the **first fruits** of the harvest of salvation that is to come, just as Jesus in his resurrection is "the first fruits" of the harvest of the dead (cf. 1 Cor. 15:20-23; Rev. 1:5). Likewise, the Holy Spirit, granted to the church on earth, could be viewed as "first fruits" of the future consummation (Rom. 8:23). Here the church on Mount Zion is the "first fruits" of the harvest that belongs to God and the Lamb.

Fifth, they are an offering to God. Like the sacrificial offerings brought to Jerusalem's temple, they are **spotless,** without blemish (Exod. 12:5; Lev. 23:12-13; cf. Eph. 1:4; Phil. 2:15; Col. 1:22), because they have been redeemed *and* have kept themselves "undefiled" from idolatry (v. 4), **and in their mouth no lie was found.** Unlike idolatrous humanity which "exchanged the truth about God for a lie and worshiped and served the creature rather than the Creator" (Rom. 1:25), the followers of the Lamb were not deceived by the serpent/dragon (12:9), or by his minion, or by heretical prophets and apostles (2:2, 14, 20). Religion is the realm in which lies flourish, then and now, and where concern for truth is eroded by slogans.

John's interpretive comment identified the characteristic features which are also the conditions that must be met by the church if she is to be with the Lamb on Mount Zion. The redeemed are virgins (female or male), disciples, first fruits, a spotless sacrificial offering, and people of truthfulness. This vision exhorts the church to raise its vision concerning its nature as God's alternative community on earth.

The Announcement and Execution of the Final Judgment (14:6-20)

This unit is the counterpart to the vision of the redeemed and draws a series of sketches which are elaborated later. The section has three parts: (A) announcement of judgment by three angels (vv. 6-11); (B) encouragement to the saints (vv. 12-13); and (A′) the execution of judgment (vv. 14-20). Six angelic actors appear in this section: three angels in vv. 6-11 prior to the call for endurance and three other angels in vv. 14-20 subsequent to it. Hence the call for endurance (B), directed to John's hearers, is the focus of this section. Moreover, also the one "seated on the cloud" like "a son of man" is preceded and followed by three angels. He is therefore positioned as the fourth among seven heavenly agents. That means that he is the central actor, even if he apparently does nothing in six of the seven episodes.

The Angel in Midheaven (14:6-7). **Another angel** appears in **midheaven,** like the eagle of 8:13, with a message that concerns all **who dwell on earth.** But in contrast to the eagle that announced three woes, the angel flying in midheaven is the messenger of good news, proclaiming an **eternal gospel** for all people. According to Mark 13:10, the gospel "must first be preached to all nations" before the end arrives, and the angel of 14:6-7 does just that. The offer of repentance and salvation at the very last moment precedes the judgment. The **eternal** gospel (singular) is the opposite of the transient gospels (plural), proclaimed in edicts and inscriptions.

There is a famous inscription of a letter of the proconsul Fabius Maximus to the provincial assembly of Asia, recommending that Caesar Augustus's birthday be celebrated as the beginning of a new era and as the beginning of the official year. The reason for this was that "he restored stability, when everything was collapsing and falling into disarray. . . . His birthday signifies the beginning of life and real living." In response to the proconsul's letter the Asian assembly noted "that the birthday of our god [Augustus] signaled the beginning of *good news* [Greek, *euangelia*, gospels, plural] for the world because of him" (Danker).

John probably knew of this decree, since it had been published in many cities of Asia Minor. The most complete inscription comes from Priene, south of Ephesus. At any rate, he used the word "gospel" only here, and he employed it in a context that sets forth his alternative vision to the imperial cult. To be sure, he must have known of the Christian usage of "gospel," but his "eternal gospel" is a summons to turn away from the worship of the beast (13:4, 8, 12, 15). John did not identify the gospel here in terms of the kerygma of the crucified and resurrected Christ (cf. 1 Cor. 15:1-5). Instead, the "eternal gospel" is the final call prior to the judgment, directed to every nation, tribe, tongue, and people: **Fear God** rather than the triumvirate of beasts. **Give him glory** rather than to the transient glitter of culture. **Worship him** rather than the emperor. The central issue is worship! It will heat up, once the beast rises from the abyss. John's gospel involves repentance, a radical break with the dominant culture. It is similar to the summons issued by John the Baptist and by Jesus: "Repent, for the kingdom of heaven is at hand" (Matt. 3:1; cf. Mark 1:14). Repent = fear God, give him glory; for the kingdom of heaven is at hand = **for the hour of his judgment has come.** The word "judgment" occurs here for the first time, though we have met its synonym "wrath" in the sixth seal and the seventh trumpet (6:16 and 11:18). John's good news includes God coming to judge the world in righteousness (Ps. 9:8). "He will shatter kings on the day of his wrath. He will execute judgment among the nations" (Ps. 110:5-6). Judgment involves an act of sorting out, and the one who does the sorting out is God, the creator of **heaven and earth.** This angelic announcement links up with the promise of the interlude: "no more delay" (10:6-7), and with the thanksgiving of the seventh trumpet (11:18).

History is not an endless series of cycles of days, months, years, and millennia. It has a beginning, creation, and a goal, the judgment and the kingdom of God. At the end, it will be clear to everyone who God is and what the world's idolaters were all about. This end, however, has already made its appearance in the Lamb who was slain and who is alive among his followers (14:1-5). He stands behind this final gracious summons before the end. Through his angel, the central actor in this series of seven agents (14:14) invites us to recognize our limitations and weaknesses, to acknowledge our accountability, and to surrender to God, who has given us all that we are and have. **Worship God.** Turn to him from your neurotic pursuits of gods, godlets, and whatnots.

The Second Angel (14:8). The second **angel** proclaims a prophetic judgment oracle: **"Fallen, fallen is Babylon the great, she who made all nations drink the wine of her impure passion."** The Greek verb has *past* tense (*epesen*), even though from John's time perspective Babylon's fall lies in the future. But because the decision about its doom has already been made in heaven, the angel can announce it with a prophetic past tense as if Babylon's fall had already happened. From the perspective of heaven, it is an accomplished fact. Moreover, the story of Babylon's destruction will be told in Revelation 17–18, another indication that the sequence of visions in John's book is not identical with the sequence of time. John narrated his visions in evolving cycles.

Babylon is introduced without explanation, probably because its identification with Rome was part of the tradition known to John's churches. This code name for Rome (cf. 1 Peter 5:13) was not used in order to cause confusion about which city was meant but in order to reveal its true nature as a world power at enmity with God's purpose. John combined prophetic oracles of Isaiah (21:9) and Jeremiah (51:7-8a), referring to it as Babylon **the great,** alluding to Dan. 4:30-31. Babylon is the beast's capital, the opposite of Mount Zion. Rome's self-aggrandizement, like Nebuchadnezzar's, shall be brought low. Like Babylon of old, so Rome represents the power of godlessness, injustice, and brutality behind a glitter of culture. **She made all nations drink the wine of** *the wrath of her fornication* (RSV is weak here: **her impure passion**). Two ideas are combined. Rome intoxicated the Gentile nations of the empire with the idolatry of the emperor cult (= fornication). That intoxication will lead to the persecution of Christians (= the wrath resulting from her idolatry). Soon we will also hear of the wine cup of *God's* wrath which the worshipers of the beast will have to drink (v. 10). We are reminded again that "one is punished by the very things by which one sins" (Wis. Sol. 11:16; cf. 12:23).

The Third Angel (14:9-11). While the second angel pronounced a *collective* verdict against the beast's capital, the third angel threatened *individuals* ("if any one . . ."). God's judgment will fall on **any one** who, in spite of the final summons of v. 7, **worships the beast and its image** (cf. 13:15) and **receives** the **mark** of 666 on **his forehead or on his hand** (cf. 13:16-18). Worship is the issue! Two traditional images are blended to picture the punishment of idolaters. One is the story of the destruction of Sodom and Gomorrah through fire and sulphur (Gen. 19:24; cf. Luke 17:29). The other is the notion of hell (Gehenna) and hell fire which can be traced back to the "valley of Hinnom," southwest of Jerusalem, where, at one time, human sacrifices by fire had been offered (2 Chron. 28:3; Jer. 7:31; 32:35). During the intertestamental period, "Gehenna" came to be used as the designation for eternal damnation; it was translated as "hell," in distinction from "Hades," the place of the dead. Hell, then, is pictured as a fiery abyss and place of torment (*1 Enoch* 90:26-27; *2 Bar.* 85:13-15; 2 Esdr. 7:36 located the end-time "furnace of hell" opposite paradise). This tradition is present not only in Revelation but also in the Gospels (cf. Matt. 5:22, 29-30; 13:42, 50; 23:15; 25:41; Mark 9:43-48). The worshipers of the beast receive God's final "No!"

Carl Gustav Jung finds "a veritable orgy of hatred, wrath and vindictiveness" in Revelation at this point (*Answer to Job*, 1972, p. 125), and for D. H. Lawrence the Apocalypse was the Judas in the New Testament (p. 66). Yet vindictiveness or an orgy of hatred is not what John sought to arouse. His aim was not to "gloat" over the fate of the opponents but rather to motivate the call for endurance addressed to Christians in the next verse. This call is, as we have seen, the literary focus of this subsection. The third angel has a wholesome message for lackadaisical, lukewarm Christians: Fish or cut bait! Of course, the idea of a final judgment is unacceptable to bourgeois writers and theologians. For John and the rest of the New Testament authors, it is God who may turn out to be the ultimate enemy. The supreme threat to our own world is not communism, capitalism, socialism, or any other ism or lie, but God, coming to judge the world and each of us in his righteousness. That is offensive, because we do not like to be exposed, stripped of our phony facades, and even less do we like to be punished for what we have done. The third angel vividly propounded the truth, that it is a disaster to reject the gospel. Worship God! (v. 7); it is a matter of life and death.

John's Call for Endurance and a Beatitude (14:12-13). In the light of the final judgment, believers are admonished not to apostatize but to *endure,* that is, to **keep the commandments of God** (cf. 12:17) **and the faith of Jesus;** better: "faithfulness toward Jesus," or perhaps "the faithfulness which Jesus exhibited" (cf. 2:13). The vision of the fate of those who refused the eternal gospel is not an occasion for gloating but cause for a solemn warning, not to worship our work and play with our worship. John's call for endurance is confirmed by two witnesses, by a nameless **voice** requesting him to include the beatitude in his letter, and by the Holy **Spirit.**

13—The beatitude is the high point of the call for endurance. **Blessed are the dead who die in the Lord henceforth.** Since Easter, death is no longer the end of a believer's relationship to God. Death is the reality to which, with few exceptions, the Old Testament has no answer other than this: the dead "will not live; they are shades, they will not arise" (Isa. 26:14). "For Sheol [the realm of the dead] cannot thank thee, death cannot praise thee; those who go down to the pit [the grave] cannot hope for thy faithfulness." Only the living person "thanks thee, as I do this day" (Isa. 38:18-19). Only a few apocalyptic texts of the Old Testament sound a different note in the face of the inevitability of death (Isa. 25:8; 26:19; Dan. 12:1).

But through Easter a new language concerning death and resurrection exploded within the church. Christ can be honored and glorified through life *or* through death (Phil. 1:20-23; cf. Rom. 8:38-39; 14:8-9; John 5:24; 11:25-26; etc.). A whole new perspective on life and death developed, finding expression in a new language of faith and praise and in a new attitude toward dying. Because the God of Abraham, Isaac, and Jacob did a new deed by raising Jesus from the dead, breaking at this one point the wall of death that surrounds all of us, death has been thoroughly relativized. To **die in the Lord** or "in Christ" means that our dying is determined by Jesus' death and by his resurrection. To "die in the Lord" also suggests that faith in the Lord Jesus has been kept to the end of one's life (cf. 1 Cor. 15:18; 1 Thess. 4:16; Phil. 1:21, 23). From **henceforth** refers to Christians who die between Easter and the parousia. From John's perspective it points especially to those who die under persecution caused by the beast. The beatitude is part of the closing bracket (inclusion). The opening bracket is the prophetic oracle of 13:10. What is stated negatively in terms of predestination in 13:10 is stated positively as beatitude in 14:13. The reader therefore hears that God does not surrender his own to the brutality of the beast (13:10) but grants salvation (14:1-5) and a beatitude (14:13) to all who "die in the Lord henceforth."

"Blessed indeed," says the Spirit, speaking through the prophet John, and he adds a reason. They are blessed because **they may rest from their labors.** The dead believers are not in torment, having "*no rest*" (14:11), nor is theirs a shadowy ghostlike existence in Sheol. They enter God's "rest" (Heb. 4:1-11), and **their deeds,** their works, **follow them** as witness either in the first resurrection (20:4-6) or in the final judgment (20:12-13). Their works disclose whether or not they followed the Lamb (14:4). God does not forget their **labors,** be it their daily toil, or their faithful endurance under pressure. This has nothing whatsoever to do with legalism or calculation of merits. For a Jew, like John, a saying like *Pirke Aboth* 6:10 would have been acceptable: "In the hour of death, it is not silver or gold or precious stones or pearls that accompany him, but Torah and good works alone." John would have added "faithfulness toward Jesus" to Torah (cf. 14:12).

The Final Judgment (14:14-20). It had been announced by each of the three angels. Now it is being executed by **one like a son of man** in the company of three other angels. This vision consists of two scenes—the grain harvest (vv. 14-16) and the gathering of the vintage (vv. 17-20). A difficult question arises at this point. Do these two scenes portray one and the same judgment in different images, or do the two scenes refer to two aspects and two different results of the final judgment? To put it another way, does the grain harvest signify the gathering of the righteous, while the vintage discloses the destruction of the beast worshipers in "the wine press of the wrath of God"? We shall sketch four different approaches to this vision.

First, the image of the harvest can be used for the gathering of the elect (e.g., Matt. 9:37). John implied it in 14:4 when he spoke of the redeemed as a "first fruits" offering. It is indeed probable that the harvest image is meant to be understood positively. It would interlock on one side with the vision of the followers of the Lamb who are "first fruits" and who learn a new song (14:1-5). On the other side of the harvest, we hear of the praise of the redeemed who sing the song of Moses and the Lamb (15:2-4). Also in favor of making a distinction between the grain harvest of the righteous and the vintage of the idolaters is the omission of gory details as well as the absence of a reference to God's wrath in the description of the grain harvest (vv. 14-16). These verses could be John's interpretation of a Christian apocalyptic tradition such as Mark 13:27. "And then he [the Son of man] will send out the angels and gather his elect from . . . the ends of the earth" (cf. Mark 4:29; Matt. 13:36-43). John's vision in two parts would, in this case, portray two kinds of eschatological judgments for two kinds of people. The followers of the Lamb as well as those who heeded the summons of the eternal gospel are gathered like grain. The worshipers of the beast are thrown into the "great wine press of the wrath of God."

Second, many of John's symbols and images are ambivalent and defy exact identification. The two images are borrowed from Joel 3:13, where they refer to only one judgment over the same people. "Put in the sickle, for the harvest is ripe. Go in, tread, for the wine press is full. The vats overflow, for their wickedness is great." We also note that John's text does not speak of the elect in vv. 14-16 but only of the harvest. **The earth was reaped.** Moreover, the parallels in the two scenes ("the sharp sickle," the state of the grain and the grapes being "ripe," the identical command, "Put in your sickle and reap") would seem to indicate only one judgment theme involving only God's enemies to whom the judgment had already been announced. The two scenes would be mere variations on the same theme.

Third, if we take both the similarities and the differences between the two scenes into account, then the first scene may merely relate the harvest in general, by one like a son of man at the appointed hour. This harvest may include believers and unbelievers alike. Nothing is said of their fate in the first scene (vv. 14-16). What happens to the harvest of the beast worshipers after the reaping is of no concern in the first scene. Only the event of reaping, and its agent, are important. Thus one could understand it as a harvest that includes all humans. Later on we hear that the conquerors of the beast will sing the song of Moses and of the Lamb (15:2-4), while the followers of the beast have entered into the winepress of God's wrath (14:17-20).

Fourth, still another approach to this vision would take into consideration that chap. 14 is a preview anticipating 20:4-6 as well as 20:11-15. If this were granted, then the followers of the Lamb on Mount Zion (14:1-5) are the candidates for the millennial reign with Christ (20:4-6). They are clearly not subjected to the general judgment in 20:11-15, as we shall see. One might then draw the conclusion that the followers of the Lamb in the preview of 14:1-5 will not be subjected to the general judgment of 14:14-20 either. In that case the harvest and the vintage take place for all human beings, including those who responded at the last minute to the gospel (14:6-8 cf. 11:13), *except* the followers of the Lamb. Their future is "the first resurrection" and the millennial reign with Christ (20:4-6), not the final judgment of 14:14-20 and its parallel in 20:11-15. John, however, does not tell us everything at once.

Our approach will be that John's vision presents a preview of salvation (grain harvest) and of judgment (vintage harvest). There is no need to regard vv. 15-17 as another interpolation, as Charles suggested. The harvest image connects with the gospel of the first angel (14:6-7) and with the conclusion of the interlude (11:13). This theme is taken up in 15:3-4 when God is addressed as "king of the nations" to whom "all nations shall come" and whom all "shall worship." These are "all" who have been gathered in the grain harvest. The question concerning the judgment of the followers of the Lamb is left open for the time being in the letter.

John brought together several threads in order to articulate this vision: the Synoptic apocalypse (Mark 13:10, 27), Dan. 7:13, and Joel 3:13; and, for the vintage, he is dependent on Isa. 63:1-6.

14-16—The figure of the **one like a son of man** is the central actor in 14:6-20. The reader's attention is prodded by the introductory exclamation **and lo** (cf. 4:1; 14:1). The title Son of man is avoided by John both here and in the inaugural vision (1:13). The comparison "like a son of man" comes from Dan. 7:13, where it symbolizes "the saints of the Most High" in contrast to the beastlike nature of pagan empires. The Son of man appears as an individual eschatological agent of salvation in the *Similitudes* of *1 Enoch* (37–71; cf. 2 Esdras 13); in the Gospels this title is used exclusively by Jesus himself. Why John avoided the titular usage of Son of man, even though it had its firm place in Christian apocalyptic traditions (Mark 13:26; Luke 9:26), can only be surmised. (See below.) Christians would, of course, recognize Jesus in the son of man-like person. The **golden** wreath (RSV, **crown;** Greek, *stephanos*) on his head (also worn by the 24 elders, 4:4) shows him to be superior to ordinary angelic agents. The **sharp sickle in his hand** designates him as judge of the earth. Moreover, he is **seated** on a **white cloud,** which is the vehicle for his parousia (cf. Mark 13:26; Acts 1:9-11). His *sitting* on a cloud recalls the theme of John's letter: Behold he is *coming* with the clouds (1:7). Yet, oddly, John's visions never refer explicitly to Jesus' "coming" at all (cf. Dan. 7:13). This may be due to the influence of Joel 3:12, where it says that Yahweh will "*sit*" to judge the nations. Also it is odd that **another angel,** coming **out of the temple,** should give a command to him, ordering him to commence the harvest. Other visions picture the immediacy of Jesus and God without an intermediary. This has led some interpreters to suggest that an angel, not Jesus, is the one like a son of man. A better hypothesis would propose the use of a Jewish-Christian tradition by John. In it, "son of man" was not a title. The tradition did not speak of his "coming" on a cloud but of his sitting on one, and, without embarrassment, it advocated an "angel Christology."

The command of the other angel to Jesus uses the language of Joel 3:13a and declares that **the hour to reap,** that is, the hour of judgment (14:7), **has come, for the harvest of the earth is fully**

ripe, whether in terms of the "endurance of the saints" (14:12) or in terms of worship of the beast (14:9). **So he who sat upon the cloud swung his sickle on the earth, and the earth was reaped.** What happened to the harvest once reaped is told in the next two scenes (vv. 17-20 and 15:1-4).

17-20—The Grapes of Wrath: The vision of the previous verses continues without interruption. The harvest scene had not spoken of a separation, a sorting out, of wheat from tares (Matt. 13:30). Neither does the vintage vision, but it presents a picture of violent destruction which is a preview of 19:11-21 (19:15 uses the same imagery of treading "the wine press of the fury of the wrath of God"). The absence of any reference to Jesus Christ in these verses should not mislead us into thinking that he has nothing to do with the carnage portrayed here. A reading of 19:11-20 will refute such notions.

And another angel came out of the temple in heaven, and he too had a sharp sickle, just like that of the one seated on the cloud (v. 14). And just as the one seated on the cloud was commanded to commence the harvest with the words, **Put in your sickle and reap** (vv. 15 and 18; cf. Joel 3:13), so the same command is now given by yet another angel (v. 18). This last one came **out from the altar,** the place where the martyrs wait for justice (6:9-11), where "the prayers of the saints" ascend to God's throne (8:3-4), asking for the coming of the kingdom and for justice. The execution of God's judgment is related to the church's worship. This is indeed surprising.

This angel is further designated as the one **who has power over fire.** Assignments of different elements of nature to particular angels are found in *1 Enoch* 60:11-21 (cf. Rev. 16:5). Also, this particular angelic job description suggests the use of a Jewish-Christian tradition. An angel who has power over **fire,** a symbol of judgment (cf. 2 Thess. 1:17; Matt. 18:8), tells another angel to begin the judgment. **So the angel swung his sickle on the earth and gathered the vintage of the earth.** Thus far the parallelism is more or less maintained with the previous image of the harvest.

Now, however, comes something new which constitutes the climax of this scene. First the angel threw the vintage **into the great wine press of the wrath of God.** Second, **the wine press was trodden outside the city,** and, third, **blood flowed from the wine press, as high as a horse's bridle, for one thousand six hundred stadia,** which is about 180 miles, the approximate length of Palestine.

The image of the winepress is taken from Isa. 63:3b-6, where Yahweh speaks: "I trod them [the nations, especially Edom] in my anger and trampled them in my wrath; their lifeblood is sprinkled upon my garments, and I have stained all my raiment. . . . I trod down the peoples in my anger, . . . and I poured out their lifeblood on the earth." In Isaiah it is Yahweh, in 19:11-21 it is Christ, and here it is an angel who executes this carnage of **blood** flowing **as high as a horse's bridle** (cf. *1 Enoch* 100:1-3: "the horse shall walk through the blood of sinners up to his chest"). The dimension of this bloodbath is 1,600 stadia. This is to be interpreted either geographically, the length of Palestine from Tyre to El-Arish, or, more likely, symbolically. Sixteen hundred is the square of four (the number of the world and its four corners, 7:1) multiplied by the square of ten which signifies totality. If so, the carnage of condemnation covers the whole world. More important is the comment that the winepress **was trodden outside the city.** Caird's interpretation that outside the city was the place of martyrdom of the faithful does not commend itself. This **city** is the elect with God and the Lamb in their midst (cf. 20:4-6, 9; 21:1—22:5, 14-15). The faithful people of God are not touched by the vintage of wrath, as John had already conveyed on several occasions (interlude of chap. 7; 11:1-2; 14:1-5). **Outside the city** means outside the new Jerusalem, as we shall see.

The Seven Bowls of Wrath (15:1—16:21)

Prelude in Heaven (15:1-8)

This vision serves a dual purpose. On one hand it forms the climactic conclusion of the church's struggle with the beasts which was introduced in the interlude 10:1—11:13. This struggle is framed by "portents" in the sky (12:1, 2; 15:1) which mark the center section (12:1—16:21) as a unit. Moreover, this vision forms an inclusion with 14:1-5 around the announcement of judgments (14:6-20) and contrasts the fate of the conquerors with those who entered the winepress of the wrath of God (14:17-20).

On the other hand this vision serves as prelude in heaven for the bowl septet, because 15:1 introduces the **seven angels with seven plagues, which are the last, for with them the wrath of God is ended.** When the seventh bowl is poured out, we hear, **It is done** (16:17). Yet John's vision narrative is not finished but continues. Out of the seventh bowl evolve the visions of the judgment on Babylon (chaps. 17–18), just as out of the seventh seal the trumpet visions had evolved.

Revelation 15:2-4 gives us a second preview of the church of the millennium (cf. 7:9-17), and, like the first, it places the emphasis on worship. Salvation is worship in heaven, beside the sea of glass, singing the song of Moses and the Lamb. The liturgy in heaven which began in chap. 4, which was interrupted by seals and trumpets, which became audible again in 7:12; 11:15-18; 12:10-12; and 14:2-3, is now expanded by the hymns of the conquerors. The victorious church has learned to sing the new song (14:3). With his hymns, doxologies, and acclamations, John did not just draw a contrast between the church and Roman imperial court ceremonial, but he also wished to interpret the drama of his visions and to highlight the importance of worship.

Since our prelude in heaven introduces the last septet of judgment visions (16:1-21), we do well to recall the sequence of the three angelic announcements of judgment (14:6-10): first, general judgment (14:6-7); second, judgment on Babylon (14:8); and third, judgment on the worshipers of the beast (14:9-10). This sequence is now inverted, and John will narrate in reverse order, first, the judgment on the worshipers of the beast (16:1-21); second, judgment on Babylon (17:1—19:10); and, finally, third, the general judgment (20:11-15; or 19:11—20:15). This reversal parallels the sequence in the elimination of the antagonists. The supreme antagonist, Satan, who was introduced first will be destroyed last, while the two beasts who were introduced after him will be destroyed before him. The reversal has logical, not chronological, significance.

1—The structure of the prelude is A (v. 1) -B (vv. 2-4) -A′ (vv. 5-8). **Another portent in heaven, great and wonderful,** interconnects with the portents of 12:1-3. The bowls of wrath will be God's response to the dragon's fury against the woman and her child. The verse also functions as title of the new section (Bousset), announcing its theme. **Seven angels with seven plagues . . . are the last, for with them the wrath of God is ended** (15:1; cf. 16:17).

2-4—The center of the heavenly overture is occupied by the victors in heaven who have **conquered the beast** and have refused to be identified with Antichrist, that is, with **the number** (666) of the beast's **name.** They are not just martyrs but *all* who were faithful unto death (2:10; 14:13) and who in the practice of their faith bore the name of the Lamb and of his Father (14:1). They conquered the devil "by the blood of the Lamb and by the word of their testimony" (12:11); they endured (13:9-10; 14:12) and now they celebrate their exodus, their deliverance from Sodom and Egypt, from Babylon/Rome (cf. 11:8), from the world characterized by idolatry. They are in heaven **beside the sea of glass** (4:6). That this sea is **mingled with fire** (cf. 8:5) alludes to the judgments of chap. 16 and to the Red Sea that brought judgment on the Egyptian oppressors. Another exodus has been enacted, more glorious than the first. Therefore the conquerors in heaven have **the harps of God in their hands,** instruments that the 24 elders also play (5:8). **And they sing the song of Moses, the servant of God, and the song of the Lamb.** These are not two songs but one. Just as in former times at Israel's exodus, after its deliverance at the Red Sea, a hymn of deliverance was sung (Exod. 15:1-21), so now those who endured (13:9-10; 14:12) and were delivered by the blood of the Lamb (5:9-10) raise their voices in praise of the **Lord God the Almighty.** Israel's deliverance in the exodus, which is the very heart of the Old Testament, has its typological correspondence in the eschatological deliverance of God's people at the end of time. Moses and Jesus are the agents of God's deeds of deliverance at the beginning and the end of the story of God's people. The designation of Jesus as the Lamb gives an additional depth to this typology. Just as the blood of the Passover lamb was effective at the exodus from Egypt, so the blood of the Lamb is effective in the eschatological exodus from Egypt, Babylon/Rome.

The hymn itself consists of Old Testament phrases and recalls Moses' victory song (Exod. 15:1-18) and to a lesser extent his farewell song (Deut. 32:1-43). Two rhetorical questions are based on Jer. 10:7 and Ps. 86:9: **Who shall not fear and glorify thy name, O Lord?** The answer obviously is: no one. **For thou alone art holy.** The statement that **all nations shall come and worship thee,** literally, "in your presence," has troubled some interpreters as being out of place because it suggests universal salvation, unless worship here means "grudging recognition" of God's superiority (so Mounce). But the Old Testament background of v. 4 is the hope and promise of the pilgrimage of the Gentile nations to Mount Zion (Isa. 2:2; 66:19-21; Jer. 16:19; Mic. 4:2-3). The invitation offered by the angel with "the eternal gospel" (14:6-7) has not been in vain. Not all Gentiles will perish in the apocalyptic upheavals. Therefore in 11:13, and here in 15:14, John took up the Old Testament promise of the pilgrimage of Gentiles to Mount Zion. They have learned the lesson at last that God's judgments are **just and true,** that God is not a tribal deity, or a member of a pantheon, but the sovereign **king of the ages** (so RSV; other manuscripts read "King of the *nations*"). Their future **worship** (future tense!) shows that they will become part of the one people of God in the end, that is, after the general judgment (20:11-15). The conquerors of the beast, however, shall sing this hymn of praise already prior to the general judgment, during the millennium (cf. 20:4-6). The hymn, like the chorus of Greek drama, interprets the meaning of the catastrophes to come. God's acts of judgment have salvation and worship as their ultimate goal.

5-8—The third part of this heavenly prelude begins with the opening of the **temple of the tent of witness.** The heavenly counterpart of the tent appears, which symbolized God's presence with his people during the years of their sojourn in the desert (Exod. 25:9; Heb. 8:5). The **seven angels** process out of the heavenly temple-tent. They are clothed like priests in white **linen.** Their status is indicated by **golden girdles,** symbols of royalty and high priesthood (cf. 1:13). They are commissioned by one of the four living creatures (4:6-8), who transfers to them **seven golden bowls full of the wrath of God.** In 5:8 the golden bowls of incense symbolized the prayers of the church and of martyrs crying out for justice (cf. 8:2-5). The injustices and oppressions that have risen from the earth are soon to be hurled back in just retribution (cf. 2 Thess. 1:16). God himself is behind this judgment, executed by his angels. Therefore, the **temple** in heaven **was filled with smoke,** symbolizing his **glory** and **power** (Exod. 19:18; Isa. 6:4; 1 Kings 8:10. **And no one could enter the temple until the seven plagues of the seven angels were ended.** No one may interfere during the execution of his wrath.

The First Six Bowls (16:1-21)

The bowl cycle parallels and intensifies the destruction caused by the trumpet cycle, even if no death toll of humans is given in chap. 16. In both cycles first four plagues afflict the earth, the sea, the sweet water, and the heavenly bodies. The next two deal with powers of the underworld in warlike images. The Euphrates River plays a role in the sixth plague of each series. Between the sixth and the seventh in each series we find an interlude, which in the bowl series is rather short. The seventh trumpet and bowl are accompanied by loud voices in heaven (or from God's throne), followed by the proclamation of the reign of God and his Messiah on earth (11:15) and of the completion of his wrath, "It is done!" in 16:17. Both conclude with lightning, thunder, earthquake, and hail (11:19; 16:18). These two series recapitulate, not pedantically, but artistically, prophetically, from different perspectives and with greater intensity the day of wrath, which was present already in the sixth seal (6:16-17).

What are the significant new emphases in the bowl series in distinction from the trumpet series? We already noted the intensification of the plagues in this last septet. In four of the bowl plagues, we find references to the dragon, the beast, the false prophet, the beast worshipers, and Babylon. The effect of these references is a historization of the bowl plagues in distinction from those caused by the trumpets. John now deals with events in the near future that will destroy the beast's domain. The kings from the east, the Parthians and their satellites, will cross the Euphrates (v. 12). The application of mythic elements to envisioned historical events enabled John to introduce the perspective which perceives the execution of God's judgment in and through expected historical catastrophes. In vv. 5-7 he interrupts the bowl series with a judgment doxology that articulates the principle of divine retribution. This principle is to be applied to all the bowl plagues. Moreover, this interruption also suggests that all bowl plagues are directed against the beast worshipers, not against ordinary sinners. In addition to the interruption, we also find an interlude in vv. 13-16 which is introduced as a new vision with "and I saw." The theme of the interlude will be unfolded in the parousia vision of 19:11-20. Appended to this interlude is a word of Jesus and a beatitude, exhorting the reader/hearer and reflecting the epistolary quality of John's "book."

The First Four Bowls (16:1-9). The bowl plagues begin with a formal commissioning of the angels (15:5—16:1) by **a loud voice from the temple** telling all seven angels to **"Go and pour out on the earth the seven bowls of the wrath of God"** (16:1). The commissioning is followed by the execution of the divine order; for example, **the first angel went and poured his bowl on the earth.** The next three pour their bowls on three other elements of the cosmos—salt water, fresh water, and, the most important element in the sky, the **sun.** The next item of the pattern indicates their effect and extent (frequently introduced in the Greek text with *kai egeneto*). For instance, the extent of the second plague was that **every living thing died that was in the sea.** Finally at the conclusion of some of the plagues (vv. 9, 11, 21), the reaction of the people is indicated and their reaction applies also to the other plagues: They **cursed God** (literally, they "blasphemed," cf. 13:5-6!) and **did not repent** (vv. 9, 11, 21; cf. 9:20-21). The hearts of the beast worshipers had become hardened like Pharaoh's. Their reaction differed from the response elicited by the gospel's final call (14:6; cf. 11:13; 15:4). For the worshipers of the beast there is no hope. But the plagues also affect all of nature. Crime, creation, and divine retribution are interrelated.

The image of **the bowls** in this septet has a twofold Old Testament background. Bronze pots and basins were used as cult vessels in the temple (Exod. 27:3). Moreover, Jeremiah was commanded to "take from my hand this cup of the wine of wrath, and make all the nations to whom I send you drink it. They shall drink and stagger and be crazed because of the sword which I am sending among them" (Jer. 25:15-16). John fused the priestly bowls of the temple with Jeremiah's goblets of God's wrath. The angels coming out of the temple (15:6) perform a judgment ritual that is parallel to 8:3-5. But whereas in chap. 8 the angelic ritual functions as prelude to the trumpet cycle, here the whole cycle is a heavenly ritual, which reenacts, on a cosmic scale, the Egyptian plagues prior to Israel's deliverance. The cosmic scale of the first four plagues shows that from John's point of view these plagues will commence in the future. They elaborate the sixth seal.

The first, fourth, fifth, and seventh bowls, as well as the interlude, disclose that God's wrath will be focused on the worshipers of the imperial cult and followers of Antichrist. The pouring of the first bowl on the **earth** recalls the sixth Egyptian plague (Exod. 9:10-11), but its extent is not localized. All worshipers of the beast and only those **who bore the mark of the beast** receive **foul and evil sores** as mark of God's judgment. The second bowl parallels the first Egyptian plague (Exod. 7:17-21). The water of **the sea . . . became like the blood of . . . dead** people. It rots and can no longer sustain life, and **every living thing** of the sea

died. Note the intensification of the parallel in the trumpet vision (8:8-9). The third bowl, like the third trumpet, is directed against the fresh water supply, but now the **rivers and the fountains of water . . . became blood** (cf. Ps. 78:44). Without water, life cannot be sustained. Now John interrupts the series with an audition in order to interpret the first three plagues.

5-7—The interpretation has the form of a psalm (vv. 5-6) and a response (v. 7). The psalm is quite similar to the song of the conquerors (15:2-4) and is given by **the angel** in charge **of water** (cf. 7:1; 14:18). Different elements are related to different angels (cf. *1 Enoch* 60:11-24; 66:1-2) who guard them and complain to God about pollution and abuse of their entrusted elements. Now, however, instead of raising accusations about water pollution, the angel intones a judgment doxology acclaiming the justice of God. The opening lines parallel the song of the victors (15:3). God, "the king of the nations" (15:3), is addressed as **thou who art and wast,** just as in 11:17. The clause "who is to come," found in 1:4, 8; 4:8, is omitted, because God's coming in judgment is the subject of this septet (cf. 11:17). His judgments are **just,** not spiteful nor capricious, even though to John's church, this may be far from self-evident. His people must hear time and again that, contrary to their present experience, God's judgments are righteous (cf. Ps. 119:137). A "person is punished by the very things by which he or she sins" (Wis. Sol. 11:16; cf. Rom. 1:22-32; Acts 7:42). In agreement with this principle and the principle of corresponding retribution, the people who **have shed the blood of saints** and of their leaders, the Christian **prophets,** to them God has **given . . . blood to drink.** Of course this is to be understood metaphorically, not literally. Those who are "drunk with the blood of the saints" (17:6), having made war on them (13:7) and on the prophets (11:7), are given **blood to drink** (16:6). God's judgment fits the crime. The sarcasm of the angel's judgment doxology is as obvious as the identity of the recipients. They are the followers of the beast who have turned against God's faithful people and their prophetic leaders. **It is their due!** which in Greek *(axioi eisin)* repeats a phrase of 3:4, but now with a sarcastic tone. God's judgment corresponds to the crime.

And I heard the altar cry in response to the angel's doxology. The **altar** is here personified and acts as spokesperson for the martyrs whose souls lie beneath it (6:9-11). Their petition for vindication is fulfilled by God coming in judgment upon their murderers. **True and just are thy judgments,** the voice from the altar calls out. God's identity, his truth and righteousness, is revealed in that murder will not go unpunished.

8-9—The fourth angel poured his bowl on the sun, and it was allowed to scorch people with fierce heat. The sun receives a special commission. **It was allowed** (Greek, *edothē*), authorized, to mete our judgment by fire. This effect differs from the fourth trumpet plague (8:12) and from the sixth seal (6:12), but it relates to the promise of 7:16: "The sun shall not strike them [the conquerors], nor any scorching heat." The pouring of the fourth bowl extends the plagues of this series to all parts of creation—earth, sea, rivers, and the sun in the sky. Yet the reaction to the plagues among the earth dwellers is not repentance and acclamation of God but cursing, blaspheming his name (cf. 13:1, 4-5), probably by maintaining the emperor cult.

We should remind ourselves again that the verb past tenses are part of the style of visions and auditions and should not mislead us into thinking that John is describing or interpreting experiences that happened in his (immediate) past. Even though Satan's throne is already present in Pergamum (2:13), Rome has not yet become drunk with the blood of the saints (17:6) from John's perspective, nor has it yet been given blood to drink (16:6), nor has the fifth angel already poured his bowl on the beast's throne (16:10). The cosmic dimension of the plagues also requires their futuristic interpretation.

The Fifth Bowl (16:10-11). The fifth bowl is directed against the **kingdom** and **the throne of the beast.** The beast's **throne** symbolizes its authority and power which it had received from the dragon (cf. 13:2). The beast's **kingdom** refers to the extent of its power and includes all followers and worshipers. For John, Rome, the city, the emperor, and the imperial cult were historic manifestations of the beast's throne and kingdom. Now the beast's **throne** and **kingdom** are under attack. The effect was **darkness,** like the ninth Egyptian plague (Exod. 10:22; cf. Rev. 8:12). Probably John would have us understand this **darkness** not only as an eclipse of the sun but also metaphorically, as God handing idolatrous Rome and its followers over into the darkness of the imperial cult (cf. Acts 7:42a; Rom. 1:22-32; Wis. Sol. 11:15).

Their reaction can be no other than to curse **the God of heaven** (v. 11), the "God who has power over these plagues" (v. 9). They **curse** him because their religion is being destroyed. Those whose hearts are hardened cannot and shall not repent. Simultaneously their hardness and darkness constitute God's just judgment. John knew the story of the Egyptian plagues and was quite aware that just as the scorching sun shall not smite the people of God (7:16), so likewise the darkness shall not cover them. Even though "thick darkness" descended upon the land of Egypt and shall descend upon the kingdom of the Antichrist, "the people of Israel had light" (Exod. 10:23) and so will the church.

The Sixth Bowl (16:12). **The sixth bowl,** as well as the sixth trumpet, refers to the **great river Euphrates** which was the eastern frontier of the Roman empire. That great river **dried up, to prepare the way for the kings from the east.** The sixth trumpet vision had pictured a vast mythical cavalry army coming from the Euphrates, swarming across the land and killing one-third of the people (9:13-19). This mythical army is now historicized. The **kings from the east,** the Parthians, and their vassals are ready to invade the empire. The Euphrates River has ceased to exist as protective natural boundary. An invasion from the east is imminent. According to Isaiah (11:15) and Jeremiah (51:36), the miracle of the deliverance at the Red Sea (Exod. 14:21) will be repeated during the end time for the remnant of Israel in Assyria and Babylonia. In John's vision, however, it will not be Israel but the enemies of Rome, the kings of the east and their armies, that will cross the river dryshod.

The hearer would now expect to be told about an invading cavalry army of Parthians and their satellites, about Nero's return and revenge on Rome. Instead, John postponed the vision of Rome's destruction to the following chapters (17:15-18) and he introduced an interlude.

Interlude (16:13-16)

And I saw initiates a new vision which contains a new subject that is related to the Parthian invasion and yet quite distinct from it. The actors in this interlude are not the kings from the east but the demonic triumvirate of **dragon** (cf. chap. 12), **beast** (cf. 13:1-8), and **false prophet** (cf. 13:11-18). **Three foul spirits like frogs** (cf. Exod. 8:2) issue from their mouths. These froglike spirits **are demonic spirits** agitating for war. With deceptive propaganda and **signs,** miracles, that seem to legitimate their propaganda, they manage to assemble **the kings of the whole world . . . for battle on the great day of God the Almighty.** It is apparent that **the kings from the east** are *distinct* from the **kings of the whole world** (Greek, *oikoumenē*). The *oikoumenē* is the civilized world of Rome and its vassal kings in sharp distinction from the **east** of the barbarians. What is not yet clear is how these two groups of kings (vv. 12 and 14) will be related to each other. Will the invading Parthian forces (with Nero in the lead) be met by the armies of Rome and its satellites for the final battle at **Armageddon?** Will they annihilate each other and in so doing execute God's judgment on themselves? Or will there be a different scenario? The hearer is kept in suspense during the sixth bowl vision and during the interlude. All he hears is when and where the battle will take place. It will take place on the **great day of God the Almighty,** which is the day of final judgment promised by the prophets (Joel 3:9-13; Zeph. 1:14-18; Isa. 13:4-22; Ezekiel 38–39; *1 Enoch* 56:5-8). The place of the battle **is called in Hebrew Armageddon,** literally, the mountain of Megiddo. Megiddo, situated on a plain, was the site of many a battle (Judg. 5:19; 2 Kings 9:27; 23:29). Yet there is no "mount" of Megiddo, and the name has eluded all attempts to define it geographically. For instance, it was thought to be a reference to Mount Carmel nearby. But that mountain is never called Mount Megiddo in the Old Testament, a fatal flaw in that interpretation. For John, Armageddon is wherever the eschatological battle of the great day of the Lord is fought.

The coming of the great day of the Lord prompted John to break the story of his vision and interject an exhortation to watchfulness (v. 15). This interjection is meant to serve as key to unlock the mythic symbols of the interlude. Their meaning is not to be found in our calculations concerning the time and speculations about the geographic location of the battle to end all wars. Their point is that we, the readers/hearers, ought to be prepared to meet our maker and Lord. **"Lo, I am coming like a thief!"** This word of Jesus addresses directly, through John, the readers and hearers of this letter, and it should impress upon them the futility of calculations (cf. Matt. 24:42-44; 1 Thess. 5:2; 2 Peter 3:10) and admonish them to alertness. **Blessed** are those who are **awake, keeping** their **garments that** they **may not go naked and be seen exposed!** No calculations and speculations will function as fig leaves and hide our nakedness on the day of the Lord. Christians who sleep securely with their apocalyptic timetables under their pillows will march **naked** into captivity (cf. Ezek. 23:26-29). Implicit in the beatitude is a solemn warning, not to lose their status as kings and priests unto God for which they are destined (5:9-10; 7:9). Incidentally, only in 3:3 and here is the **thief** identified with Christ.

The Seventh Bowl (16:17-21). **The seventh** bowl is poured **into the air, and a loud voice came out of the temple, from the throne** announcing, **"It is done!"** (cf. 10:6-7; 11:15; 15:1). We are also reminded of the "third woe" prior to the seventh trumpet; it is now completed. The interlude in 10:6-7 had promised that *the end* would come in the days of the seventh trumpet call. And it did! Just as the trumpet cycle evolved out of the seventh seal, so the bowl cycle evolved out of the seventh trumpet, reaching its climax in the proclamation, **It is done!** These cycles deal with the same eschatological future. Each culminates in the day of the Lord (cf. 11:15-19) which from John's point of view was imminent. In short, the three septets do not describe successive historical periods. **It is done!** leads us to the threshold of eternity but not beyond. There were **flashes of lightning, loud voices, peals of thunder.** The seventh bowl, poured **into the air,** without which nothing can live, is accompanied by manifestations of theophany (cf. 4:5; 8:5; 11:19). However, these manifestations of God's coming to judge the world in righteousness have still another function which becomes apparent in the **great earthquake** and the **great hailstones.** They function in the seventh bowl plague as instruments of God's judgment itself. The **great earthquake** is identified as one that **had never been since men were on the earth, so great was that earthquake.** This great earthquake connects the seventh bowl with the sixth seal (6:12) which had introduced the day of the Lord in the seal septet. **It is done!** relates to the church's struggle with imperial Rome (chaps. 12–13), to the scene on Mount Zion (14:1-5), and to the song of Moses and the Lamb by the conquerors (15:1-4). Therefore the announcement **It is done!** must also include the fall of Babylon/Rome (cf. 14:8). And it does! **The great city was split** by the great earthquake **into three parts, and the cities of the nations fell, and God remembered great Babylon, to make her drain the cup of the fury of his wrath.** Babylon/Rome is made to drink the cup of God's wrath (cf. Jer. 25:15-16) in retribution for her "passion" with which she intoxicated the nations through the imperial cults (14:8). The **great city** is none other than Babylon/Rome, the heart of the empire, the instigator of the emperor cult and of the church's future oppression. **It is done!** means that the judgment of Rome is completed—here by an earthquake of tremendous proportions, later, in chap. 17, by something else. John himself gives us quite a few pointers against understanding his symbols and images literally, the way some modern fundamentalists do.

The images of Babylon and the beast will be related with some new nuances in chap. 17, even though from one perspective both symbolize the Roman empire. Moreover, the announcement, **It is done!** must also include the rest of creation. **And every island fled away, and no mountains were to be found** (cf. 20:11). The life on this earth, as we know it, is herewith finished. But what is happening to the worshipers of the beast? **And great hailstones, heavy as a hundredweight** (about 66 lbs.) **dropped on** them, and they, quite naturally, **cursed God for the plague of the hail** (cf. Ezek. 38:18-23).

The beast worshipers remain obdurate to the end and in the end. Their great city, Babylon, has fallen (14:8), having drained the "cup of the fury of his [God's] wrath" (16:19). Nevertheless, the power behind Babylon, the demonic trinity, has not yet been overthrown, even though the outcome of the great conflict between God and Satan has been decided ever since the Lamb opened the seals of the scroll (5:6-14; cf. 12:7-12). Though while "it is done," it is not yet done and John will communicate a new climactic series of visions.

■ The Revelation of the Climactic End (17:1—22:5[9])

Any good speech ought not to end with a whimper but with a climactic high point. John did just that. Moreover, his last section balances his first (chaps. 4–11) and narrates the consummation of the sovereign reign of God and Christ on earth in judgment and salvation. The section itself is carefully structured (*A-B-A'*). The introduction, the conclusion, and the theme of 17:1—19:10 (A) have an exact parallel and countertheme in 21:9—22:19 (A'). Compare the introduction 17:1-4 with 21:9-11, and the conclusion 19:9-10 with 22:7b-9. The theme of the harlot Babylon finds its countertheme in the bride of the Lamb, the new Jerusalem. The center B (19:11—21:8) is the high point of this section and of the whole letter, climaxing in the only word of God in direct discourse (21:5-8) found in the body of John's letter (cf. 1:8).

In this concluding section John incorporated diverse apocalyptic traditions from his churches. He will narrate a radically different version of the final judgment in 20:11-15 from the one in 14:14-20. The same holds true of the destruction of Babylon which in the seventh bowl vision was caused by God's angel through "a great earthquake such as had never been" (16:18-20). In the new section, Babylon's demise is told quite differently (17:15-18), and yet a third version is given in 18:21. His endeavor to include different traditions, subjecting them to his design, prompted him not only to incorporate carnage at the parousia (19:11-20) but to repeat it a thousand years later at the annihilation of Gog and Magog (20:7-10). Obviously, Ezekiel's prophecy against God was important enough, if not to John then to some of his people, to merit his authoritative interpretation. The same is true of messianic interim-kingdom speculations that circulated among his people. He had to deal with them, even as he had to deal with the spiritualizing, gnosticizing notion that the believers' resurrection has happened already in baptism. He attended to these and other questions among his people not by means of argumentation but through setting his visions before them and drawing them into those visions.

The visions of his climactic conclusion picture his double theme: negatively, the cleansing of God's creation from all idolatry and from every power hostile to God and his Messiah, through a series of judgments; positively, the establishment of a new creation, free from idolatry, death, and the power of the devil and his minions, with God in the midst of his people worshiping him, reigning as coregents with Christ and being glorified by the light of God and the Lamb which is life eternal. John would expect us to understand by now that the sequence of his visions may not be translated into a chronological sequence of post-parousia events, lest we also conclude with fundamentalists and "behold!" with academicians who lack imagination that God destroys his creation (20:11) one verse after he has completed his cleansing (20:7-10).

The Judgment of Babylon and the Triumph of God (17:1—19:10)

This section evolves from the seventh bowl vision. It contains three parts (17:1-18; 18:1-24; 19:1-10) and expands the announcement in 14:8 of Babylon's fall and the reference in 16:12 to the army of the kings from the east. Two new versions of Babylon's doom are presented. Chapter 17 depicts Babylon as the great harlot, interprets the identity of the beast, and climaxes in the destruction of the harlot by the beast. Chapter 18 brings reflections and laments of different groups on Babylon's doom, culminating in an angelic symbolic action of Babylon's destruction (18:21) and in an indictment. Babylon/Rome is guilty of murder (18:24). The third part contains the liturgy of the triumph of God (19:1-8).

The Great Harlot and the Beast (17:1-18)

The vision of the harlot (vv. 1-6) is followed by an angelic interpretation of the beast (vv. 7-14) and concluded with the annihilation of the harlot by the beast and its forces (vv. 15-18). Again we can see that John's literary sequence is not organized in terms of a temporal sequence. Certainly, the Lamb's conquest of the beast (v. 14) comes, in terms of time, not *before* but *after* its war against the harlot (v. 16).

Introduction to the Vision (17:1-3a). One of the angels with the bowls (chap. 16) assists the seer in receiving a new vision. Later on the same angel will interpret the vision (vv. 7-18). The pattern of vision and interpretation is traditional (cf. Dan. 7; 2 Esdras 13). The introduction (vv. 1-3a) connects the vision of the harlot on the beast with the seventh bowl and thereby indicates that chap. 17 is an enlargement of a segment of the bowl plagues. Simultaneously the angel's invitation, **Come, I will show you the judgment of the great harlot** functions as superscription of the section up to 19:10 (cf. 15:1). The designation of cities as harlots has its antecedent in the Old Testament (cf. Isa. 1:21; 23:16-18; Ezek. 16:15-21; 23:1-2; Nah. 3:1-4). Basic to this indictment is the sin of idolatry, denounced as fornication by the prophets (e.g., Ezek. 16:15-17; Jer. 1:21; 13:27). The capital city played the harlot with its vassal **kings** and made **the dwellers on earth** drunk **with the wine** of her **fornication,** leading them into the fascination and intoxicating stupor of the emperor cult. Worship is the issue also in this chapter. The great harlot is said to be **seated upon many waters,** which echoes Jer. 51:23. There the geographic site of old Babylon was meant. With its Euphrates River on one side and its network of many canals, old Babylon felt secure. In our text the many waters support the symbolic identification of Babylon with Rome and indicate Rome's worldwide influence. Its fleet of ships extended its power and returned with the wealth of nations (cf. 18:11-19). Some Roman coins depict the goddess Roma (Latin, *Dea Roma*) with the river-god Tiber. The Tiber is the river that flows through the capital to its seaport of Ostia. For John, the goddess Roma, whose cult was quite popular in Asia Minor, was nothing but a whore.

The angel **carried** John **away in the Spirit,** in a state of ecstasy, into the **wilderness.** Two other transportations are mentioned in Revelation (4:1-2, into the open door of the heavenly throne room; 21:10, to a high mountain). The desert to which John is translated "in the Spirit" is here the symbol of Babylon's fate (Isa. 19:22; Jer. 51:26, 29, 43), not a place of protection by God (as in 12:6, 14). Because Babylon/Rome shall become desolate, like a desert, John is carried there **in the Spirit** (cf. Acts 8:39).

The Woman and the Beast (17:3b-6). **I saw a woman sitting on a scarlet beast.** Goddesses were occasionally pictured as seated on a horse or a lion. This **scarlet beast** with its **seven heads** and **ten horns** and **blasphemous names** is Satan's royal representative (11:17; 13:1-8, 14) and the incarnation of all evil. The **woman** and the **beast** are actually two images, yet together they express the harmony of evil. But they are also distinct from each other. The woman represents the capital city; the beast on which she sits is the empire. In the opening vision the harlot and the beast, though distinct, operate in unison. Later the beast will turn against her, but by then the beast will not represent the empire but an individual (vv. 10-11, 16). This woman is artfully contrasted with the other woman, the glorious queen of heaven, the symbol of the church of God (12:1). And she is also contrasted with "the Bride" of Christ (21:2, 9).

The woman was arrayed in purple and scarlet, and bedecked with gold and jewels and pearls. Purple is the color of royalty and sovereignty. Scarlet is the color of the beast, and she is overloaded with gold and jewels and pearls, blatantly parading her luxury. The contrast with the woman who represents the city of God and Bride of the Lamb (chap. 21) is obvious. The people of God are clothed in white garments of "fine linen," which are the righteous deeds of the saints (19:8; 3:18; 7:9). Babylon/Rome wallows in the ill-gotten gain of its imperialistic policy. She holds **in her hand a golden cup full of abominations and the impurities of her fornication.** John's perspective prevented him from perceiving any benefit that Rome might have brought to the Mediterranean world. As an apocalyptic seer he went far beyond moralists such as Tacitus, for whom Rome was the city "where all things hideous and shameful from every part of the world find their center and become popular" (*Annals* 15.44). Rome is compared to a "filthy sewer" by Seneca, and Juvenal hurled his satire against the capital in which "corruption reigns supreme" (*Satire* 3). The **abominations** which fill her **golden cup** are her idolatries, her spiritual **fornication,** culminating in the imperial cult. **On her forehead was written a name of mystery.** Perhaps John alluded to the practice of prostitutes in Rome having to wear their names on a headband. Her known name is **Babylon the great, mother of harlots and of earth's abominations.** This code word for Rome originated after A.D. 70 in Jewish circles (*Syr. Bar.* 67:7; *Sib. Or.* 5.143, 159) because Rome, like Babylon of old, had destroyed Jerusalem and its temple and had humiliated its people. This identification was taken over by some Christian groups (1 Peter 5:13) and became part of John's tradition. Rome was the origin of the imperial cult and therefore the **mother** of the *harlots* (of *male* priests! see comments on 14:4) who performed in the cult all over the Roman world. But what is the **name of mystery**? The secret name of Rome and its goddess Roma was believed to be AMOR, love, *Roma* spelled backwards. This would undergird John's association of the capital with harlotry. She represents the opposite of the love that Christ extends to his people (1:5) and that they should extend to each other (2:4).

With **and I saw,** John introduces the result of Rome's harlotry. **The woman** was **drunk with the blood of the saints and the blood of the martyrs of Jesus** (cf. 11:8-10; 13:7, 10; 16:6; 18:24; 19:2). The murder of the witnesses of Jesus is the apex of Rome's idolatry. The history of Rome's murder of Christians began with Nero in A.D. 64 when they were "covered with skins of beasts . . . torn by dogs . . . nailed to crosses . . . doomed to the flames and burned to serve as nightly illumination" (Tacitus, *Annals* 15.44). With local persecutions in the past as background, John envisions worse to come at the end of time. And he **marveled.** He had expected to see **the judgment** (v. 1) of the harlot. Instead, he sees a gaudy prostitute in luxury, riding high and mighty and drunk with her wine. (Note the vision sequence from the destruction of great Babylon in 16:19 to the intoxicated prostitute Babylon in 17:6 riding on the back of what seems to be absolute power.)

The Interpretation of the Beast and the Harlot (17:7-18). Verse 7 is a transition from John's vision to the angel's interpretation. John's amazement is a literary device that gives the angel an opportunity to explain **the mystery of the woman, and of the beast** to him and his readers. The interpretation of the woman comes last (vv. 15-18) because she will be the subject of the next chapter. This arrangement facilitates the transition.

8-14—The interpretation of the beast fluctuates between representing the empire with its seven heads, its emperors or kings (v. 10a), on one hand, and an individual figure, the Antichrist, on the other (vv. 8a and 11-14, 16). The reason for this fluctuation lies in the fact that an emperor or king represents his realm. **The beast,** the angel explained, **was, and is not, and is to ascend from**

the bottomless pit and go to perdition. This language imitates the threefold predicate of God and reflects John's use of the Nero tradition. In contrast to God, "who is and who was and who is to come" (1:8), the beast **was,** it existed and reigned in the past; but it **is not,** it does not live and rule in the present. It will **ascend from the bottomless pit** in the last days (11:7), make war on the saints in the power of the dragon (13:2b, 7), and it will **go to perdition** (cf. v. 14; 19:20). This beast is the Antichrist, who will come straight from the abyss (11:17), with features like Nero. But the abyss is also the place from which chaos monsters, subdued in primordial times, shall emerge in the end and be destroyed (Isa. 27:1; *2 Bar.* 29:4; 2 Esdr. 6:52). Hence the appearance of the beast is grotesque, because John fused the Nero legend with the Danielic Antichrist and the apocalyptic idea of the destruction of primeval monsters in the end time.

The dwellers on earth whose names have not been written in the book of life . . . will, when they encounter the beast, **marvel . . . because it was and is not and is to come.** The appearance of the Antichrist who existed in the past but does not live now among the earth dwellers at present will arouse their excitement. The reason for their fascination will be that his past existence and his subsequent absence are followed by his appearance among them. The solution to the mystery concerning the beast's identity is found in the legend of the returning Nero, to which the "wound unto death" (13:3, 12, 14) and the mysterious number 666 already referred (13:18). All human beings, except the Christians, will be awed by the appearance of Antichrist, which will look like Nero's reappearance. In him who ascends from the realm of chaos, all the evils of the godless empire will be incarnated. His ascent from the abyss for his eschatological parousia is a demonic parody of Christ's descent from heaven at his parousia. Of course, the awed earth dwellers cannot perceive that the Antichrist will end in final **perdition.**

Two interpretations are given for the **seven heads** of this beast from the abyss. One, they are the **seven hills** or mountains, on which the woman is seated. Never mind that she is also **seated** on many waters (vv. 1, 15) and on the beast (v. 3). Just about everybody in John's churches would know that Rome is called the city on seven hills.

Second, the seven heads **are also seven kings.** "King" was used in the eastern part of the empire in place of emperor or Caesar (cf. 1 Peter 2:13, 17; 1 Tim. 2:2). **Five** emperors **have fallen;** they have died, perhaps they even died violently. **One is,** one Caesar reigns at John's time of writing which would be a sixth Caesar/King. **The other,** the seventh Caesar, **has not yet come, and when he comes he must remain only a little while.** The reign of the seventh Caesar will be short. There is no agreement as to who was the first Roman emperor in this series. But actually this question is less important than the realization that for John the present Roman emperor would be succeeded by only one more emperor, whose tenure would be short. And then the beast, the Antichrist, will make his parousia, ascending from the abyss, and all idolaters **will marvel** (v. 8)

As for the beast that was and is not, it is an eighth but it belongs to the seven (v. 11). It is obvious that the **beast** here refers to an individual emperor who was one of the seven Roman emperors but whose eschatological appearance as Antichrist marks him as an eighth. Clearly, John's formulation alludes to the Nero legend (cf. v. 8). As a historical emperor he was one of the seven, but as Antichrist he will appear as an eighth. At this point we should keep in mind the multilayered nature of apocalyptic prophecy. While John made use of the Nero legend, he never identified the Antichrist explicitly as Nero. Since the Roman Senate had declared Nero a public enemy, John would have had nothing to fear had he made the identification explicit. For him, the number **seven** is primarily a symbolic number indicating completeness. When he identifies the Antichrist as an **eighth,** then he suggests that the Antichrist will be someone so novel in evil as to signal a new beginning. But on the other hand he belongs to the seven, which means that the evil can already be detected in the imperial cult of Asia Minor.

The problem of how the emperors prior to the appearance of the eighth are to be identified is therefore a secondary problem. It has not resulted in a generally agreed upon solution. The series of Roman Caesars is thus: (1) Julius Caesar, died 44 B.C.; (2) Augustus, 27 B.C. to A.D. 14; (3) Tiberius, A.D. 14 to 37; (4) Caligula, A.D. 37–41; (5) Claudius, A.D. 41–54; (6) Nero, A.D. 54–68; (7) Galba, Otho, Vitellius, in the confusion after Nero's death, A.D. 69; (8) Vespasian, A.D. 69–79; (9) Titus, A.D. 79–81; (10) Domitian, A.D. 81–96. (11) Nerva, A.D. 96–98; (12) Trajan, A.D. 98–117.

Without discussing the multitude of diverse suggestions that have been offered, we will begin with Irenaeus's statement that Revelation was written during the time of tenure of emperor Domitian. If Irenaeus's statement is correct, as I think it is, then *Domitian* would be the *sixth* Roman emperor, reigning at John's time, and would be succeeded by a seventh of brief duration. Then the **eighth,** the Antichrist, would make his appearance. Counting back from Domitian and omitting the three "interim" Caesars of A.D. 68–69, we would arrive at Caligula as the first of the **five** who **have fallen** which may indicate a violent death. Interestingly enough, not only was Caligula the first Roman emperor installed after Christ's execution but he also died a violent death. Claudius was poisoned by Nero's mother; Nero committed suicide; of Vespasian, Jewish tradition reported that he died a most painful death in agony (cf. 2 Esdr. 12:26). His son Titus, some Jewish circles believed, was murdered with the sword of his brother Domitian (cf. 2 Esdr. 12:28). All of these five were regarded by some as enemies of the people of God. Of Caligula's attempt to erect his statue in Jerusalem's temple we know through Josephus (*Ant.* 18.261–275; cf. Mark 13:14).

Claudius ordered the banishment of Jews and Jewish Christians from Rome (Acts 18:2). Nero murdered Christians as scapegoats (Tacitus, quoted above). Vespasian and Titus destroyed Jerusalem and its temple, an act that was repulsive also to Christian Jews like John. Finally, Domitian, the sixth emperor (counting from Caligula and omitting the interim Caesars), is remembered as promoter of the imperial cult in Asia Minor. A temple in his honor was built in Ephesus. At any rate, the five emperors beginning with Caligula have a definite anti-Christian coloring.

The emperor ruling at John's time, according to this hypothesis, would be Domitian. He is to be succeeded by a *seventh* who **has not yet come** and whose tenure will last **only a little while** (v. 10). The Antichrist will be **an eighth,** a new incarnation of evil, a monster, ascending from the abyss, not a "king" like Vespasian,

Titus, or Domitian. Yet, since this monster **belongs to the seven** (v. 11), some anti-Christian traits are present in the rule of the Caesars at John's time, whoever they may be. In short, John's vision of the Antichrist is meant to sharpen the eyes of his audience concerning the nature of the totalitarian, self-deifying state of their present and dispel the illusion that relations between church and empire will gradually improve.

12-14—The angel interprets the meaning of the **ten horns** of the beast. They represent **ten kings**—not ten Roman kings of the past but **ten kings** who shall appear simultaneously with the beast in the future (cf. 16:12). At present they do not rule. But with the beast's appearance they shall receive royal **authority as kings for one hour, together with the beast.** These future ten kings will be **of one mind and give over their power and authority to the beast,** the Antichrist. These ten kings are the vassals of Antichrist who is to come. Again the legend lies in the background that Nero will return allied with the vassal of Parthia (cf. 16:12).

Before John narrated the destruction of the harlot by Antichrist and his cohorts, he anticipated the final war described in 19:11-21 (cf. 16:14-16) in which Antichrist will go to perdition (v. 11). He and his ten vassals **will make war on the Lamb, and the Lamb will conquer them,** because the Lamb that was slain is **Lord of lords and King of kings** (cf. 19:16) rather than present or future Roman emperors. The title "king of kings" was used by Babylonian great kings and applied to God in Judaism (cf. *1 Enoch* 9:4; 63:4; 84:2; 2 Macc. 13:4). Its usage here shows, first, that Christ receives titles reserved for God in the tradition. Second, Christ is Lord over the earth; it is not just in heaven where he exercises his authority. Third, he is Lord already now and has a legitimate claim upon the earth. Finally, he will be made manifest on the last day as Lord over this world. **And those with him are called and chosen and faithful** and participate in the war against Antichrist (cf. 19:11, 19). Yet neither here nor in chap. 19 do we find a battle scene.

15-18—Before the Antichrist will "go to perdition" (vv. 8 and 11), he and his followers have a task to perform according to God's plan. This task involves the harlot by **the waters** (cf. v. 1). Now the waters represent **peoples and multitudes and nations and tongues** who are subject to her. However, an open revolt against the harlot/Rome occurs, instigated by the beast/Antichrist and the **ten horns** (vv. 12-14), his vassals. Up to this moment the harmony between beast, empire, and capital city had been maintained. In vv. 3-6 the harlot (Rome) sits on the beast, the empire. In vv. 8, 10-14, the beast appears as Antichrist, but there is no indication that the alliance with the empire has been terminated. Now the liaison is broken and the Antichrist turns against Rome, which is the supreme divine irony. **The ten horns that you saw,** the vassal kings of the Antichrist (v. 12), **they and the beast** (v. 11) **will hate the harlot** (Rome). Their hatred means war against the capital, which would agree with one form of the Nero legend. The beast becomes the agent that will destroy the nerve center and power base of the evil empire which had also been symbolized as beast (vv. 3-6). John's audience might hear that the returning Nero with his Parthian cavalry will make Rome **desolate** (same Greek word stem as in "desert," or "wilderness," v. 3). The gaudy harlot will be stripped of her garments and left **naked.** The Antichrist and his allies will **devour her flesh** (Ps. 27:2; Mic. 3:3) **and burn her up with fire.** The background to the gory annihilation of the capital is, on one hand, Tacitus's description of the murder of the Christians of Rome (quoted above) in conjunction with the law of just retribution and, on the other, Ezekiel's prophecy of Jerusalem's destruction (Ezek. 23:22-35). The great city, which has played the harlot, will be hated by her former love, who shall strip her of her clothes and jewels and leave her naked, and her members shall be "devoured by fire." The enemies of God and his people shall mete out justice on themselves. Evil turns against itself, because God **has put it into their hearts to carry out his purpose.** In their struggle for domination of the world, the beast and its minions are part of God's plan. Even an Antichrist with the characteristics of a returning Nero must serve his purpose and do so without knowing it. John sharpened the vision of his audience. The leaders who believe that they manage, control, and preside over the affairs of the world are, quite ironically and unknowingly, led to do God's bidding. The irony and sovereignty of God is revealed through John to his churches, in order that they may not lose courage. The God who uses the Antichrist to do his bidding is one whose ways are not our ways and whose judgments are both unsearchable and ironic (cf. Rom. 11:33-36).

18—Once more the identity of the great harlot is disclosed, though most readers/hearers would have known it through v. 9. But vv. 15-18 also serve as transition to the next chapter and therefore it helps to state explicitly that **the woman that you saw is the great city which has dominion over the kings of the earth.** The woman is the capital of the empire, Rome.

Two additional comments: (1) "The kings of the earth" (v. 18) are Rome's vassals (cf. 18:9). They must be distinguished from the "ten kings" who are allies of Antichrist (v. 12) aiding in the destruction of Rome. (2) In 17:14, the "ten kings" are involved in the war against the Lamb, but in 19:11-21, it is "the kings of the earth" (19:19) and "the beast" that make war against the Lamb. The two groups of kings had already appeared in 16:12-14 as "kings from the east" crossing the Euphrates and "kings of the whole world" who will assemble for battle at "Armageddon" at the behest of the satanic trinity. The reason for this confusion lies in the dual role of the Antichrist. As the incarnation of the empire's anti-God forces, the Antichrist wages war against the Lamb together with Rome's vassals, who are called "the kings of the earth" (16:13-16; 19:11-21). As the executor of God's judgment on Rome, the Antichrist in Nero-like form returns with his allies, called "the ten kings" or "the kings of the east" (16:12; 17:12, 15-18). Naturally, the Antichrist must be present at the final battle at Armageddon which seals his doom (16:16; 17:14; 19:19-21).

In conclusion: We should avoid superimposing the Nero legend upon this chapter to such an extent that we interpret John as predicting the fulfillment of that legend. Rather, his use of the legend, like his use of the Old Testament, is determined by his expectation of the imminent end. The Nero legend aided John to show: (1) The continuity and the discontinuity between his present and his envisioned future with respect to the Antichrist. Antichrist is the eighth but belongs to the seven (17:11). (2) The irony of God in using his antagonists to execute his judgment.

The Fall of Babylon (18:1-24)

John used only one verse to narrate Babylon's destruction (17:16), but 24 verses celebrate the significance of the city's overthrow, signaling the end of the old order. The announcement of Babylon's fall by an **angel** with **great authority** (A, vv. 1-3) is followed by the audition of **another voice from heaven** (B, vv. 4-20) and concluded with a symbolic action and its interpretation (A′, vv. 21-24). The chapter reaches its climax in the indictment of v. 24: Babylon/Rome is guilty of murder.

The central section, vv. 4-20, contains different forms. An admonition (vv. 4-5) is addressed to **my people** to **come out** of Babylon. Next are two commands to execute judgment on Babylon and the reasons for doing so (vv. 6-8). In vv. 9-19, we find a series of three laments or dirges over the fall of the great city by the kings of the earth (vv. 9-10), by the merchants who gained their wealth through Rome (vv. 11-17), and by the shipmasters and "all whose trade is on the sea" (vv. 18-19). In radical contrast to their laments, the section closes with a call for rejoicing (v. 20). This call discloses the purpose of the prior dirges. Their purpose is not to evoke the reader's solidarity and sympathy with the sorrow of the kings, merchants, and seafarers but to reveal the significance of God's judgment on Babylon through the reaction of these three groups. Like a Greek play, so Revelation 18 tells the reader, through the eyes of these spectators, what is happening and how Rome's destruction affects them.

The Angel's Announcement (18:1-3). **Fallen, fallen is Babylon the great!** (cf. 14:8). The past tense of the angel's announcement indicates that in God's sight the great city is already destroyed even if within time and space its destruction is still a matter of the future. Its ruins will be inhabited by **demons** and impure

bird(s) (cf. Isa. 13:21-22; 34:11-15; Jer. 50:39). The announcement itself is a parody of a funeral song (cf. Isa. 21:9). A threefold reason for Babylon's doom is given, **for all nations have drunk the wine of her impure passion.** They drank the abominations of the imperial cult (cf. 17:2, 4-6; 14:8). Literally, humanity drank the wine of the wrath of Rome's fornication. The wine of her wrath resulted in the murder of Christians and non-Christians alike (v. 24). Hence, God made her "drain the cup of the fury of his wrath" (16:19; 14:10). **The kings of the earth** are Rome's allies in distinction from the kings of the east (16:12; 17:16). These leaders in the worship of the goddess Roma have thereby **committed fornication with her.** Idolatry is spiritual harlotry. **And the merchants of the earth have grown rich with the wealth of her wantonness.** Rome's self-glorifying power was supported by the idolatry of allied kings and nations. It bore results with the rise of a new class of business magnates who gained fabulous wealth through the empire, while the majority of the population lived in poverty and was burdened by taxation. Through economic threats on one hand (cf. 13:17) and the lure of riches on the other, Rome advanced its idolatry, crushing those who opposed her imperialistic claims.

Another Voice from Heaven (18:4-20). The speech of **another,** unspecified, **voice from heaven** ends in v. 20. At first the reference to **my people** suggests that the speaker is God himself. But v. 5b ("God has remembered her iniquities") distinguishes between the speaker and God. Hence, the voice belongs to another angel.

4-5—The admonition **Come out of her, my people** is spoken to Babylon's doom and alludes to Jer. 51:45, to the exodus from Sodom (Gen. 19:12-14; cf. Rev. 11:8) and Egypt, and to the flight from Jerusalem at the time of its doom (Mark 13:14). Yet this admonition should be understood metaphorically rather than literally. It is not an exhortation to Roman Christians to leave the city but rather to break with the empire's idolatrous culture and life-style and to avoid compromise (cf. the seven messages of chaps. 2 and 3). Only if the church is an exclusive fellowship, separated from the idolatrous city, only if it is nurtured by God's word in "the desert" (12:6, 14) apart from the idolatry of civilization, only if the church engages in a spiritual exodus from Rome/Egypt/Sodom (11:8), only then can God's people withstand the assaults of Satan (12:6, 14), escape the judgment of God and not **share in her plagues** that fall on Babylon/Rome. John's critical program of "Christ against culture" (Niebuhr) has been ignored by churches at their own spiritual peril. The church may not become society on Sunday, through compromise and accommodations. If it does, it ceases to be **my people.**

6—The angel's voice exclaimed, **Render to her** (Babylon/Rome) **as she herself has rendered, and repay her double for her deeds; mix a double draught for her in the cup** of abomination **she mixed.** This command to execute divine vengeance is not addressed to God's people. It is addressed either to the angels of judgment or perhaps (according to the context) to the Antichrist and the ten kings (17:12, 16-17). They are the unwitting instruments of God's wrath. The **double** punishment means nothing more or nothing less than full retribution (cf. Jer. 50:15, 29; 16:18; 17:18; Isa. 40:2). Drinking from the **cup** is an image for suffering God's judgment (14:10), and, simultaneously, it is an image of Rome's idolatrous arrogance (14:8; 18:3). Rome's sin and God's judgment correspond in that God's wrath is mixed in the same cup from which she gave the nations to drink (18:3).

7-8—The ground for her destruction lies in Rome's self-glorification and abysmal ignorance concerning her own eternity. **A queen I sit, I am no** (poor) **widow, mourning** (and sorrow) **I shall never see.** But Rome, the self-styled eternal city, shall be brought down **in a single day. Pestilence and mourning and famine** shall suddenly overtake her and **she shall be burned with fire** (17:16; cf. Isa. 47:8-9; Jer. 50:31-32; 51:25, 30). The execution of God's judgment in this book is on one hand the result of cosmic catastrophes caused by God or his angels (11:13; 16:18-19), and on the other hand it is caused by anti-Christian humans who function as the ignorant executors of just retribution (16:12; 17:16). **Mighty is the Lord God who judges her.** The one who brought judgment to Jerusalem through the might of Babylon and who stirred up "the spirit of a destroyer against Babylon" (Jer. 51:1) shall execute justice in Babylon/Rome.

9-10—The lament of the kings, which is the first of three, has its model in Ezekiel 26–27, where the same three groups of mourners appear (cf. Ezek. 26:15-19; 27:11-30). **The kings of the earth,** Rome's allies in its provinces, **will weep and wail** when they see her burning and exclaim in terror. **Alas! alas! thou great city. . . . In one hour has thy judgment come.** This lament is repeated by the merchants (vv. 16-17) and the shipowners (v. 19). **Alas** or woe (Greek, *ouai*) is typical in funeral laments (1 Kings 13:30; Jer. 22:18). Suddenly and unexpectedly in but **one hour** doom has overtaken the **great city** that had wallowed in unparalleled luxury and bragged of its might. The **kings** are not identifiable rulers but types of those rulers who profited from Roman idolatry, exploitation, and luxury. The Greek verb *strēniaō,* to live in luxury, is found only in 18:7, 9 in the New Testament (cf. 18:13). Here they stand **far off,** at a safe distance, watching the great city burn without coming to her aid but mourning their own loss.

11-13—The **merchants** are the big international import-export wholesale merchants whose profits rose through Rome's exploitation of the provinces. They too **weep** loudly because **no one buys their cargo any more.** Their sorrow is purely selfish—loss of profits, not admiration for the city's virtues. They enumerate their cargoes of luxury items, of **gold, silver, jewels and pearls, fine linen, purple, silk and scarlet,** cargoes of expensive *thyia,* **wood** of African citrus trees preferred by the wealthy Romans for their furniture, **all articles of ivory, all articles of costly wood, bronze, iron and marble,** and so forth. The list closes with cargoes of **slaves,** literally, "of bodies," to which John added, **that is, human souls.** The slave traders regarded their cargo as mere "bodies." Rome's life-style was possible only because slaves provided cheap labor. When human beings are treated as merchandise to enable a life-style of leisure and luxury to flourish, then the mandate to love the neighbor is strangled, just as the first commandment, to love God above all, is drowned in the wantonness of idolatry. To be sure, the phrase **human souls** (cf. Ezek. 27:13) could in ordinary speech mean "human merchandise," synonymous with "bodies." By adding both terms, John indicated his view of the inhuman institution of slavery, of the exploitation and degradation of human beings by the wholesale merchants.

14—In this verse a shift occurs to the second person (cf. 13:9-10) as Babylon/Rome is addressed directly. **All** of Rome's **dainties** (Greek, *liparos*, sumptuous) and **splendor** are lost forever. Here wealth was proverbial. According to the Talmud, "Ten measures of riches came down to the world; nine were taken by the Romans and one was left for the rest of the world" (Billerbeck, 1:826). Suetonius's book *The Twelve Caesars* bristles with stories and references to the excessive waste, luxury items, and delicacies squandered by emperors. Thus, for instance, Vitellius (*Suetonius* 9, 13), who reigned less than one year (A.D. 69), held a dinner in honor of the goddess Minerva, which called for pike livers, pheasant brains, peacock brains, flamingo tongues, lamprey milk, and so forth. "Ingredients collected in every corner of the empire from the Parthian frontier to the Straits of Gibraltar were brought to Rome" by ship. Moreover, that emperor invited himself for dinner at a cost to his host of no less than 4,000 pieces of gold.

15-19—Like the kings, so the **merchants** who **gained** their **wealth** from Rome, the capital of big business in John's day, **will stand far off** from the doomed city and loudly bewail their financial loss. Their lament is continued by the ship captains, shipowners, and sailors who had grown **rich by her wealth. The great city** has been destroyed **in one hour** (cf. vv. 10, 16-17, 19).

If we look at the verb tenses of this chapter, John's lack of interest in a chronological sequence of events becomes obvious. In v. 3 the fall of Babylon is announced in the past tense. In v.

4 the command for the exodus from Babylon must have been issued prior to Babylon's fall. In v. 8 her destruction is told in the future. Likewise, the mourning of the three groups is told in the past tense (v. 17), the present tense (v. 11), and the future tense (vv. 9 and 15).

20—The lament of Rome's friends is interrupted with a call for rejoicing, issued to the inhabitants of heaven. **Rejoice over her** destruction, **O heaven** (cf. 12:12). If modern students are offended by this exhortation, they should realize that they do not share John's perspective of solidarity with the oppressed. They cannot understand the longing for justice on the part of the exploited and persecuted. Nor can they perceive God's judgment in terms of the punishment and destruction of oppressive and murderous powers. Rome's slaughter of Christians under Nero was, for John, only the beginning of what in the end will turn into worldwide slaughter of God's people (13:7; 18:24). Above all, John is dependent on Jer. 51:45-48. There the call for an exodus from Babylon (cf. Rev. 18:4) is followed by the promise that "the heavens and the earth, and all that is in them, shall sing for joy over Babylon['s]" doom. John transformed Jeremiah's *promise* of rejoicing into a *call* for rejoicing, and he substituted the **saints and apostles and prophets** for Jeremiah's people on earth. This threefold group comprises those members of the church who have suffered martyrdom. The last line of v. 20 states that **God has given judgment for you** against Babylon/Rome. This conclusion requires that the saints, apostles, and prophets especially had to suffer from the cruelty and godlessness of Rome. Thus v. 20 connects to 6:9-11; 13:7, 15; and 18:24. It would therefore not be right to see in the saints, apostles, and prophets the members of the church on earth and its leaders. Rather, they are the martyrs whose souls are "under the altar" in heaven, and the reason for heaven's rejoicing is that with Babylon's destruction God has executed his justice **against her** and **for** them. Their vindication (cf. 6:9-11) is reason for them to join in the triumphant joy of heaven, a theme that John will expand in 19:1-8. The reference to **apostles** is probably an allusion to the martyrdom of Peter and Paul in Rome during Nero's reign. Moreover, the witness of apostles and Christian **prophets** is basic for the church's life in the interim between Christ's exaltation and his parousia (cf. Eph. 2:20; 4:11). Once again, it becomes clear that for John, God's judgment is the negative side of the vindication-salvation of his faithful people. The message of judgment on Babylon/Rome is gospel for the church.

A Symbolic Action and Its Interpretation (18:21-24). The laments of the political and commercial profiteers of Rome's largesse (vv. 9-19) are bracketed with dirges by angels. Thus far in chap. 18 we have heard of Rome's destruction through the eyes of viewers who look at her collapse from the outside. Now we receive an inside view of her desolation, as the angel interprets his symbolic action and addresses Babylon/Rome in the second person (vv. 22-23).

Before the rejoicing in heaven commences (18:20; 19:1-8) **a mighty angel took up a stone like a great millstone and threw it into the sea.** Similar prophetic actions that illustrate and effect a future event are found in the Old Testament (e.g., 1 Kings 11:29-32; Isa. 8:1-4; 20:1-6; Jer. 19:1-13; 32:6-15). Here it is an angel who performs a symbolic action that recalls Jer. 51:63. A book containing Jeremiah's announcements of judgment on Babylon was to be bound to a stone and thrown into the Euphrates with the words: "Thus shall Babylon sink, to rise no more, because of the evil that I [Yahweh] am bringing upon her." John did not describe Babylon/Rome's doom in detail. Instead, he substituted the angel's symbolic action and its interpretation. **So shall Babylon the great city be thrown down with violence, and shall be found no more.** The symbolic action guarantees the occurrence state in the interpretation. Six times these few verses (vv. 21-23) repeat the words **no more,** which sound the death knell of Babylon's doom. The silence of death hovers over the doomed city. Expanding on Ezek. 26:13, the angel tells us that the sounds of merry making, of **harpers and minstrels, of flute players and**

trumpeters, shall be heard in thee no more, neither the arts and crafts. In the morning there shall be no grinding of handmills preparing the daily ration of grain, and in the evening no lamp will shine. Life has come to an end in desolate Babylon, and hence there are no weddings. Once more, Babylon's guild is stated. First, Rome's **merchants** had become the **great men,** the princes **of the earth** (cf. Jer. 27:35 LXX). Their arrogance, based on wealth, led to the exploitation of the poor on one hand and sorcery on the other. Sorcery, like fornication (17:2; 18:3), should be understood metaphorically in spite of the fact that both were common in Rome (e.g., *Sib. Or.* 5.162-166: "You [Rome] will be utterly desolate for all ages . . . because you desired sorcery. With you are found adulteries and illicit intercourse with boys," who were frequently slaves). The magic of wealth represented by the merchant princes operated in conjunction with Rome's idolatrous city culture and deceived **all nations.** The religious economic cooperation with Rome was the presupposition for the merchants' quest for wealth. Hence the call "Come out of her, my people" (v. 4) demands disentanglement from the tentacles of the magic of wealth and the snares of the economic life of the city (cf. Isa. 23:17-18; Nah. 3:4 LXX; cf. Rev. 2:18-25; 3:14-17).

The second and concluding indictment of Rome is given in the third person. **In her was found the blood of prophets and of saints, and of all who have been slain on earth.** Rome is guilty of murder. It killed Christians and non-Christians alike. Clearly Rome here is the symbol of the empire's persecution and of its brutal policies toward freedom-loving people.

Two examples from Tacitus: He tells us in *Annals* 13.39-41 of the Roman general Corbulo and his campaign against the Armenians (A.D. 58/59). The Armenian fortress Volandum was captured and "all adult inhabitants were massacred without the loss of a single Roman soldier. . . . The nonmilitary population was sold at auction; the rest of the booty fell to conquerors." After that the legions advanced toward Armenia's capital, Artaxata, which surrendered. Nevertheless "the city was fired, demolished and leveled to the ground." One of the reasons given for putting the city to the torch was that its mere surrender gave no "glory" to the Roman legions. This was Roman logic. The capture of a peaceful city brought neither advantage nor glory to Rome. Therefore it had to be leveled to the ground. Small wonder that there was hatred against Rome among certain classes of people in the east as well as among Jews for Jerusalem's destruction. But also from the rest of the empire we hear of freedom fighters, or brigands as the Romans called them.

The same Tacitus placed a speech into the mouth of a Celtic chieftain of Britain named Galgacus. Facing the Romans, he addressed his people: "To us who dwell on the uttermost confines of the earth and of freedom, this remote sanctuary of Britain's glory has up to this time been a defense. Now, however, . . . the yet more terrible Romans [have come] from whose oppression escape is vainly sought by obedience and submission. Robbers of the world, having by their universal plunder exhausted the land, they rifle the deep. If their enemy is rich, they are rapacious; if he be poor, they lust for domination. Neither the east nor the west has been able to satisfy them. . . . To their robbery, slaughter and plunder, they give the lying name of empire. They create a desert and call it peace" (*Agricola* 30).

John's concluding indictment of Rome (18:24) shares the same perspective of people who were disgusted with Rome's greed, oppression, and murder. Yet psychologizing John's attitude toward Rome in terms of hatred and envy (Yarbro Collins, *Crisis*, 154-160) misses his theological perspective. What is at stake for him is the first commandment and the establishment of God's justice on earth, a justice that Rome has trampled underfoot.

The Hymn of Triumph (19:1-10)

Just as 15:1-4 served both as climax of the prior section and as prelude to what follows (cf. 15:1), so the Hallelujah chorus is the grand finale of God's judgment on Babylon/Rome (17:1—19:10); simultaneously it serves as prelude to the center section (19:11—21:8). The destruction of the harlot is the reason for the hallelujahs and also the presupposition for the judgment of the demonic triumvirate in the center section. John's grand finale and final prelude are also the last hymnic section in his book and the only time the hallelujahs are sounded. Worship is the response of the elect to their vindication by God. These hymns were composed by John, because they refer to details found in prior visions or auditions. They also contain traditional elements from the church's worship.

These hallelujahs are ecstatic exclamations of praise befitting the arrival of the eschatological salvation. They are distinct from the general praise and thanksgiving given for God's goodness, manifested daily in food, drink, and health. Rather, they are sung in response to the admonition of 18:20. Heaven is to rejoice over the destruction of the whore Babylon, intoxicated with abominations (17:5-6). The eschatological jubilation begins in heaven (19:1-4) and is joined on earth by "all" of God's servants (19:5-8). It forms a fitting counterpart to the self-centered laments of the kings, merchants, and sailors (18:9-19).

John made use of a Jewish tradition that connected the hallelujah with the end time of judgment and salvation. "One hundred and three sections of psalms were spoken by David, but he said 'Hallelujah' first when he saw the fall of the ungodly" (Billerbeck, 2:725; Berak.9b). The **great multitude in heaven** are not just angels but the company of conquerors who kept the faith. The church triumphant after judgment joins the heavenly host in praise and acclamation (cf. 7:9-10; 15:2-5). Later we will hear why those who died in faith can now sing Hallelujahs (cf. 20:4-6). **Hallelujah** means "Praise Yahweh" and is generally translated, "Praise the Lord." It is found at the beginning of some psalms (e.g., Psalm 106; 112; 113; 117) or at their conclusion (e.g., Psalm 104). Revelation 19 is the earliest evidence of Christian use of this Old Testament prayer formula and its only occurrence in the New Testament.

Hallelujah! those who witnessed Babylon's doom are called upon to praise the Lord. His **salvation and glory and power** (cf. 7:10; 11:15; 12:10) are manifested first of all in his victory over his enemies (cf. 11:18; 17:16). **His judgments are true and just** (cf. 15:3; 16:7) because **he** justly **judged the great harlot** for corrupting the earth and for shedding **the blood of his servants** (6:9-10; 13:7, 15; 16:5-6; 17:6; 18:24). Babylon's destruction manifests God's sovereignty on earth and vindicates his servants (cf.

6:9-11). **Hallelujah!** The power base of Antichrist, the center of disease, from which spreads deadly infection, has been removed. **Salvation and glory and power belong** not to Caesar, the self-styled savior, lord, and god, but **to our God** who comprises present, past, and future, life and death, salvation and disaster. Hence, at the end of this section we hear the admonition, "Worship God" (v. 10) and—by implication—do not worship the emperor, empire, or Dea Roma. The posture of "my country, right or wrong" is idolatry.

Once more the same heavenly choir bursts into **Hallelujah! The smoke from her goes up for ever and ever** (cf. 17:16; 18:8-9). The resounding hallelujahs are grounded in God's judgment over the "destroyers of the earth" (cf. 11:18). The doom of the great harlot is the beginning of a new order of justice.

And the twenty-four elders and the four living creatures, who are mentioned for the last time, **fell down and worshiped God who is seated on the throne** and sang the antiphony, **"Amen. Hallelujah!"** (cf. Ps. 106:48). Their antiphony links this heavenly chorus to "the new song" of 5:8-14 and 14:3 and to the song of Moses and the Lamb (15:3-4). With **Amen** they confirm the praise of the church triumphant and incorporate it into their eternal liturgy (4:8; 7:11-12). With **Hallelujah!** they call for further praise of the Lord.

5—An unidentified **voice** coming **from the throne** now calls on God's people to praise him. In this call the hallelujah of the elders and creatures is extended. **"Praise our God, all you his servants, you who fear him, small and great."** Since **all** servants are admonished to praise **our** God, this call from heaven is directed to the church on earth. It would hardly make any sense to admonish the members of heaven to praise him, because they do so already (vv. 1-4). The believers on earth, including those who, in the last minute, have come to **fear** God (14:6-8; 11:13; 15:4), must join in the heavenly chorus (cf. 5:13). His **servants** are the faithful members of the church on earth (cf. 2:20; 7:3; 22:6). **Small and great** (cf. Ps. 115:13; Rev. 11:18), without distinction of rank and status, **all** servants of God in heaven and on earth participate in the eschatological antiphony that is now called for.

6-8—Hallelujah! The earth is cleansed from Babylon's idolatry and ready for the presence of God and the Lamb. The great multitude of God's people on earth respond to the heavenly chorus. Their voice is **like the sound of many waters and like the sound of mighty thunderpeals,** as they join the heavenly chorus. Sociologically, the Christians were small groups of no-accounts, scattered across the empire, but their worship unites them already now into one great multitude. And on that day when they are bidden to join the angels' Hallelujah, their many voices in diverse tongues will converge, like the sound of many waters, and merge in harmony with heaven's liturgy echoing like mighty thunderpeals. John's letter began on the Lord's day with a vision of the Lord whom we worship (1:9-20). Throughout his letter he narrated scenes of worship (7:9-12; 11:15-18; 14:1-4; 15:2-4). During worship in heaven the scroll was received by the Lamb and with it the authorization to complete the salvation accomplished through his death (chaps. 4–5). John's letter will conclude with the vision of the new Jerusalem as place of worship. For him, worship embraces all of life because it involves us in God's all-embracing activity and expands our vision to his future. Worship unites a creation fragmented by idolatry, the breeder of all vices.

Hallelujah! Two reasons for joining in heaven's praise are given. **For the Lord our God the Almighty** (the Pantocrator) **reigns** (cf. 11:15). The almighty creator has at last established his reign on earth, so that his purpose and will are done on earth as in heaven. He reigns because he has won his victory over the anti-God forces on earth embodied in the idolatrous power of the capital. Only when all powers of evil have been destroyed does God reign with finality. God's people on earth are therefore exhorting themselves: **"Let us rejoice and exult and give him the glory."**

A second reason for rejoicing with Hallelujah is: **For the marriage of the Lamb has come, and his Bride has made herself ready.** This means that the promised parousia of Christ is taking place. The end has come and with it a new beginning. One aspect of the new beginning is the marriage of the Lamb, a union of Christ and the church in his glory. The church's wedding garment has been *given* to her (Greek, *edothē*). Redemption is the gift of grace, and she wears it as bridal dress. Made of **fine linen, bright and pure,** her dress is noble, in stark contrast to the gaudy clothing of the intoxicated harlot (17:3-6). The symbol of the **marriage** discloses the nature of God's eschatological reign in terms of love and faithfulness, joy and care, understanding and intimacy. In the Old Testament, Israel is compared to a woman betrothed to Yahweh. Hence she owes him fidelity (Hosea 2; Isa. 54:6; Ezek. 16:7-8). Moreover, Isaiah depicted the messianic time of salvation as a wedding feast (61:10; 62:5), and Jesus designated the time of his ministry as a wedding time (Mark 2:19). He compared the kingdom of heaven to "a king who gave a marriage feast for his son" (Matt. 22:2). After Easter, the church saw in Jesus the bridegroom who is to come in order to be reunited with his bride, the church (2 Cor. 11:2; Eph. 5:23, 33). John used this tradition here; later he combined it with the image of the new Jerusalem (see 21:2, 9) and thereby he gained a double contrast. As the new Jerusalem, the church is the opposite of the great city Babylon; as Bride of the Lamb, she is the opposite of the great harlot. It was important for John that his people should understand that the future belongs to God and his Messiah, that he will lead his church into the glory of the consummation. Therefore the church is to be an alternative to society already before the parousia. Hence he added a comment for his people: The **fine linen** of the church's wedding garment is **the righteous deeds of the saints.**

This explanatory comment, appended by John to the Hallelujah antiphony resounding from earth, has frequently been interpreted as an interpolation, added to the text by a later copyist (Bousset, Charles, and others). At first glance one might agree that the white garments either symbolize God's saving gift or the believers' obedient deeds (cf. 6:11), but not both. But there are at least two other considerations. First, John did relate white garments to Christian obedience (cf. 3:18). While Christians received them as a gift (**it was granted** to the church to be clothed thus; 19:8), the question is whether or not they preserve them **bright and pure** (cf. 14:4-5). Their acts of obedience relate to Christ's deed of redemption (1:5-6; 5:9-10) in the same manner as Paul's exhortations relate to his doctrine of justification. For Paul, the justification of sinners is not a justification of sin (cf. Rom. 6:1) but a challenge to "walk in newness of life" (Rom. 6:4; cf. Phil. 2:12-14).

Second, the Greek word (*dikaiomata*) that is translated with **righteous deeds** could be translated with "just judgments." The same word with this meaning occurs in 15:4, where it expresses *God's* judicial sentences on the nations. God's *dikaiomata* are revealed not only in condemnations but also in forgiveness and acceptance. Only because of the latter can the "nations come and worship" God (15:4). If we take this meaning into consideration, then the church's wedding garment of fine linen consists of *God's* just judgments, including his pronouncements of forgiveness granted to the saints (genitive objective) rather than in obedient acts done by them. Either way, John's explanatory comment makes sense, though the first suggestion is the easier one.

9-10—Three words spoken by an angel and a comment by John conclude this section by focusing our attention upon the church on earth. **"Write this,"** an angel said, **"Blessed are those who are invited to the marriage supper of the Lamb."** This is the fourth of the seven beatitudes in Revelation (1:3; 14:13; 16:15; 19:9; 20:6; 22:7, 14). John no more described the marriage of the Lamb than he gave details about the destruction of Babylon or the war with the beasts and Satan (cf. 17:16; 18; 19:19-20; 20:9-10) or the description of the feelings of the damned in hell. He omitted such details because his intention was not to entertain but to exhort his people and expand their vision by interpreting the end time for them.

In the previous verses, John had depicted the church collectively as the Bride of Christ. In this beatitude the church is seen as individual believers who are guests **invited to the marriage supper of the Lamb.** Only a pedant will find these divergent images of the church as Bride and as guests to be incongruous. The roots of a banquet as image of salvation lie in the Old Testament. The great banquet of Yahweh, according to Isaiah, is to be held on Mount Zion. Then, "he will swallow up death for ever, and the Lord God will wipe away tears from all faces, and the reproach of his people he will take away" (Isa. 25:6-8). The great feast of Yahweh becomes a messianic banquet (cf. *3 Enoch* 48:10) to which his people will flock from the four corners of the earth "and sit at table in the kingdom of God" (Luke 13:29; cf. Matt. 26:29). **Blessed are those who are invited** (cf. Luke 14:15) to share in the eschatological union of Christ and the church which signals a new creation (21:1-4, 9-10). Simultaneously, the promise of the beatitude is also an exhortation not to forfeit the invitation through sloth or compromise.

Then the angel **said to me, "These are true words of God."** The angelic legitimation does not vouch for just the beatitude but for the whole section beginning with 17:1. For John's people, this section climaxes in the beatitude which involves them directly. A similar legitimation, occurring in 22:18-19, applies to the whole letter. The church under pressure needs to hear that they are blessed and invited to **the marriage supper of the Lamb** (cf. Matt. 5:10-11), that his parousia will lead to a new beginning, not to a terrible ending.

The last scene (v. 10) has three parts: an action of John, a word by the angel, and a concluding explanatory comment by John. Several important themes are raised in this verse. His attempt to prostrate himself before the angel, that is, **to worship him,** by an act of total submission is cut short. **"You must not do that! . . . Worship God."** Neither angel nor beast (13:15) may become objects of our worship and allegiance. Angels are at best servants and, as such, subject to criticism (cf. the criticisms in the messages to the angels of the seven churches). It is a matter of the first commandment, a matter of life and death, whom one worships. Idolatry can take many forms, including that of angel worship which John attempted (as a literary device; cf. also 22:8) and which was apparently practiced by some churches of the region (cf. Col. 2:18; *Ascension of Isaiah* 3:15; Justin, *Apol.* 1.6). His point, however, is obvious. If not even the angel who mediated and interpreted the visions and auditions to John is to be worshiped, how perverse would it be to worship community angels, not to mention emperors or beasts. Moreover, a true angel knows his assigned place and function, something that self-deifying Caesars have blatantly transgressed. **I am a fellow servant,** the angel told John, **with you and your** sisters and brothers. From this perspective, angels do not rank higher than any member of the church. In relation to God, they and the believers on earth are servants, mediators of the message. While the **brethren** of 22:9 are identified as prophets, such an identification is not made here or in 1:9 and 12:17. The absence of identification with prophets seems to suggest that "the brothers" are the members of the community. Their membership is specified: they **hold the testimony of Jesus** (1:2, 9; 12:17). It is here where the church's true authority lies, not in hierarchical structures of ministerial offices, nor in hierarchies of angels, but in the testimony that Jesus himself bore (genitive subject). His life and death disclosed the essence of faithful witness and what it means to bear witness (1:5; 3:14), and his testimony is continued in the lives of believing sisters and brothers. **"Worship God"** is the final and absolute command of the angel. This command precludes "fornication" with the harlot (v. 2), or worshiping the image of Antichrist (13:4, 15), even as it precludes the worship of angels.

John concludes with another explanatory comment. **For the testimony of Jesus is the spirit of prophecy.** Some interpreters view this sentence as the conclusion of the angel's speech, which is improbable. Others regard this sentence as an interpolation by a later hand, even though there is no manuscript evidence for omitting the sentence. To be sure, it is not easy to see how this sentence relates to the preceding imperative, **"Worship God,"** for which it should supply the *rationale* ("For . . ."; Greek, *gar*). One might begin by pointing out that **the spirit of prophecy** is the Holy Spirit operating through prophets. The criterion of true prophecy is found in the *testimony* that *Jesus* bore, and the whole church (John's brothers and sisters) is engaged in prophetic ministry, extending the testimony of Jesus. The **testimony of Jesus** points us back to the beginning of John's letter. Through an angel, Jesus has shown John what is to take place soon (1:13). Hence the content of John's letter is prophecy (cf. 22:18). What the *Spirit* tells the seven churches is part of the testimony of *Jesus*, and therefore the church as a prophetic community ought to be able to distinguish true prophecy from the "beguiling" prattle of false prophets like Jezebel (2:20; cf. 2:2) or the miracles and proclamations of the beastlike prophet of Antichrist (13:11-17).

Now we have to take one more step and understand this last sentence as rationale for the imperative "Worship God." The conjunction **for** suggests that the testimony of Jesus demands worship of God (thou shalt have no other god, godlet, angel, or beast) and so does the Holy Spirit as well as the interpreting angel. **"Worship God"**—this demand is made by Jesus and his angel, by the Spirit speaking through prophets and prophetic communities who keep the testimony of Jesus. Worship God! finds its fulfillment in the hallelujah choruses on the last day, in heaven and on earth.

The Parousia, Final Judgments, and the Final Salvation (19:11—21:8)

The center section of the climactic conclusion begins with the parousia of Christ (19:11) and ends with the vision of a new heaven and earth and of the new Jerusalem (21:1-8) which also contains two auditions. Both are introduced with "Behold." In the second, God himself is speaking in direct discourse, validating the visions of the new order, proclaiming **It is done!** and issuing the law of the new order (21:5-8). Out of 21:1-8 the final section (A′) evolves (21:9—22:10) which expands the picture of the new Jerusalem. Just as chaps. 17 and 18 elaborate the fall of Babylon, announced in the seventh bowl vision (16:19), so the description of the new

Jerusalem in 21:9—22:10 expands the climactic vision and auditions of 21:1-8. The compositional parallel structure discloses that the new Jerusalem is the antithesis of Babylon/Rome, even as the Bride of the Lamb is the antithesis of the harlot.

The seventh trumpet blast (11:15-19), which fulfilled the promise of the interlude (No more delay! 10:5-7), praised God for destroying the destroyers of the earth (11:18). He did so in the bowl plagues and its sequel (16:1—19:10), and he continues to do so in 19:11—20:3; and 20:7-10. These visions present different aspects of the final judgment.

The seventh trumpet praised God also for rewarding his "servants, the prophets and the saints" and all who fear his name "both small and great" (11:18). He did so in the marriage of the Lamb (19:6-8), accompanied by the great Hallelujah in heaven and on earth, and he continues to do so in 20:4-6 and 21:1-8. Finally, the seventh trumpet announced the victory of God and of his anointed One. "The kingdom of the world has become the kingdom of our Lord and of his Christ, and he shall reign for ever" (11:15). This vision of God's reign on earth is unfolded in new images in 20:4-6; 21:1-8; and, last, in 21:9—22:5. These visions present different aspects of the final salvation.

Chapter 13 displayed the Antichrist as beast and as parody of the Messiah. After the sixth bowl a new vision announced the battle at Armageddon (16:13-16). In 17:14 we heard that the Antichrist and his ten kings "will make war on the Lamb." This confrontation is now told in the threefold vision of 19:11-21. The counterpart to "the marriage supper of the Lamb" (19:9) will be "the great supper of God" (19:17). Both are aspects of the parousia. Creation is to be cleared of Antichrist and his cohorts (19:11-21; 20:1-3, 7-10), because the parousia ushers in the millennial reign of Christ in the new Jerusalem (20:4-6; 21:1—22:5).

John structured the material in this section in nine visions and two auditions, introduced by **then** (or **and**) **I saw, I heard, he . . . said** (19:11, 17, 19; 20:1, 4, 11, 12; 21:2, 3, 5; the second "I saw," in 20:4 RSV, is absent in the Greek text). Moreover, he introduced the time reference of 1,000 years six times into Satan's two-stage elimination (20:1-10). He apparently dealt with a hot issue in his churches, which is also indicated by the fusion of diverse traditions.

The thematic and chronological relationships between the visions become clear if we look at the composition of this section according to its vision markers.

- **A** The parousia, 19:11-16
- **B** The gory supper, 19:17-18
- **C** The elimination of the beasts and their followers, 19:19-21
- **D** Two visions: the two-stage elimination of Satan at the beginning and the end of the millennium, 20:1-3, 7-10; the millennial reign with Christ, 20:4-6

- **D′** Two visions: the great white throne and the disappearance of earth and sky, 20:11; the final judgment of the dead, 20:12-15
- **C′** The new heaven and earth and the abolition of the sea, 21:1
- **B′** The new community, the new Jerusalem, the Bride, the presence of God, 21:2-4
- **A′** The word of God, 21:5-8

Note that A to D focus on Christ; D′ to A′ center on the activity of God (cf. 1:7-8). We shall briefly consider the thematic relationships between the visions.

A and **A′**: The names of the parousia-Christ are "Faithful and True" and "The Word of God" (19:11, 13) and so is the word spoken by God (21:5). Christ's parousia (19:11-16) signals God's declaration: "It is done!" (21:6). His title "King of kings" (19:16) has its correspondence in the "Alpha and the Omega" of God (21:6) whose eschatological plenipotentiary he is. The sharp sword issuing from his mouth and the winepress wrath correspond to the threat uttered by God in 20:8.

B and **B′**: "The great supper of God" in 19:17-18, which pictures the gory end of "all" people, is the antithesis to the new community in which "death shall be no more" because God dwells with his people (21:2-4).

C and **C′**: The elimination of the two beasts and their followers from the earth (19:19-21) has its counterpart in the vision of a "new heaven and earth" and in the abolition of "the sea" from which the first beast came (21:1; cf. 13:1).

D and **D′**: The millennial imprisonment of the dragon, or Satan, in the abyss gives John the opportunity to introduce the millennial reign of the saints with Christ which will be unfolded in 21:1—22:5. Their "first resurrection" is their reward in distinction from the final judgment of the rest of humanity. Satan's final attempt to deceive fails as miserably as his battle with Michael (20:7-10; cf. 12:7-9).

The thematic relations should be kept in mind as we interpret the sequence of visions and the chronological references in chap. 20.

Christ's Victory over Beasts and Vassals (19:11-21)

The narrative contains three visions introduced by "then [and] I saw" (vv. 11, 17, 19). The hallelujah of 19:6-8 accompanied the marriage of the Lamb. The marriage is the symbol that the parousia has taken place and the church has entered life eternal. John narrated neither a marriage ceremony nor a messianic war scene. The destruction of Babylon through Antichrist was an eschatological event within history, prior to Christ's parousia. With the new vision of the parousia of Christ (19:11-16), a series of final judgments begins and we are confronted again with the great day of wrath (6:16-17).

The Parousia of Christ (19:11-16). Suddenly our eyes are raised from John's churches on earth (19:9-10) to **heaven opened. And behold** (v. 11) invites us to join John's vision of the revelation of Jesus Christ at his parousia. In 4:1 only a door was opened into heaven so that revelation could be received (cf. 11:19; 15:5), but now the whole heaven is **opened** wide to let the Messiah and his army pass. Before a description of the rider is given, we hear, in John's typical fashion, first about the horse (cf. 1:12-13; 4:2

[first the throne]; 14:14 [first the white cloud]; 20:11 [first the white throne]). **Behold, a white horse!** Also the preview of Antichrist given in the opening of the seal showed him on a **white** horse (6:2). The horse is an animal of war and white is the heavenly eschatological color (cf. 3:4-5; 6:11). One would have expected the Messiah to ride on a donkey instead, in accordance with Zech. 9:9 (cf. Mark 11:7; John 12:14-15). But at his parousia the Messiah appears, not in the lowliness of the suffering servant, but in the majesty of the eschatological warrior whom no one can withstand. The rider **is called Faithful and True,** the first of four references to his name in vv. 11-16. Though Codex Alexandrinus omitted **is called,** thereby regarding "Faithful and True" as messianic tributes rather than as a name of the Messiah, most modern interpreters consider "is called" to be original (see Metzger). His name symbolizes his action (cf. 3:12, 14). By coming and doing what he is about to do, the Messiah discloses the essence of his name, faithfulness and truth, which are also the attributes of Yahweh and his word (v. 13b). When the Messiah **judges and makes war** he establishes God's justice with the goal of final salvation (cf. 15:3; Isa. 11:4-5). In the *Psalms of Solomon* we read that the Lord Messiah is "to destroy the unrighteous rulers, to purge Jerusalem from Gentiles . . . to smash the arrogance of sinners . . . to destroy the unlawful nations with the word of his mouth" (*Pss. Sol.* 17:22-24, 32). The Messiah of Revelation has gained this authority by his death (5:9) in which his faithfulness and truth as witness to God were made manifest in the past (1:5; 3:14). Now he will make war against those who oppose God and persecuted the saints (13:7).

His eyes are like a flame of fire (cf. 1:14; 2:18), nothing is hidden from him. The **many diadems** on his head not only symbolize his legitimate power and authority over the world in contrast to the beast's (13:1; 12:3) but also include the victories that his followers have won through their faithfulness (cf. 2:10; 3:21; 12:11; 1:6; 5:10). **And he has a name inscribed which no one knows but himself.** Naturally some interpreters have tried to improve John's letter by second-guessing the unknown name and thereby missing John's point. Though John gives three names in vv. 11-16, he generally avoided Christological titles (exception: 1:1, 5; 20:4, 6; 22:21). Son of man is not a title in Revelation, but, as in Daniel, a comparison. Lamb is also not a title, but an image that describes functions. John's reticence to employ titles may result from his awareness of the mystery of Christ. None of the traditional names or titles fully express the mystery of the Messiah. His unknown name of v. 12 is his "new name" granted to victors (3:12). The traditional names and titles, including those of vv. 1, 13b, and 16, express aspects of his person and work but do not disclose the mystery of his very being. This is also true of the **name by which he is called** in John's own time: **The Word of God.** Again, some interpreters regard this name (v. 13b) as a later addition made by a copyist. But there is no manuscript evidence to justify such a surgical procedure. **The Word of God** expresses Christ's relationship to God. In him, God himself speaks and acts.

In distinction from John 1:1-3, Revelation does not develop a Christology of preexistence, nor does it refer to the role of the Logos as mediator in creation. Rather, the title "Word of God" recalls Wis. Sol. 18:15-16: "Thy all-powerful world leaped from heaven, from the royal throne, into the midst of the land that was doomed," which was Egypt at the time of the exodus when the firstborn were struck down. The word of God is then compared with "a stern warrior carrying the sharp sword of thy authentic command" (cf. Heb. 4:12). The series of names finds its high point in the title **King of kings and Lord of lords** (v. 16; 17:14; 1 Tim. 6:15; Deut. 10:17). The parousia reveals Christ's universal rule. He, not Caesar, legitimately bears this title and fulfills its function, because "worthy is the Lamb who was slain" to receive power, honor, and glory (5:12). At his parousia he executes the final phase of God's plan for his creation. This name is written **on his robe and on his thigh.** The background of a name written on the thigh may be Isa. 11:5: "Righteousness shall be the girdle of his waist, and faithfulness the girdle of his loins." Other suggestions for understanding this strange location for a name recall inscriptions found on the thighs of statues.

At his parousia the Messiah **is clad in a robe dipped in blood** (v. 13). This image received the stimulus from Isa. 63:1-6 where Yahweh's garments are splattered with the blood of his enemies on "the day of vengeance." John, however, reversed the image. The blood is his own, the Messiah's blood, the blood of him whom his opponents have "pierced" (1:7), the blood that either redeems (1:5-6; 5:9-10) or condemns. The heavenly armies that follow him on **white horses** are **arrayed in fine linen, white and pure.** If these armies (plural) contain not only the angelic hosts but also the martyrs, then their garments are white because they have washed them "in the blood of the Lamb" (7:14); "the fine linen is the righteous deeds of the saints" (19:8) who have conquered (12:11). From the warrior-Messiah's **mouth issues a sharp sword.** This weapon is the word of God (1:16; 2:12) which effects destruction (cf. Isa. 11:4; 49:2; *Pss. Sol.* 17:39; 2 Thess. 2:8) and salvation because it is the "testimony of Jesus" (19:10). **He will rule** the nations **with a rod of iron** (2:27; 12:5; Ps. 2:9 LXX) and **tread the wine press of the fury of the wrath of God the Almighty.** The image of the winepress in which his opponents are trampled underfoot (cf. 14:19; Isa. 63:3; Joel 3:13) is combined with the image of God's cup of wrath which is given them to drink (14:10; 16:19). Both images denote judgment in terms of total destruction. It should be noted that in this picture of the warrior-Messiah coming to execute God's judgment on his enemies, it is he alone who goes to battle, the sword is his and so are the blood-spattered garments. Moreover, we should note that John avoids a description of a battle scene. The word, the pronouncement of judgment by him who is the word of God, is all that is needed.

The Great Supper of God (19:17-18). In a new vision, John saw an **angel standing** on (rather than RSV **in**) **the sun,** calling **all the birds** to gather **for the great supper of God, to eat the flesh of kings, . . . of captains, . . . of mighty men, . . . of horses and their riders, . . . free and slave, . . . small and great.** Rank and status are irrelevant. This gory supper is the counterimage to the "marriage supper of the Lamb" (19:9). Its antecedent lies in Ezek. 39:17-20: "Speak to the birds . . . , gather . . . to the sacrificial feast which I am preparing for you . . . and you shall eat . . . the flesh of the mighty." Both suppers are prepared by God and both disclose the twofold antithetical effect of "The Word of God" on humans. Judgment or salvation, death or life, the grizzly supper or the marriage feast, are brought about by the same God and his word. The outcome of the battle between God's agent and rebellious humanity is already decided when Christ appears. Even before the battle, the lines are drawn, the invitation is issued to dispose of the corpses of his enemies, the destroyers of the earth (11:18).

The Third Vision (19:19-21). This third vision elaborates 17:14 without narrating a battle scene. **The beast,** the Antichrist and incarnation of Satan, his lackey, the **false prophet** which is the beast from the land (chap. 13), and the **kings of the earth with their armies** gathered for **war** against the Messiah. Only the outcome of the battle is told. The beast and the false prophet are **thrown alive into the lake of fire. And the rest were slain by the sword** of the word of God and **all the birds were gorged with their flesh.** Thus ends the battle of Armageddon (16:13-16). The climax of history is not the progress of humans from ape to angel but the destruction of the forces of Antichrist. The miracles, **the signs,** by which the false prophet had led humans astray prior to the end did not save him in the end. He and **those who had received the mark of the beast** and had **worshiped its image** (13:13-18) had come to irreversible and everlasting ruin. The **lake of fire** is the equivalent to Gehenna, hell (cf. Matt. 5:22; 18:9; Mark 9:43). It is the place of condemnation in distinction from Hades, the place of the dead. Hell's first residents in Revelation are the Antichrist and the false prophet. They will be joined by the dragon, by Death and Hades, and by all over whom God speaks a final negative verdict (20:10, 14-15).

Satan Removed into the Abyss (20:1-3)

The context: The proclamation of the seventh bowl "It is done!" announced the accomplished destruction of Babylon (16:17). Its doom was then elaborated with new images and from new perspectives (chaps. 17–18). The antithesis to its doom are the Hallelujah choruses which celebrated the reign of God and the marriage of the Lamb (19:1-10). With Antichrist's power base laid waste (16:17—18:24), John's vision of 19:11-21 moved from the seventh bowl (16:17) to elaborating the sixth and the fifth bowl. The brief reference to the battle of Armageddon (16:16) became the subject of 19:11-21. The outcome of this battle is the destruction of Antichrist and the false prophet together with their supporters. Thus Christ's parousia signifies not only the marriage of the Lamb (19:6-8), attested through hallelujah choruses in heaven and on earth, it also involves clearing the earth of all anti-God forces. The interlude after the sixth bowl had also mentioned the dragon whom John's hearers know to be the ultimate cause of evil. The elimination of the antagonist who had been mentioned first (chap. 12) is narrated last. Moreover, his elimination is narrated in two visions, representing two stages that are separated by a thousand years (20:1-10).

Such a two-stage elimination of Satan was unknown in the Old Testament, the Jewish and Christian tradition. Therefore the question arises, Why would John introduce it at this point? He could have knocked off the dragon together with the other two beasts in 19:20, as any attentive hearer would have expected. The answer to this question is of necessity hypothetical, since our knowledge of the religious context of the communities that John was addressing is rather limited and dependent primarily on what he said. I am suggesting that John had at least three reasons for presenting the elimination of Satan in two stages. One, it gave him the opportunity to undercut the gnosticizing idea that the believers' resurrection had already happened in their baptism (cf. 2 Tim. 2:18). Two, it gave him the opportunity to reinterpret the apocalyptic notion of a preliminary messianic interim kingdom, prior to the appearance of the kingdom of God, and to introduce the millennial reign with Christ as the beginning of the eternal kingdom. Three, he could interpret Ezekiel's Gog-Magog prophecy, which may have bothered some of his people.

1-3—After the judgment of Antichrist and the false prophet comes the devil's turn. In a new vision John saw an angel descending from heaven who simply **seized the dragon, . . . bound him for a thousand years, and threw him into the pit,** the abyss, a cavern beneath the sea (cf. 11:7; 13:1). What God had accomplished in primal times when he bound and imprisoned the powers of chaos will be repeated in the end time (Isa. 24:21-22). The first stage of the dragon's defeat was his expulsion from heaven (12:7-9). His next defeat was inflicted by those who "have conquered him by the blood of the Lamb and by the word of their testimony" (12:11). The "short" time in which he could vent his fury on God's people on earth (12:12, 13-17) has now ended. His thousand-year imprisonment in the abyss constitutes his preliminary punishment and the total liberation of the earth from sin, idolatry, and the devil. He can **deceive the nations no more.** The anti-God nations have been eliminated already (19:21). Who those nations of v. 3 are and where they come from will be discussed when we meet "Gog and Magog" in v. 8. Here we note that with **the dragon, that ancient serpent, who is the Devil and Satan,** in the abyss, the ultimate cause of evil is removed from the *earth.* His removal is an aspect of Christ's parousia.

Interlude 1: The Millennial Reign with Christ (20:4-6)

These three verses have caused more confusion than any other in this letter and their interpretations by second- and third-century chiliasts were the reason why quite a few bishops and synods in Eastern churches did not want to include Revelation among the canonical writings of the New Testament.

The difficulties that interpreters have had with this text in centuries past continue to this day. The magisterial commentary on Revelation in English by R. H. Charles illustrates rather well the problems that scholars encountered in the concluding chapters. Charles found the text beginning with 20:4 to the end of Revelation so confusing that he theorized that John must have died before completing his work and that beginning with 20:4 a "faithful but unintelligent disciple" tried to bring his master's work to conclusion. Unfortunately this disciple produced an ending "full of confusion and contradiction," making it "impossible for us to accept the text as it stands" (Charles, 2:144–147). While German scholars thought that the text beginning with 20:4 came about by the fusion of two sources or authors (Bousset), or three (Johannes Weiss), or four (Spitta), Charles was satisfied with just one, but a rather unintelligent one. "We stand aghast at the hopeless mental confusion that dominates the present structure of these chapters," beginning with 20:4 (Charles, 2:145).

The difficulties that Charles had with the present text were largely of his own making. First, he assumed that John meant to compose an apocalyptic timetable, and therefore Charles saw interpolations and dislocations of the text even prior to 20:4. For instance, the first four trumpets (8:7-12) were regarded as an interpolation, because their cosmic catastrophes belong to the end, not in chap. 8. The price he had to pay for rejecting the recapitulation theory was his hypotheses of transpositions and later additions in the text. Second, he ignored that John wrote a letter, not a treatise on the "Semitic philosophy of religion" and of history (Charles, 2:144). Through his letter, John addressed specific people and communities, and he exhorted them also in his new Jerusalem vision to abstain from idolatry, fornication, and so forth. Charles found these references of 21:8, 27; 22:15 to be absolute contradictions to the nature of the new Jerusalem and the new creation (Charles, 1:l-lv; 2:145–226). True enough, but irrelevant. He missed the significance of the letter genre for interpreting Revelation. Third, Charles, like many before and after him, failed to see that John's millennium is not a preliminary messianic interim but the beginning of the eternal kingdom of God and of his Messiah (cf. 11:15). Charles's penetrating questions and the difficulties he encountered with the text enable us to pursue an alternative to his solution which begins by leaving the text as is.

When we consider the historical context in which John wrote, it seems probable that already in some of his messages (chaps. 2–3) he was also arguing against gnosticizing notions of an overly realized eschatology. The false apostles, the Nicolaitans and Jezebel (2:2, 15, 20), presumably spoke of their baptism, or rebirth, in terms of their "first resurrection" (cf. 2 Tim. 2:18). At any rate, the expression "the first resurrection" was foreign to apocalyptic traditions. On the other hand a letter like Ephesians could say that God "raised us up [the living believers] with him [Christ], and made us sit with him in the heavenly places" (Eph. 2:5-6). Ideas like these could be developed into the notion that our "first resurrection" has taken place in baptism and that our present life is to be unencumbered by tribulations and crosses but lived according to the knowledge of the depths of God or of Satan and that the future has little importance for us. If this describes part of John's context, then the interlude (20:4-6) gave him an opportunity to set the record straight. "The first resurrection" for him presupposes the death of believers and the parousia of Christ. It will take place in the millennial kingdom, not before. First comes death, and only then the resurrection, just as it is also in 1 Corinthians 15, not the other way around, as gnosticizing teachers held. Realized eschatology, which John affirmed (1:5-6; 5:9-10), is inseparable from its future dimension. The millennium signals "the first resurrection."

No one denies that John's context was also characterized by diverse apocalyptic traditions. I am suggesting that he and his people were aware of speculations concerning a temporary messianic interim kingdom prior to the appearance of the eternal reign of God. Traditions about a preliminary messianic interim kingdom are *not* found in the Old Testament or in the New Testament. They appear among some rabbis, for example, Rabbi Akiba (martyred about A.D. 135), who thought that the Messiah's reign would last 40 years on the basis of Ps. 90:15 in conjunction with Deut. 8:2-3. Other rabbis reached different conclusions concerning its duration all the way up to 7,000 years. (For details, see Billerbeck, 3:824-827). Messianic interim kingdom speculations appear also in the apocalyptic tradition of Judaism. According to 4 Ezra 7:26-33, the Messiah shall rule for 400 years on earth over those who are alive at the time of his coming. Then the Messiah as well as all human beings shall die and the world shall return to primeval silence for seven days, as it was at the beginning. After that follows the final judgment. Also in *2 Baruch* the Messiah's rule on earth is of limited but unspecified duration. When his time is over, he returns to heaven and the final judgment commences (*2 Baruch* 29–30; cf. 40:2-3).

There are two reasons why we may assume that John was aware of apocalyptic messianic interim kingdom traditions. One, they do turn up in Papias and in subsequent chiliasts of the church. We know that in the aftermath of the catastrophe of A.D. 70 Jewish Christians such as Philip and his four prophesying daughters (Acts 21:8-9) moved from Palestine to Asia Minor (Eusebius, *C.H.* 3.33.3). John himself may have been one of them. Some of them brought apocalyptic messianic interim traditions with them which later appeared in chiliasts like Justin, who was converted in Ephesus around A.D. 130. These Jewish Christians of John's time may have hoped that the Messiah Jesus would return, rebuild Jerusalem, fulfill the prophecies concerning the Jewish people, and convert them. And then, after a messianic interim, the resurrection of the dead, the final judgment, and the kingdom of God would come. Naturally this reconstruction is hypothetical. But, we may ask, where did chiliasts, like Justin, get their ideas? Not from our letter, but through other persons' traditions. Moreover, we know that in chap. 11 John incorporated Jewish-Christian traditions about Jerusalem. And it is fairly clear that in the text before us, 20:4-6, he dealt with and changed a messianic interim tradition. For him, there is to be no rebuilding of historic Jerusalem by the Messiah. All that is left is its name, the new Jerusalem, which will be borne by a community that shall descend from heaven.

Two, John's literary structure suggests that he combined the sequence of Ezekiel 37–48 with another sequence found in an apocalyptic tradition similar to 4 Ezra 7 and that he gave a new twist to both. John followed the outline of Ezekiel 37–48 in his concluding chapters. Thus the millennial reign with its resurrection of the saints (20:4-6) alludes to Ezekiel 37; the battle of Gog and Magog (20:7-10) alludes to Ezekiel 38–39. In his new Jerusalem vision he made use of Ezekiel 40–48. His modifications of Ezekiel's visions are most obvious in the absence of a temple within the new Jerusalem (21:22), in the vision of the final judgment (20:11-15) which is lacking in Ezekiel, and in what looks, at first sight, like the notion of a messianic interim reign which is also not found in Ezekiel. With respect to a messianic interim kingdom, followed by a final judgment, apocalyptic traditions, similar to 4 Ezra 7, supply the missing link.

While John retained the notion of a final judgment, he radically reinterpreted the idea of a preliminary messianic kingdom. In contrast to apocalyptic traditions, like 4 Ezra 7, he insisted that it will not be the living who shall reign with Christ but the dead martyrs and saints who are raised from the dead (20:4-6). Moreover, and even more important, those who reign with Christ after their resurrection shall no more die, just as the resurrected Christ shall not die at the end of the millennium. When Gog and Magog march against them (20:7-10), they are secure. Fire consumes their enemies, as Ezekiel had promised, and Satan receives a punishment worse than he had before. Nor does the disappearance of earth and sky bother the resurrected saints (20:11). Why should it? It does not seem to bother God (20:11). So why should it trouble those who have death behind them and Christ and God before them? How could it disturb the coregents of Christ who serve as priests of God (20:6)? John felt no need for a vision telling us, his hearers, that the millennial saints will be secure, when earth and sky flee away (20:11). If we, John's hearers, have paid any attention to the text (rather than figuring out dislocations and interpolations), we ought to know by now that the saints have been "sealed" and that cosmic cataclysmic upheavals do not destroy them (cf. 7:1-8). Just as the Egyptian plagues did not bother Israel of old, so (John told us twice) their eschatological counterparts, the trumpet and bowl plagues, are not directed against the saints, because they are God's eschatological people, redeemed by the blood of the Lamb. So why should the dissolution of earth and sky in 20:11 affect the resurrected Christians, when it did not affect the believers before the last day, according to 6:16—7:8? This question has to be answered by the advocates of the messianic interim theory! Our hypothesis is that John was aware of messianic interim kingdom speculations and that he undercut them. For him, the millennium is the beginning of the consummated kingdom of God and his Messiah and not a preliminary kingdom which is to be superseded by God's eternal kingdom.

What, then, should we make of the "new heaven" and the "new earth" (21:1) in relation to the millennium? The new heaven and earth are referred to in one single verse. They are important only as the place for the saints, the new Jerusalem (21:2). The new heaven and earth are our heaven and earth without idolatry, death, and the devil, but with God and Christ in the midst of his people. This new world is indeed the millennial world, even as the new Jerusalem is none other than "the beloved (millennial) city" (20:9). This conclusion is reinforced by the last beatitude of the epilog. There John's hearers are called blessed, provided they wash their robes that they may **enter the city by the gates** (22:14). This invitation to enter the city by the gates is undergirded by Jesus' threefold promise in the epilog: "Behold, I am coming soon" (22:7, 12, 20). The **gates** of the city link the beatitude with the gates of the new Jerusalem (21:12, 21, 25), even as the promise of Christ's imminent coming links **the city** of 22:14 with the millennial city of 20:9 and the heavenly city of 21:2—22:5. It would be rather absurd to assume that, from John's point of view, the invitation in the form of a beatitude to "enter the city by the gates" (22:14) could find its fulfillment only a thousand years after the (second) coming of Christ. But such absurdity would have to be maintained if the identity of the city in 22:14; 21:2; *and 20:9* were to be denied. But if the city in the three texts is the same city, namely, the heavenly "new" and "beloved" Jerusalem, then the idea of a preliminary messianic interim has vanished like smoke into nothingness.

The same conclusion, that the new Jerusalem of 21:2—22:5 is identical with the beloved millennial city of 20:9, is reached when we consider the first appearance of the image of "the new Jerusalem" in the promise to the conquerors of 3:12. As in the epilog, so here Jesus' promise "I am coming soon" is explicitly stated (3:11). Again we would argue that it would be absurd to think that the presence of the conquerors in the new Jerusalem would be realized a millennium after Christ's parousia. But if both cities are identical (3:12 and 20:9), then there is no basis for turning the millennium into a messianic interim.

One final example: 21:2, 9 refer to **the Bride of the Lamb** and identify the Bride as the new Jerusalem, coming down out of heaven from God. In 19:7, 9 the Bride has made herself ready and "those who are invited to the marriage supper of the Lamb" are called blessed. One can hardly imagine that the bride will have to wait a millennium before the marriage supper commences. If not, then there is no messianic interim kingdom, distinct and separated from the new Jerusalem. Moreover, the Bride appears once more in the epilog, where she is identical with the present faithful church of John's time. "The Spirit and the Bride say, 'Come.' " The Bride, the present church through whom the Spirit is speaking, calls upon Jesus to come. His parousia signals the consummation of the union, the marriage supper (19:7, 9) and with it the revelation of "the Bride, the wife of the

Lamb" (21:2, 9). In short, a messianic interim kingdom is as improbable as an interim marriage. On the contrary, the millennium is not an interim but the beginning of the life of the world to come, inaugurated by Christ's parousia.

Thus far we have suggested a hypothesis, namely, that John was aware of messianic interim kingdom speculations and that he modified them by undercutting them in his millennium vision. In contrast to modern interpreters, we hold that John did not reconcile two, originally distinct, eschatological expectations: the national expectation which hoped for a messianic kingdom of unlimited duration on earth (e.g., *Psalms of Solomon* 17) and the apocalyptic expectation of a transcendent eternal kingdom beyond history. While 4 Ezra 7 clearly reconciled both expectations by making the messianic kingdom into a temporary interim on earth, prior to the final judgment and eternal life in "the paradise of delight" (4 Ezra 7:36), John did not follow this pattern. We have shown that, for him, there is no interim that is superseded by something more glorious than the millennium.

We now have to comment briefly on the way John structured his material. He created a two-stage elimination of the devil with a thousand-year interim in between. That is the only interim he will allow, the devil's interim. Between the devil's imprisonment in the abyss and his demise in the lake of fire the earth is free from his deception for a thousand years (20:3, 7). When he makes his final appearance on earth he meets his final doom. His two-stage elimination created space for an interlude on the millennial reign with Christ and on the Gog-Magog prophecy. The millennium signals the inauguration of the eternal reign of Christ and God (cf. 7:9-17; 15:2-4; 19:6-8), even as the destruction of Gog-Magog completes the eternal doom of Satan (20:10). This interlude in two parts shows a new beginning and a final ending. The new beginning will be elaborated in 21:1—22:5. As for the devil, he is finished, and God's proclamation in 21:5, "It is done!" applies also to him. Satan's two-stage destruction, placed on either side of the millennium vision, indicates the protection and invulnerability of the resurrected saints (cf. 7:1-8; 11:1-2, 11-12; 20:8-9).

The sequence of visions from 19:11 to 21:8 is both logical and chronological: first, aspects of the parousia of Christ to whom the church owes its redemption (19:11—20:10; cf. 1:7 and chap. 5); and second, aspects of the parousia of God to whom the world owes its existence and who as "the Alpha and the Omega" determines judgment and salvation (20:11—21:8; cf. 1:8 and chap. 4).

4-6—Most of v. 4 (from **Then I saw thrones** to **or their hands**) is one sentence in Greek. The construction of this sentence is difficult and raises several questions. Typically, John mentioned the seats first (cf. 4:2; 14:14; 19:11; 20:11) and only then those sitting on them. But what kind of **thrones** are these and who are the ones sitting on them? Are these judgment thrones on which the heavenly court is seated in accordance with Dan. 7:9-10? In that case, John envisioned the heavenly tribunal, consisting perhaps of the 24 elders (4:4), taking their seat on judgment thrones in order to pronounce a verdict, because the authority to execute judgment was given, **committed,** to them. This interpretation is possible, but so is another one.

The background of this verse is Dan. 7:22. There "judgment was given for the saints," they were vindicated and they "received the kingdom." In this case, the thrones that John saw are royal thrones rather than judgment thrones, and those who are sitting on them are the vindicated saints. Moreover, he saw a second group, the martyrs who had been **beheaded** and who had **not worshiped the beast** (cf. 13:2-18). They too received the justice that the beast had denied them. They were rewarded for their faithful perseverance unto death (2:10; 11:18) in answer to their prayer (6:9-11). Their position on thrones fulfills Christ's promise to the conquerors (3:21) that they will reign with him. While it is not easy to decide between these two interpretations, I would lead toward the second alternative in view of v. 6c ("they shall reign with him a thousand years").

Grammatically it is possible to distinguish two groups of martyrs that are connected by **and who** (Greek, *kai hotines*). The second group would consist of those who resisted the worship of the Antichrist and bore the consequences (13:7, 15). The first group would be the martyrs prior to the appearance of the beast. However, it is also possible that our text envisions only one group, namely, the martyrs. Therefore some interpreters have limited the millennial reign with Christ to martyrs only. Psychologically this would be rather devastating for those Christians in John's churches whose husbands, wives, children, parents, and grandparents had died in faith without martyrdom. They would be lumped together with the rest of humanity and would have to wait for another thousand years after the parousia until their turn would come in the final judgment. Perhaps, but not likely! Moreover, we must take note that in v. 9 we hear of "the camp of **the saints**"; the meaning of saints in Revelation cannot be restricted to martyrs only.

John was aware of representative figures (e.g., the two witnesses of chap. 11, the harlot of chap. 17). It is quite possible that he did envision only one group in v. 4, namely, the martyrs. They would then function as representatives of the whole church that resisted compromise, overcame lukewarmness, and persevered in the faith. Just as Shadrach, Meshach, and Abednego in Daniel represented "the saints of the Most High" (Daniel 3; 7:22), so the martyrs here represent the faithful church. There is no reason to limit the millennial reign to martyrs only. Christ's promises to the conquerors are not exhortations to martyrdom (cf. 2:26; 3:21). His promise of 5:9-10 (cf. 1:6) is addressed to all the saints, not just to martyrs. The faithful people of God, ransomed from many nations, are a "kingdom" because they have been elected to reign with Christ (5:10; 20:6; 22:5). The vision does not tell us where the thrones are located. Hearers who paid attention would assume that these thrones are in heaven, because thus far all thrones, with the exception of those belonging to Satan and the beast, were located there. However, in the second part of the interlude we hear that "the saints" and "the beloved city" are on earth. We will have to wait to find out how they got there (cf. 21:2, 9-10).

They came to life again, **and reigned with Christ a thousand years. The rest of the dead did not come to life** again **until the thousand years were ended. This is the first resurrection.** The souls of the martyrs under the altar had asked, Lord, "how long" until our vindication comes about (6:10)? When we now hear that they came to life again (Greek, *ezēsan*) and when this is identified as "the first resurrection," then coming to life can only refer to their "bodily" resurrection from the dead, not to some spiritual immortal life of souls. The Greek verb here is identical with the verb in 1:18 and 2:8 which beyond doubt refers to the resurrection of Christ, who is "the first-born of the dead" (1:6). The resurrection of the saints is also implied in John's statement, "The rest of the dead did not come to life until the thousand years were ended" (v. 5). With death behind them, with Satan exiled from the earth, the resurrected saints reign with Christ **a thousand years,** which is the beginning of their eternal reign.

A **thousand** years equals the third power of ten (ten times ten times ten) and symbolizes the ideal time or a new quality of time. It is the time of the resurrection and of the revelation of the reign of Christ, which until then had been hidden under tribulations demanding endurance (cf. 1:9). It is most doubtful that John arrived at the number 1,000 as a result of combining Ps. 90:4 (a thousand years are but a day in the sight of God) with Gen. 2:1-3. In that case, he would have understood the seventh day as the day of the Messiah lasting a thousand years. However, in distinction from other apocalypticists and second-century chiliasts, John did not indulge in speculations concerning the duration of history on the basis of a world-week. At any rate, we should note the symbolic significance of all numbers in this book as well as the fact that we are dealing here with "time" beyond our time. A thousand years indicates a long time, in contrast to three and a half years (11:2-3; 12:6, 14; 13:5). Equally important is the realization that John did not describe the reign of the resurrected saints over others. The objects of their rule are not mentioned but only the reversal of their former condition; they had been dead, but now their true status is revealed as coregents with

Christ and as **priests of God** (cf. 1:6; 5:10). There is no evangelistic activity envisioned here (contrary to Caird and others), because no people other than the saints are on earth (19:21). The focus does not lie on diverse activities but on freedom from all evil, including death. With a beatitude John addresses the hearer/reader. **Blessed and holy is he who shares the first resurrection!** The first resurrection constitutes the reward of God's faithful people who are raised from the dead to new life with Christ a long time before "the rest" of humanity shall meet their maker. In short, the millennium is nothing other than the *special* resurrection of Christians that precedes the *general* resurrection of the dead. We suggested that the phrase "the first resurrection" may have been a slogan of people who connected it with their baptism. Be this as it may, John interpreted it along traditional Christian (Pauline) lines. In 1 Thess. 4:16 we read; "The dead in Christ will rise *first*" (cf. 1 Cor. 15:23). John interpreted their precedence in terms of a temporal priority of a thousand years. **Over such the second death has no power.** The second death refers to the condemnation in the final judgment (20:14-15). Implicit in the beatitude is an exhortation for John's hearers and readers to persevere lest the second death catch up with them. For the resurrected saints, the final judgment has happened already in that justice was done for them and they live in all eternity as kings and priests in freedom and in worship. Their reign and worship are the antithesis of the idolatry and brutality of the beast.

Interlude 2: Satan Cast into the Lake of Fire (20:7-10)

We suggested that John's second reason for constructing a two-stage elimination of Satan with a thousand-year period in between lay in his, or his people's, interest in Ezekiel's Gog and Magog prophecy. He could also allude to a parallel and a contrast with Genesis 3. Just as Satan entered the garden in the beginning, so in the end he is permitted (he "must," v. 3) to appear on an earth that has already been cleared of idolatry and death. Note, the dead are not on earth but in the netherworld, in Hades (20:13). The resurrected saints do not die at the end of the millennium, even as the resurrected Messiah does not die again, contrary to 4 Ezra 7:29. So then the devil makes his encore on an earth freed from sin and death. Too bad for him!

This episode shows Satan's perversity and futility. Having been beaten in heaven (12:7-12) and twice on earth (12:11; 20:1-3), he tries again his old trick of deception (20:3, 8, 10), just as he had done in the beginning (Gen. 3:4). This is why Satan is called here "that ancient serpent" (20:2). Now he deceives **the nations which are at the four corners of the earth, that is, Gog and Magog, to gather them for battle; their number is like the sand of the sea.** For Ezekiel, Gog from the land of Magog was the leader of an army, probably of Scythians, that would march against Jerusalem from the north and would be destroyed with fire and brimstone (Ezek. 37:1—38:22). Since Ezekiel's time, Gog and Magog had been thought of as rulers of a mythical army. For John, the nations of Gog and Magog are an army of demons from the netherworld (cf. 9:1-11, 16-19). Passages led from "the four corners of the earth" to the realm of demons below. When this demonic army, in numbers like the sand of the sea (cf. 9:16), **marched up** and **surrounded the camp of the saints and the beloved city,** it is all over. No battle takes place, for the battle has already been won by the slain Lamb, the Lion of the tribe of Judah, and victory needs only to be revealed on earth. Hence **fire came down . . . and consumed them** and Satan was cast into the lake of fire. From there the abyss would have looked like a cozy place. **The beloved city** is the counterimage to "the great city" (11:8). It cannot be located on a map, for it is none other than the new Jerusalem. The protection of the saints, the folly of the devil, and the elimination of the underworld are the theme of this subsection.

The Judgment of the Dead (20:11-15)

The Great White Throne (20:11). A new vision, the sixth of seven judgment visions, brings a new aspect of the parousia, which is the overthrow of heaven and earth. While John related the millennium chronologically to the general judgment (20:5), he did thus relate it to the dissolution of the world. The latter, we remember, had already happened at the opening of the sixth seal when "the sky [the same Greek word as "heaven"] vanished like a scroll that is rolled up" (6:14). No answers are given to silly timetables or questions such as: How can there still be a sea to give up the dead (20:13), when the earth has already vanished (20:11)? Where does the great white throne stand since earth and heaven have passed away? On the sea? What will happen to the saints who reigned with Christ when the earth is literally pulled out from underneath them and the sky also disappears? Would they not experience "a second death" in spite of 20:6? We should keep in mind that John's images change like pictures of a kaleidoscope and that his images are metaphors used to express eschatological aspects. John's point in this vision is that with the parousia not only Christ, but God, becomes visible. His majestic great **throne** radiates the color of heaven, **white** (2:17; 3:4-5; 4:4; 7:9; 14:14; 19:11). From the presence of him who is the Holy One, the earth, polluted by idolatry, greed, and bloodshed, must flee (cf. Dan. 2:35 with reference to the king's image "not a trace of them could be found"). John expected not only the transformation of the church through the resurrection of the saints and martyrs but also the transformation of the whole world. Both are aspects of the parousia, and the sequence of visions should not be translated into a temporal sequence. A world free from idolatry and death differs radically from the present one. Once again, the dissolution of our earth and sky does not affect the resurrected saints any more than it affects God or Christ. The saints already live on the new earth, or, if you will, in a dimension free from idolatry, sin, death, and the devil that have left their imprint on our world.

The General Judgment (20:12-15). A preview, strikingly different from the present vision, had been presented in 14:14-20. There "one like a son of man" was sitting on a white cloud reaping the earth's harvest with his sickle. Here it is God seated on the great white throne before whom the dead appear. Both visions are aspects of the same truth: God, Christ, shall come to judge the living (19:11-21) and the dead (cf. 1:7-8). Consistency would have required a reference to "the second resurrection" (cf. 20:5-6). Though this is obviously implied, John avoided speaking of a second resurrection in this vision. For him the concept of "the first resurrection" was important, probably because his opponents had located it in their baptism, rebirth, or reception of the Spirit. At any rate, the resurrected saints are not subjected to the general judgment of this vision, because only the **dead** are judged. The judgment and vindication of the faithful church, represented by the martyrs, took place at the beginning of the millennium (20:4; cf. 3:5).

John's emphasis in this vision is threefold. First, no one is so **great** that he or she could escape God's judgment, and none are so **small** and unimportant that they will be overlooked. Even "the sea gave up the dead," and those eaten by the fish are not forgotten either (*1 Enoch* 61:5). All will have their day in court before him whose eyes pierce through the facades behind which humans hide their true being. Second, two different kinds of **books** are opened. In one set of books is written **what they had done,** and the dead are judged accordingly. This notion is found in apocalyptic traditions (Dan. 7:10, "the court sat in judgment, and the books were opened"; cf. *1 Enoch* 90:20; 4 Ezra 6:20). Nothing is forgotten, whether good or bad (cf. Matt. 25:37-40). Also Paul, the preacher of justification by faith alone, insisted that God's judgment is according to works (Rom. 2:6-16; 14:10-12; 1 Cor. 3:13-15; 2 Cor. 5:10; 9:6; 11:15; Gal. 6:7; cf. Col. 3:25; Eph. 6:8; 2 Tim. 4:14; 1 Peter 1:17; Matt. 7:13-27; Acts 10:42; 17:31; etc.). The final judgment reveals whether our faith, worship, and confession are genuine or phony. In this respect faith and worship are like fire. Just as fire clings to fuel, so faith clings to God's word of promise. And just as fire produces heat and light, so faith and worship produce endurance (1:9), love (2:4, 19), patience (3:10; 13:10), the conquest of idolatry (12:11), doing what is right

(22:11), keeping the commandments of God (14:12), and persevering in the testimony of Jesus and the word of God (20:4). The redemption through "the blood" of Christ (5:9; cf. Rom. 3:24-25) is to find expression in conduct, that is, in doing what is right (22:11). Conversely, the principle that a person is what he or she does will result in the exclusion of "the cowardly, the faithless, the polluted, . . . murderers, fornicators, sorcerers, idolaters, and all liars" (21:8; cf. 21:27; 22:3, 15). For John, the relationship to God and Christ, established by divine initiative (5:9), has to be lived and expressed in conduct, in works, otherwise faith degenerates into a "wretched, pitiable, poor, blind, and naked" illusion (3:17).

Just as the **books** (plural) containing the records of good and bad works are mentioned twice, so the vision contains two references to **the book of life** (singular! 20:12, 15; cf. 3:5; 13:8; 21:27). Also the idea that the names of the elect are written in a book is traditional (e.g., Phil. 4:3; Luke 10:20; Dan. 12:1; *1 Enoch* 47:3). John did not relieve the tension between personal accountability and divine election but depicted it by juxtaposing two kinds of books, that is, the book of life and the record of works. Divine election and human responsibility may not be balanced on the same ledger. Before the judgment throne we cannot invite God to a recital of our good works, nor can we blame him by pointing to the omission of our names from the book of life. This book of life is under the control of the Lamb (21:27) who "loves us [present tense] and has freed us from our sins" and has elected us coregents with him and "priests to his God" (1:6). This election, ratified by the blood of the Lamb, must be ratified by the elect with their lives, their conduct, and their death (cf. 3:5; 14:13).

Perhaps an additional significance of the "book of life" in this vision may lie in John's distinction between the empirical Judaism of his time and place (cf. 2:9; 3:9) and faithful Israel. John, who was so deeply immersed in Moses, the prophets, and psalms, may have alluded to Israel's election with this symbol of the book of life (cf. Exod. 32:32-33). Certainly, John did not consign faithful Israel of the old covenant to the lake of fire.

The negative formulation of v. 15 (if anyone's name was not found in the book of life, he or she was thrown into the lake of fire) serves as contrast between the millennial reign on one side (20:4-6) and the new Jerusalem on the other (21:2-4). It should not lead us to the false conclusion that the final judgment resulted in the universal condemnation of all to "the lake of fire" (e.g., Rissi). The text is silent on the question of how many were saved, because the judgment is God's sovereign prerogative and revelation is not the communication of information to satisfy curiosity.

The third and final emphasis of this vision lies in the abolition of death. The earth had already been liberated from death at "the first resurrection." Now, with the demons destroyed (20:7-10) and the judgment of the dead completed, the netherworld will be cleared of its last two residents. **Death and Hades were thrown into the lake of fire.** Again John is dependent on Christian tradition. "The last enemy to be destroyed is death" (1 Cor. 15:26; cf. Isa. 25:8). Death and Hades (the realm of the dead) are pictured here as two personified beings of the netherworld (cf. 6:7-8). Their destruction is final. They, together with the satanic triumvirate, are the only ones mentioned explicitly to be subjected to the lake of fire. As in the case of all humans, their fate is left unspecified.

The New Jerusalem and the Final Word of God (21:1-8)

We have tried to show that the vision of the millennial reign with Christ (20:4-6) tells us of the inauguration of the new life of the world to come, and the vision gave a preview of it. This preview, sandwiched between the two stages of Satan's elimination, established that "the beloved city" (20:9) consisted of the resurrected saints and martyrs who had been vindicated and who were reigning as kings and worshiping God as priests. They are the new creation because the devil, sin, death, demons, and all the forces of chaos are unable to touch those who have been raised from the dead to new life. Neither the destruction of this world (20:11) nor the final judgment (20:12-15) impinges on them, and therefore John has no vision of their transformation when the present earth is dissolved. The millennial reign with Christ constitutes the reward of the saints and their precedence over the rest of humanity. It is not an interim that ends with the final judgment but the beginning of the new world without end. Therefore John unfolded his millennial vision in 21:1-8, *after* the general judgment vision rather than before.

We have seen that John changed the meaning of some traditional symbols at crucial points, for example, the Messiah is the conqueror through his death rather than through the use of military might; the people of the messianic millennium are not the present generation of the living but the resurrected saints and martyrs; neither they nor the Messiah shall die during or at the end of the millennium, contrary to 4 Ezra 7:29; the new Jerusalem is not the restoration of the present earthly city in the geographic area of Israel/Palestine but the life and reign of the people of God redeemed by the Lamb (5:9-10) and resurrected by God (20:4-6).

In his preview (20:4-6) John had depicted the resurrected saints as sitting on "thrones" and as reigning with Christ (20:4-6). Those "thrones" were presumably thought to be in heaven. Of the 34 occurrences of "throne" prior to chap. 20 all, except Satan's throne (2:13) and the throne of the beast (13:2; 16:10), are thrones in heaven. However, in 20:9 the saints and "the beloved city" are on earth. How did they get there? The new double vision (21:1-2) unfolds the preview and tells us that the new Jerusalem came down **out of heaven,** that is, **from God.**

21:1-8 is the climax of the series of visions that begins with the parousia vision (19:11) and simultaneously it introduces the following section (21:9—22:5). Thus it serves a dual function, as does 15:1-4 or 19:1-10. The double vision (vv. 1-2) is interpreted by a "voice from the throne" and confirmed by God himself. Up to this point the consequence of the parousia was depicted primarily negatively in a series of judgment visions that cleansed the earth and the netherworld from all evils. Now the positive side is shown in one grand picture which elaborates 20:4-6. The importance of this section can also be seen in that here is the only instance, apart from 1:8, when God himself speaks directly. Thus this section is also the high point of the whole letter, and a reader who wishes to know what John's letter is all about may well be directed to these eight verses. Genesis 1:3 brings the Bible's first word of God: "Let there be light" and our section has God's last word in which he guarantees the fulfillment of his promise.

Because this section is the high point of the whole letter, all compositional lines meet here. The promises to the conquerors of the first septet are fulfilled in the promise of inheritance (v. 7). The hymns and acclamations of the throne room visions (vv. 4-5) are realized in the presence of God among his people on earth. The cosmic destructions wrought by the sixth seal (6:12-17), continued in the trumpet and bowl visions and taken up in the general judgment vision (20:11), have given way to a new heaven and a new earth. The woman, clothed with the sun and crowned with stars (12:1), pursued by the dragon but not defeated (12:4-17), now appears as bride adorned for her husband (21:2). The victory scenes of interludes and previews (7:1-17; 11:11-13; 14:1-5; 15:2-4), the Hallelujah chorus and its response (19:1-8), the rejoicing that the marriage of the Lamb with the Bride clothed in fine linen has come (19:7-8)—all these lines, and more, merge in our scene.

A New Heaven and a New Earth (21:1). **Then I saw a new heaven and a new earth; for the first heaven and the first earth had passed away, and the sea was no more.** A new beginning is made which is as different from the world of our experience as the resurrection is from death. The background of this verse is Isaiah's promise: "Behold, I create new heavens and a new earth; and the former things shall not be remembered" (Isa. 65:17). This promise is now fulfilled even as "the mystery of God" (10:7), his secret, connected with the seventh trumpet call (11:15-19) is now revealed. It is not a renewal of the present creation any more than resurrection is a resuscitation of the present body. Not a renewal is envisioned here as it was expected in *1 Enoch* 45:4-5 or *2 Bar.* 32:6. Nor is it a poetic comparison as in Isaiah, who compared Israel's deliverance from exile with a new act of creation while focusing his hope upon an earthly renewed Jerusalem. For John, it is a **new** creation in which neither death nor chaos, symbolized by **the sea,** has a place. The latter was the abode of the beast (13:1) and of chaotic forces. John did not derive the idea of the disappearance of the sea from the Old Testament, but there are some parallels in apocalyptic literature to this effect (e.g., *Test. Levi* 4:1; *Sib. Or.* 5:158; *As. Mos.* 10:6). The new creation is not an object of cosmological speculation but serves as context for the heavenly Jerusalem.

The New Jerusalem (21:2). **And I saw the holy city, new Jerusalem, coming down out of heaven from God, prepared as a bride adorned for her husband.** This vision reinterprets Isa. 65:18, where the idea of a new earth is related to a renewed Jerusalem in the land of Israel (cf. Isa. 54:11-17; 60:1). In Tob. 13:16 we read: "For Jerusalem will be built with sapphires and emeralds, her walls with precious stones, and her towers and battlements with pure gold. . . . All her lanes will cry 'Hallelujah! . . . Blessed is God, who has exalted you for ever' " (cf. Isa. 54:11-14). This hope for a glorious Jerusalem within history was modified by the apocalyptists. A preexistent heavenly Jerusalem, which is not seen at present but which shall appear at the end, is found in some apocalyptic traditions (e.g., 4 Ezra 7:26; 10:54; *2 Bar.* 4:2-6).

By placing the vision of the new heaven next to the vision of the new city, John indicated that the two are inseparable from each other. The new city determines the new creation, and we might note that only here and in 3:12 does the name of the city, **Jerusalem,** occur in this book and both verses refer to the eschatological, not the historical, city of God. Of it we hear that it shall be **coming down out of heaven from God.** There is no "rapture" of the saints in this book. Only the Messiah has been "caught up to God" (12:5). While Paul envisioned that on the last day the Christians, dead or alive, shall be "caught up" in the clouds "to meet the Lord in the air" (1 Thess. 4:16-17), John described the opposite movement. The new Jerusalem, the resurrected saints and those approved in the final judgment, come down from heaven upon the new earth, so that heaven and earth become one.

The beauty of the new city of God is compared to a **bride adorned for her husband,** the Lamb. The fabric of her wedding gown is "the righteous deeds of the saints (19:8). Cities as women or goddesses were part of John's context. Jerusalem, or Zion, was presented as a woman by prophets and apocalyptists who hoped for her renewal or her eschatological transformation on the last day (e.g., Isaiah 54: 61:10; Jer. 4:31; 4 Ezra 9:38—10:54). Romans presented their capital as goddess with a cult of her own. For John, the woman, adorned as a bride, is a community of no-accounts in the present order which is awaiting their own descent from heaven and which, inspired by the Spirit, calls "Amen. Come, Lord Jesus!" requesting his coming not after the millennium but "soon" (22:17, 20).

Also Paul referred to a heavenly Jerusalem who is "our mother" (Gal. 4:25-31). For him, Christians are citizens not of historic Jerusalem, which represents the law and hostility to the gospel, but of "Jerusalem above," the kingdom of God, our "commonwealth" in heaven, which bestows freedom and the gifts of the Spirit. It is from the heavenly city that the church awaits the Savior and the final consummation (Phil. 3:20; cf. Heb. 11:10; 12:22; 13:14). For John, the heavenly city is the antithesis of "the great city," whether Babylon/Rome or historic Jerusalem, where "the Lord was crucified" (11:8). If Jews threatened Christians in Smyrna and Philadelphia with "the second death" (2:9, 11) and with exclusion from the end-time people of God (3:7, "key of David"), then the promise of becoming a "pillar" in God's temple, that is, in the "new Jerusalem," represents the countervision to those threats (3:12). By identifying the new Jerusalem as "the bride" of Christ, John also suggests that love, intimacy, and faithfulness constitute the relationship between the community and its Lord, both now (22:17) and in the ultimate future.

An Audition (21:3-4). The first audition interprets the double vision of vv. 1-2; the second brings God's solemn confirmation. The first speaker is represented as **a loud voice from the throne** (cf. 19:5), announcing the presence of God among his people. **Behold** has the force of "Pay attention now!" and John placed this attention-getter strategically at important points. **The dwelling of God is with men** (Greek, *anthrōpoi*). **He will dwell with them, and they shall be his people** (the better manuscripts read "peoples," Greek, *laoi*), **and God himself will be with them.**

The basic promise over Israel's history is the preamble to the first commandment: "I am the Lord your God, who brought you out of the land of Egypt, out of the house of bondage" (Deut. 5:6). From this follows the convenantal promise: "I will make my abode among you . . . and will be your God, and you shall be my people" (Lev. 26:11). The prophets proclaimed a new realization of this promise: "I will make a covenant of peace with them; it shall be an everlasting covenant. . . . My dwelling place shall be with them; and I will be their God, and they shall be my people" (Ezek. 37:26-27; cf. Jer. 31:33; Zech. 2:14; 8:8). This promise of a perfect communion with God is now fulfilled. What the tabernacle and the temple represented as hope, shadow, and type has been attained. The decisive feature of the "holy city, new Jerusalem" is God's presence, unencumbered by sin and evil. No longer shall the throne be in unapproachable majesty and distance in heaven, but the **dwelling,** the residence of the three times holy creator (4:8), shall be among his creatures. The new Jerusalem, all of it, will be God's temple, and therefore there is no need for a special temple (21:22). All shall be priests with direct access to him, worshiping the Almighty, who has come among them, thereby fulfilling the first commandment.

As an aside we should note the significance of John's use of Ezek. 37:27 in v. 3. He had used this chapter from Ezekiel already in his millennial vision, 20:4-6. He had then, following Ezekiel's sequence, moved on to Ezekiel 38–39 in the Gog-Magog episode, and he will allude to Ezekiel 40–48 in his concluding vision (21:9—22:5). His return to chap. 37 of Ezekiel in the text before us (21:3) is significant because it ties our section (21:1-9) to the millennial vision of 20:4-6. This link supports our contention that the millennial vision of 20:4-6 is elaborated in 21:1—22:5. This link also answers the question why the resurrection is never mentioned explicitly in 21:1—22:5. It need not be, because it is the core of 20:4-6.

Some modern interpreters have argued that God's residence will be among generic humanity, among all **men,** who shall be **his peoples** (cf. RSV footnote). Hence John would have held an unlimited universalism of salvation in which no one is excluded, except the devil and his two minions. Some have gone so far as to hold that according to John "the lake of fire" is a kind of evangelical purgatory, from which people, condemned in the final judgment (20:15), can find eventual release (Rissi). One might wish that John had embraced such universalistic notions, but he did not, as vv. 7 and 8 clearly demonstrate. "The peoples" around God are the conquerors (21:7) and those who have not ended in the lake of fire (20:15). The meaning of the plural "peoples" has shifted from indicating unbelievers (cf. 7:9) to referring to the saints and the acquitted (21:3). The plural points to the universality of the community of salvation which originated from "every tribe and tongue and people and nation" (5:9), and not just from Israel. (See comments on 21:24-27.)

He will wipe away every tear from their eyes, and death shall be no more, neither shall there be mourning nor crying nor pain any more, for the former things have passed away (cf. 7:17b). Suffering and sorrow, pain and death, which are the signature of "the former things," of the first earth (v. 1), shall disappear in the new world as consequence of God's presence among his people. We should note that the result of God's residence in the holy city is, first, his ministering to the citizens, his consoling them. Second, the effect of his presence with them can be described only negatively, as absence of pain, sorrow, and death. The Koran deals with this subject differently. There the righteous enter gardens of delight, recline on jeweled couches, drink of the purest wine, eat the fruit they desire, and have as companions "chaste virgins" (pp. 110, 335). For John, life in the new Jerusalem is not a quantitative increase of delights that can be experienced already in the present, but it involves a new creation which cannot be sketched adequately, except in negative terms. The phrase "shall be no more" echoes the lament over Babylon (18:9-19).

The Final Word of God (21:5-8; cf. 1:8). Up to this point, God has been dealing with John's churches by proxy, as it were. Now he speaks to them and solemnly vouches for the content of 21:1-4, and he commands John to put this guarantee in writing (cf. 19:9c; 22:6). **Behold, I make all things new.** This is the most important pronouncement in the whole letter. Alluding to the promise to the exiles of Isa. 43:19 and using the present tense instead of the future, God himself summarizes the content of the whole letter which finds its goal in the **new** creation and the **new** Jerusalem. All the exhortations of the message septet, all the judgment visions of the seal, trumpet, and bowl cycles, all the previews of the final victory, are summed up in God's own declaration.

Second, he orders John: **Write this, for these words are trustworthy and true.** John's churches, to whom he writes, are to know that his message is legitimated not only by an angel but by God himself.

Next we hear: **It is done!** (Greek, *gegonan;* literally, "they have happened"). The words through which God promised a new creation have been effective. Just as the words of God: "Let there be . . ." brought about the first heaven and earth, so his words of promise will accomplish the new creation. For when God speaks, something happens. His word of judgment and salvation does not return to him empty (Isa. 55:11; Wis. Sol. 18:15). Just as the exclamation in the seventh bowl vision, "It is done!" (16:17) signaled the completion of the wrath of God as promised (15:1; cf. 10:6-7; 11:18a), so "It is done!" it is finished signals the completion of the new Jerusalem on earth.

The ultimate guarantee of the trustworthiness of God's word is grounded in the very nature of God himself. **I am the Alpha and the Omega, the beginning and the end** (cf. 1:8; also 1:17; 2:8; 3:14; 22:13). In God, past and future are held together. He is not just the creator in the past and thus upholder of the status quo, but the sovereign Lord of the future who upsets every status quo. His future design does not end with the abyss, the lake of fire, or the final judgment, but with a new creation free from sin, death, and the devil. Because God's nature is thus, therefore the church can wait with confidence for the fulfillment of his design.

To the thirsty I will give water **from the fountain of the water of life without payment** (cf. Isa. 55:1; Rev. 7:17). This promise is also related to the present (22:17b). Future salvation and present redemption are always by grace alone and not by merit. All people thirst for fulfillment, and the question is whether they still their longings at the fountain of the water of life or at the watering holes of the world. This promise of God should make each hearer think. He or she, not the community, is addressed here. The gift of God freely given "without price" (cf. 1:5; 5:10) must be put to use and expressed in their lives and conduct. Otherwise Christians live with a fatal illusion (of. 3:14-22).

He who conquers shall have this heritage, and I will be his God and he shall be my son. The conquerors who are "rewarded" (cf. 11:18c) have drunk from the water of life and set forth the strength received from drinking at God's fountain by rejecting idolatry and by persevering in faithful obedience. Their inheritance is to live with God in the new Jerusalem. This heritage realizes the promises of all conqueror texts in the seven messages. But more, in words similar to the messianic prophecy of 2 Sam. 7:14 (cf. Ps. 2:7) God announces that the conqueror shall have a new status as God's **son.** Not only Jesus will be Son of God, that is, Messiah and King (cf. 11:15) but each true Christian, female or male, shall be heir to the messianic promise and reign with Christ forever (22:5). A democracy of kings and queens is promised by God for the consummation. What the French revolution had hoped to accomplish, Liberty, Equality, Brotherhood and

Sisterhood, a dream so shamefully betrayed and drowned in blood, will come true according to God's promise. Then there will no longer be ecclesiastical hierarchies, no more officeholders with fancy titles manipulating "subordinates" under the guise of "service" and ripping off the people of God for their own self-aggrandizement. All shall be kings and queens, coregents with the Son-Messiah, and the equality of God's creatures shall at last be realized.

8—This threat is addressed to the present churches. It does not imply that the people listed in this catalog of the damned are part of the new world. From John's point of view, they should not even be part of the present church (2:2, 6, 14, 22). The reverse side of the heritage of the conquerors is the rejection, ratified by God, of a group of evildoers. Their fate will be "the lake of fire." This catalog should be read in conjunction with its parallels here (cf. 9:20-21; 21:27; 22:3, 15) and in other parts of the New Testament (cf. Rom. 1:29-32; 1 Cor. 6:9-11; Gal. 5:19-21; Col. 3:5) and with the traditions of the Old Testament covenantal obligations (e.g., Deuteronomy 5; 27–28; Isa. 52:1, cf. Rev. 21:27; Ezek. 44:9). The list of exclusion begins with **the cowardly** and ends with **all liars,** thereby giving emphasis to these two groups. In between we hear of groups that characterize the behavior of Babylon which is thus set over against the conquerors, the new Jerusalem. For the **polluted** (Greek, *ebdelygmenoi*), see 17:4 (RSV, "abominations"; Greek, *bdelygma*). These include not just pagans but also those Christians who participate in the abomination of the imperial cult or eat meat sacrificed to idols. They are in continuity with those Israelites who "consecrated themselves to Baal, and became detestable like the thing they loved" (Hos. 9:10). "Detestable" is the same word in the LXX as "polluted" here. For **murderers,** see the indictment of murder pronounced against Babylon in 18:24 (cf. 17:6). It is unlikely that Christians at John's time were guilty of killing, even though this catalog of rogues is addressed to them rather than to the world outside the church. Hence on a second level "murderers" may refer to instigators of strife within the community who stab others in the back, metaphorically speaking, and then proceed to cover it up with the feathers of the "Spirit," with phony, pious rhetoric. The **fornicators** embrace diverse forms of sexual promiscuity which were denounced already by Hellenistic moralists (e.g., Musonius Rufus, frag. 12, written during the first century A.D.). The warning is to be heard both literally as an injunction against extramarital and homosexual sex and metaphorically as a demand to abstain from pagan cultic rites. **Sorcerers** or magicians sought to manipulate the gods in order to achieve desired goals. They represented the broad spectrum of an international religious underground in Greco-Roman society, known to us through magical papyri, amulets, gems, and tablets with spells. The practice of magic constituted one religious milieu from which members of John's churches came. Ephesus was world famous in antiquity as a center for magical arts (cf. Acts 19:19). Hence John referred to sorcerers not only here but also in 9:21 and 22:15, and he accused Babylon of deceiving all nations with her sorcery (18:23). **Idolaters** are those who worship false gods and in so doing represent Babylon. This catalog of rogues, whose irrevocable fate will be **the second death** in the lake of fire, should function as a blunt warning to Christians then and now.

The list is headed by **the cowardly** who choose personal well-being over faithfulness to the testimony of Jesus. It is not fear of persecution that is condemned but lack of endurance. The cowardly are linked with the **faithless**—professing Christians who are void of faith. And the list is concluded and summarized with a reference to **all liars.** Religion and politics are the realm of lies, a realm that includes false Christian apostles (2:2), Jews who make false claims (2:9; 3:9), Jezebel and her followers (2:20), the advocates of the "teaching of Balaam" (2:14), and, last but not least, "the false prophet" of the imperial cult (16:13; cf. 13:13-14; 19:20). The practice of speaking lies (RSV, "falsehood") is excluded in the holy city (21:27; 22:15). In contrast to gnosticizing Christians who think that salvation is their irrevocable possession already now, John's blunt warning in the form of God's last word to his church on earth is meant to point out the deadly danger that threatens each of us, then and now. Because religion and politics are the realm of lies, our book contains three legitimations of its truthfulness and trustworthiness. Two of them are given by an angel (19:9; 22:6), but the high point is the confirmation by God himself (21:5). And in contrast to "the faithless" and the "liars," the church's Lord is called "Faithful and True" (19:11), because he is "the faithful and true witness, the beginning of God's creation" (3:14), who in the end shall reveal, establish, the truth of God against the lies of false religion and politics.

This climactic conclusion of a series of judgment visions serves at the same time as prolog to the Jerusalem vision (21:9—22:5). Thus each verse of this prolog is picked up in the last vision: v. 1, the new earth, is developed in 22:1-5. the new paradise; v. 2 is taken up in 21:9-11; v. 3 in 21:22-23; v. 4 in 22:2; v. 5 in 22:6; v. 6 in 22:1; v. 7 in 22:4; and v. 8 in 21:27 and 22:3a.

The New Jerusalem (21:9—22:5 [9])

This section develops the climactic proclamation of salvation in 21:1-8. It also describes the city of God as the antithesis of Babylon. Already the overall structure of the third part of the body of the letter discloses the existence of a relationship between Babylon and the city of God: A, 17:1—19:10; B, 19:11—21:8; A′, 21:9—22:5 (9). The parallels and contrasts between the two visions demonstrate that the new Jerusalem is the very antithesis of Babylon, symbol of idolatry and exploitation. Consider the following parallels and contrasts:

BABYLON	**CITY OF GOD**
Introduction	*Introduction*
An angel of the bowl plagues approaches John (17:1)	An angel of the bowl plagues approaches John (21:9)
Invitation: "Come, I will show you" (17:1)	Invitation: "Come, I will show you" (21:9)

"the great harlot" (17:1)	"the Bride, the wife of the Lamb" (21:9)
"in the Spirit" John is carried into the "wilderness" (17:3)	"in the Spirit" John is carried to a "great, high mountain" (21:10)
The harlot is "seated upon many waters" (17:1)	The Bride is "coming down out of heaven from God" (21:10)
Vision The harlot Babylon is arrayed in purple and scarlet, with gold, jewels, and pearls (17:4; 18:16-17)	*Vision* The Bride Jerusalem has "the glory of God, its radiance like a most rare jewel, like a jasper, clear as crystal" (21:11)
A "name" on her forehead (17:5)	God's name on their foreheads (22:4)
The mother of "abominations" (17:5)	Nothing "unclean," no "abomination" shall enter (21:27; 22:3a)
Their "names" are not written in "the book of life" (17:8)	Their "names" are written in "the Lamb's book of life" (21:27)
"The kings of the earth" shall destroy "the harlot" (17:15-18)	"The kings of the earth shall bring their glory into it" (21:24)
Babylon, a "dwelling place of demons" (18:2)	The new Jerusalem, "the dwelling of God" (21:3, 22)
Babylon's doom (18:1-3, 9-19)	Jerusalem's eternal glory (21:10—22:5)
Conclusion Beatitude (19:9) with imminence of the eschaton ("marriage supper of the Lamb")	*Conclusion* These words are true (22:6); imminence of the eschaton ("I am coming soon," 22:7)
"These are true words of God" (19:9)	Beatitude (22:7)
Angel worship (19:10)	Angel worship (22:8)

"You must not do that!" (19:10)	"You must not do that!" (22:9)
"Worship God" (19:10)	"Worship God" (22:9)

One more parallel should be added. We have already seen that 21:1-8 functions as climax of its section (19:11—21:8) and at the same time as prolog of the new Jerusalem vision (21:9—22:5[9]). The same is true of the seventh bowl vision (16:17-21). It concludes the section that begins at 12:1. The seven bowl plagues are identified as "the last, for with them the wrath of God is ended" (15:1). The seventh bowl announces, *"It is done!"* (16:17), the "great city" is split into three parts, "the cities of the nations" fall, and "great Babylon" has to drain "the cup of the fury of his wrath," even as islands and mountains disappear. In turn, this climactic conclusion of the bowl judgments serves as prolog to the doom of Babylon vision (17:1—19:10). Thus the antithetical parallels between 16:17-21 and 21:1-8 become clear.

Just as the seventh bowl vision signals the destruction of the world and the downfall of Babylon and the completion of judgments, so the prolog of 21:1-8 reveals a new heaven and earth, the appearance of the city of God and the manifestation of the final salvation. The conclusion of judgment as well as the consummation of salvation is marked by *"It is done!"* (16:17; 21:6).

A psychologizing interpretation may conclude that the new Jerusalem vision functions as "compensation" for the oppressive situation of poverty and powerlessness of John's hearers. Their feelings of "envy" are compensated by the hope of incredible wealth, of gold and precious stones in the future, even as their aggression finds release in the vision of the destruction of the powerful. Like a schizophrenic who cannot cope with the harsh realities of the present and therefore withdraws into a world of "elaborate fantasies," John lapsed into pessimistic mythology and transferred his aggression to the future (cf. Yarboro Collins, *Crisis*, 154–160).

A psychological hermeneutic can destroy most theological texts. In John's story the Christians do not receive the riches of Babylon, nor do they reign over others as their subjects in the city of God. It seems to me that our apocalyptic epistle is not a narrative of compensation for poverty and persecution experienced. Rather, through his symbolic story, John endeavored to reveal who God and Christ are with respect to past, present, and, above all, with respect to the future. The great issue is: Whom do we and should we worship? This is the issue of the first commandment. John's symbolic, cartoon-like theological drama seeks to shock its hearers and draw them into his vision of God and the Lamb that was slain. It is he, "the faithful witness" unto death, who reigns, and he, the Crucified One, discloses how Christians reign with him, namely, under tribulations. If it were otherwise, they would not reign with him. Moreover, John's symbolic narrative seeks to reveal who the enemies are, which means whom the church must resist. The danger that beset John's churches consisted of compromise, cultural accommodation and assimilation, which was all the greater since neither persecution by the state nor abject social poverty determined their present. He saw idolatry running rampant in the world, heretics propagating their teaching within the church, and church members comfortable and self-satisfied thereby denying the witness of the crucified King. Faithfulness toward the Lamb that was slain requires rejection of idolatry and therefore involves separation from the world of Rome which in turn results in inevitable tribulation. Finally, the hope for the new Jerusalem is not a lust for compensation for real or imagined deprivation but a hope grounded in the slain Lamb. The Crucified One does reign, and therefore neither death nor idolatry shall reign in the end.

John had drawn his hearers into an initial experience of the vision of God sitting upon his throne, receiving the worship of the heavenly court and holding a scroll in his hand (4:1—5:1). Yet God himself said nothing in the throne room or in the visions that followed. Ingeniously John had delayed bringing a new word of God until the climactic scene of 21:1-8. "Behold, I make all things new." The following vision serves as exposition of this word of God and its context. After an introduction (21:9-10), John at once presents the essential characteristics of the city of God (21:11), followed by a general description of its external features (21:12-14) and its external measurements (21:15-21a). Then he gives a picture of the internal features of the city and its people (21:21b-27). Last, he presents the city as the new paradise (22:1-5). The vision reaches its concluding high point in the eternal worship and reign of God's priests and kings (22:5).

What are some antecedents of this vision? Ezekiel's vision of a new temple (Ezekiel 40–48) serves in part as model for John's reinterpretation. Like Ezekiel, John is placed on a high mountain, sees an angel with a measuring rod, describes the structure, the river of paradise, and other details in language reminiscent of Ezekiel. Yet the thrust of his vision differs. Whereas in Ezekiel the temple is the focus of chaps. 40–49 and the city appears merely as an aside, we can clearly see that John's vision deals exclusively with the city and that his new Jerusalem has no temple (21:22). Such an expectation is remarkable and without parallel in the Old Testament or in apocalyptic literature. He transferred features of Ezekiel's temple to his description of the city of God (e.g., v. 11, cf. Ezek. 43:2; vv. 12-13, cf. Ezek. 40:30-35; v. 15, cf. Ezek. 40:3-5; v. 16, cf. Ezek. 43:16; etc.) because for John the whole city is the "dwelling of God" (21:2), his temple. Moreover, he used traditions concerning Jerusalem's renewal, such as Isa. 54:11-17; 61:1-22; 62:1-12; 4 Ezra 8:52; 10:27; 44:54-55. The result is that his magnificent vision depicts the eschatological community not only as an alternative to Babylon but also as the fulfillment of promises made to Israel as well as to the conquerors, and as the realization of utopian hopes centered on Hellenistic cities and their people.

The City (21:9-21)

Introduction (21:9-10). This introduction also indicates that the new Jerusalem is the anti-image of Babylon. No one can be a citizen of both! To dwell in the new Jerusalem is to renounce the harlot. One of the seven bowl angels, an agent of God's wrath against the worshipers of the beast (16:1-21), enabled John to see the heavenly city. God's judgment, executed by that angel, serves to bring about the new creation. In contrast to Ezek. 40:2 the **high mountain** to which John was carried **in the Spirit** is not a topographical spot on a map but a symbolic place of revelation concerning the consummation, in contrast to the desert where Babylon's desolate state was revealed. The image of Jerusalem as **Bride** and **wife** intimates that the marriage of the Lamb (19:7) is taking place. Yet this picture is not developed further, though it suggests beauty and rejoicing (19:7-8) and the love of Christ for his people (cf. 1:5, "He loves us"; cf. Isa. 54:5; Hosea 1–2). The image of **the holy city Jerusalem,** rather than the marriage, dominates the vision. The city of God comes down to earth, unlike Ezekiel's temple which comes to rest upon a mountain. In Ezekiel the mountain delineates the temple from the city—the former being more holy than the latter. Not so in John's vision, where the city *is* the temple. For him, however, the new Jerusalem and the old Babylon have one thing in common. Both are on *earth.*

The Essential Characteristics of This City (21:11). It glows with **the glory of God,** its iridescent **radiance** sparkles **like a most rare jewel, like a jasper, clear as crystal.** The city's main feature is God's glory, the presence of his very nature. Unlike Ezekiel, where the glory must enter the temple through a gate and therefore remains distinct from the temple (cf. Ezek. 43:2-5), the glory of God is constitutive of the new Jerusalem. The brilliance of the heavenly city recalls the throne room vision (cf. 4:3).

External Features and Measurements (21:12-21a). Every ancient city was surrounded by a wall (cf. Isa. 26:1) The **great, high wall** in this vision symbolizes beauty, security, and demarcation (cf. 21:27; 22:3). Yet these are not the walls of a prison. **Twelve gates** with the names of the **twelve tribes** of Israel inscribed on them (cf. Ezek. 48:31-34) and guarded by **twelve angels** remain open day and night (cf. 21:25). The twelve tribes are no longer identical with the Old Testament covenant people, because the

twelve foundations of the wall are identified as **the twelve apostles of the Lamb.** The church as "the Israel of God" appears in Gal. 6:16, and the apostles function as the church's "foundation" in Eph. 2:20. In short, the new Jerusalem symbolizes the fulfillment of the promises made to Israel and the establishment of the perfected people of God, transfigured by the glory of God and in continuity with the apostles' teaching.

The names of the twelve tribes and twelve apostles also connect the city of God with past history in which Israel has a historical priority with respect to the church and its apostles. One would therefore have expected Israel's tribes to function as foundation stones of the wall and to find the apostles' names on the gates, rather than vice versa. John, however, transformed the image. Israel's tribes whose doors were closed to uncircumcised outsiders in the past will have their names inscribed on the open doors of the new city. Thus the open gates with Israel's names on them are also an invitation to present Israel to consider the beauty of the future Jerusalem. The foundations of this city bear the historical names of the apostles because their witness to God's eschatological fulfillment constitutes the foundation of the city of the future.

The measuring of the city by an angel is reminiscent of Ezek. 40:5-15; 45:1-2, where we find foursquare measurements. In distinction from 11:1-2, where the measuring of the sanctuary signifies protection, the measuring of the new city functions as an angelic interpretation of the new Jerusalem. **The city lies foursquare** and measures **twelve thousand stadia** (about 1,400 miles) on each side, and its **height** is the same as its breadth. In short, the city has the form of a cube, like the Holy of Holies (cf. 1 Kings 6:20). Hence the city needs no separate temple, because in its totality the city is the temple filled with the presence and glory of God. The city's dimensions stagger the imagination. Foursquare is a symbol of perfection, the cube form is a symbol of holiness; the city of God is a square of the twelve thousand of the tribes of Israel (7:4-8), which make up 144,000, reflected in the **hundred and forty-four cubits** of the **wall.** All of John's numbers have symbolical values and yet the size and height of the city, reaching from earth to heaven and coming down from heaven, may have reminded John's hearers of the ancient astrological notion of the city of the stars, the heavenly temple of the gods. Some earthly temple cities, like Babylon, were built foursquare, as a counterpart to the heavenly city (Herodotus, 1.178). Among Jewish writers it was envisioned that the renewed Jerusalem would extend as far as Joppa or Damascus, with a height that reaches up to the throne of glory (Billerbeck, 3:849). For John, such dreams are surpassed in the perfect cube of the city of God in which heaven and earth, God and his people, are one. Perhaps the new city is also meant to be a counterimage to the quest to reach the heavens through the building of the tower of Babel (Gen. 11:1-9).

The discrepancy between the height of the city and the measurement of the **wall** (about 1,400 *miles* to approximately 220 *feet*) is so tremendous as to be ludicrous. Therefore some interpreters have taken the wall measurement to refer to the width, the thickness of the wall, rather than to its height, pointing out that John had already told us that the wall is "great" and "high" (21:12). Perhaps they are right, but we ought to realize that a wall 1,400 miles high must be wider than 220 feet. In short, the picture is not a realistic one.

Other interpreters have suggested that the difference between the height of the wall and the height of the city symbolizes the distinction between the perfected church on one hand and all of humanity on the other. We note that the apostles' names are inscribed on the foundations of "the wall" rather than of the city. However, if only "the wall" were to symbolize the eschatological Israel, then it would seem that "the city" cannot symbolize a universal, cosmic salvation of humanity as a whole, as has been suggested. Rather, we would have to say that the enormous size of the city indicates an enormous group of originally "non-Christian" people who in the final judgment were accepted by God, "registered" in "the Lamb's book of life" (20:11-15; 21:27) and incorporated into the one perfected people among whom God and the Lamb are present and worshiped (22:3-4). We may recall the song of the redeemed: "All nations shall come and worship thee" (15:4). At the end "the rest [of the people of the great city] were terrified and gave glory to the God of heaven" (11:13), and before the end an angel with an eternal gospel issued the command: "Fear God and give him glory . . . worship him" (14:7). So then, if the discrepancy in height between the wall and the city were to refer to two types of humans within the one perfected people of God, then the above interpretation might be on target.

But there is a more obvious solution to this problem. The walls of the city are so low, comparatively speaking, because their purpose is not defense and protection but beauty and demarcation (21:8, 27; 22:3, 15). At any rate, universal salvation is not the message this vision seeks to communicate; otherwise "the lake that burns with fire" together with God's last pronouncement in this book would merely be a joke (20:8).

The wall was built of jasper, while the city was pure gold, clear as glass. The symbolism emphasizes not obscene riches and wanton luxuries in which the redeemed indulge but the radiant glory and holiness of God which transfigures his people. **The foundations of the wall of the city were adorned with every jewel.** Then follows a list of twelve precious or semiprecious stones. Charles gave an ingenious interpretation to this list on the basis of an A.D. 1653 publication that refers to Arabic and Egyptian monuments which contained the stones of 21:20 in reverse order and identified them with the signs of the zodiac (Charles, 2:165-169). Unfortunately these Arabic documents can no longer be located, and some scholars have doubted whether they ever existed.

Eight of the twelve stones have parallels in the LXX version of the stones in the high priest's breastplate (Exod. 28:17-20; 36:17-20; cf. Ezek. 28:13). Moreover, these stones are related to the twelve tribes (Exod. 28:21). How did the stones from the high priest's breastplate become foundation stones in the new Jerusalem? From Isaiah we hear: "Behold, I will set your stones in antimony, and lay your foundations with sapphires. I will make your pinnacles of agate, your gates of carbuncles, and all your wall of precious stones" (Isa. 54:11-12; cf. Tob. 13:16-17). A fragment from Qumran relates Isaiah's foundation stones to the stones of the high priest's breastplate and to the eschatological community (4QpIs, frag. 1). Philo as well as Josephus links the stones of the high priest's breastplate to the twelve signs of the zodiac (*Life of Moses* 2.133; *Ant.* 3.3.186), which represent the gates of the heavenly city.

Once again John transformed a tradition. The gates refer to the tribes of Israel, not to twelve precious stones (v. 12), and are made of pearls (v. 21). The jewels are foundation stones, and the names of the apostles are inscribed on them (v. 14). The inscription of the stones with the names of the apostles indicates that the city of God is based on the foundation of their testimony to Jesus. Their testimony to Jesus is that "he loves us" and has redeemed us by his blood so that we shall be coregents with him and priests of God (1:5-6; 5:9-10). The connection of the stones with the high priest's breastplate discloses the eschatological worship of God's new high priests (22:3). We should also note that the list of John's stones and their sequence differs from any other list known to us. He probably grouped them in four groups of three stones each for euphonic reasons (Farrer, 219). The last stone in the first three groups ends with the Greek letter "n". Moreover, the four-square shape of the city required four groups of three stones each.

A different approach has been suggested recently. Taking the first and last Greek letters of the first four stones, we receive the abbreviation of "Jesus Christ," as commonly used in Greek manuscripts. Then taking the first Greek letters of the remaining stones (but omitting the sixth stone, because the number 6 has negative connotations), we might obtain the following cryptogram: "Iesous Christos Soter, Christos Basileus Telos, Christos Hyios Anthropou," meaning: Jesus Christ is Savior, Christ the King is the End (or, Christ is the King and the End; cf. 19:16; 22:13), Christ is the Son of Man (*NTS* 33, 1987, 154). The meaning of the cryptogram would constitute the foundational witness of the apostles.

Attractive as this conclusion might be, its difficulties lie not only in the omission of the sixth stone, which in Greek also begins with the letter "s", but also in the absence of the Christological title "Savior" in this book. We are on firmer ground when we perceive the foundation stones as depicting the contrast between the new Jerusalem and the jewels of the harlot Babylon (17:4; cf. 18:12, 16), and this contrast is also part of the apostles' witness.

The **twelve gates** of the city of God are made of **twelve pearls.** Pearls were not regarded as jewels before Hellenistic times, but then they were highly valued (cf. Matt. 7:6; 13:45-46). Their size here staggers the imagination. Likewise the city (v. 18), its main **street** is **pure gold, transparent as glass.** In iridescent splendor the city emits the radiance of the glory of God that permeates it.

The People (21:22-27)

The internal features of the city and its people are described: The street of gold moves the vision into the city and its most startling feature, the absence of a temple. **I saw no temple.** The old Jerusalem was dominated by Mount Zion and its temple, and only because of the temple was Jerusalem the city of God. As Psalm 46 confesses: "God is in the midst of her, she shall not be moved. . . . The Lord of hosts is with us; the God of Jacob is our refuge." Jewish prophetic and apocalyptic end-time hopes always included an expectation for the renewal of the temple, irrespective of whether the end was conceived as taking place within history or beyond history (cf. Dan. 8:14; Ezekiel 40–46; *1 Enoch* 93:7; *Jub.* 1:17). This point of view, according to which the renewed temple guarantees God's presence among his people also in the eschaton, is radically transformed in John's vision. **No temple!** and a reason for its abrogation is given. The city's **temple is the Lord God the Almighty and the Lamb.** Instead of a divine presence mediated by the cult in a geographic holy location, the new Jerusalem as a whole and in all its parts is the temple of God and the Lamb. What does that mean?

In the first place, the astronomical dimensions of the city reveal "a great multitude" of "saints" which no human could "number." They come from "every nation, from all tribes and peoples and tongues." They "have washed their robes and made them white in the blood of the Lamb" (7:9, 15). All are admitted to the city of God, except those who are excluded according to 20:11-15; 21:8, 27. This international new humanity is the temple of God, and therefore this humanity is the new Jerusalem.

In the second place, where God and the Lamb are, there is the temple of the new city. Hence the cubically shaped city in the form of the Holy of Holies exists *in* God and the Lamb rather than vice versa, as was the case with the old temple. In short, the saints dwell in God and in the Lamb. The conquerors of Philadelphia are therefore promised to be pillars "*in* the temple" (3:12), which in the light of 21:22 means *in* God.

In the third place, even though God and the Lamb are the city's temple (21:22), so that the city, the saints, dwell in them, at the same time the city is "the dwelling place" of God and the Lamb (21:3). This means that God and Christ dwell *in them.* Therefore the new Jerusalem is the city of God, his temple, in which he and the Lamb are present. (For the church as temple in which God is present, see 1 Cor. 6:19-20; 2 Cor. 6:16—7:1; Eph. 2:19-21; 1 Peter 2:4-10; cf. 1QS 5:5-6; 8:4-10; 11QT).

In the fourth place, the reciprocal indwelling of God and the saints in the ultimate future begins with the millennium of 20:4-6 and contrasts sharply with the fate of the saints in the penultimate future. Then another city will be "drunk with the blood of the saints" (17:6) even as the victorious saints will conquer Babylon's idolatry "by the blood of the Lamb" and their own testimony (12:11). Moreover, John's vision of the ultimate future of the saints also contrasts with Jewish threats against the church. The fate of the saints will not be "the second death" (2:9, 11) but the reciprocal indwelling of God and the followers of the Lamb. Furthermore, with respect to those Christians who imagine that their "first resurrection" has happened already, that they already dwell in God and God in them, that the eschaton is thoroughly realized (cf. John 14–17), our vision insists on a futuristic eschatology. The new Jerusalem is not yet present, our resurrection has not yet happened (cf. 20:4-6), because idolatry, death, and the devil are still rampant, threatening even the church (e.g., 2:14, 24).

In the fifth place, the reciprocal indwelling of God and the saints means nothing less than the future glorification of the followers of the Lamb. The negative aspect of the city stated: There is "no temple." Stated positively, the whole city is engulfed in the glory of God radiating in it and from it. The saints no longer stand "before" God, but live "in" him, being completely surrounded by him, even as he lives "in" them. Thus they become "partakers of the divine nature" (2 Peter 1:4; cf. Phil. 3:20-21; 1 Cor. 15:45-55). Their transfiguration in glory does not obliterate the distinction between God and the saints and advocate pantheism, or some fusion of God and them into one single being. The vision clearly distinguishes between the city and God, but it no longer separates them (cf. vv. 24-26). Not God's "essence" but his "energies," his glory, beauty, love, and holiness permeate and transfigure the saints (the city), so that—to borrow the language of the Greek fathers—they become gods without ceasing to be humans (cf. John 10:34). This future union between God and his people is the focus of this vision.

The city has no need of sun or moon to shine upon it, for the glory of God is its light, and its lamp is the Lamb. All darkness and alienation belong to the past, the city is suffused with the light of divine glory, and Isaiah's prophecy has come about: "The sun shall be no more your light by day, nor . . . the moon . . . by night; but the Lord will be your everlasting light, and your God will be your glory" (Isa. 60:19). John is not conveying astronomical information, but he is using traditional imagery to depict life that will never grow old, resurrection life beyond death (20:4-6), life free from sin and the devil and infused with the light of the glory that radiates from God and the Lamb.

Because John continues to make use of traditional images from Isaiah 60, we hear: **By its light shall the nations walk; and the**

kings of the earth shall bring their glory into it, and its gates shall never be shut by day—and there shall be no night there; they shall bring into it the glory and the honor of the nations (cf. Isa. 60:3-6, 11). These nations and kings are no longer idolatrous Gentiles and their rulers but the true people of God (contrary to Caird, Schüssler Fiorenza, and others). Nor do we agree that the text of 20:4—22:20 was "put together by a faithful but unintelligent disciple" of John after John's death (so Charles, 2:147). Rather, John uses here the traditional image of the pilgrimage of the Gentiles to a renewed Jerusalem within history (Isa. 60:3-11) in order to show its fulfillment beyond history. For him, "the nations" are not the idolaters who had offered "their riches to the city of the Antichrist" (contrary to Beasley-Murray) but the saints. Just as the meaning of "peoples" in 21:3 no longer refers to idolaters and unbelievers but to the saints, so likewise the same change in meaning has occurred with respect to "nations" and "kings of the earth." The idolatrous nations and kings have perished (19:20-21; 20:15; 21:8).

Jerusalem's citizens are "the nations" because they come from every nation (7:9), and they are "the kings of the earth" because they rule with Christ (20:4-6), the King of kings. "Their glory" is God's glory reflected by them. The spatial images of bringing into or entering the city mean to participate in the city's life. The image of entering is not meant to convey the idea that the nations live "outside" the city, for outside the city of God there is nothing—except the lake of fire. Nor are the open gates an invitation, addressed to Jews and Gentiles who found themselves in the lake of fire, to come and enter the city (contrary to Rissi, 74, 78). The open gates indicate that the city of God is not a jail, nor can there be any threat to it (cf. 20:9). However, the conquerors shall never "go out of it" (3:12), because God and the Lamb are their future.

Lest anyone should think that the "nations" and their "kings" are not the saints, John adds an implicit exhortation for his audience in the seven churches: **But nothing unclean shall enter it, nor any one who practices abomination or falsehood, but only**

those who are written in the Lamb's book of life. John addresses his churches, challenging them to faithfulness and warning them against compromises. The meaning is the same as in 20:8. "Unclean" (Greek, *koinon*) occurs in Revelation only here and alludes to texts like Isa. 52:1: "there shall no more come into you [Jerusalem] the uncircumcised and the unclean," that is, non-Jews. In 11QT 45-47 the exclusion of everything unclean from the renewed Jerusalem is carried so far as to ban all latrines from the holy city, locating them at a distance from the city that is farther away than the distance that may be walked on the sabbath. Hence the people would have to refrain from relieving themselves on the sabbath, a practice adopted by the Essenes (cf. Josephus, *War* 2.147-149; Yadin, 294–301). For John, "unclean" refers to the list of 20:8; "abomination" (Greek, *bdelygma*) is the same as idolatry. "The Lamb's book of life" is the register containing the names of the conquerors and of all whom God accepted in the final judgment (20:12-15). Hence John's hearers know who "the nations" and "kings" are that participate in the life in God's temple.

Paradise (22:1-5)

The ideal Hellenistic city tried to integrate nature by incorporating parks and gardens within its extended walls. John not only placed the new Jerusalem upon a new earth but he saw it as paradise. On this note the Bible began (Gen. 2:8), and it ends with the picture of the city, not as a teeming jungle of bricks, imprisoning angry humanity, but with the city as a lovely garden. This concluding vision draws a picture of the end like the beginning (cf. *Barnabas* 6.13). It also suggests the utopian realization of the Hellenistic ideal city in which nature and culture together with diverse people from different nations are integrated into a harmonious community. With his vision John intimates that God and the Lamb are key to this utopia.

In addition to Genesis 2, John recalled and modified Ezekiel's picture of a river originating in the temple and flowing into the Dead Sea, with trees lining the riverbanks and bearing fresh fruit each month and with fish swarming in the formerly stagnant waters of that sea (Ezek. 47:1-12). But the new Jerusalem has no separate temple building that is distinguishable from the city, and therefore **the river of the water of life, bright as crystal,** flows from **the throne of God and of the Lamb.** The source of life eternal, symbolized by crystal-clear water like the heavenly sea (4:6), lies "in" God and "in" the Lamb that was slain. The river does not flow outside the city, but **through the middle of the street of the city** (for a different translation, see RSV footnote). We should probably envision the river running down the middle of the broad main street (Greek, *plateia*), with **tree**(s) **of life** growing on either side of the riverbanks—an entire avenue of trees of life flanking both banks of the river. They bear fruit without interruption. No famine, no worry where the next meal is coming from. There is sufficient food for all, and one goal of the ideal city has been met. A second trait is the absence of disease. **The leaves** possess healing powers (cf. Ezek. 47:12), preventing illness and promoting health and vigor. This is another Greek ideal which corresponds to the Hebrew hope of life without suffering (21:4). Nothing accursed shall be part of the new city-paradise (cf. Zech. 14:11). The curse of Genesis 3 has been lifted and its place is taken by the life-giving **throne of God and of the Lamb.** The new paradise differs from the first in that "the ancient serpent" (20:2) has no more power to deceive the elect but has been relegated to the abyss and to the lake of fire.

With a grand finale the vision ends: **His servants shall worship him; they shall see his face, and his name shall be on their foreheads. . . . The Lord God will be their light, and they shall reign for ever and ever.** God's servants are priests (1:6; 5:10) who, like Jewish high priests, bear the name of God on their foreheads (cf. Exod. 28:36-38) in contrast to the mark of the beast (13:16). The question, Whom do people worship? remains the paramount question to the end of time and of John's letter. To be in paradise is to be in God's presence, not just once a year and then only within the Holy of Holies, like the high priests of old. It is to see God face-to-face, in contrast to the godless who on the last day cry, "Hide us from the face of him who is seated upon the throne" (6:16). Communion with God face-to-face, which even Moses was not privileged to attain (Exod. 33:20-23), involves the transformation of our being. "We shall be like him, for we shall see him as he is" (1 John 3:2). The eschatological worship consists of the vision of God, and as the invincible light of God shines upon the worshipers, they are transformed into his likeness. As such, they share in the sovereign reign of God who is "first among equals," a hope that the Roman principate did not fulfill as it degenerated into a monster, into the likeness of the dragon (13:1-4, 11-12). To see God means heaven has become the world and the world is the city of God. The city is a paradise and citizenship is kingship. No subordination of fellow citizens, male or female, no oppression of others or social deprivation, but inclusiveness of different peoples and equalization of social classes. This is paradise on earth. What Old Testament prophets and Hellenistic utopians had hoped for, that shall be, when God speaks, "Behold, I make all things new," at the beginning of the millennium.

■ Epilog and Epistolary Conclusion (22:6[10]-21)

This concluding section, which at first seems to be a collection of haphazardly arranged sayings, serves several functions. In the first place, we have already seen that 22:6-9 corresponds to 19:9-10 and thus serves as conclusion to the new Jerusalem vision, parallel to the conclusion of the Babylon vision. At the same time these verses are part of the epilog which, with its epistolary benediction (v. 21), forms an inclusion with the prolog of 1:1-8 and reminds us that this book is meant to be a letter to the seven churches of Asia. Note the following parallels between the epilog and the prolog:

1. Compare 22:6 with 1:1: Authentication of the whole book; God is the ultimate origin of the revelation of Jesus Christ; God who through angels as his heavenly agents, and Spirit-filled

prophets as his earthly agents, communicated in visions and auditions "what must soon take place," namely, the final "revelation of Jesus Christ."

2. Compare 22:7-8 with 1:3: Beatitude to those who "keep what is written therein," who keep "the words of the prophecy of this book," for "the time is near," which means that Jesus is coming "soon."

3. Compare 21:8 with 1:9 and 1:2b: "I John" can testify to the visions and auditions found in this book, to all I "heard and saw."

4. Compare 22:12 with 1:7: The parousia as recompense.

5. Compare 22:13 with 1:8: God and also his Messiah as "the Alpha and the Omega." As "the Alpha," Christ has "freed us from our sins by his blood and made us a kingdom, priests to his God" (1:5-6); as "the Omega" he shall soon be "coming with clouds" for judgment (1:7; 22:12) and for salvation (20:4-6; 21:9—22:5).

6. The epistolary benediction (22:21) and the epistolary prescript establish this writing as a letter.

In the second place, the epilog clarifies once more that John would have us understand the content of his epistle, not in terms of predictions of future historical events according to a timetable, but as prophecy (22:7, 18-19). His visions and exhortations unveil, reveal, the hidden dimensions of the church and of the world in the present and the future. Hence in the epilog John made use of *prophetic forms of speech:*

1. Beatitudes and parousia announcements in the first person singular: "**Behold, I am coming soon. Blessed** is he who keeps the words of the prophecy of this book" (vv. 6-7); "**Blessed** are those who wash their robes, that they may have access to the tree of life."

2. Announcement of judgment in the first person singular: **"Behold, I am coming soon, bringing my recompense, to repay every one for what he has done"** (v. 12).

3. An oracle of doom and of encouragement and a list of rogues: **Let the evildoer still do evil, and the filthy still be filthy;** their judgment is assured. **And** let **the righteous still do right, and the**

holy still be holy (v. 11). The demarcation between the elect and the reprobate is final, but the saints must persevere. **Outside are the dogs and sorcerers and fornicators and murderers and idolaters, and every one who loves and practices falsehood** (lies) (v. 15). Jews frequently referred to Gentiles as "dogs," while Christians pinned this label on (Jewish) heretics (cf. Matt. 7:6; Phil. 3:2; 2 Peter 2:22). In John's list, "dogs" is either an equivalent to "the polluted" of 21:8 or it has the additional meaning of sodomite, or male prostitute. The background might be Deut. 23:18: "You shall not bring the hire of a harlot, or the wages of a dog, into the house" of God. In either case, this list draws a sharp line between the community and the outsiders (cf. 2:14, 20). ***"Liars"*** once again summarizes this catalog as in 21:8. A parallel to the exclusion of immoral persons is found in Hellenistic mystery religions: "If there be any atheist, or Christian, or Epicurean here spying upon our rites, let him depart in haste" (Lucian, *Alex.* 38).

4. The epilog contains two self-identifications of Christ, beginning with "I am": **"I am the Alpha and the Omega, the first and the last, the beginning and the end"** (v. 13). We have already noted that this oracle virtually identifies Christ with God (cf. 1:8, 17; 21:6), who in the beginning created all things (4:11) and at the end speaks: "Behold, I make all things new" (21:5). Christ reveals himself as the Alpha and the Omega through his prophet in the epilog. He is the victim, whose death had always been his (and God's) victory and the beginning of redemption. He is the **first**born of the dead (1:5, 17), and now in the end he has been revealed before all in John's vision as the victor (19:11—22:5). The end, "the Omega," is not an event but a person.

"I am the root and the offspring of David, the bright morning star" (v. 16). According to Isa. 11:1, "There shall come forth a shoot from the stump of Jesse, and a branch shall grow out of his roots." In this self-disclosure Jesus reverses Isaiah's image. He, the risen Messiah who is "the beginning of God's creation" (3:14), is "the root" from which David came and he is David's promised descendant. Hence he is the source of David's line, "the root," as well as David's "offspring," the promised Messiah, the Lion of the tribe of Judah (cf. 5:5; cf. Mark 12:35-37). This is a daring Christological conception, and it probably represents John's answer to Jewish anti-Christian polemics. In the message to Philadelphia, Jesus disclosed himself as "the one who has the key of *David.*" He therefore, not the Jews who trouble the community, will decide who is included and who is excluded from the new Jerusalem, the city of God and of the new David (2:8-13).

In the designation "the bright morning star" several traditions meet. First, Balaam had announced that "a star shall come forth out of Jacob" (Num. 24:17). Second, this text was understood messianically in Qumran (4QT 9-11) and in the *Testaments of the Twelve Patriarchs* (*Test. Levi* 18:3; *Test. Judah* 24:1). Third, while "the star" is a familiar messianic symbol among Jews (e.g., Bar Kochba), we have no Jewish text that speaks of the Messiah as "the morning star." This is none other than Venus, the "Day Star," the brightest and the largest star (planet) in the opinion of antiquity. This "morning star" signaled victory over all the other stars that represent nations. Venus could be related to male deities and kings. In Isaiah's taunt against the king of Babylon we hear, "How you are fallen from heaven, O Day Star, son of Dawn" (Isa. 14:12-14). When Jesus promised the conquerors in Thyatira that he would give them "the morning star" (2:28), he was promising them a share in his millennial reign after the defeat of the powers of darkness (19:11—20:6). He can make such a promise, because he is "the morning star," the eschatological victorious conqueror. In short, these self-designations combine Jewish and Hellenistic ideas in order to set forth the uniqueness of Christ.

We should also be aware that the resurrected Jesus speaks through John not only in his self-disclosure but also in vv. 7, 12-16, and 20a. Because Jesus speaks through him, John is in fact a prophet even though he never claims the title "prophet" for himself. His words, his narration of visions and auditions, are prophecy also when they are mediated by an angel. For this angel has been "sent" by Jesus (22:16) and by God (1:1; 22:6).

5. Last, John included a solemn warning against tampering with his prophecy (vv. 18-20a). In Deut. 4:2 we read, "You shall not add to the word which I command you, nor take from it" (cf.

Deut. 13:1; *1 Enoch* 104:10-13). The *Letter of Aristeas* concerning the Greek translation of the Old Testament stated: "There should be no revision . . . and they [the elders] commanded that a curse should be laid, as was their custom, on any one who should alter the version, by any addition or change" (*Letter of Arist.* 310-311). John clothed his warning in the form of the law of retribution. **If any one adds to** the words of prophecy in this book, **God will add to him the plagues described in this book, and if any one takes away from the words of the book of this prophecy, God will take away his share in the tree of life and in the holy city.** The importance of this law of retribution is seen in that it is bracketed by two different speakers in vv. 18 and 20: **I** (John) **warn every one** (Greek, *martyrō*, v. 18); **He** (Jesus) **who testifies** (Greek, *martyrōn*) **to these things** (v. 20) and who is coming soon likewise prohibits tampering with John's prophecy. **These things** (v. 20) include John's prophetic warning of vv. 18-19. His lengthy letter was also a substitute for his personal presence, and he was quite aware that prophets like Jezebel and others would find his message rather objectionable (cf. 2:2, 14-15, 20-23). He had therefore started his letter with a blessing on the "lector" who would read his message during the community's worship (1:3), and he now concludes it with a threat against those who would tamper with it. In so doing, he seems to imply that his "words of prophecy" would be read more than once.

In the third place, John's epilog repeatedly emphasizes his expectation of the imminent end. God's angelic agent communicated **what must soon take place** (v. 6), and he told John, **the time is near** (v. 10). Therefore John may **not seal up the words of the prophecy of this book** (v. 10), in contrast to Dan. 12:4 (cf. *1 Enoch* 1:2). Daniel had predated himself and his visions into the Babylonian period and therefore had to "seal up the vision, for it pertains to many days hence" (Dan. 8:26), that is, to the author's real present. John has no need of pseudonymity and predating, for the eschaton has already come with the death and resurrection of Christ and the time to the end is short; Jesus is coming soon (vv. 6c, 7a, 10, 12, 20; cf. 1:1; 2:16; 3:11). Also note: There is no reference to an interim kingdom in the epilog! The reason seems obvious. John's millennium (20:4-6), which appears with the imminent coming of Jesus, signals the beginning of the new Jerusalem and of the new paradise to which v. 14 refers.

We should keep in mind that all of John's visions are determined by the expectation of the imminent end, as his epilog abundantly demonstrates. We may recall that the dragon's time on earth is short (12:12) and that the church's persecution will last but a short time (11:1-2; 13:5). The imminent-end expectation undergirded the urgency of the call to repentance (2:16), to perseverance (2:25; 3:11), to bringing one's life into conformity with the commandments of God (cf. 12:17; 22:14) and cutting out lackadaisicalness (3:15-22). The epilog links the imminent coming of Christ (vv. 7, 12, 20) with the urgency of taking John's prophecy seriously and "to *keep* the words of the prophecy of this book" (v. 7; cf. 1:3).

In the fourth place, the epilog reflects the situation within the churches, because the epilog is to serve as bridge between the world of visions and auditions on one side and the world of the hearers on the other. There may be a connection between the Christological designation "morning star," the Balaamites of chap. 2, and "the sorcerers" of 22:15 (cf. 21:8; 18:23; 9:21), especially since the Gentile prophet Balaam was denounced as chief sorcerer and magician among Jews. But we can no longer see that connection. Perhaps John merely wished to declare: what some hope to gain from Venus, the bright morning star (an angel?), this has been realized by Christ in his resurrection and will be realized at his parousia. He fulfills not only the Jewish expectations of a Davidic Messiah but also the dreams of Gentiles that focus on stars.

At any rate, the epilog gives the impression that persecution by the state and the demands of the emperor cult were not the issues of the moment. They loom on John's horizon, in the near future, but the present problems are related to the rogues' catalog (v. 15), to threats from Judaism (2:8-11; 3:7-13), and from syncretism. The last of the seven beatitudes in Revelation draws the contrast between the "Blessed" and those who are, or should be, and certainly will be "outside" the community of Christ (22:14-15).

Blessed are those who wash their robes, that they may have the right to the tree of life and that they may enter the city by the gates. The verb tense for **wash** is present participle, which signifies an ongoing activity rather than a past action as in 7:14. Their present moral behavior is depicted with the image of a continuous activity of washing their robes. And their moral behavior should maintain the once and for all redemptive washing received in baptism and maintain it to the end. The contrast to the rogues in the verse that follows (22:15) is as obvious as the contrast with the majority of Christians in Sardis who had "soiled their garments" (3:4). Access to "the tree of life" in paradise is promised to the Ephesian conquerors and entry to "the city" to those in Philadelphia.

It is odd that in spite of the rebuke by the angel (19:10), John for the second time falls down **to worship at the feet of the angel** (22:8-9). The mere repetition of this curious action and the fact that it occurs also in the epilog, which forms a bridge between the world of John's visions and the world of John's hearers, underscores the problem of angel worship among churches in Asia. The identification of stars with angels is reflected in 1:20, and astrology had a broad base in the ancient world. The details of the angel worship in Asia and Phrygia are unknown to us, but not its presence (cf. Col. 2:16-18). In this strange episode John undercut angel worship by making a fool of himself, having to be rebuked a second time and hear a second time: **"You must not do that! . . . Worship God."** If not even the angelic agent of revelation may become an object of worship, then there is no room for this syncretistic practice in the church. And just as John, the prophet, had to obey, so should his hearers follow his example and the angel's command. But more, John restructured the significance of angels. Even the angelic agent of revelation is but a **fellow servant** with the prophets on earth and with Christians who are not prophets but **who keep the words of this book.** The imperative "Worship God" constitutes the commission of John and of his hearers to do just that. The sisterhood and brotherhood of prophets exist not above but within the worshiping community.

In the fifth place, the epilog authenticates John's book in the highest possible degree. God, Christ, and the angel vouch for the reliability of the whole message, its visions, promises, and warnings. **The Lord, the God of the spirits of the prophets, has sent his angel** not just to John but through him also to **his servants** (22:6), that is, to the other prophets of the seven churches. The "spirits" of prophets, their prophetic inspiration, may not be autonomous, mouthing what feels right at the moment. Inspiration is to be theonomous. Hence several times the epilog emphasizes that John's message has its source in God (22:6b; 21:5b), Christ (22:16a, 20), and the angel (22:6a). This stress on reliability and authentication reflects the threat from false prophets like Jezebel, the Nicolaitans, and their emissaries. For John the source of his authority does not lie in the title "prophet" but in God, Christ, and the angel of revelation, and so, in contrast to Jezebel, John avoided the title "prophet" for himself, even though the angel implied it (22:9). Since his message is confirmed and guaranteed by the highest authorities, John utters a solemn threat, a curse, upon those who would dare to change that message (22:18-19).

The fact that John never mentioned bishops and elders should not lead us to conclude that the seven churches addressed by John were without them but were led by prophets only (cf. Bornkamm, Satake). He wanted his letter to be read to and heard by the whole community rather than just by its bishop and elders. John's view of church leadership contains an interesting dialectic. On one hand, all believers are and shall be kings and priests and hence a hierarchical structure has no place in the church. On the other hand, prophets are not only members within the church but also God's spokespersons over against the church, as demonstrated by his seven messages. Thus John distinguished the (true) prophets from the saints and simultaneously related them closely to each other (cf. 11:18; 16:6; 18:20, 24; 22:9). Moreover, the prophets in the Apocalypse were probably not local leaders but itinerant prophets, perhaps within a region, and John may have been their leader. At any rate, they knew him. Yet his prophetic leadership was rejected by prophets like Jezebel, and therefore he emphasized the divine authority of his message and pronounced a curse on those who would alter it (22:18-19).

In the sixth place, the most important function of this epilog is to serve as bridge from the world of visions and auditions to the worship of the assembled community. John expected his letter to be read during the communities' gatherings, and therefore he had opened his letter with a beatitude for the reader, the lector (singular), and the hearers (plural) and he noted that it was "on the Lord's day" that he was commissioned to write to the seven churches (1:3, 10).

By listening to the reading of the letter, the hearers were drawn into his visions and reexperienced them. As they followed from vision to vision, it was like walking through a maze with seals being broken, trumpets blowing, beasts arising, bowls pouring out wrath. They experienced the reality of the hidden God whose ways are not our ways and whose judgments stagger the imagination, who appears as a moral enigma in the light of the tragedies and catastrophes that befall self-assured idolatrous humanity. They were also enveloped in the triumphant worship in heaven and heard the admonition, "Fear God and give him glory . . . worship him who made heaven and earth" (14:7). And at last they heard the voice of God himself: "Behold, I make all things *new* . . . It is done!" and they saw the "new" which will never grow old, the new Jerusalem, the future city of God and their city, and their ultimate future became present as they participated in John's visions.

Being drawn into the vision of the future kingdom of God has profound consequences, for it alters one's perspective. A new vision of what God, Christ, the world, and worship are all about strengthens, modifies, or changes one's outlook, hope, and conduct. When Luther gained a new perspective on the righteousness of God, it was so powerful an experience that it propelled him right out of the church of his day. When Augustine read Rom. 13:13-14 it opened up a new world for him; it was "as though the light of confidence flooded into my heart and all the darkness of doubt was dispelled."

John's epilog signals the exit from the visions and the entry into the life of the community, specifically its worship. The hearers are led back from the vision of the future paradise (22:1-5) to their present, and in their present they must be able to rely on John's words as word of God (22:6). Therefore the author reveals himself: **I John** stand behind my visions and auditions (22:8), and through John, Jesus addresses the hearers directly: **I Jesus** have sent this testimony **to you** (plural, 22:16). So then, at the exit are the two persons, John and Jesus. For the hearers of the recital John represents the historical continuity between the recital and the prophet they know. Jesus represents the theological continuity beginning with their redemption via the recital that they had just heard, to his presence in the Eucharist which they are about to celebrate, and to his final appearance in glory in which they hope to participate. Both John and Jesus lead the assembled hearers into the celebration of the coming of Jesus in the Eucharist. Not that John quotes from the eucharistic liturgy any more than he quoted from the Old Testament, but he certainly alludes to the liturgy in the closing verses (vv. 14-21). Compare the following liturgical transitions:

1 Cor. 16:20, 22	*Didache 10:6*	*Rev. 22:14, 15, 17, 20*
Greet one another with a holy kiss.	If any one is holy, let him come	Blessed are those who wash their robes
If any one has no love for the Lord, let him be accursed.	If any one is not, let him repent	Outside are the dogs
Maranatha (Our Lord, come!)	Maranatha (Our Lord, come!)	Amen. Come, Lord Jesus!

The announcement of Jesus' imminent coming, which is highlighted in the epilog (cf. 22:12; 3:11; cf. 16:15 and 22:14), requires an answer from the worshiping community which had listened to John's letter. **The Spirit and the Bride say, "Come." Let him who hears say, "Come."** After the reading, the community, which is "the Bride," prays in the power of the Spirit for the coming of Jesus in the Eucharist. His coming and presence in the Holy Supper are his pledge and sign of his future coming. Just as he comes to the gathered community through the prophetic word of John and through the recital of the Apocalypse, so he comes to them in the Eucharist. And the recital of this letter as well as the celebration of the meal looks back to his coming in the past when he accomplished redemption by shedding his blood (1:5; 5:9). The hearing of this letter and the celebration of the Eucharist look forward to his coming in glory when his faithful followers shall reign with him in millennial bliss. **"Surely I am coming soon." Amen. Come, Lord Jesus! The grace of the Lord Jesus be with all the saints.** Thus the recital of the Apocalypse leads into the celebration of the communion with our Lord Jesus Christ. Worship is not an individualistic affair between me and sweet Jesus. It is the community's political statement concerning the kingdom, power, and glory of God and his Christ (11:15) *on earth*. Therefore worship of God and Christ must be in radical opposition to idolatry within state and society. For such worship the church needs the **grace** of God and of the Lord Jesus as stated in the beginning (1:4) and at the end (22:21) of this letter. No other apocalypse ends with a benediction like that. But the church lives by grace, and grace shall sustain it through the turmoils of the future until we reach the consummation in the life of the world to come. The grace of our Lord Jesus be with you too!

SELECTED BIBLIOGRAPHY

I. Commentaries on Revelation in English

Anon. *Revelation: Its Grand Climax at Hand!* Brooklyn, N.Y.: Watchtower Bible and Tract Society, 1988.

Beasley-Murray, G. R. *The Book of Revelation.* New Century Commentary. Grand Rapids: Eerdmans, 1978.

Caird. G. B. *A Commentary on the Revelation of St. John the Divine.* Harper's New Testament Commentary, New York: Harper & Row, 1966.

Charles, R. H. *A Critical and Exegetical Commentary on the Revelation of St. John.* 2 volumes. International Critical Commentary. New York: Charles Scribner's Sons, 1920.

Collins, A. Yarbro. *The Apocalypse.* New Testament Message 22. Wilmington, Del.: Michael Glazier, 1979.

Corsini, E. *The Apocalypse: The Perennial Revelation of Jesus Christ.* Translated and edited by Francis J. Moloney, S.D.B. Good News Studies. Wilmington, Del.: Michael Glazier, 1983.

Ford, J. Massyngberde. *Revelation: Introduction, Translation and Commentary.* Anchor Bible. Garden City: Doubleday, 1975.

Hemer, C. J. *The Letters to the Seven Churches of Asia in Their Local Setting.* Journal for the Study of the New Testament Supplement Series 11. Sheffield: JSOT Press, 1986.

Jeske, R. L. *Revelation for Today: Images of Hope.* Philadelphia: Fortress Press, 1983.

Kealy, S. P. *The Apocalypse of John.* Message of Biblical Spirituality 15. Wilmington, Del.: Michael Glazier, 1987.

Ladd, G. E. *A Commentary on the Revelation of John.* Grand Rapids: Eerdmans, 1972.

Lilje, H. *The Last Book of the Bible: The Meaning of the Revelation of St. John.* Translated by O. Wyon. Philadelphia: Muhlenberg Press, 1957.

Mounce, R. H. *The Book of Revelation.* The New International Commentary on the New Testament. Grand Rapids: Eerdmans, 1977.

Schüssler Fiorenza, E. *Invitation to the Book of Revelation.* Garden City: Doubleday, 1981.

Sweet, J. P. M. *Revelation.* Westminster Pelican Commentaries. Philadelphia: Westminster Press, 1979.

II. Commentaries on Revelation in German

Billerbeck, P. *Die Briefe des Neuen Testaments und die Offenbarung Johannis*, in H. Strack and P. Billerbeck, *Kommentar zum Neuen Testament aus Talmud und Midrasch.* 2nd edition, vol. 3. Munich: Beck, 1954.

Bousset, W. *Die Offenbarung Johannis.* 6th edition. Göttingen: Vandenhoeck & Ruprecht, 1906. Reprint, 1966.

Kraft, H. *Die Offenbarung des Johannes.* Tübingen: Mohr, 1974.

Lohmeyer, E. *Die Offenbarung des Johannes.* Tübingen: Mohr, 1926. Reprint, 3rd edition, 1970.

Lohse, E. *Die Offenbarung des Johannes.* Göttingen: Vandenhoeck & Ruprecht, 1976.

Müller, U. B. *Die Offenbarung des Johannes.* Gütersloh: Mohn, 1984.

Roloff, J. *Die Offenbarung des Johannes.* Zurich: Theologischer Verlag, 1984.

Zahn, T. *Die Offenbarung des Johannes.* 2 volumes. Leipzig: Deichert, 1922–1926. Reprint, Wuppertal: Brockhaus Verlag, 1986.

III. Bibliography to the Introduction

Bengel, J. A. *Gnomon Novi Testamenti.* 3rd edition. London: David Nutt and Williams, 1862. Published in 1742 (Stuttgart: Paulus), this book was translated into several modern European languages. English edition, Edinborough: T. & T. Clark, 1858.

_______. *Erklärte Offenbarung Johannis oder vielmehr Jesu Christi.* 2nd edition. Stuttgart: Paulus, 1773. (A comparison between Bengel and Elliott is interesting.)

Bietenhard, H. "The Millennial Hope in the Early Church." *Scottish Journal of Theology* 6 (1953): 12-30.

Bultmann, R. *Theology of the New Testament.* 2 volumes (cf. vol. 2, p. 175). New York: Charles Scribner's Sons, 1951–1955.

Charlesworth, J. H., editor. *The Old Testament Pseudepigrapha.* 2 volumes. Garden City: Doubleday, 1983–1985.

Collins, J. J. *The Apocalyptic Imagination: An Introduction to the Jewish Matrix of Christianity.* New York: Crossroad, 1987.

_______. "Introduction: Towards the Morphology of a Genre." *Semeia* 14 (1979): 1–20.

_______. "The Jewish Apocalypse," *Semeia* 14 (1979) 21–59.

Dodd, C. H. *The Apostolic Preaching and Its Developments.* London: Hodder & Stoughton, 1944 (cf. pp. 40–41).

Elliott, E. B. *Horae Apocalypticae.* 4 volumes. Reprint, St. Louis: Christian Publishing Co., 1898 (compare with Bengel).

Efird, J. M. *End-Times: Rapture, Antichrist, Millennium.* Nashville: Abingdon Press, 1986 (good introduction to millennialism).

Faid, R. W. *Gorbachev! Has the Real Antichrist Come?* Tulsa: Victory House Publisher, 1988.

Hanson, P. D. *The Dawn of Apocalyptic.* Philadelphia: Fortress Press, 1979.

_______. *Old Testament Apocalyptic.* Interpreting Biblical Texts. Nashville: Abingdon Press, 1987.

_______, editor. *Visionaries and Their Apocalypses.* Philadelphia: Fortress Press, 1983.

Hofmann, H. U. *Luther und die Johannes Apokalypse.* Tübingen: Mohr, 1982.

Jensen, J. "What Are They Saying About Armageddon?" *Currents in Theology and Mission* 13 (1986): 292–301 (about H. Lindsey's scenario and other fundamentalist interpretations).

Jewett, R. "Coming to Terms with the Doom Boom." *Quarterly Review* 4 (1984) (on H. Lindsey et al.).

Jones, B. *Domitian and the Senatorial Order.* Philadelphia: American Philosophical Society, 1979.

Jülicher, A. *Einleitung in das Neue Testament.* 6th edition. Tübingen: Mohr, 1921 (cf. p. 222).

Kennedy, G. A. *New Testament Interpretation Through Rhetorical Criticism.* Chapel Hill: University of North Carolina Press, 1984.

Kretschmar, G. *Die Offenbarung des Johannes: Die Geschichte ihrer Auslegung im 1. Jahrtausend.* Calwer Theologische Monographien 9. Stuttgart: Calwer Verlag, 1985.

Kümmel, W. G. *Introduction to the New Testament.* Revised edition, translated by H. C. Kee. Nashville: Abingdon Press, 1975, 452–540.

Lambrecht, J. "A Structuration of Revelation 4:1—22:5." In J. Lambrecht, editor, *L'Apocalypse johannique et l'Apocalyptique dans le Nouveau Testament.* Louvain: University Press, 1980, 77–104 (good discussion and critique of various proposals and his own proposal of John's "encompassing technique").

Lawrence, D. H. *Apocalypse and the Writings on Revelation.* Edited by M. Kalnins. Cambridge: Cambridge University Press, 1980 (cf. p. 67).

Lindsey, H. *The Late Great Planet Earth.* Grand Rapids: Zondervan, 1970.

Luther, M. "Preface to the Revelation of St. John, 1522" and "Preface to the Revelation of St. John, 1546 (1530)," *LW* 35:398–411. Philadelphia: Fortress Press, 1960.

McDermott, W. C., and Orentzel, A. "Silius Italicus and Domitian." *The American Journal of Philology* 98 (1977): 23–34.

McGinn, B. *Visions of the End: Apocalyptic Traditions in the Middle Ages.* New York: Columbia University Press, 1979.

MacMullen, R. *Enemies of the Roman Order.* Cambridge, Mass.: Harvard University Press, 1966.

Maier, G. *Die Johannesoffenbarung und die Kirche.* Tübingen: Mohr, 1981.

Metzger, B. M. *A Textual Commentary on the Greek New Testament.* New York: United Bible Societies, 1971, 731–769 (on the Greek text of Revelation).

Robinson, J. A. T. *Redating the New Testament.* Philadelphia: Westminster Press, 1976, 221–253 (cf. 231).

Rowland, C. *The Open Heaven: A Study of Apocalyptic in Judaism and Christianity.* New York: Crossroad, 1982.

Rowley, H. H. *The Relevance of Apocalyptic: A Study of Jewish and Christian Apocalypses from Daniel to Revelation.* New York: Association Press, 1963.

Russell, D. S. *The Method and Message of Jewish Apocalyptic.* Philadelphia: Westminster Press, 1964.

Schneemelcher, W., editor. *New Testament Apocrypha.* 2 volumes. Translation edited by R. McL. Wilson. Philadelphia: Westminster Press, 1963–1965.

Schüssler Fiorenza, E. "Composition and Structure of Revelation," *CBQ* 39 (1977): 344–366. Also in Schüssler Fiorenza, *The Book of Revelation: Justice and Judgment.* Philadelphia: Fortress Press, 1985, 159–180.

Scott, E. F. *The Literature of the New Testament.* New York: Columbia University Press, 1943 (cf. p. 282).

Stowers, S. K. *Letter Writing in Greco-Roman Antiquity.* Library of Early Christianity. Philadelphia: Westminster Press, 1986.

Thompson, L. "Domitianus Dominus: A Gloss on Statius, Silvae 1.6.84." *The American Journal of Philology* 105 (1984): 469–475.

Waters, K. "Traianus Domitiani Continuator." *The American Journal of Philology* 90 (1969): 385–405.

IV. Studies

Aune, D. E. "The Social Matrix of the Apocalypse of John." *BR* 26 (1981): 16–32.

———. "The Influence of Roman Imperial Court Ceremonial on the Apocalypse of John." *BR* 28 (1983): 5–26.

———. *Prophecy in Early Christianity and the Ancient Mediterranean World.* Grand Rapids, Mich.: Wm. B. Eerdmans, 1983.

———. "The Apocalypse of John and the Problem of Genre." *Semeia* 36 (1986): 65–96.

———. "The Apocalypse of John and Graeco-Roman Revelatory Magic." *NTS* 33 (1987): 481–501.

Barr, D. L. "The Apocalypse as a Symbolic Transformation of the World: A Literary Analysis." *Interp.* 38 (1984): 39–50.

———. "The Apocalypse of John as Oral Enactment." *Interp.* 40 (1986): 243–256.

———. "Elephants and Holograms: From Metaphor to Methodology in the Study of the Apocalypse." *Society of Biblical Literature Seminar Papers*, 1986, 400–411.

Barton, S. C., and Horsley, G. H. R. "A Hellenistic Cult Group and the New Testament." *Jahrbuch für Antike und Christentum* 24 (1981): 7–41 (on an inscription from Philadelphia).

Beale, G. K. *The Use of Daniel in Jewish Apocalyptic Literature and in the Revelation of St. John.* New York: University Press of America, 1984.

Boesak, A. A. *Comfort and Protest: Reflections on the Apocalypse of John of Patmos.* Philadelphia: Westminster Press, 1987.

Boring, E. "The Apocalypse as Christian Prophecy: A Discussion of the Issues Raised by the Book of Revelation for the Study of Early Christian Prophecy." *Society of Biblical Literature Seminar Papers*, 1974, 43–57.

———. "The Theology of Revelation, 'The Lord our God the Almighty Reigns.' " *Interp.* 40 (1986): 257–269.

Bornkamm, G. "Die Komposition der apokalyptischen Visionen in der Offenbarung Johannes," in *Studien zu Antike und Urchristentum*, Gesammelte Aufsätze, vol. 2. Munich: Kaiser Verlag, 1959, 204–222.

Bruce, F. F. "The Spirit in the Apocalypse," in B. Lindars and S. S. Smalley, editors, *Christ and Spirit in the New Testament.* Cambridge: Cambridge University Press, 1974, 333–344.

Casey, J. "The Exodus Theme in the Book of Revelation Against the Background of the New Testament." *Concilium* 189 (1987): 34–43.

Charlesworth, J. H. "The Jewish Roots of Christology: The Discovery of the Hypostatic Voice." *Scottish Journal of Theology* 34 (1986): 19–41 (an angelic being may have been called "Voice").

Collins, A. Yarbro. *The Combat Myth in the Book of Revelation.* Published by Scholars Press for *Harvard Theological Review,* 1976.

———. "Early Christian Apocalypses." *Semeia* 14 (1979): 21–59.

———. "Revelation 18: Taunt-Song or Dirge?" in J. Lambrecht, editor, *L'Apocalypse johannique et l'Apocalyptique dans le Nouveau Testament.* Louvain: University Press, 1980, 185–204.

———. *Crisis and Catharsis: The Power of the Apocalypse.* Philadelphia: Westminster Press, 1984.

———. "Introduction: Early Christian Apocalypticism." *Semeia* 36 (1986): 1–11.

———. "Women's History and the Book of Revelation." *Society of Biblical Literature Seminar Papers,* 1987, 80–91.

Court, J. M. *Myth and History in the Book of Revelation.* Atlanta: John Knox Press, 1979.

Cullmann, O. *Christ and Time.* Philadelphia: Westminster Press, 1950, 160–162.

Danker, F. W. *Benefactor: Epigraphic Study of a Graeco-Roman and New Testament Semantic Field.* St. Louis: Clayton Publishing House, 1982.

Deutsch, C. "Transformation of Symbols: The New Jerusalem in Rev. 21:1—22:5." *ZNW* 78 (1987): 106–126.

Gager, J. G. "The Attainment of Millennial Bliss Through Myth: The Book of Revelation," in P. D. Hanson, editor, *Visionaries and Their Apocalypses.* Philadelphia: Fortress Press, 1983.

Georgi, D. "Die Visionen vom himmlischen Jerusalem in Apk 21 u. 22," in D. Lührmann and G. Strecker, editors, *Kirche,*

Festschrift für Günther Bornkamm zum 75. Geburtstag. Tübingen: Mohr, 1980.

———. "Who Is the True Prophet?" in *Essays in Honor of Krister Stendahl*. *HTR* 79 (1986): 100–126.

Grabbe, L. L. "The Scapegoat Tradition: A Study in Early Jewish Interpretation." *Journal for the Study of Judaism* 18 (1987): 152–167.

Gundry, R. H. "The New Jerusalem: People as Place, not Place for People." *Nov. Test.* 29 (1987): 254–264.

Guthrie, D. *The Relevance of the Apocalypse*. Grand Rapids, Mich.: Wm. B. Eerdmans, 1987.

Hellholm, D., editor. *Apocalypticism in the Mediterranean World and the Near East*. Proceedings of the International Colloquium on Apocalypticism. Uppsala, August 12–17, 1979. Tübingen: Mohr, 1983.

———. "The Problem of Apocalyptic Genre and the Apocalypse of John." *Semeia* 36 (1986): 14–64.

Hill, D. *New Testament Prophecy*. Atlanta: John Knox Press, 1979.

Hills, J. "The Epistula Apostolorum and the Genre 'Apocalypse.' " *Society of Biblical Literature Seminar Papers*, 1986, 581–595.

Jeremias, J. "*har Magedōn*." *Theological Dictionary of the New Testament*. Grand Rapids, Mich.: Wm. B. Eerdmans, 1964–1976. 1:468.

———. "*Poimēn, poimainō*." In idem, 6:485–501.

Jörns, K. P. *Das hymnische Evangelium: Untersuchungen zu Aufbau, Funktion und Herkunft der hymnischen Stücke in der Johannesoffenbarung*. Gütersloh: Mohn, 1971.

Johnson, S. E. "Asia Minor and Early Christianity," in J. Neusner, editor, *Christianity, Judaism, and other Greco-Roman Cults*. Leiden: Brill, 1975, 77–144.

Käsemann, E. *Jesus Means Freedom*. Philadelphia: Fortress Press, 1970, 144–153.

Karrer, M. *Die Johannesoffenbarung als Brief: Studien zu ihrem literarischen, historischen und theologischen Ort*. Göttingen: Vandenhoeck & Ruprecht, 1986.

Kirby, J. T. "The Rhetorical Situations of Revelation 1–3." *NTS* 34 (1988): 197–207.

Klassen, W. "Vengeance in the Apocalypse of John." *CBQ* 28 (1966): 300–311.

Kraabel, A. T. "Hypsistos and the Synagogue at Sardis." *Greek, Roman and Byzantine Studies* 10 (1969): 81–93.

———. "Judaism in Western Asia Minor Under the Roman Empire, with a Preliminary Study of the Jewish Community at Sardis." Dissertation, Harvard University, 1968.

Magie, D. *Roman Rule in Asia Minor to the End of the Third Century After Christ.* 2 volumes. Princeton: University Press, 1950.

Minear, P. S. *I Saw a New Earth.* Washington and Cleveland: Corpus Books, 1968.

———. *New Testament Apocalyptic.* Interpreting Biblical Texts. Nashville: Abingdon Press, 1981.

Neal, B. S. *The Concept of Character in the Apocalypse with Implications for Character Education.* Washington: University Press of America, 1983.

Oberweis, M. "Die Bedeutung der neutestamentlichen 'Rätselzahlen' 666 (Apk 13:18) und 153 (Joh 21:11)." *ZNW* 77 (1986): 226–241.

Pleket, H. "Domitian, the Senate and the Provinces." *Mnemosyne* 7 (1961): 296–315.

Prigent, P. *Apocalypse 12: Histoire de l'exégèse.* Tübingen: Mohr, 1959.

Ramsay, W. M. *The Letters to the Seven Churches of Asia.* London: Hodder & Stoughton, 1904. Reprint, Grand Rapids, Mich.: Baker, 1963.

Reader, W. W. "The Twelve Jewels of Revelation 21:19-20: Tradition History and Modern Interpretation." *JBL* 100 (1981): 433–457.

Rissi, M. *Time and History: A Study on the Revelation.* Translated by G. C. Winsor. Richmond, Va.: John Knox Press, 1966.

———. *The Future of the World.* Studies in Biblical Theology, second series 23. London: SCM Press, 1972.

Schüssler Fiorenza, E. "Eschatology in the New Testament." *Interpreter's Dictionary of the Bible, Supplementary Volume.* Nashville: Abingdon Press, 1976, 271–277.

———. *The Book of Revelation: Justice and Judgment.* Philadelphia: Fortress Press, 1985.

Thompson, L. "A Sociological Analysis of Tribulation in the Apocalypse of John." *Semeia* 36 (1986): 147–174.

Topham, M. "Hanniqolaites." *Ex. Times* 98 (1986): 44–45.

Webber, R. C. "Group Solidarity in the Revelation of John." *Society of Biblical Literature Seminar Papers,* 1988, 132–140.

Whale, P. "The Lamb of John: Some Myths About Vocabulary of the Johannine Literature." *JBL* 106 (1987): 289–295.

Wilder, A. N. "The Rhetoric of Ancient and Modern Apocalyptic." *Interp.* 25 (1971): 436–453.

Wojciechowski, M. "Apocalypse 21:19-20: Des titres christologiques cachés dans la liste des pierres précieuses." *NTS* 33 (1987): 153–154.

Yadin, Y., editor. *The Temple Scroll.* 2 volumes. Jerusalem: Israel Exploration Society, 1983.

Zahn, T. *Forschungen zur Geschichte des neutestamentlichen Kanons und der altchristlichen Literatur.* 5 volumes. Erlangen: Deichert, 1881ff.

V. Works of Ancient Authors

The Ante-Nicene Fathers. New York: Charles Scribner's Sons, various dates.

Bue, F. L., editor. *The Turin Fragments of Tyconius's Commentary on Revelation.* Texts and Studies 7. Cambridge: Cambridge University Press, 1963.

Charlesworth, J. H., editor. *The Old Testament Pseudepigrapha.* 2 volumes. Garden City, N.Y.: Doubleday, 1983–1985. Contains such writings as the *Apocalypse of Abraham,* the *Martyrdom and Ascension of Isaiah,* the *Letter of Aristeas, 2 Baruch,* 4 Ezra, *Jubilees,* the *Psalms of Solomon,* the *Sibylline Oracles,* and the *Testaments of the Twelve Patriarchs.*

Danby, H., translator. *The Mishnah*. London: Oxford University Press, 1933 (*Pirke Aboth*, pp. 446–460).

Dawood, N. J., translator. *The Koran*. 4th revised edition. New York: Penguin, 1974.

Hausleiter, J., editor. *Victorini episcopis Petavrionensis opera*. Corpus scriptorum ecclesiasticorum Latinorum. Vienna, 1916 (Victorinus of Pettau).

Loeb Classical Library. Cambridge, Mass.: Harvard University Press, various dates. Contains the works of Christian authors such as the Apostolic Fathers, Eusebius, and Augustine; and of non-Christian authors such as Dio Cassius, Dio Chrysostom, Josephus, Ovid, Pliny the Younger, Plutarch, Statius, Suetonius, Tacitus, and Virgil.

Maier, G. *Die Johannesoffenbarung und die Kirche*. Tübingen: Mohr, 1981 (Tyconius).

Schneemelcher, W., editor. *New Testament Apocrypha*. 2 volumes. Translation edited by R. McL. Wilson. Philadelphia: Westminster Press, 1963–1965 (the *Apocryphon of John*, *Epistula Apostolorum*, and the *Gospel of Thomas*).

Schoedel, W. R. *The Apostolic Fathers*. Volume 5. New York: Thomas Nelson, 1967 (Papias). See also H. J. Körtner, *Papias von Hierapolis*. Göttingen: Vandenhoeck & Ruprecht, 1983.

ABOUT THE AUTHOR

Dr. Gerhard Krodel has been dean of Gettysburg Seminary and professor of New Testament since 1977. His professional education took place at the Universities of Erlangen (Ph. D., 1950) and Tübingen. He also attended Concordia Seminary, St. Louis (1950–1951), and took courses at Union Theological Seminary, New York. He served as pastor (1951–1955), taught classical languages at Capital University (1955–1958), and was professor of New Testament at Wartburg Theological Seminary (1958–1964) and at the Lutheran Theological Seminary at Philadelphia (1964–1977). He has served on the Commission on Faith and Order of the National Council of Churches and on its Executive Committee, on the Task Force on Theology of the New Lutheran Church (1983), and, since 1978, on the International Orthodox–Lutheran Dialog. He is the editor of Proclamation Commentaries (Fortress Press).